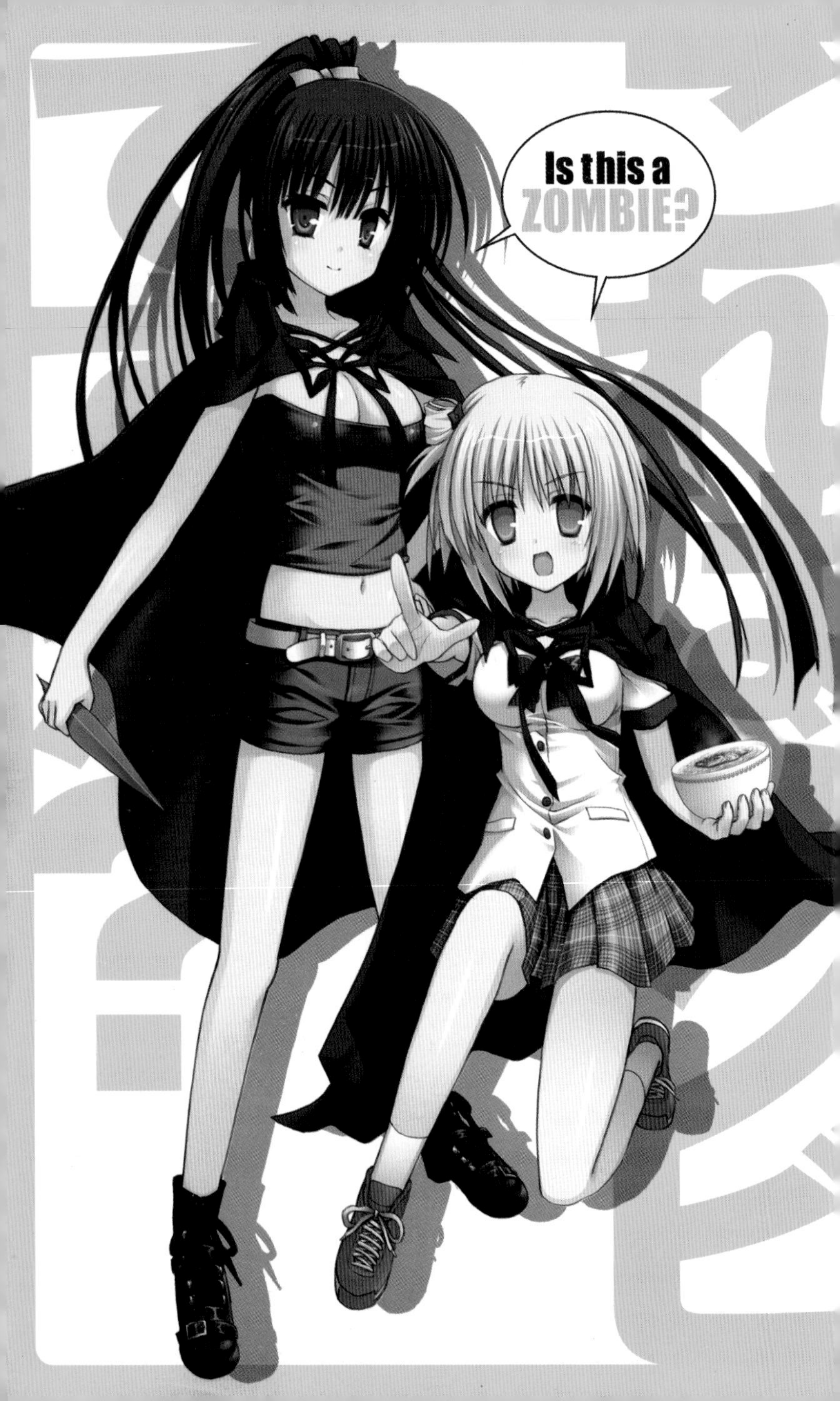
Is this a ZOMBIE?

CONTENTS

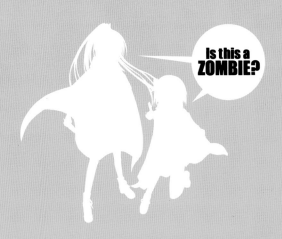

Is this a ZOMBIE?

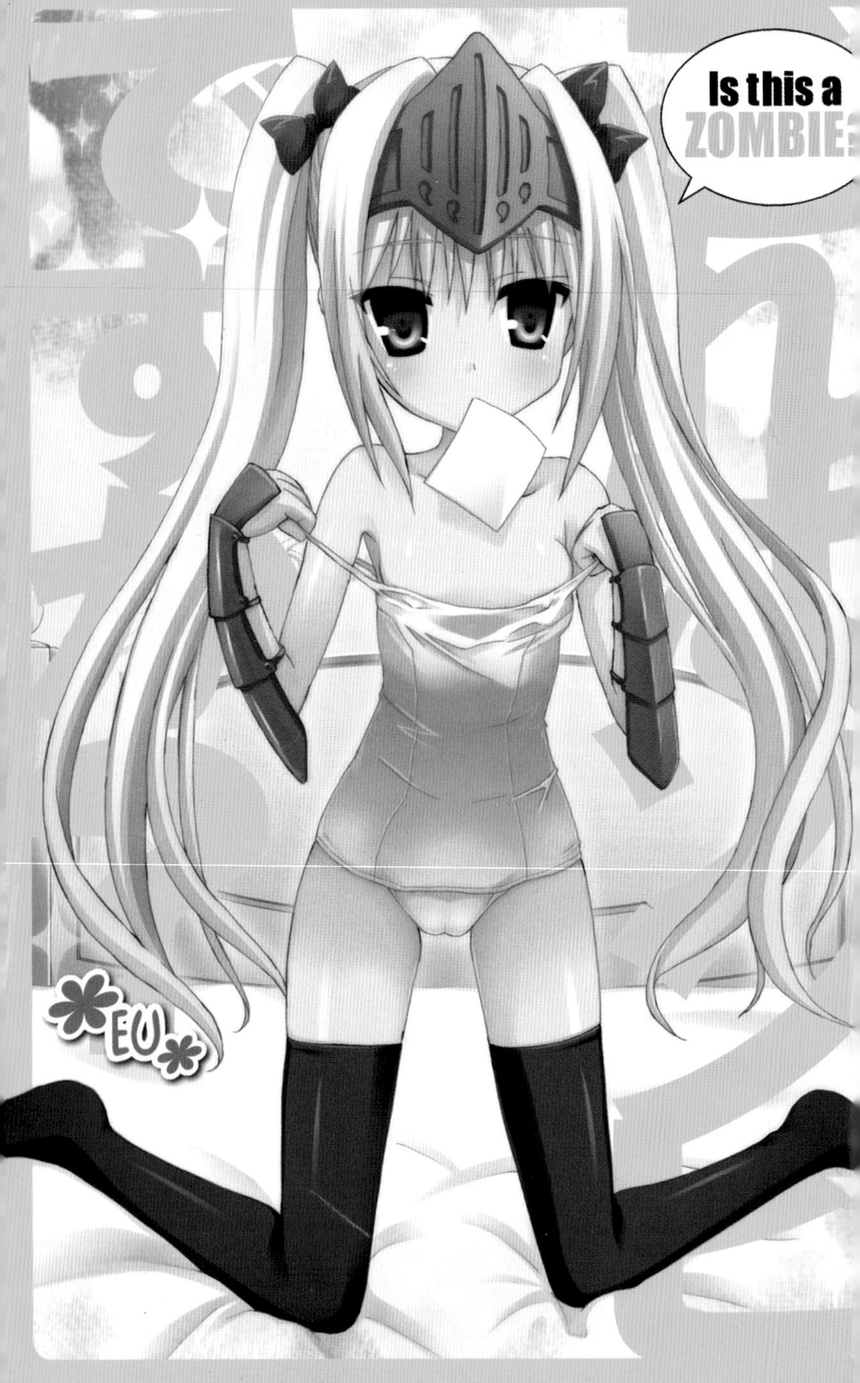
Is this a
ZOMBIE?
EU

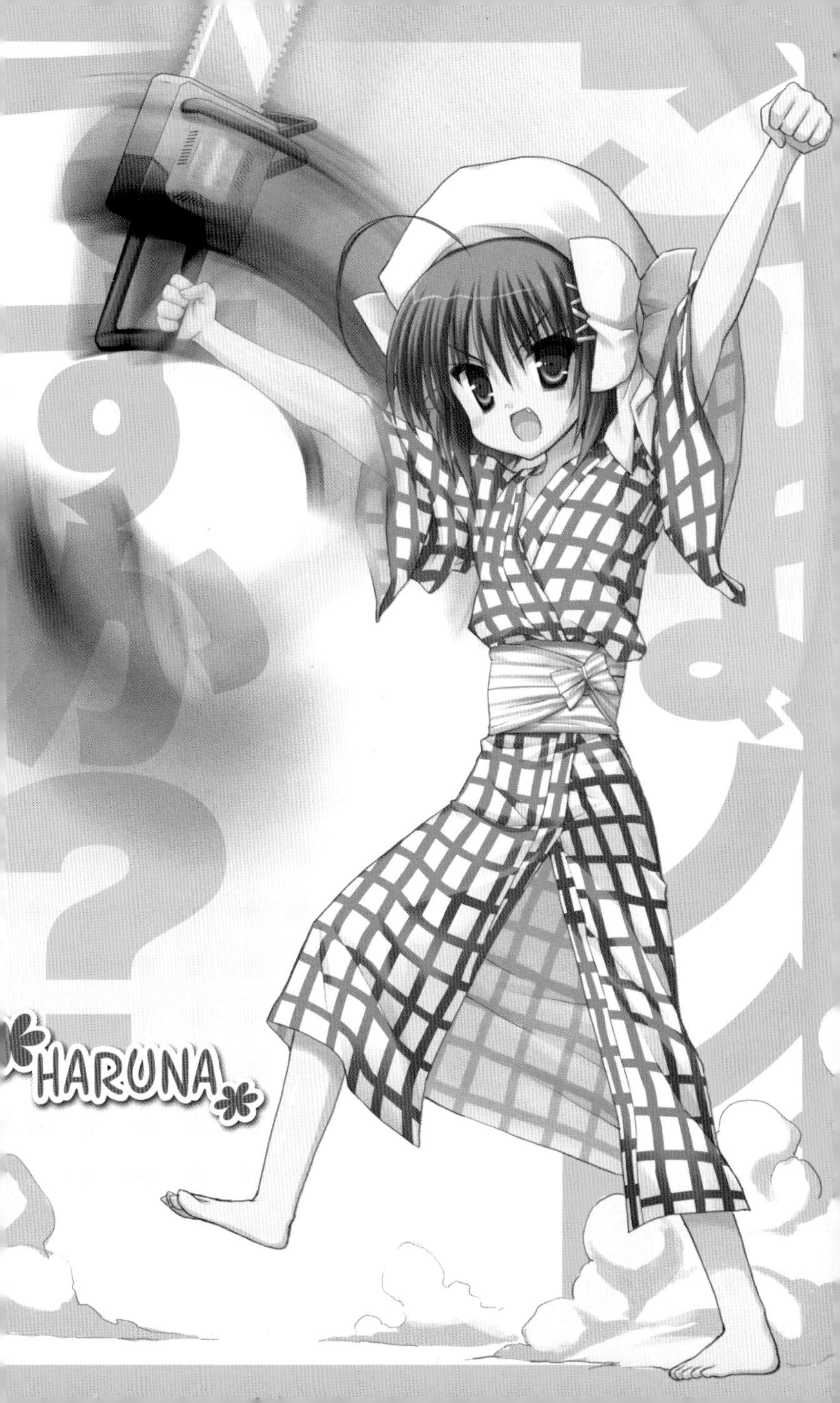
HARUNA

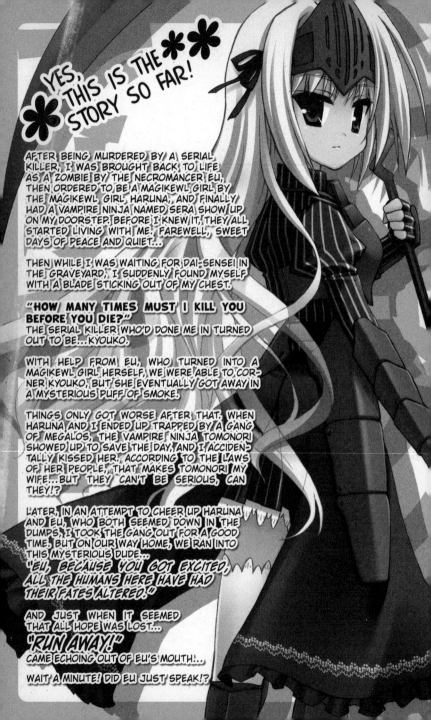

✱✱ YES, THIS IS THE STORY SO FAR!

AFTER BEING MURDERED BY A SERIAL KILLER, I WAS BROUGHT BACK TO LIFE AS A ZOMBIE BY THE NECROMANCER EU, THEN ORDERED TO BE A MAGIKEWL GIRL BY THE MAGIKEWL GIRL, HARUNA, AND FINALLY HAD A VAMPIRE NINJA NAMED SERA SHOW UP ON MY DOORSTEP. BEFORE I KNEW IT, THEY ALL STARTED LIVING WITH ME. FAREWELL, SWEET DAYS OF PEACE AND QUIET...

THEN WHILE I WAS WAITING FOR DAI-SENSEI IN THE GRAVEYARD, I SUDDENLY FOUND MYSELF WITH A BLADE STICKING OUT OF MY CHEST.

"HOW MANY TIMES MUST I KILL YOU BEFORE YOU DIE?"
THE SERIAL KILLER WHO'D DONE ME IN TURNED OUT TO BE...KYOUKO.

WITH HELP FROM EU, WHO TURNED INTO A MAGIKEWL GIRL HERSELF, WE WERE ABLE TO CORNER KYOUKO, BUT SHE EVENTUALLY GOT AWAY IN A MYSTERIOUS PUFF OF SMOKE.

THINGS ONLY GOT WORSE AFTER THAT. WHEN HARUNA AND I ENDED UP TRAPPED BY A GANG OF MEGALOS, THE VAMPIRE NINJA TOMONORI SHOWED UP TO SAVE THE DAY, AND I ACCIDENTALLY KISSED HER. ACCORDING TO THE LAWS OF HER PEOPLE, THAT MAKES TOMONORI MY WIFE...BUT THEY CAN'T BE SERIOUS, CAN THEY!?

LATER, IN AN ATTEMPT TO CHEER UP HARUNA AND EU, WHO BOTH SEEMED DOWN IN THE DUMPS, I TOOK THE GANG OUT FOR A GOOD TIME. BUT ON OUR WAY HOME, WE RAN INTO THIS MYSTERIOUS DUDE...
"EU, BECAUSE YOU GOT EXCITED, ALL THE HUMANS HERE HAVE HAD THEIR FATES ALTERED."

AND JUST WHEN IT SEEMED THAT ALL HOPE WAS LOST...
"RUN AWAY!"
CAME ECHOING OUT OF EU'S MOUTH!...

WAIT A MINUTE! DID EU JUST SPEAK!?

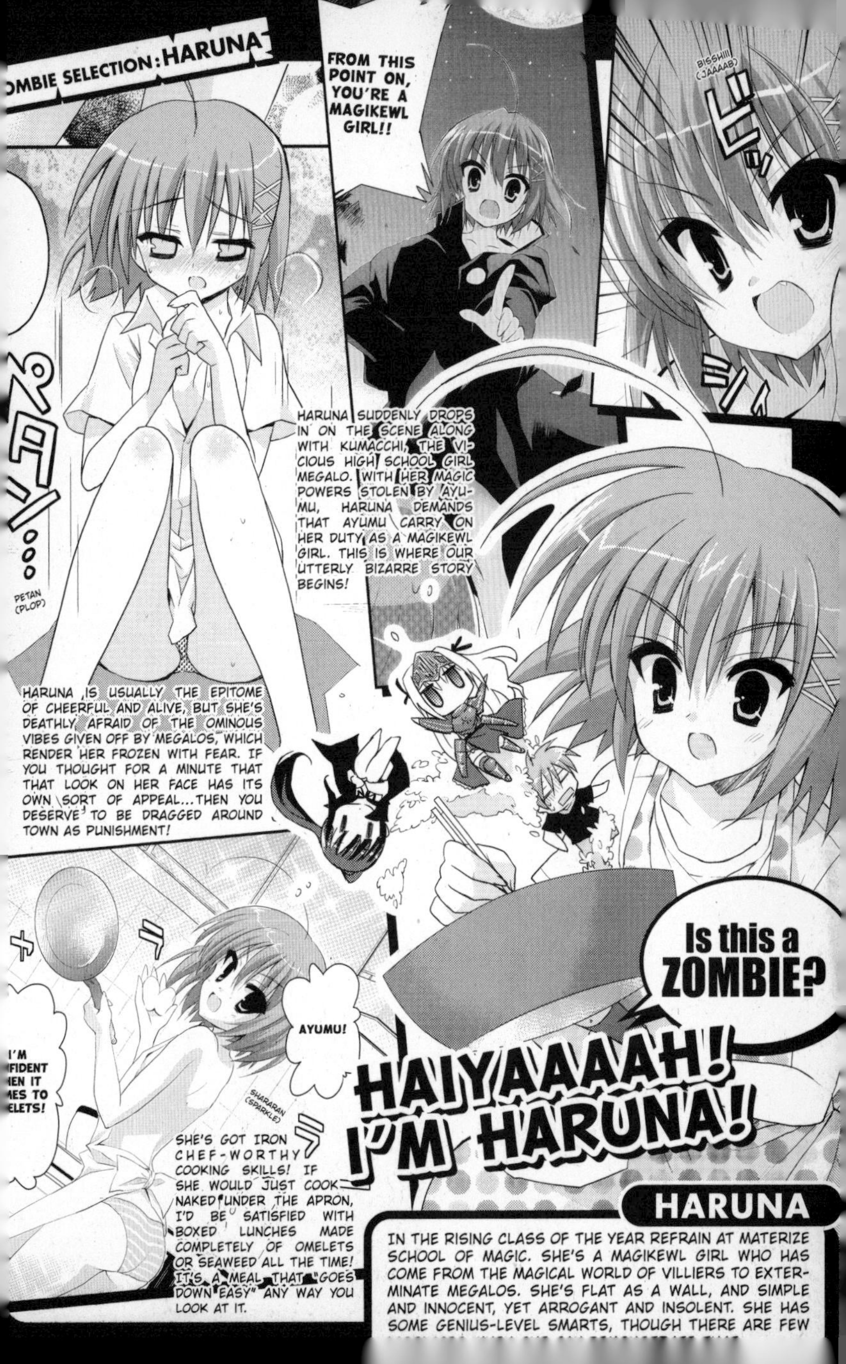
BISSHIII (JAAAAB)
FROM THIS POINT ON, YOU'RE A MAGIKEWL GIRL!!
OMBIE SELECTION: HARUNA
PETAN (PLOP)
HARUNA SUDDENLY DROPS IN ON THE SCENE ALONG WITH KUMACCHI, THE VICIOUS HIGH SCHOOL GIRL MEGALO. WITH HER MAGIC POWERS STOLEN BY AYUMU, HARUNA DEMANDS THAT AYUMU CARRY ON HER DUTY AS A MAGIKEWL GIRL. THIS IS WHERE OUR UTTERLY BIZARRE STORY BEGINS!
HARUNA IS USUALLY THE EPITOME OF CHEERFUL AND ALIVE, BUT SHE'S DEATHLY AFRAID OF THE OMINOUS VIBES GIVEN OFF BY MEGALOS, WHICH RENDER HER FROZEN WITH FEAR. IF YOU THOUGHT FOR A MINUTE THAT THAT LOOK ON HER FACE HAS ITS OWN SORT OF APPEAL...THEN YOU DESERVE TO BE DRAGGED AROUND TOWN AS PUNISHMENT!
Is this a ZOMBIE?
HAIYAAAAAH! I'M HARUNA!
HARUNA
IN THE RISING CLASS OF THE YEAR REFRAIN AT MATERIZE SCHOOL OF MAGIC. SHE'S A MAGIKEWL GIRL WHO HAS COME FROM THE MAGICAL WORLD OF VILLIERS TO EXTERMINATE MEGALOS. SHE'S FLAT AS A WALL, AND SIMPLE AND INNOCENT, YET ARROGANT AND INSOLENT. SHE HAS SOME GENIUS-LEVEL SMARTS, THOUGH THERE ARE FEW
AYUMU!
I'M
FIDENT
HEN IT
MES TO
ELETS!
SHARARAN (SPARKLE)
SHE'S GOT IRON CHEF-WORTHY COOKING SKILLS! IF SHE WOULD JUST COOK NAKED UNDER THE APRON, I'D BE SATISFIED WITH BOXED LUNCHES MADE COMPLETELY OF OMELETS OR SEAWEED ALL THE TIME! IT'S A MEAL THAT "GOES DOWN EASY" ANY WAY YOU LOOK AT IT.

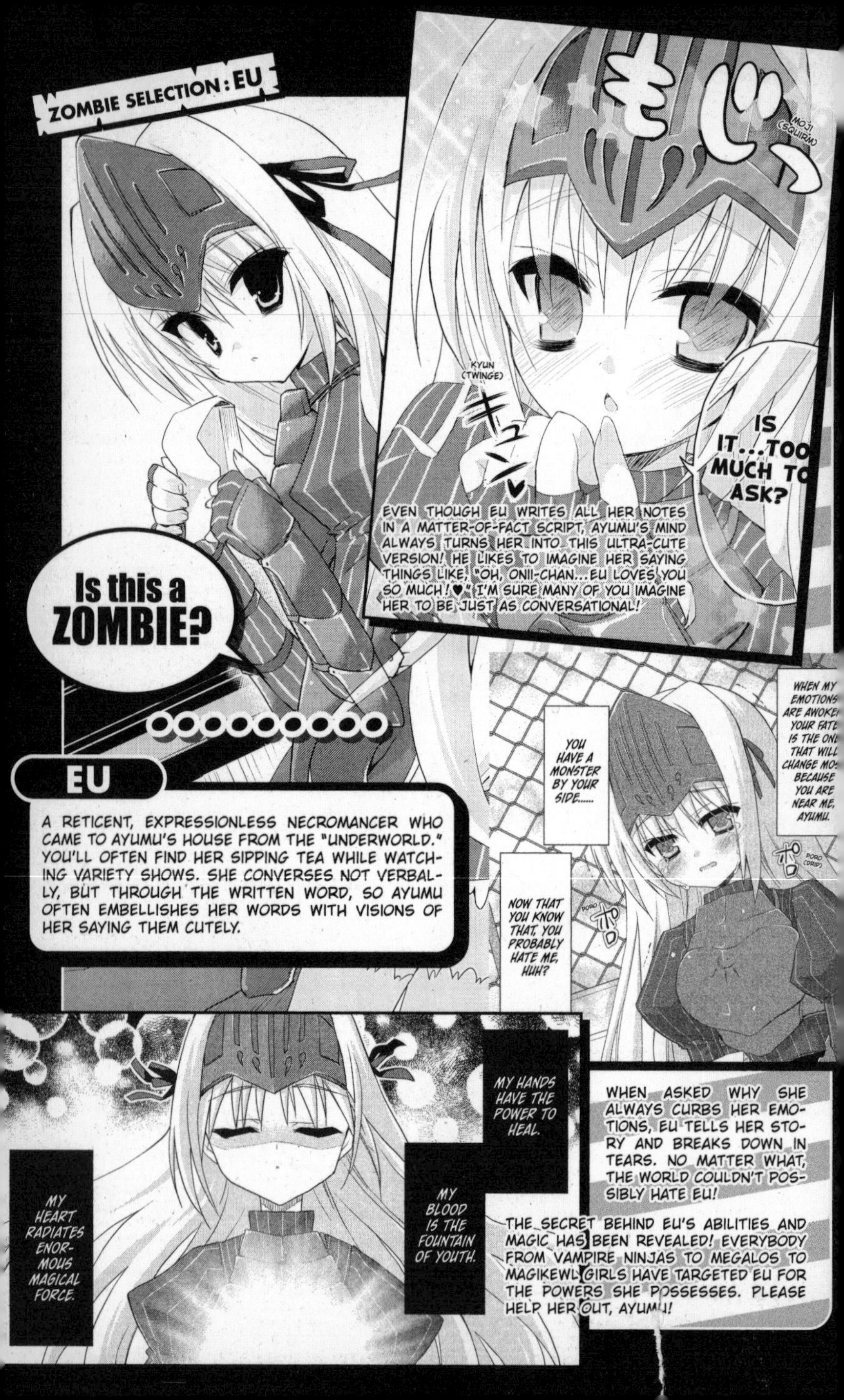

ZOMBIE SELECTION : EU
MOJI (SQUIRM)
KYUN (TWINGE)
IS IT...TOO MUCH TO ASK?
EVEN THOUGH EU WRITES ALL HER NOTES IN A MATTER-OF-FACT SCRIPT, AYUMU'S MIND ALWAYS TURNS HER INTO THIS ULTRA-CUTE VERSION! HE LIKES TO IMAGINE HER SAYING THINGS LIKE, "OH, ONII-CHAN...EU LOVES YOU SO MUCH!♥" I'M SURE MANY OF YOU IMAGINE HER TO BE JUST AS CONVERSATIONAL!
Is this a ZOMBIE?
EU
A RETICENT, EXPRESSIONLESS NECROMANCER WHO CAME TO AYUMU'S HOUSE FROM THE "UNDERWORLD." YOU'LL OFTEN FIND HER SIPPING TEA WHILE WATCHING VARIETY SHOWS. SHE CONVERSES NOT VERBALLY, BUT THROUGH THE WRITTEN WORD, SO AYUMU OFTEN EMBELLISHES HER WORDS WITH VISIONS OF HER SAYING THEM CUTELY.
WHEN MY EMOTIONS ARE AWOKE YOUR FATE IS THE ONE THAT WILL CHANGE MOS BECAUSE YOU ARE NEAR ME, AYUMU.
YOU HAVE A MONSTER BY YOUR SIDE......
PORO (DRIP)
PORO
NOW THAT YOU KNOW THAT, YOU PROBABLY HATE ME, HUH?
WHEN ASKED WHY SHE ALWAYS CURBS HER EMOTIONS, EU TELLS HER STORY AND BREAKS DOWN IN TEARS. NO MATTER WHAT, THE WORLD COULDN'T POSSIBLY HATE EU!
THE SECRET BEHIND EU'S ABILITIES AND MAGIC HAS BEEN REVEALED! EVERYBODY FROM VAMPIRE NINJAS TO MEGALOS TO MAGIKEWL GIRLS HAVE TARGETED EU FOR THE POWERS SHE POSSESSES. PLEASE HELP HER OUT, AYUMU!
MY HANDS HAVE THE POWER TO HEAL.
MY BLOOD IS THE FOUNTAIN OF YOUTH.
MY HEART RADIATES ENORMOUS MAGICAL FORCE.

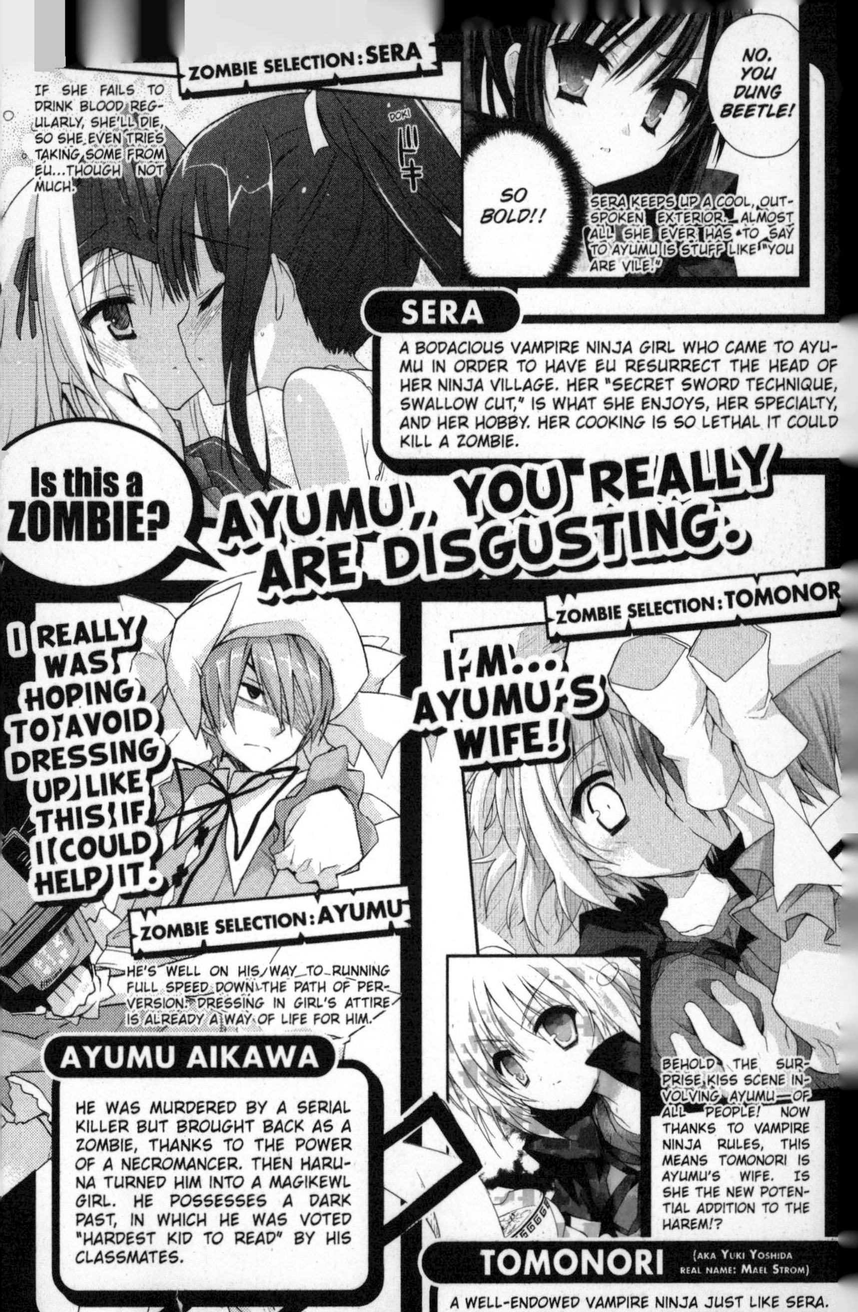
NO. YOU DUNG BEETLE!
SO BOLD!!
SERA KEEPS UP A COOL, OUT-SPOKEN EXTERIOR. ALMOST ALL SHE EVER HAS TO SAY TO AYUMU IS STUFF LIKE "YOU ARE VILE."
ZOMBIE SELECTION: SERA
DOKI
IF SHE FAILS TO DRINK BLOOD REG-ULARLY, SHE'LL DIE, SO SHE EVEN TRIES TAKING SOME FROM EU...THOUGH NOT MUCH.
SERA
A BODACIOUS VAMPIRE NINJA GIRL WHO CAME TO AYU-MU IN ORDER TO HAVE EU RESURRECT THE HEAD OF HER NINJA VILLAGE. HER "SECRET SWORD TECHNIQUE, SWALLOW CUT," IS WHAT SHE ENJOYS, HER SPECIALTY, AND HER HOBBY. HER COOKING IS SO LETHAL IT COULD KILL A ZOMBIE.
AYUMU, YOU REALLY ARE DISGUSTING.
Is this a ZOMBIE?
ZOMBIE SELECTION: TOMONOR
I'M... AYUMU'S WIFE!
BEHOLD THE SUR-PRISE KISS SCENE IN-VOLVING AYUMU—OF ALL PEOPLE! NOW THANKS TO VAMPIRE NINJA RULES, THIS MEANS TOMONORI IS AYUMU'S WIFE. IS SHE THE NEW POTEN-TIAL ADDITION TO THE HAREM!?
TOMONORI (AKA YUKI YOSHIDA REAL NAME: MAEL STROM)
A WELL-ENDOWED VAMPIRE NINJA JUST LIKE SERA. AFTER KISSING AYUMU, SHE BECOMES AYUMU'S WIFE. SHE'S BASICALLY A BIT OF AN AIRHEAD.
I REALLY WAS HOPING TO AVOID DRESSING UP LIKE THIS IF I COULD HELP IT.
ZOMBIE SELECTION: AYUMU
HE'S WELL ON HIS WAY TO RUNNING FULL SPEED DOWN THE PATH OF PER-VERSION. DRESSING IN GIRL'S ATTIRE IS ALREADY A WAY OF LIFE FOR HIM.
AYUMU AIKAWA
HE WAS MURDERED BY A SERIAL KILLER BUT BROUGHT BACK AS A ZOMBIE, THANKS TO THE POWER OF A NECROMANCER. THEN HARU-NA TURNED HIM INTO A MAGIKEWL GIRL. HE POSSESSES A DARK PAST, IN WHICH HE WAS VOTED "HARDEST KID TO READ" BY HIS CLASSMATES.

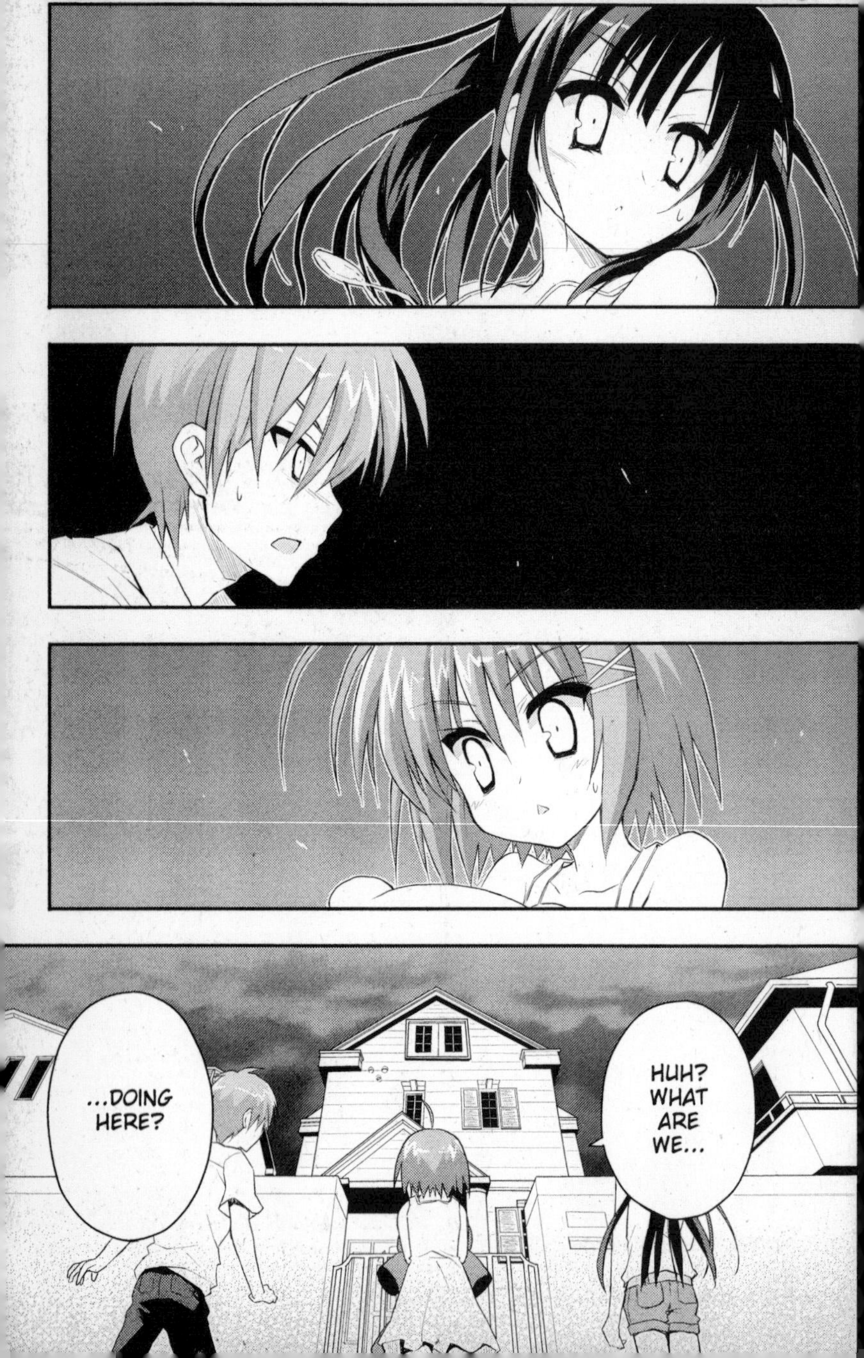
HUH? WHAT ARE WE...
...DOING HERE?

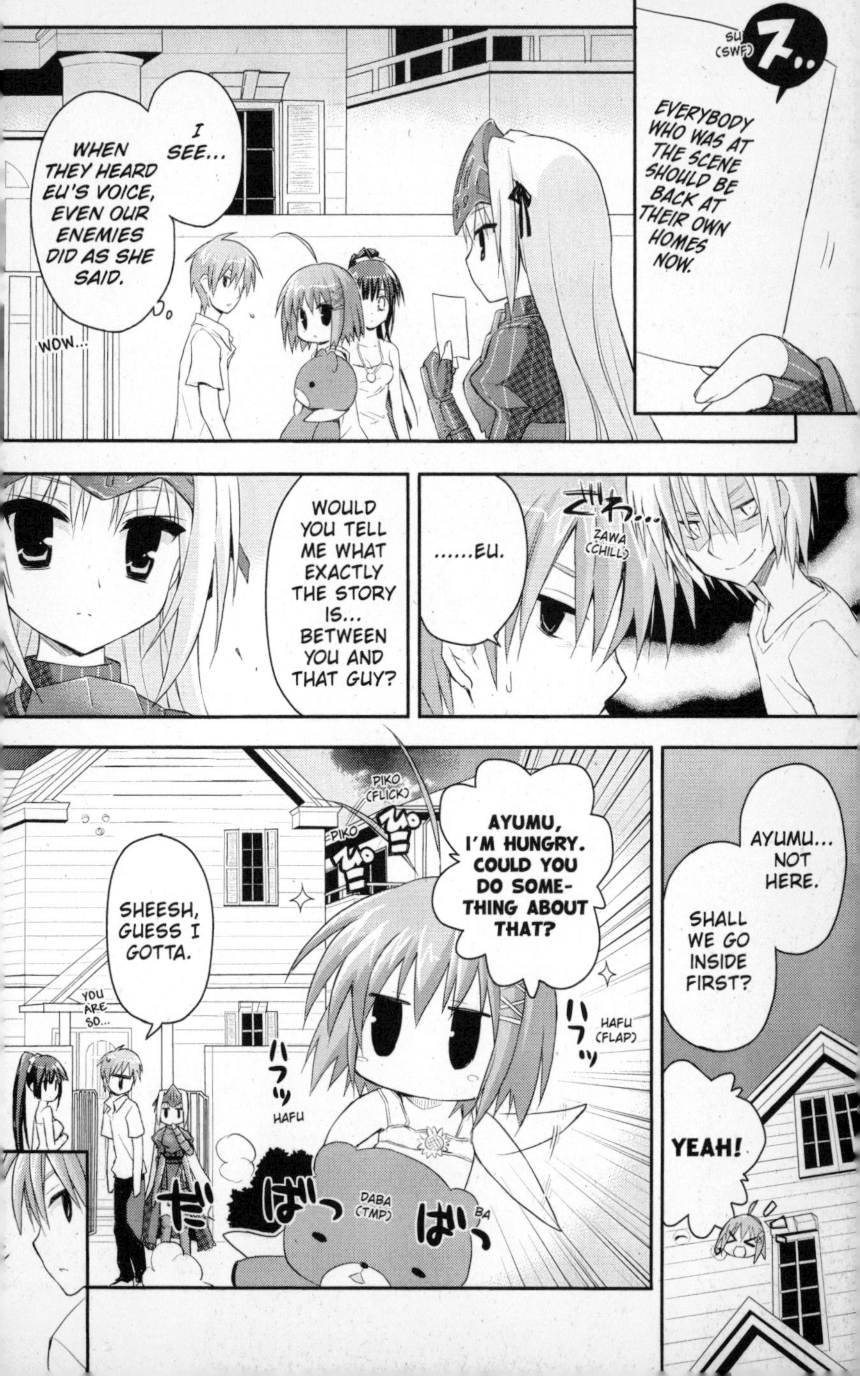
SU (SWF)
EVERYBODY WHO WAS AT THE SCENE SHOULD BE BACK AT THEIR OWN HOMES NOW.
I SEE...
WHEN THEY HEARD EU'S VOICE, EVEN OUR ENEMIES DID AS SHE SAID.
WOW...
......EU.
ZAWA (CHILL)
WOULD YOU TELL ME WHAT EXACTLY THE STORY IS... BETWEEN YOU AND THAT GUY?
AYUMU... NOT HERE.
SHALL WE GO INSIDE FIRST?
YEAH!
PIKO (FLICK)
PIKO
AYUMU, I'M HUNGRY. COULD YOU DO SOMETHING ABOUT THAT?
HAFU (FLAP)
HAFU
SHEESH, GUESS I GOTTA.
YOU ARE SO...
DABA (TMP)
BA

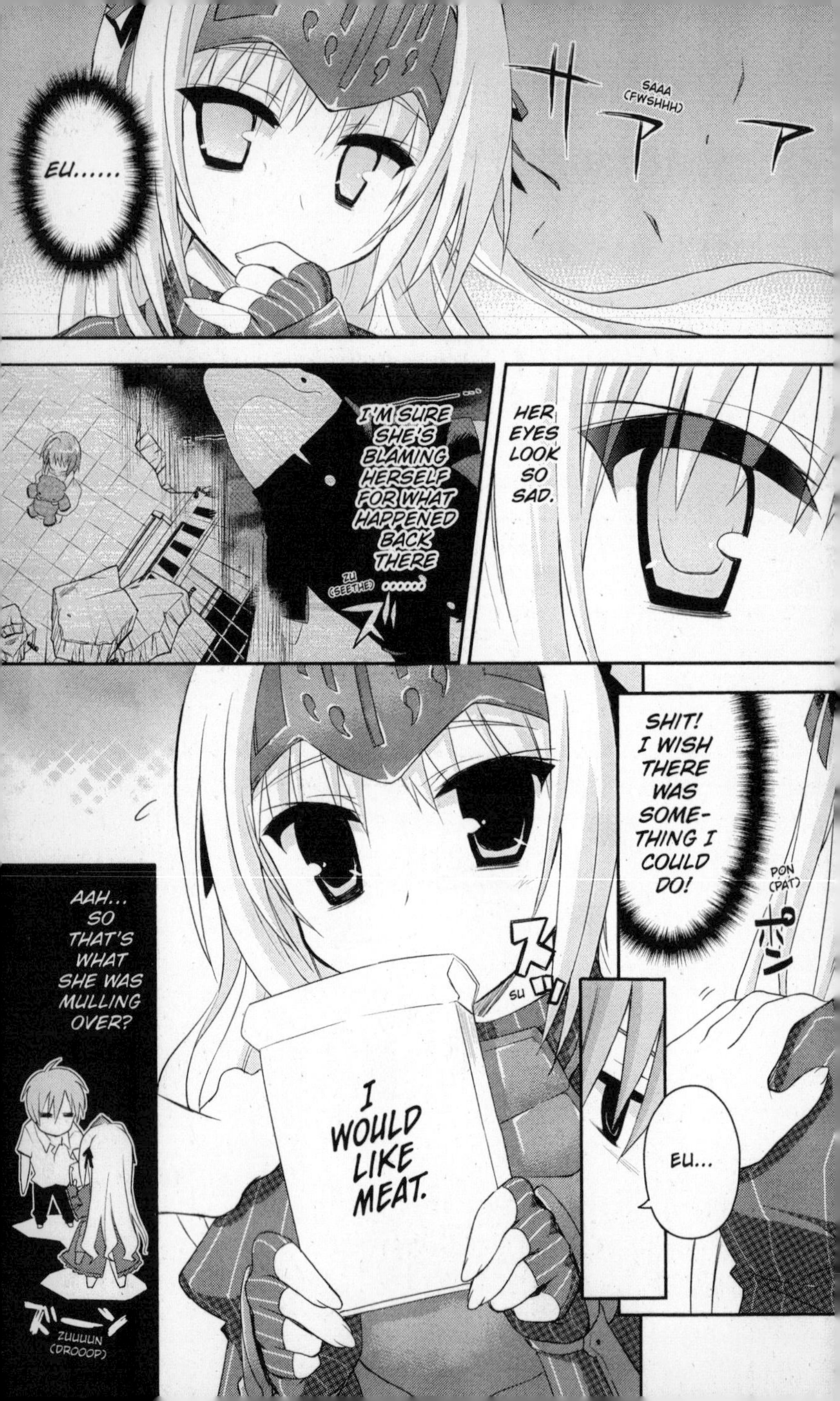
SAAA (FWSHHH)
EU......
HER EYES LOOK SO SAD.
I'M SURE SHE'S BLAMING HERSELF FOR WHAT HAPPENED BACK THERE ....
ZU (SEETHE)
SHIT! I WISH THERE WAS SOMETHING I COULD DO!
PON (PAT)
EU...
SU
I WOULD LIKE MEAT.
AAH... SO THAT'S WHAT SHE WAS MULLING OVER?
ZUUUUN (DROOOP)

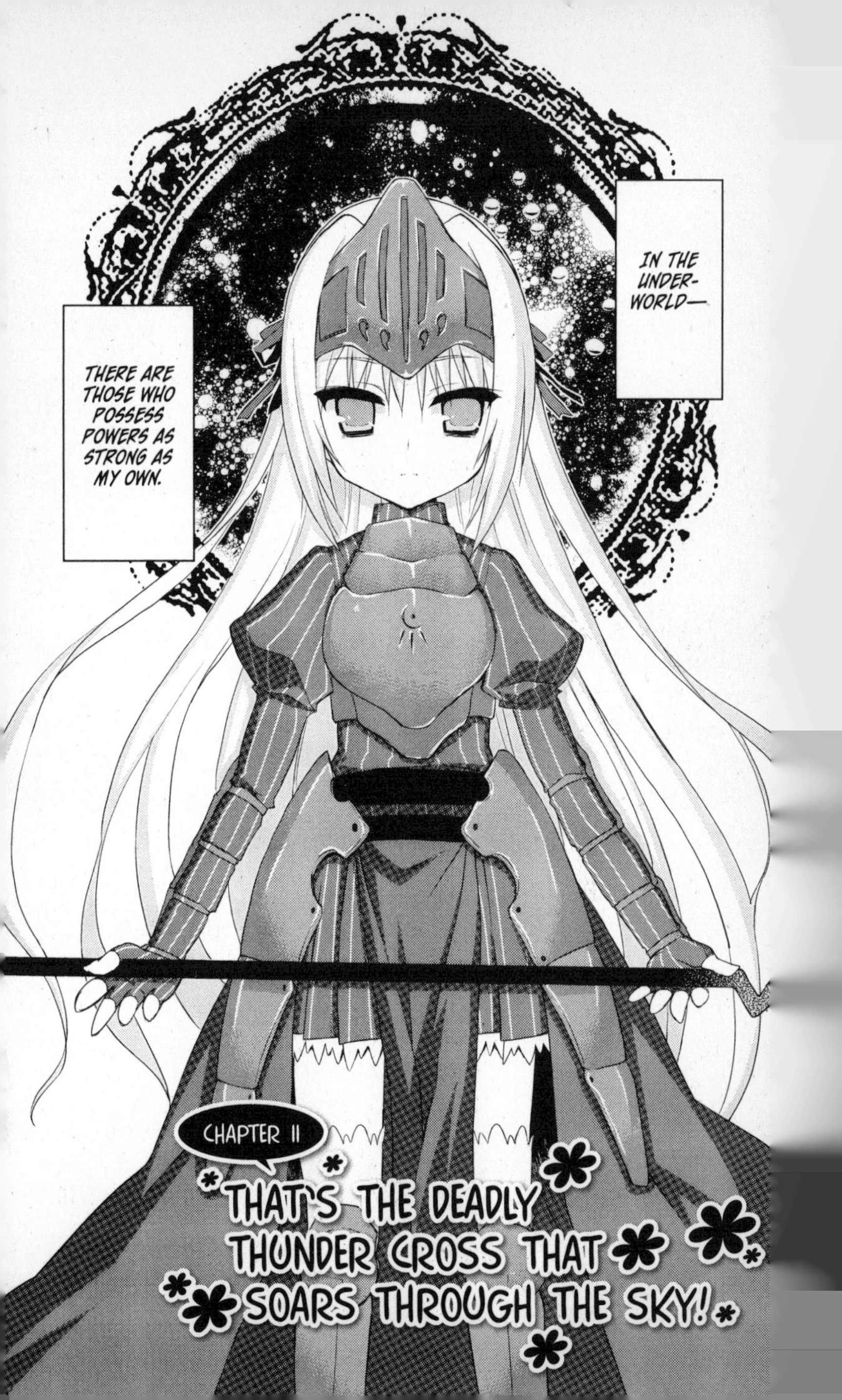
IN THE UNDER-WORLD—
THERE ARE THOSE WHO POSSESS POWERS AS STRONG AS MY OWN.
CHAPTER 11
THAT'S THE DEADLY THUNDER CROSS THAT SOARS THROUGH THE SKY!

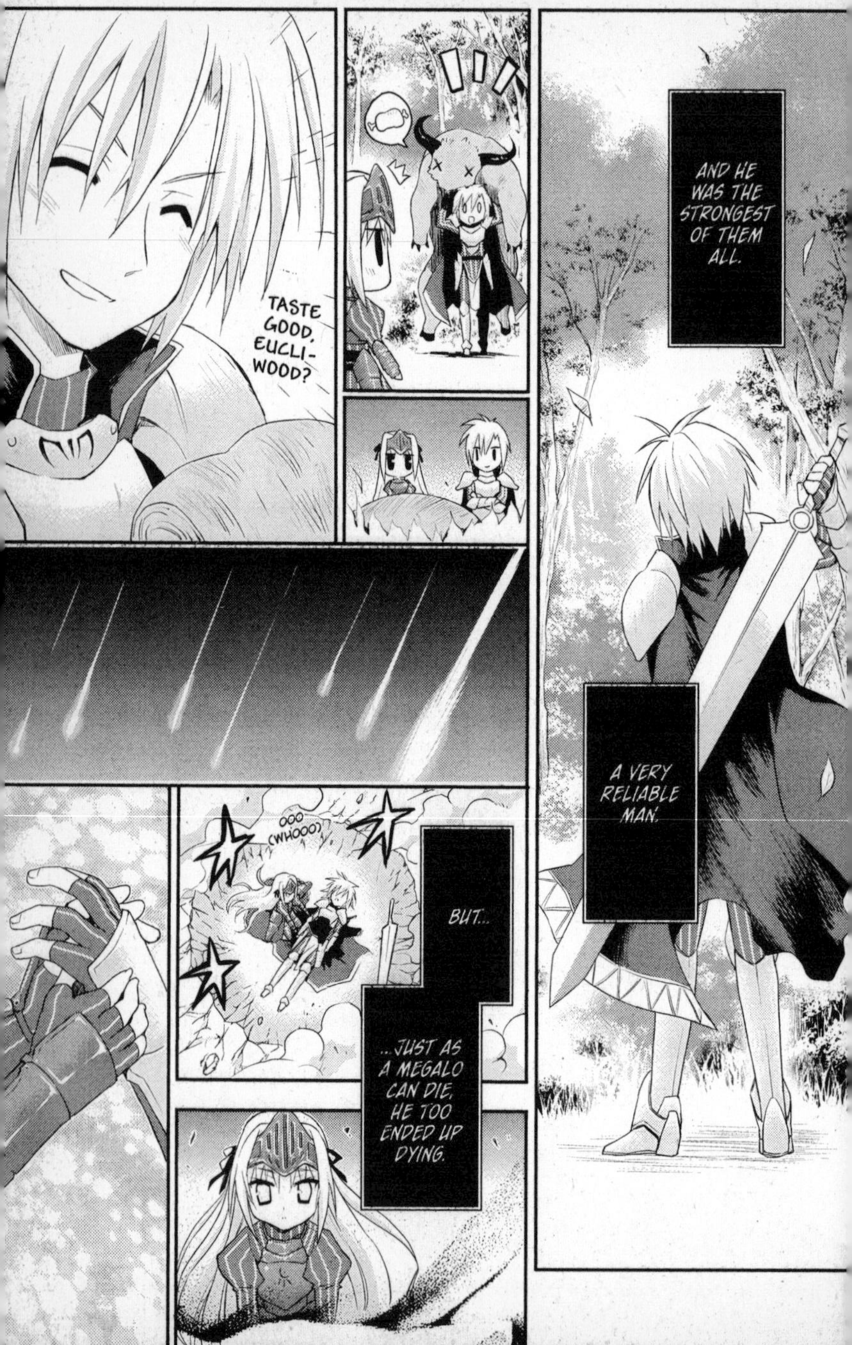
AND HE WAS THE STRONGEST OF THEM ALL.
A VERY RELIABLE MAN.
!!!
...
TASTE GOOD, EUCLI-WOOD?
OOO (WHOOO)
BUT...
...JUST AS A MEGALO CAN DIE, HE TOO ENDED UP DYING.

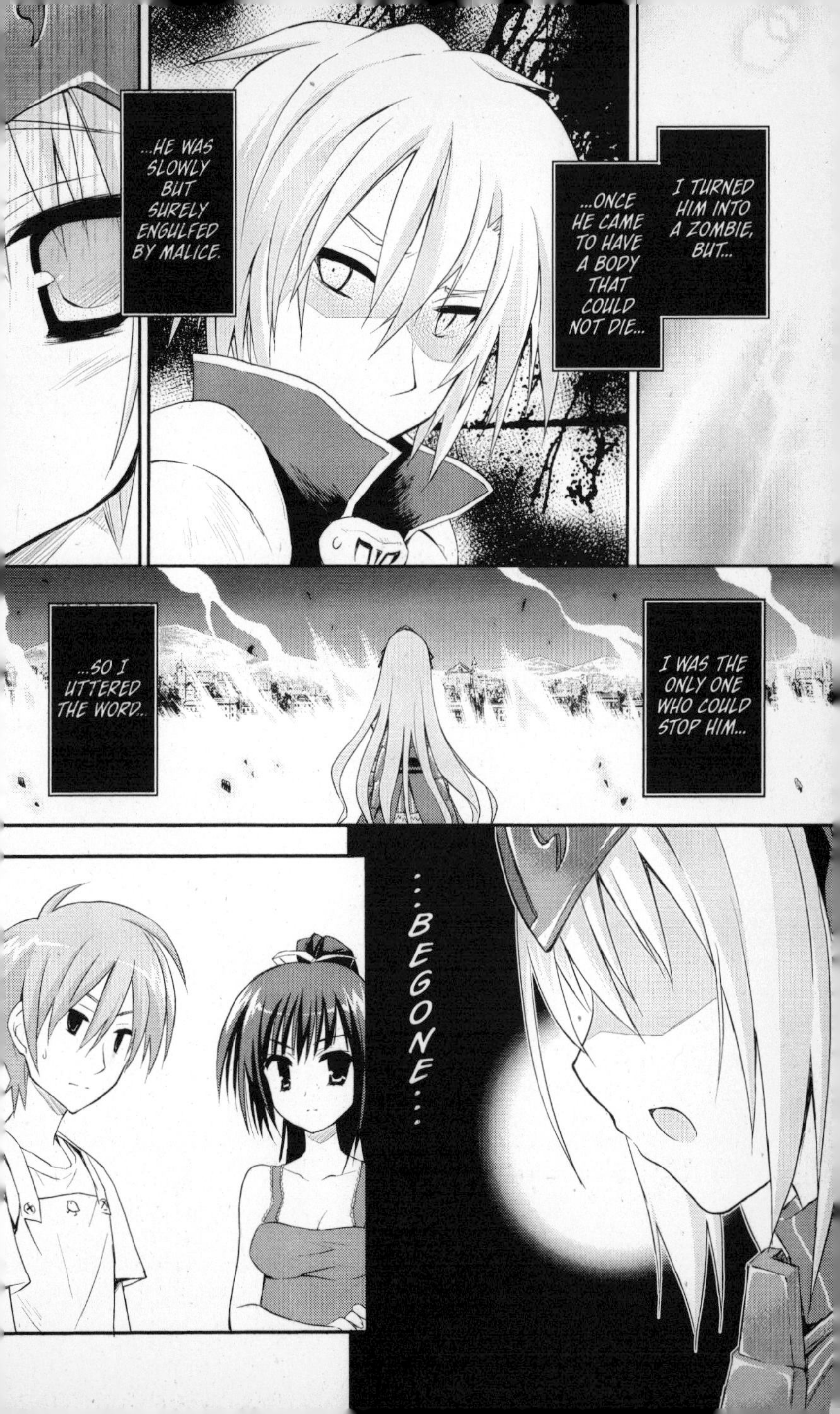
I TURNED HIM INTO A ZOMBIE, BUT...
...ONCE HE CAME TO HAVE A BODY THAT COULD NOT DIE...
...HE WAS SLOWLY BUT SURELY ENGULFED BY MALICE.
I WAS THE ONLY ONE WHO COULD STOP HIM...
...SO I UTTERED THE WORD...
...BEGONE...

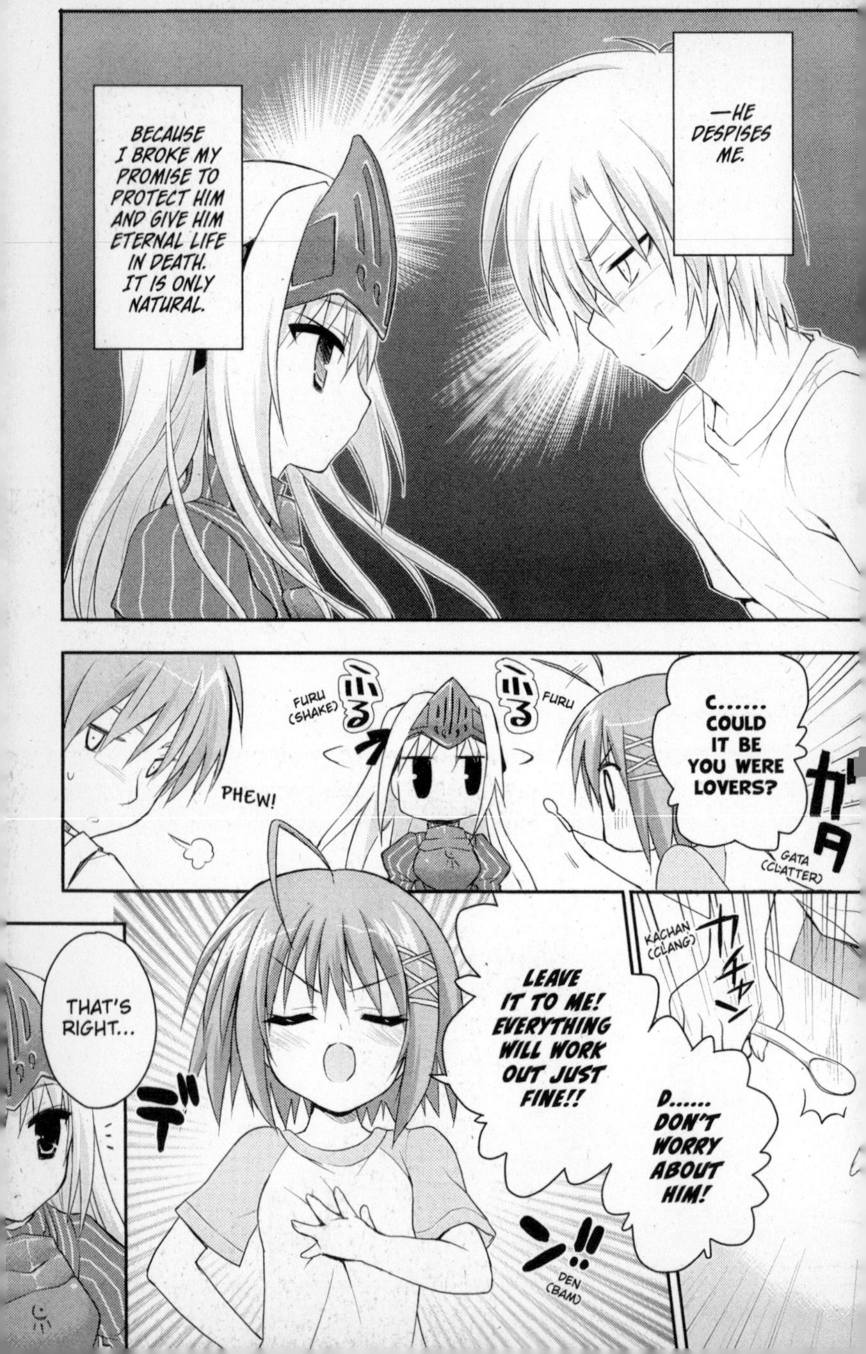
—HE DESPISES ME.
BECAUSE I BROKE MY PROMISE TO PROTECT HIM AND GIVE HIM ETERNAL LIFE IN DEATH. IT IS ONLY NATURAL.
C...... COULD IT BE YOU WERE LOVERS?
GATA (CLATTER)
FURU
FURU (SHAKE)
PHEW!
KACHAN (CLANG)
D...... DON'T WORRY ABOUT HIM!
LEAVE IT TO ME! EVERYTHING WILL WORK OUT JUST FINE!!
DEN (BAM)
THAT'S RIGHT...

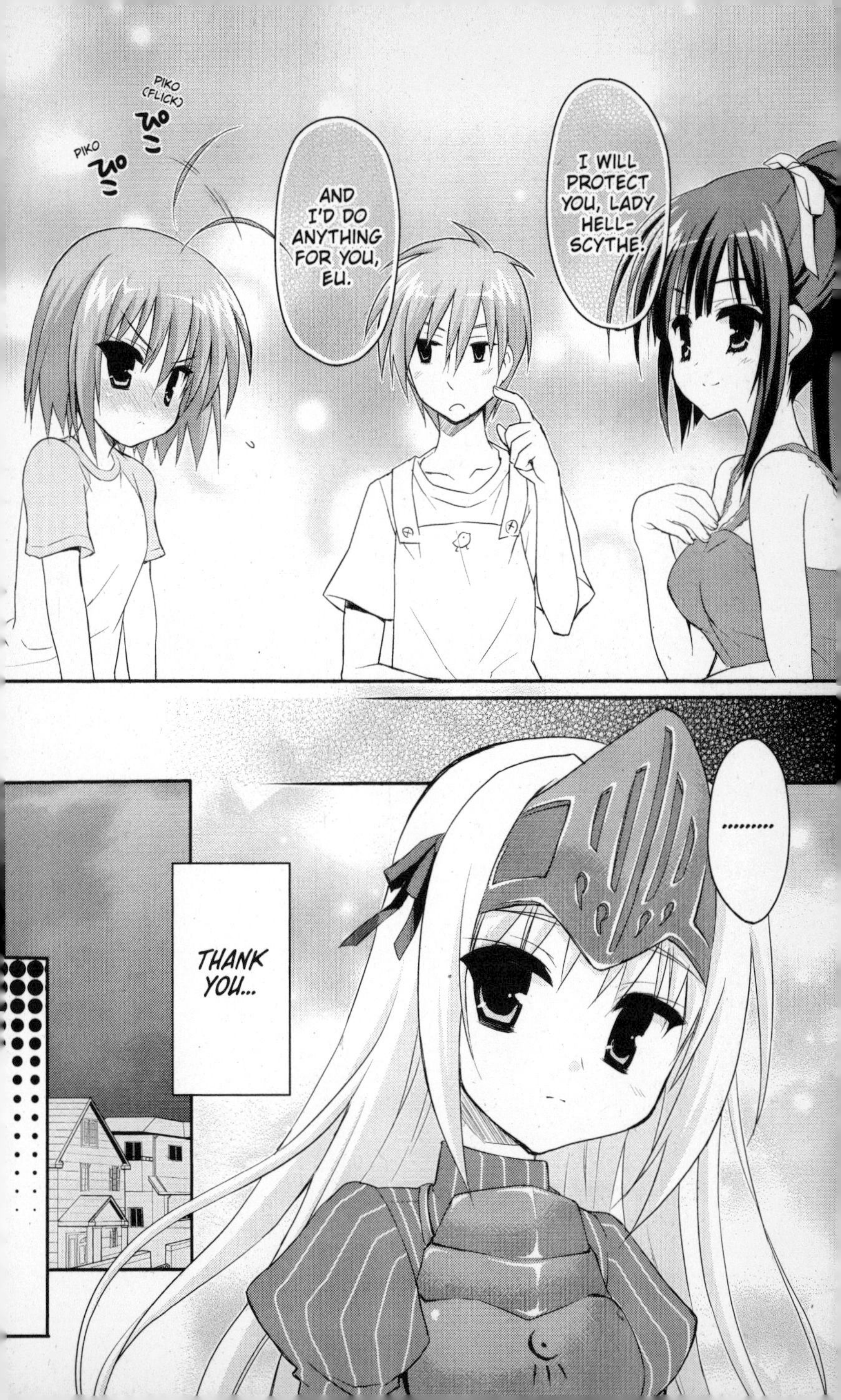
I WILL PROTECT YOU, LADY HELL-SCYTHE.
AND I'D DO ANYTHING FOR YOU, EU.
PIKO (FLICK)
ぴこ
PIKO
ぴこ
....
THANK YOU...

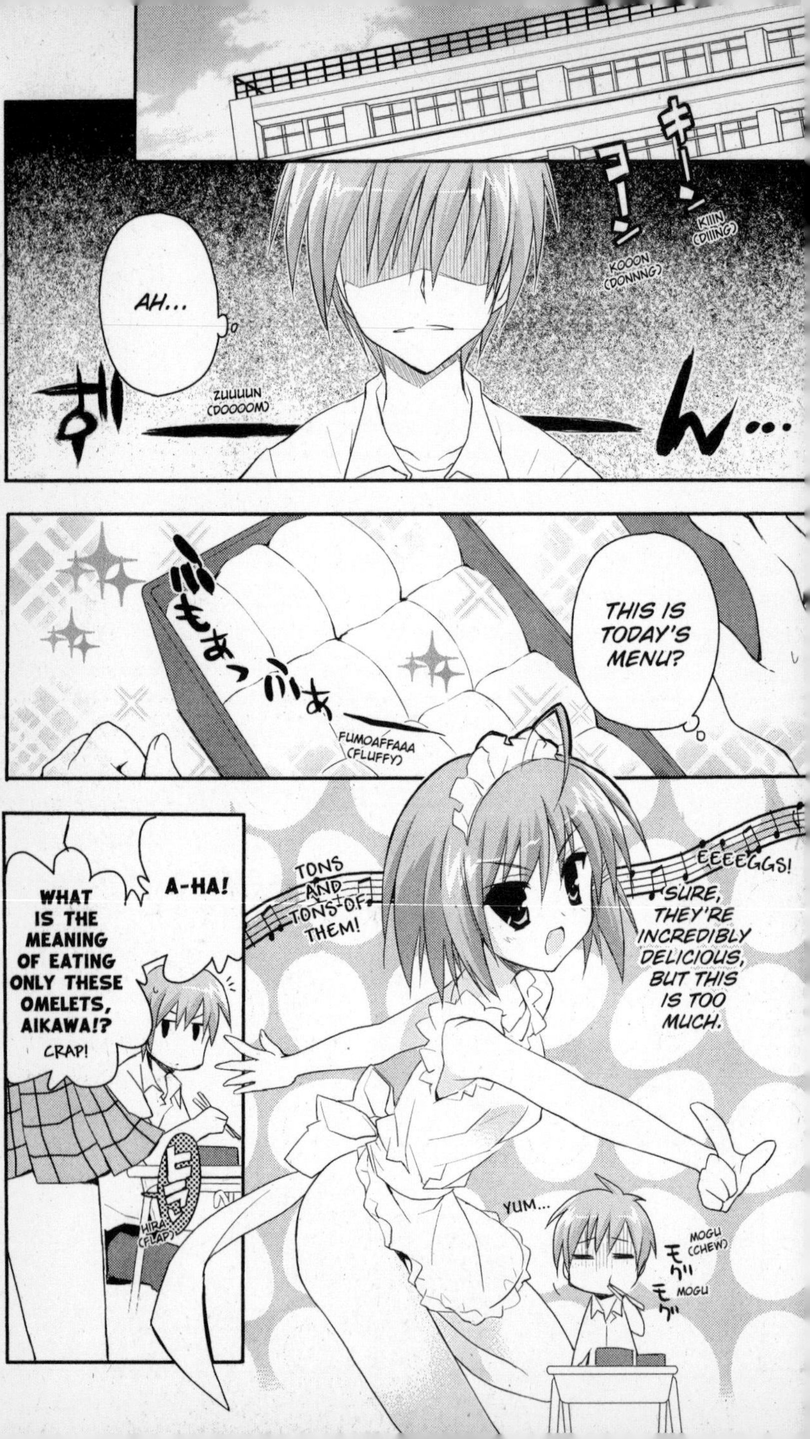
キーン
KIIN (DIIING)
コーン
KOOON (DONNNG)
ずーーん...
ZUUUUN (DOOOOM)
AH...
ふもぁっふぁー
FUMOAFFAAA (FLUFFY)
THIS IS TODAY'S MENU?
EEEEGGS!
SURE, THEY'RE INCREDIBLY DELICIOUS, BUT THIS IS TOO MUCH.
TONS AND TONS OF THEM!
YUM...
モグモグ
MOGU (CHEW) MOGU
A-HA!
WHAT IS THE MEANING OF EATING ONLY THESE OMELETS, AIKAWA!?
CRAP!
ヒラ
HIRA (FLAP)

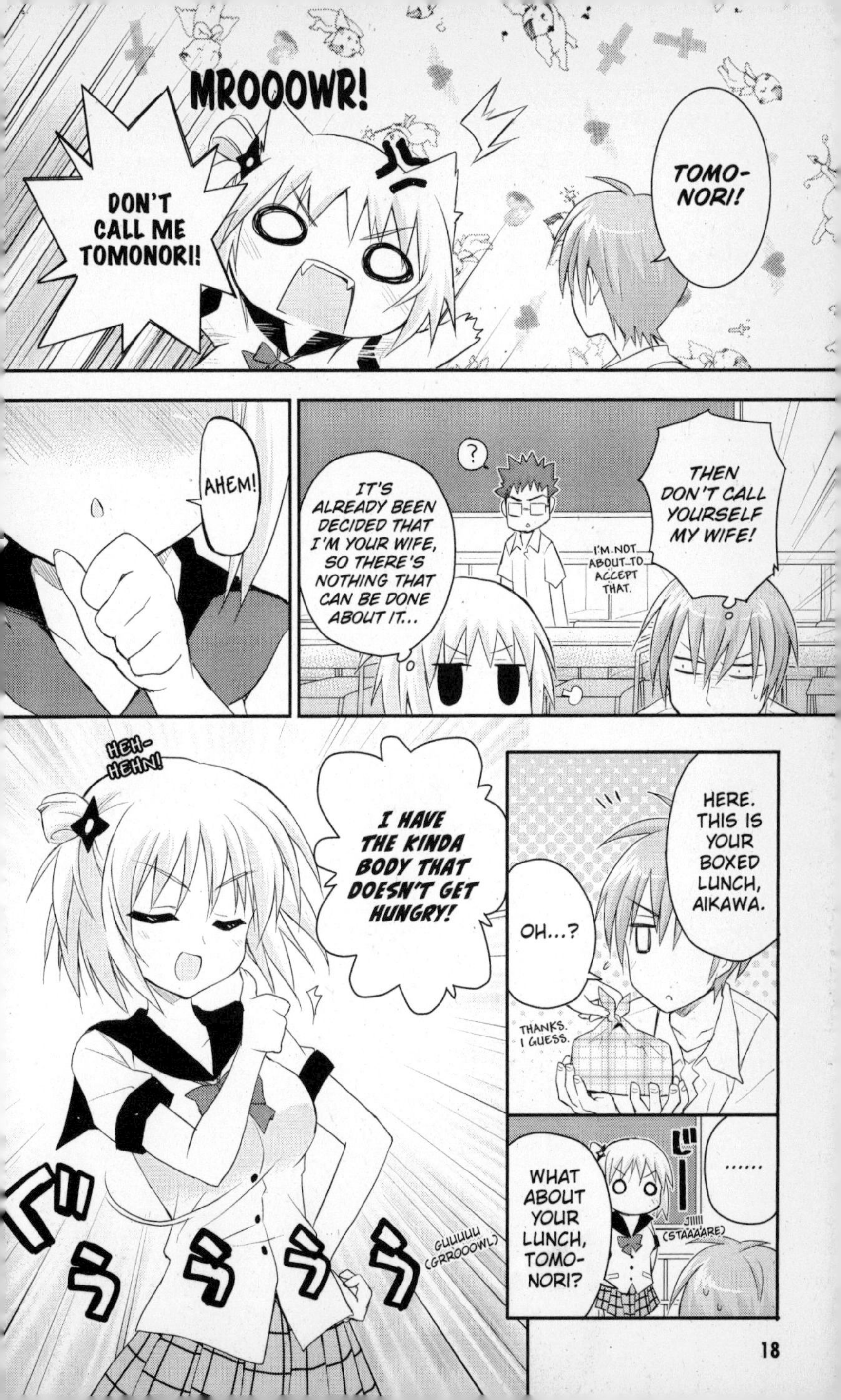

TOMO-NORI!
MROOOWR!
DON'T CALL ME TOMONORI!
THEN DON'T CALL YOURSELF MY WIFE!
I'M NOT ABOUT TO ACCEPT THAT.
?
IT'S ALREADY BEEN DECIDED THAT I'M YOUR WIFE, SO THERE'S NOTHING THAT CAN BE DONE ABOUT IT...
AHEM!
HERE. THIS IS YOUR BOXED LUNCH, AIKAWA.
OH...?
THANKS. I GUESS.
......
JIIIII (STAAAARE)
WHAT ABOUT YOUR LUNCH, TOMO-NORI?
HEH-HEHN!
I HAVE THE KINDA BODY THAT DOESN'T GET HUNGRY!
GUUUUU (GRROOOWL)

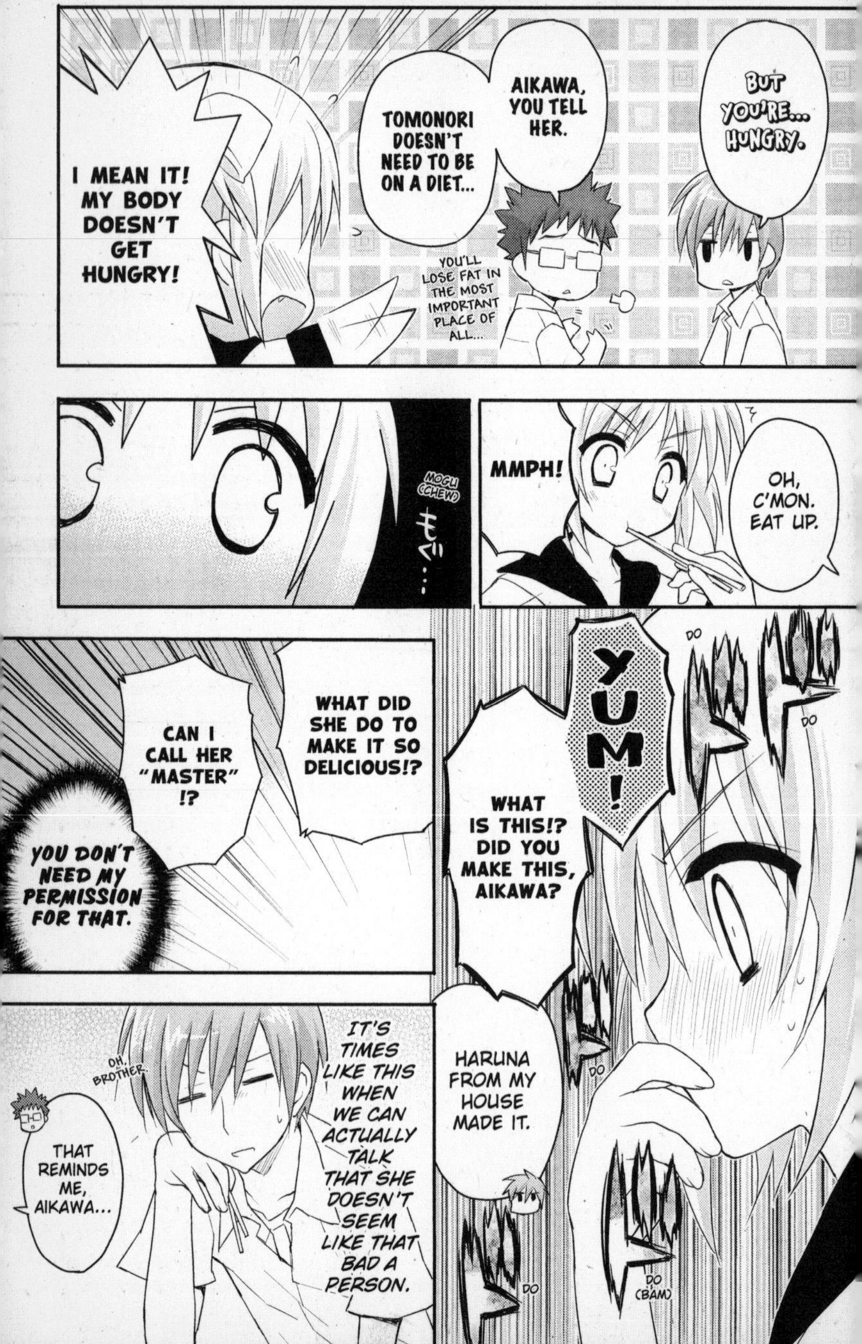

BUT YOU'RE... HUNGRY.
AIKAWA, YOU TELL HER.
TOMONORI DOESN'T NEED TO BE ON A DIET...
YOU'LL LOSE FAT IN THE MOST IMPORTANT PLACE OF ALL...
I MEAN IT! MY BODY DOESN'T GET HUNGRY!
OH, C'MON. EAT UP.
MMPH!
MOGU (CHEW)
もぐ…
DO
DO
YUM!
WHAT IS THIS!? DID YOU MAKE THIS, AIKAWA?
HARUNA FROM MY HOUSE MADE IT.
DO
DO
DO (BAM)
WHAT DID SHE DO TO MAKE IT SO DELICIOUS!?
CAN I CALL HER "MASTER" !?
YOU DON'T NEED MY PERMISSION FOR THAT.
IT'S TIMES LIKE THIS WHEN WE CAN ACTUALLY TALK THAT SHE DOESN'T SEEM LIKE THAT BAD A PERSON.
OH, BROTHER.
THAT REMINDS ME, AIKAWA...

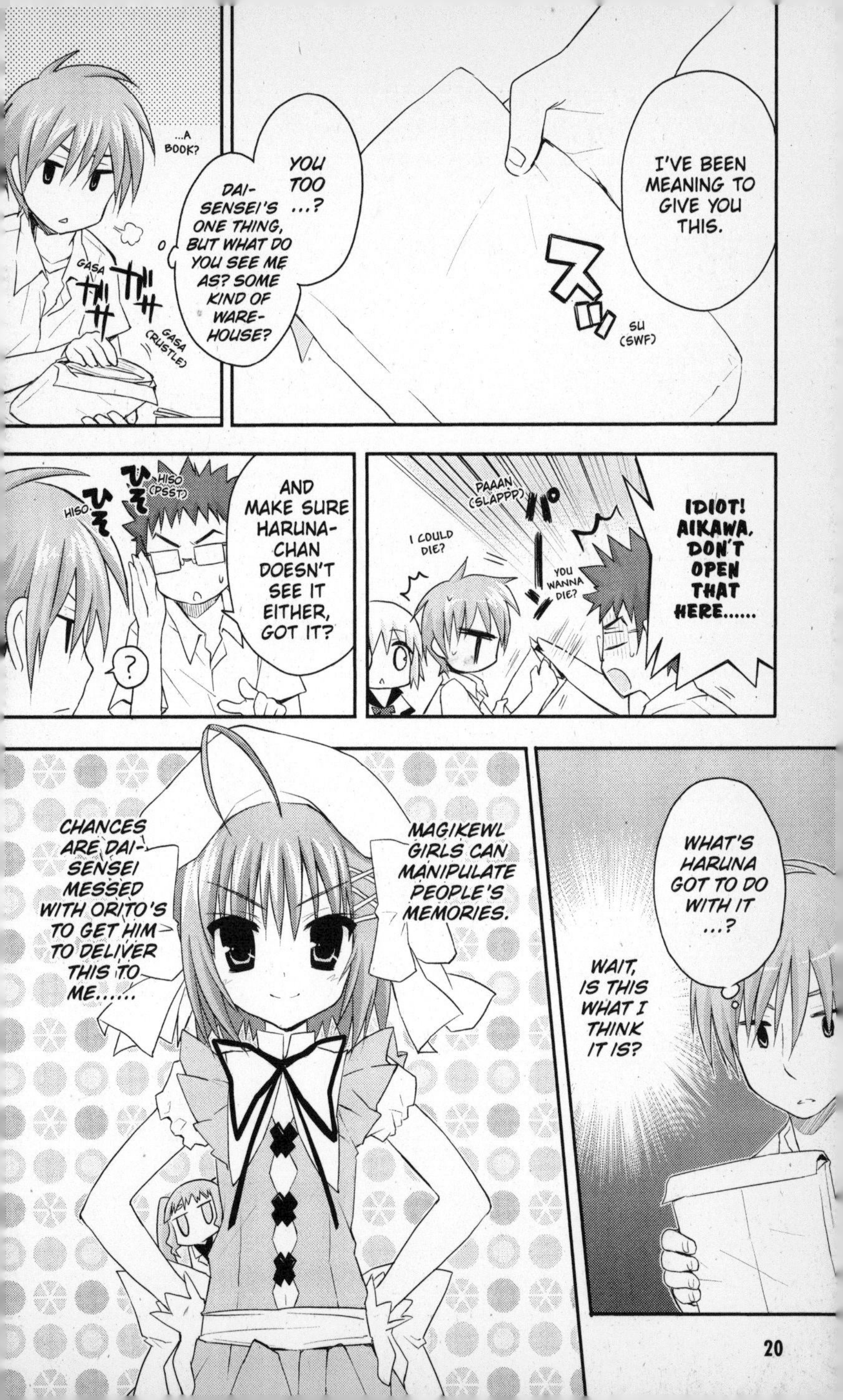
I'VE BEEN MEANING TO GIVE YOU THIS.
スッ
SU (SWF)
YOU TOO ...?
DAI-SENSEI'S ONE THING, BUT WHAT DO YOU SEE ME AS? SOME KIND OF WARE-HOUSE?
...A BOOK?
GASA
GASA (RUSTLE)
IDIOT! AIKAWA, DON'T OPEN THAT HERE......
PAAAN (SLAPPP)
YOU WANNA DIE?
I COULD DIE?
AND MAKE SURE HARUNA-CHAN DOESN'T SEE IT EITHER, GOT IT?
HISO (PSST)
HISO
?
WHAT'S HARUNA GOT TO DO WITH IT ...?
WAIT, IS THIS WHAT I THINK IT IS?
MAGIKEWL GIRLS CAN MANIPULATE PEOPLE'S MEMORIES.
CHANCES ARE DAI-SENSEI MESSED WITH ORITO'S TO GET HIM TO DELIVER THIS TO ME......

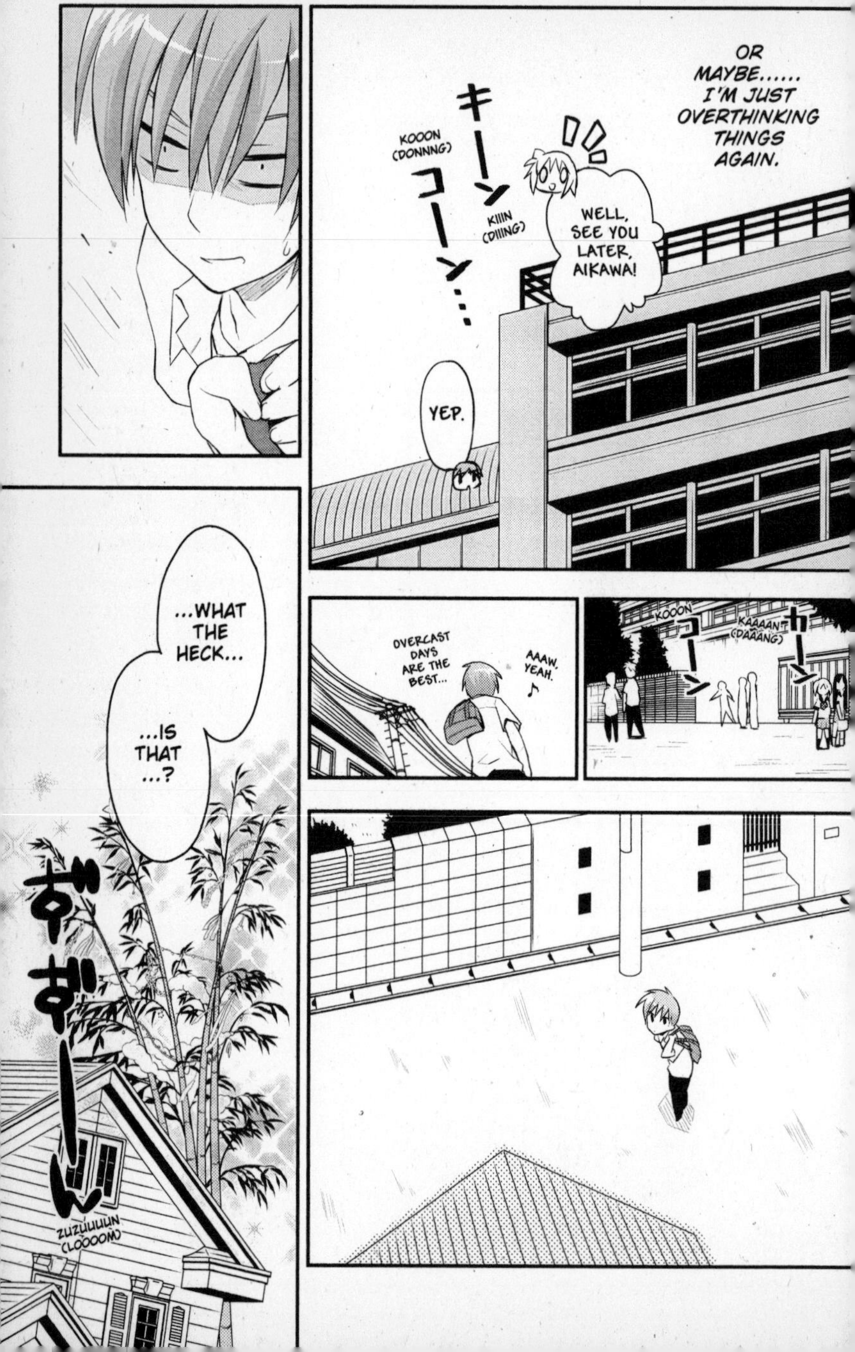
OR MAYBE...... I'M JUST OVERTHINKING THINGS AGAIN.
キーン
KIIIN (DIIING)
コーン…
KOOON (DONNNG)
WELL, SEE YOU LATER, AIKAWA!
YEP.
カーン
KAAAAN (DAAANG)
コーン
KOOON
OVERCAST DAYS ARE THE BEST...
AAAW, YEAH. ♪
...WHAT THE HECK...
...IS THAT ...?
ずずーん
ZUZUUUUN (LOOOOM)

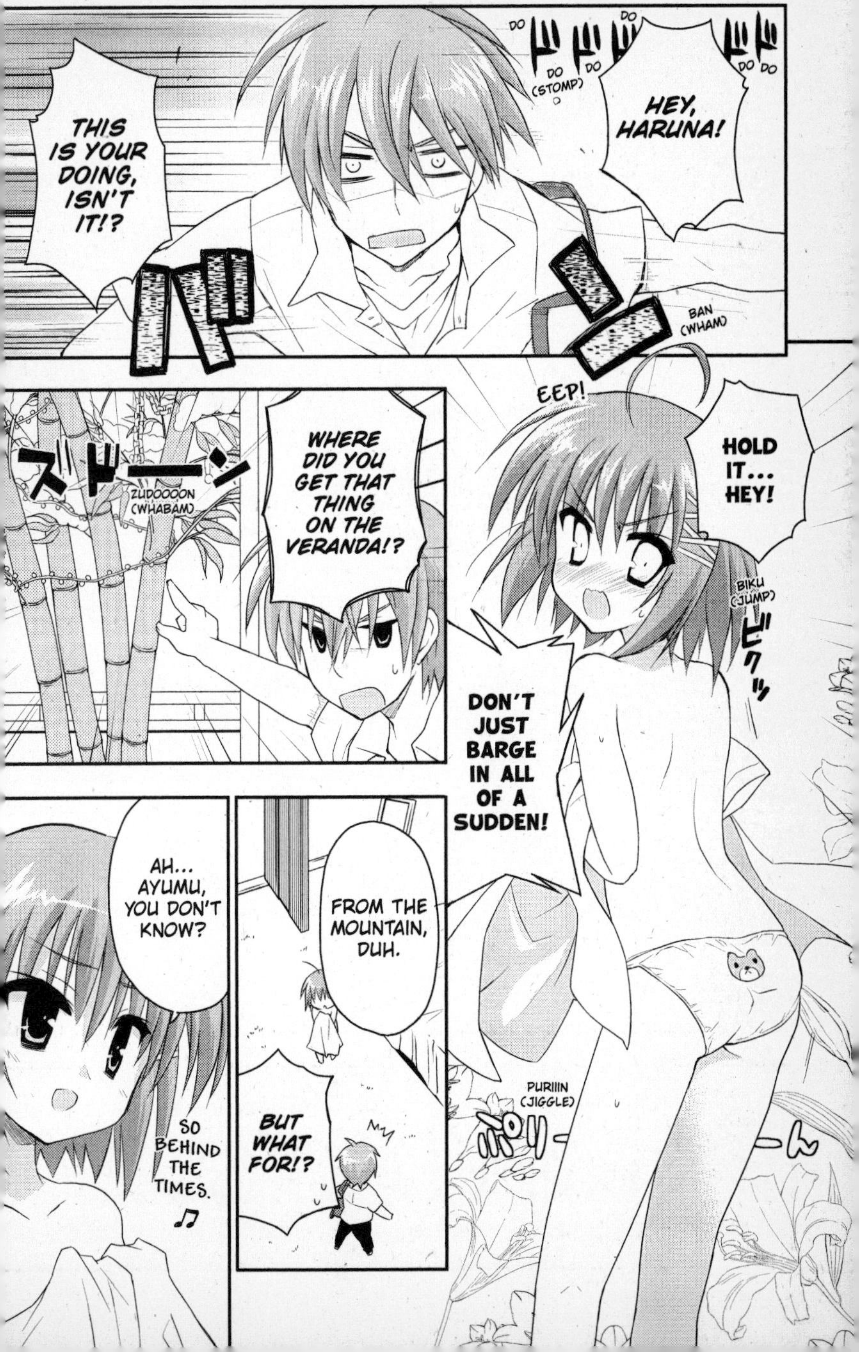
DO DO DO DO (STOMP) DO DO DO
HEY, HARUNA!
THIS IS YOUR DOING, ISN'T IT!?
BAN (WHAM)
EEP!
HOLD IT... HEY!
BIKU (JUMP)
DON'T JUST BARGE IN ALL OF A SUDDEN!
PURIIIN (JIGGLE)
WHERE DID YOU GET THAT THING ON THE VERANDA!?
ZUDOOOON (WHABAM)
FROM THE MOUNTAIN, DUH.
BUT WHAT FOR!?
AH... AYUMU, YOU DON'T KNOW?
SO BEHIND THE TIMES. ♪

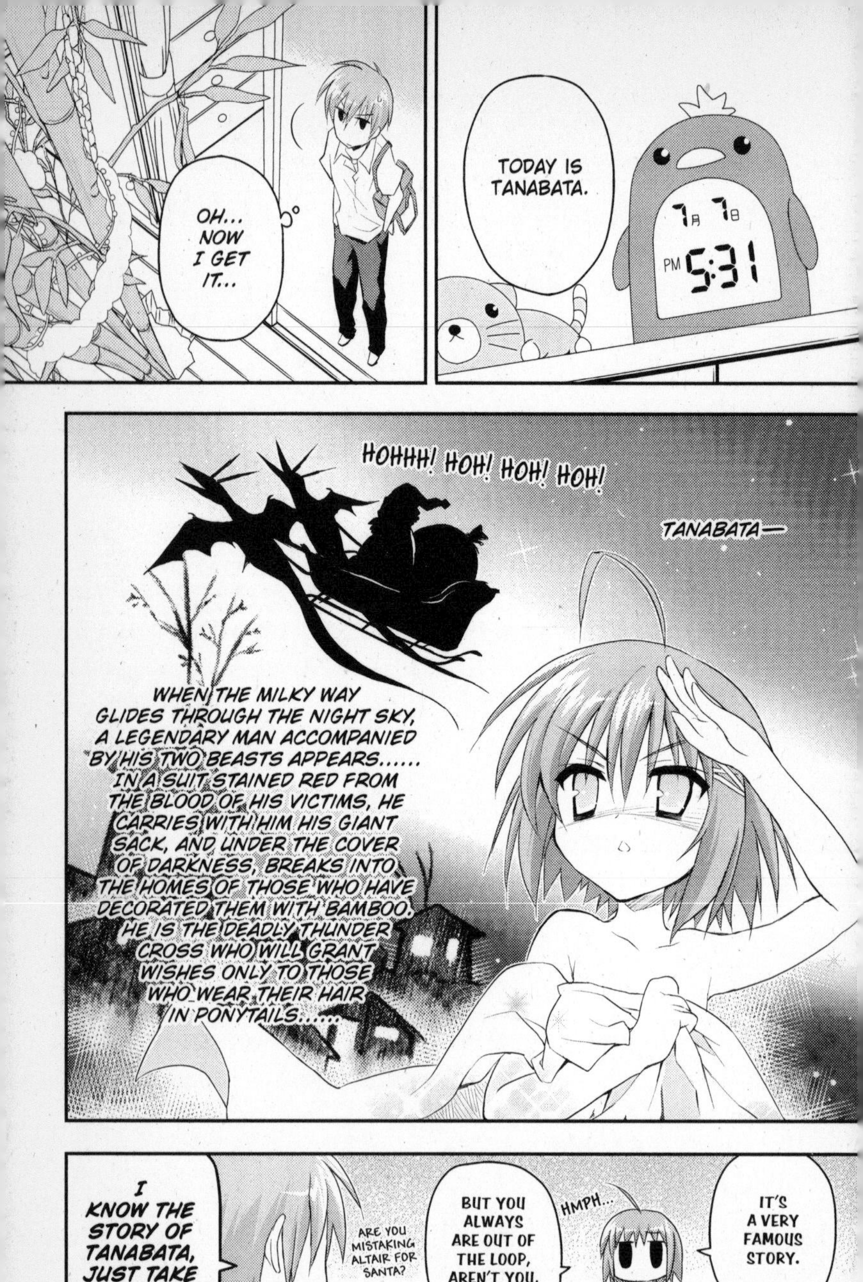

TODAY IS TANABATA.
7月 7日
PM 5:31
OH... NOW I GET IT...
HOHHH! HOH! HOH! HOH!
TANABATA—
WHEN THE MILKY WAY GLIDES THROUGH THE NIGHT SKY, A LEGENDARY MAN ACCOMPANIED BY HIS TWO BEASTS APPEARS...... IN A SUIT STAINED RED FROM THE BLOOD OF HIS VICTIMS, HE CARRIES WITH HIM HIS GIANT SACK, AND UNDER THE COVER OF DARKNESS, BREAKS INTO THE HOMES OF THOSE WHO HAVE DECORATED THEM WITH BAMBOO. HE IS THE DEADLY THUNDER CROSS WHO WILL GRANT WISHES ONLY TO THOSE WHO WEAR THEIR HAIR IN PONYTAILS......
IT'S A VERY FAMOUS STORY.
HMPH...
BUT YOU ALWAYS ARE OUT OF THE LOOP, AREN'T YOU, AYUMU?
ARE YOU MISTAKING ALTAIR FOR SANTA?
I KNOW THE STORY OF TANABATA, JUST TAKE THIS THING DOWN.

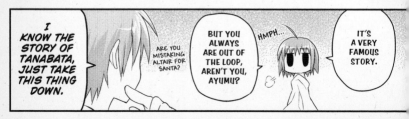

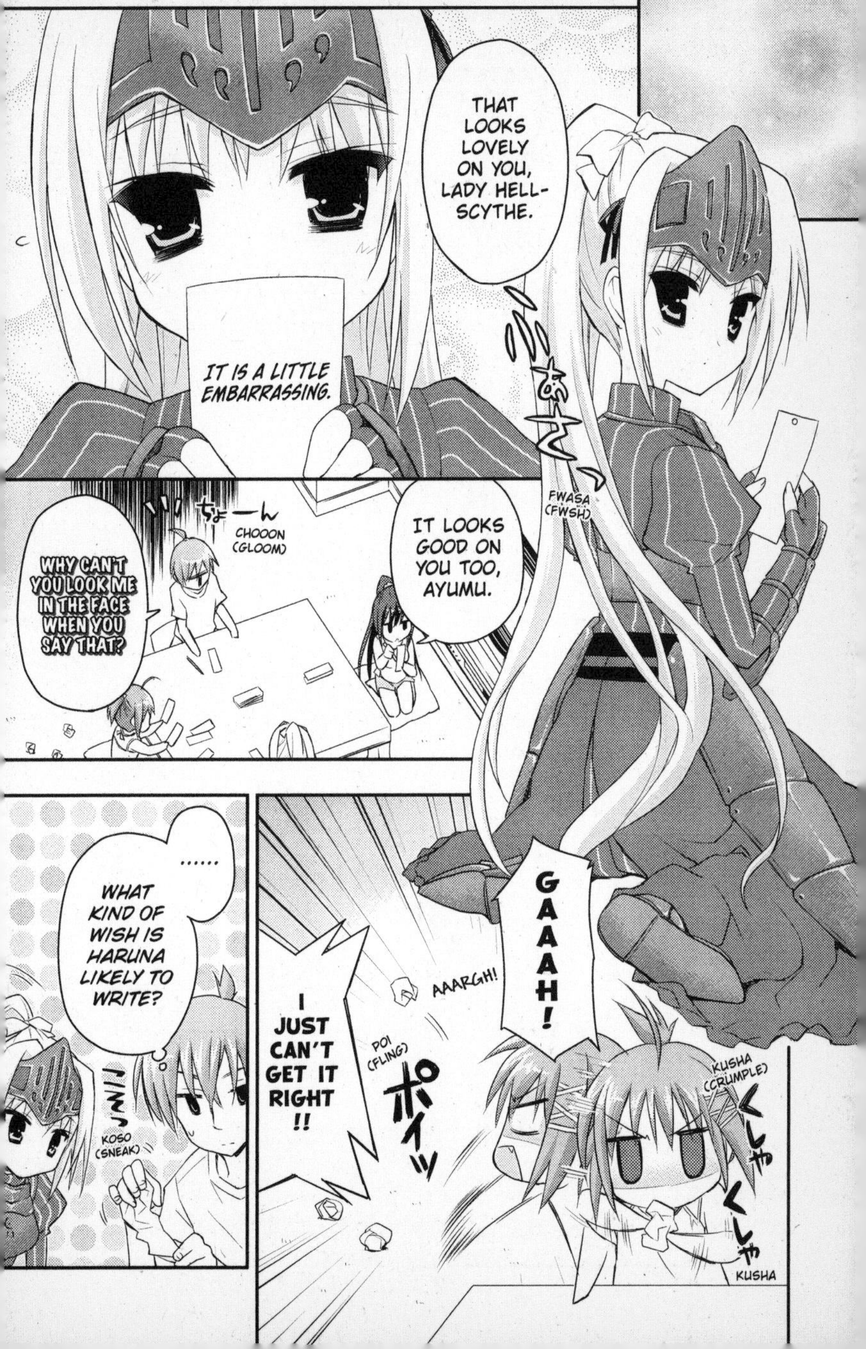
THAT LOOKS LOVELY ON YOU, LADY HELL-SCYTHE.
IT IS A LITTLE EMBARRASSING.
ふぁさっ
FWASA (FWSH)
IT LOOKS GOOD ON YOU TOO, AYUMU.
ちょーん
CHOOON (GLOOM)
WHY CAN'T YOU LOOK ME IN THE FACE WHEN YOU SAY THAT?
GAAAAH!
I JUST CAN'T GET IT RIGHT!!
AAARGH!
POI (FLING)
ポイッ
KUSHA (CRUMPLE)
くしゃくしゃ
KUSHA
......
WHAT KIND OF WISH IS HARUNA LIKELY TO WRITE?
KOSO (SNEAK)

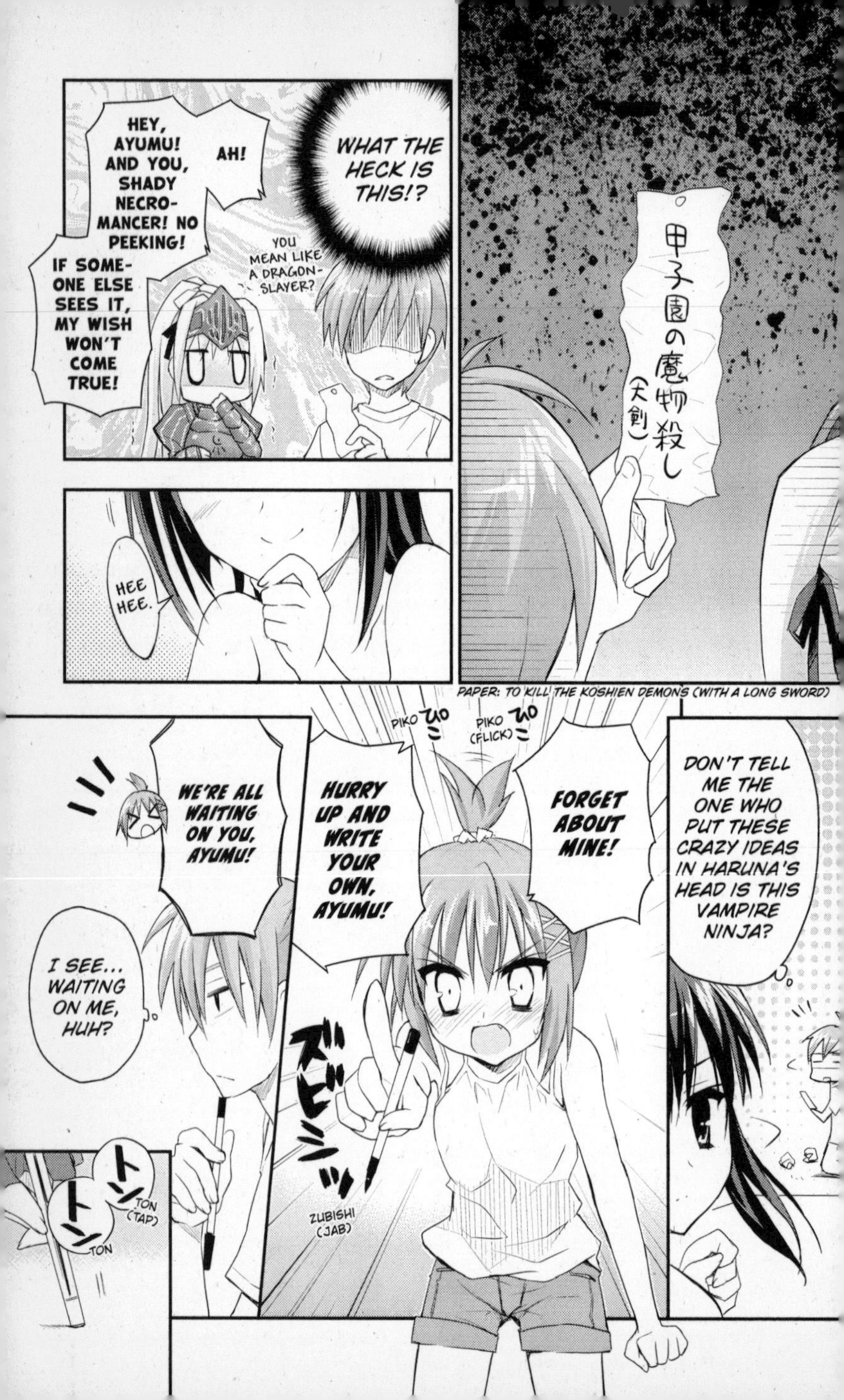
甲子園の魔物殺し(大剣)
PAPER: TO KILL THE KOSHIEN DEMONS (WITH A LONG SWORD)
WHAT THE HECK IS THIS!?
AH!
YOU MEAN LIKE A DRAGON-SLAYER?
HEY, AYUMU! AND YOU, SHADY NECROMANCER! NO PEEKING!
IF SOMEONE ELSE SEES IT, MY WISH WON'T COME TRUE!
HEE HEE.
DON'T TELL ME THE ONE WHO PUT THESE CRAZY IDEAS IN HARUNA'S HEAD IS THIS VAMPIRE NINJA?
ぴこ PIKO (FLICK)
ぴこ PIKO
FORGET ABOUT MINE!
HURRY UP AND WRITE YOUR OWN, AYUMU!
ズビシッ ZUBISHI (JAB)
WE'RE ALL WAITING ON YOU, AYUMU!
I SEE... WAITING ON ME, HUH?
トン TON (TAP)
トン TON

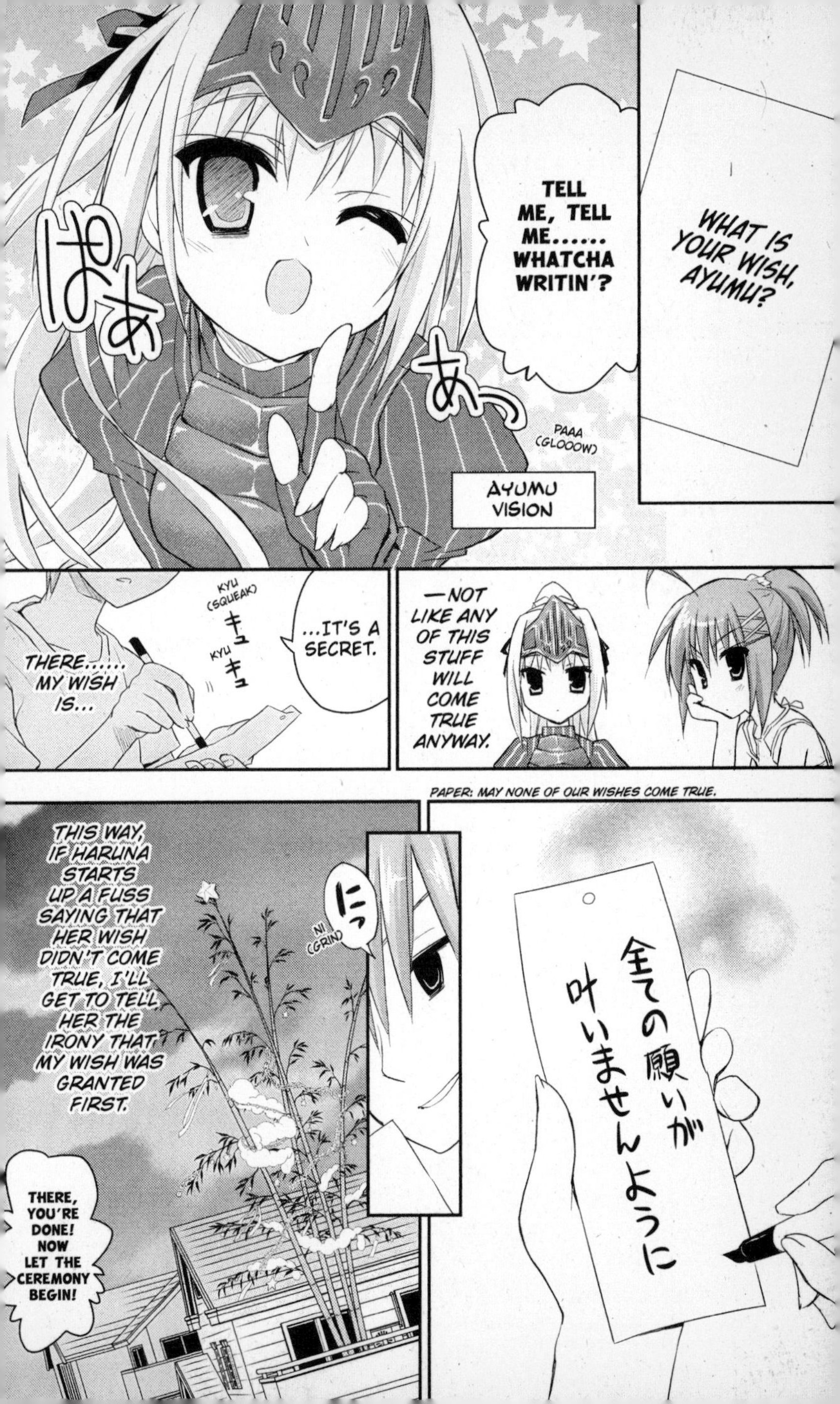
WHAT IS YOUR WISH, AYUMU?
TELL ME, TELL ME...... WHATCHA WRITIN'?
ぱあ
あっ
PAAA (GLOOOW)
AYUMU VISION
—NOT LIKE ANY OF THIS STUFF WILL COME TRUE ANYWAY.
...IT'S A SECRET.
KYU (SQUEAK)
キュ
KYU
キュ
THERE...... MY WISH IS...
PAPER: MAY NONE OF OUR WISHES COME TRUE.
全ての願いが叶いませんように
にっ
NI (GRIN)
THIS WAY, IF HARUNA STARTS UP A FUSS SAYING THAT HER WISH DIDN'T COME TRUE, I'LL GET TO TELL HER THE IRONY THAT MY WISH WAS GRANTED FIRST.
THERE, YOU'RE DONE! NOW LET THE CEREMONY BEGIN!

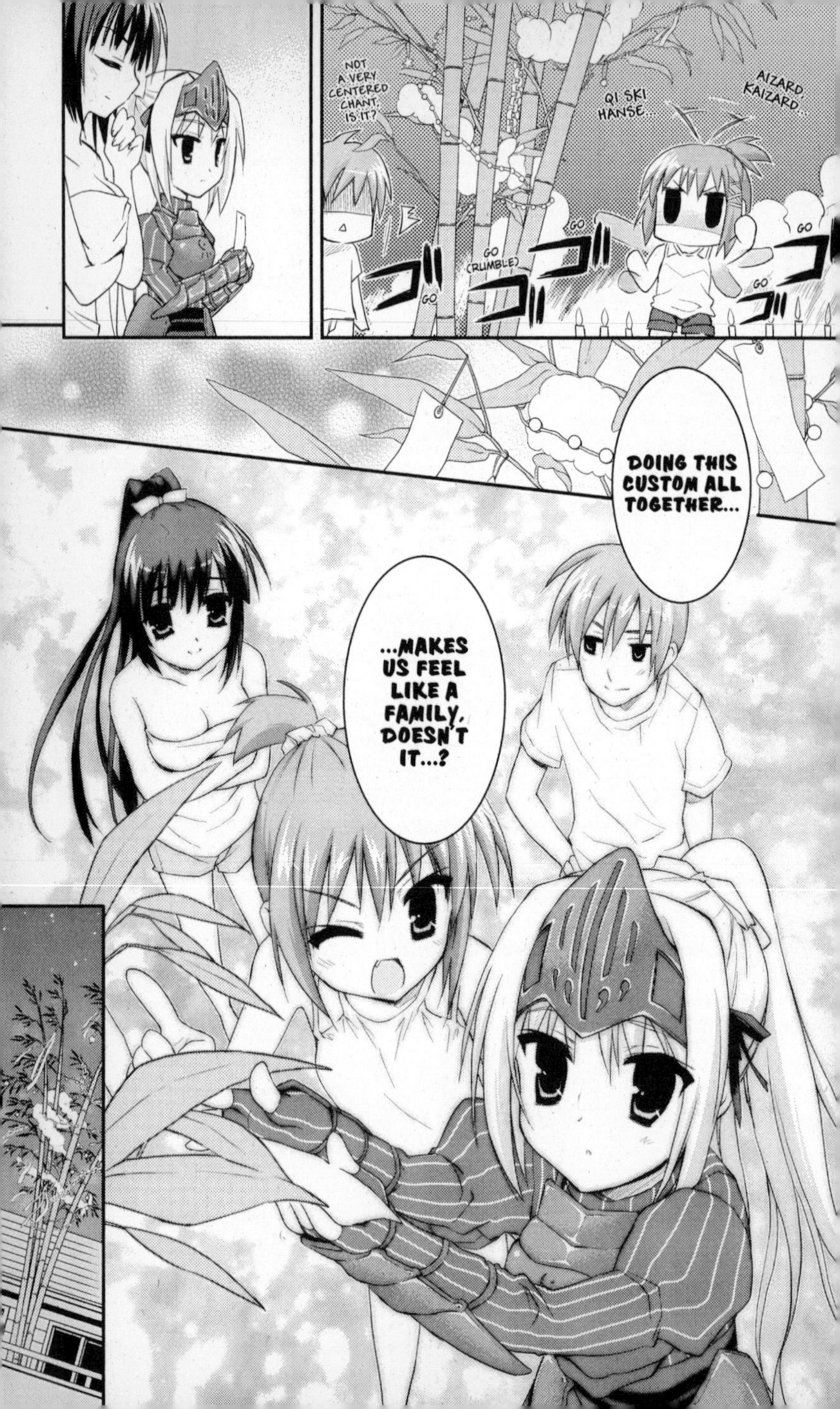
AIZARD, KAIZARD...
QI SKI HANSE...
NOT A VERY CENTERED CHANT, IS IT?
GO
GO
GO (RUMBLE)
GO
GO
DOING THIS CUSTOM ALL TOGETHER...
...MAKES US FEEL LIKE A FAMILY, DOESN'T IT...?

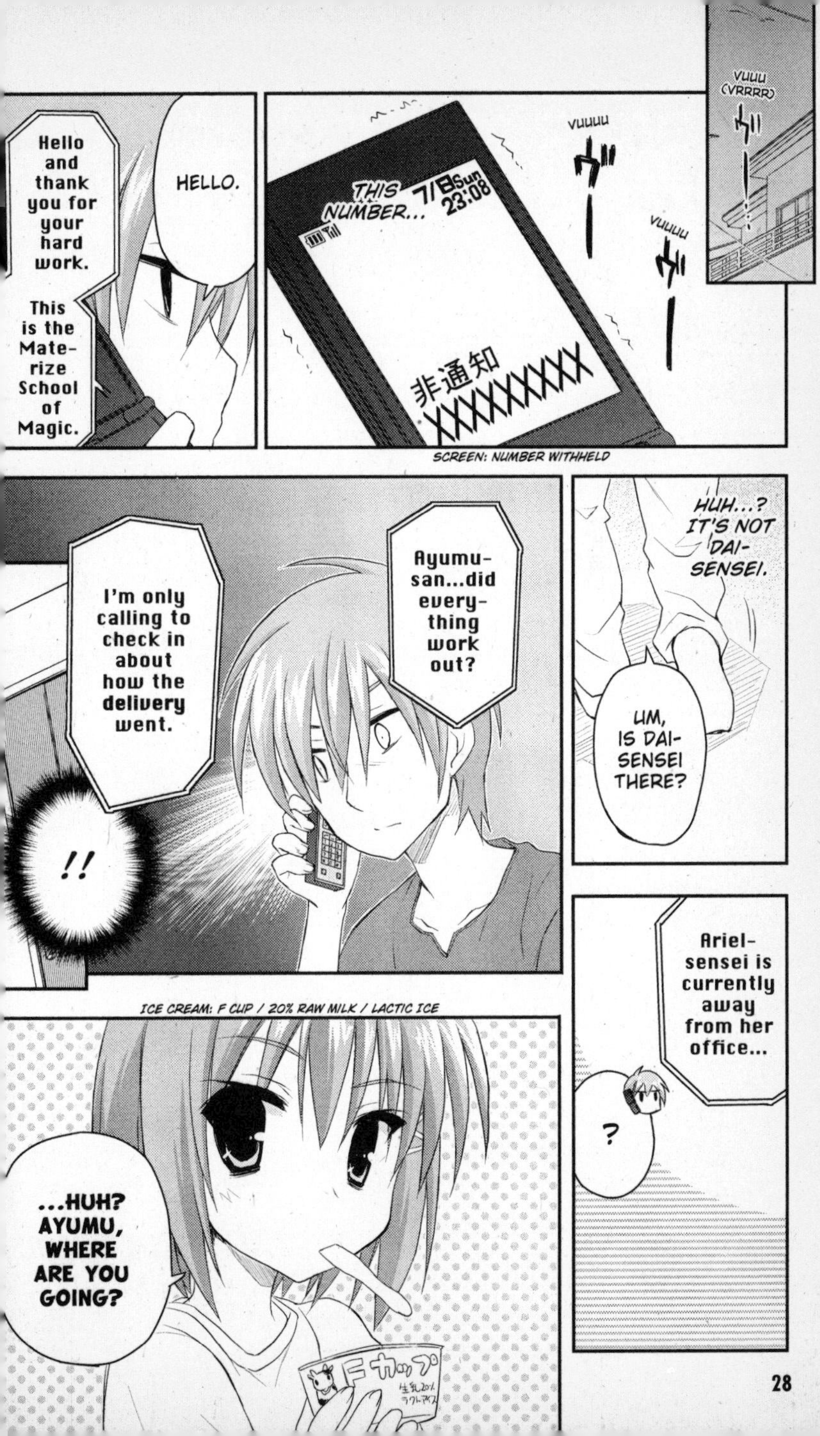
vuuu
(VRRRR)
ヴー…
vuuuu
ヴー
vuuuu
ヴー
THIS NUMBER...
7/日Sun 23:08
非通知
XXXXXXXX
SCREEN: NUMBER WITHHELD
HELLO.
Hello and thank you for your hard work.
This is the Materize School of Magic.
HUH...? IT'S NOT DAI-SENSEI.
UM, IS DAI-SENSEI THERE?
Ayumu-san...did everything work out?
I'm only calling to check in about how the delivery went.
!!
Ariel-sensei is currently away from her office...
?
ICE CREAM: F CUP / 20% RAW MILK / LACTIC ICE
...HUH? AYUMU, WHERE ARE YOU GOING?
Fカップ
生乳20%
ラクトアイス

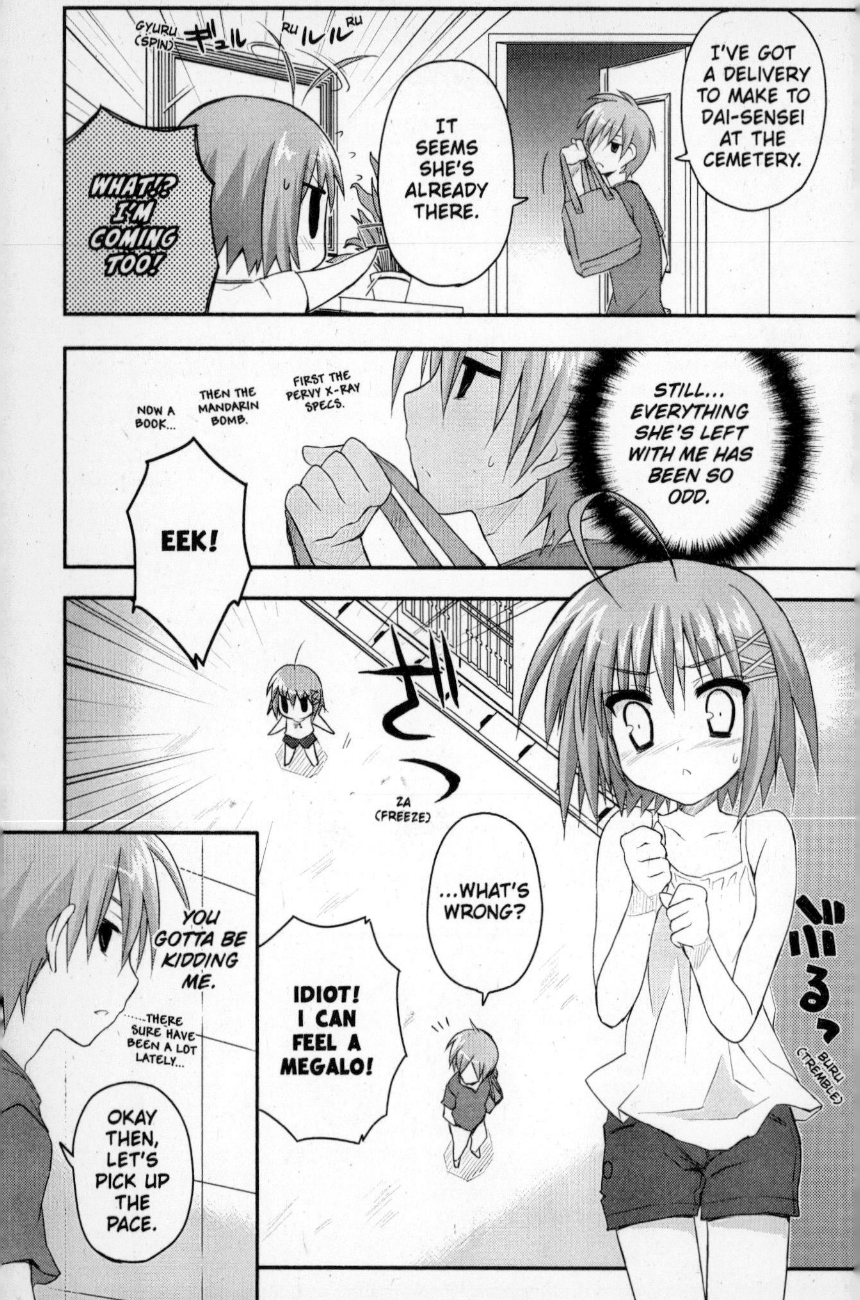
I'VE GOT A DELIVERY TO MAKE TO DAI-SENSEI AT THE CEMETERY.
IT SEEMS SHE'S ALREADY THERE.
GYURU (SPIN) ギュルルルRU RU
WHAT!? I'M COMING TOO!
STILL... EVERYTHING SHE'S LEFT WITH ME HAS BEEN SO ODD.
FIRST THE PERVY X-RAY SPECS.
THEN THE MANDARIN BOMB.
NOW A BOOK...
EEK!
BURU (TREMBLE)
ZA (FREEZE)
...WHAT'S WRONG?
IDIOT! I CAN FEEL A MEGALO!
YOU GOTTA BE KIDDING ME.
......THERE SURE HAVE BEEN A LOT LATELY...
OKAY THEN, LET'S PICK UP THE PACE.

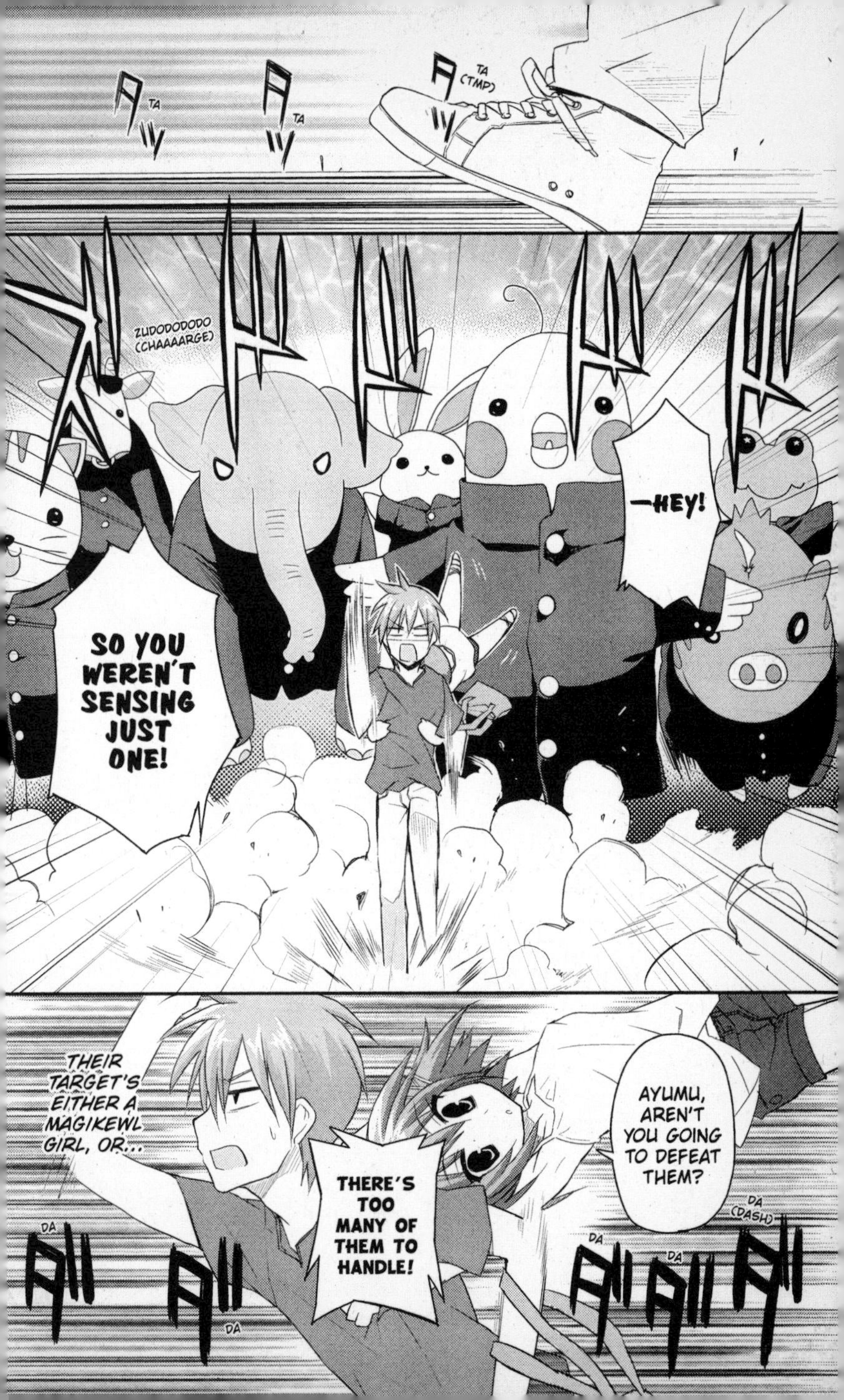
TA (TMP)
TA
TA
—HEY!
ZUDODODODO (CHAAAARGE)
SO YOU WEREN'T SENSING JUST ONE!
AYUMU, AREN'T YOU GOING TO DEFEAT THEM?
DA (DASH)
DA
DA
THERE'S TOO MANY OF THEM TO HANDLE!
THEIR TARGET'S EITHER A MAGIKEWL GIRL, OR...
DA
DA

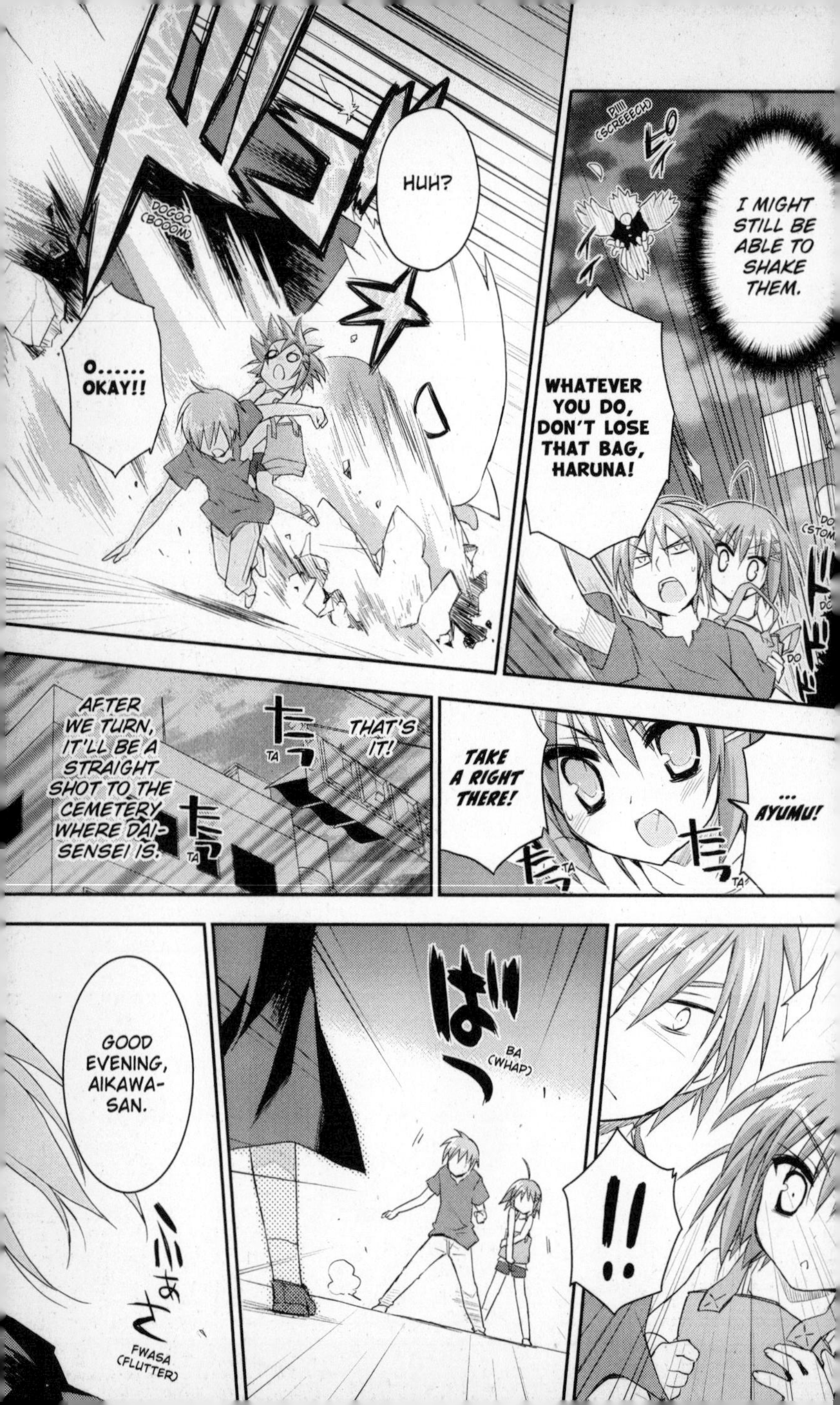

I MIGHT STILL BE ABLE TO SHAKE THEM.
PIIII (SCREEECH)
WHATEVER YOU DO, DON'T LOSE THAT BAG, HARUNA!
DO
DO
HUH?
DOGOO (BOOOM)
O...... OKAY!!
TAKE A RIGHT THERE!
... AYUMU!
TA
TA
THAT'S IT!
AFTER WE TURN, IT'LL BE A STRAIGHT SHOT TO THE CEMETERY WHERE DAI-SENSEI IS.
TA
TA
!!
BA (WHAP)
GOOD EVENING, AIKAWA-SAN.
FWASA (FLUTTER)

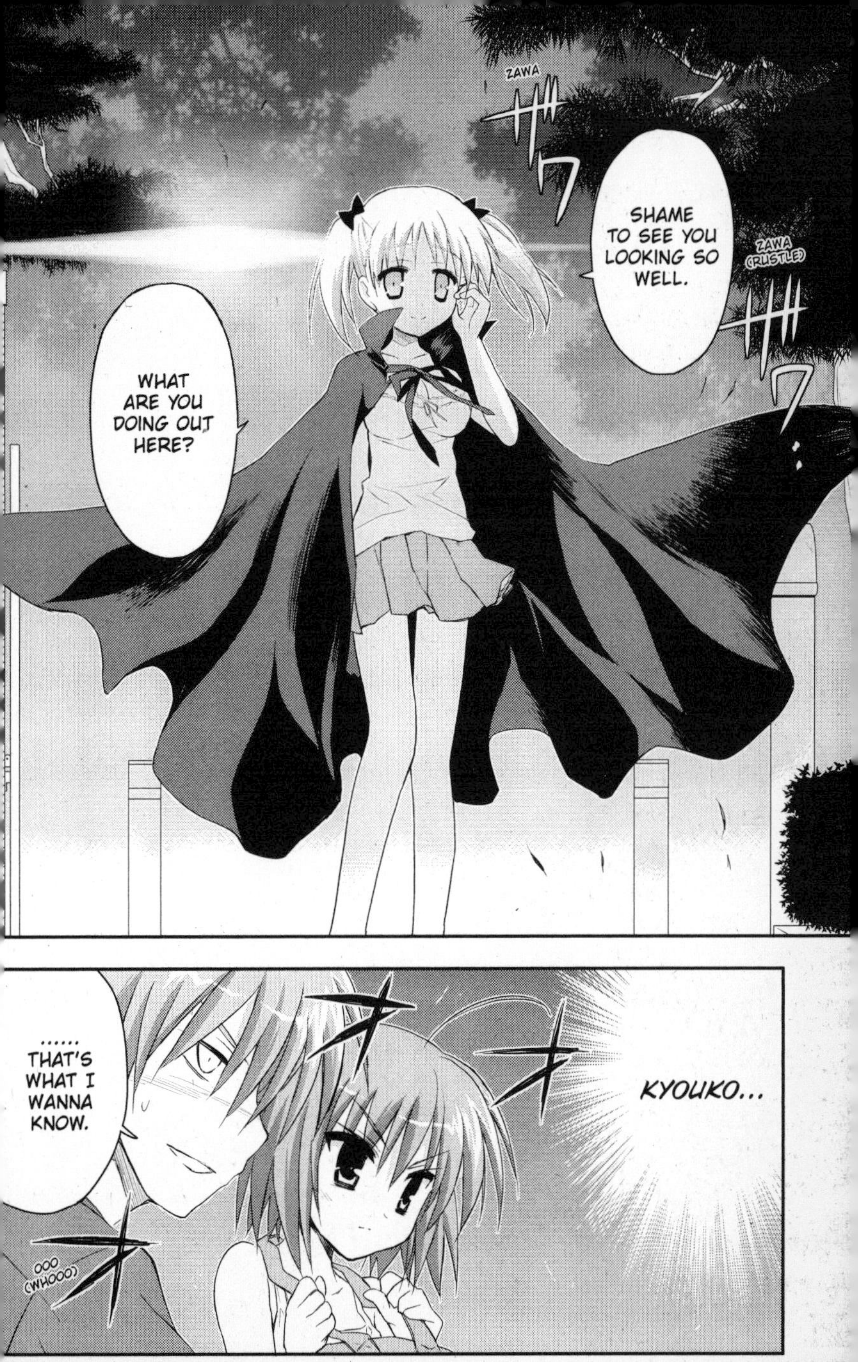
ZAWA
ZAWA (RUSTLE)
SHAME TO SEE YOU LOOKING SO WELL.
WHAT ARE YOU DOING OUT HERE?
KYOUKO...
...... THAT'S WHAT I WANNA KNOW.
OOO (WHOOO)

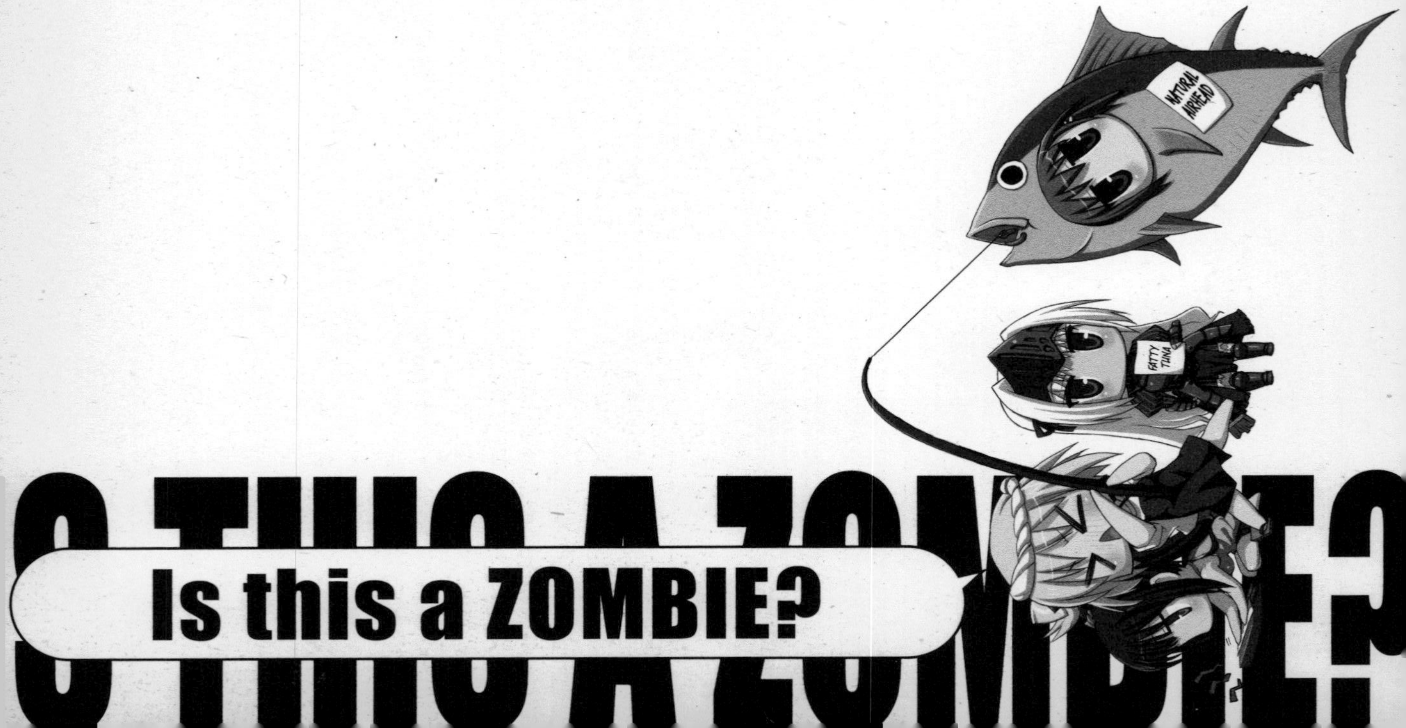
Is this a ZOMBIE?
NATURAL AIRHEAD
FATTY TUNA

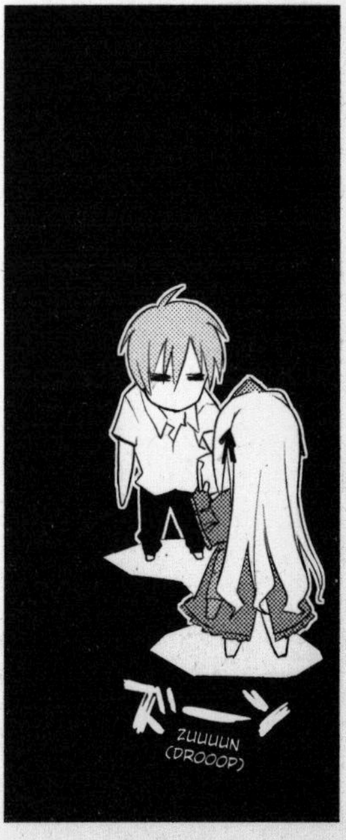
ズーン
ZUUUUN
(DROOOP)

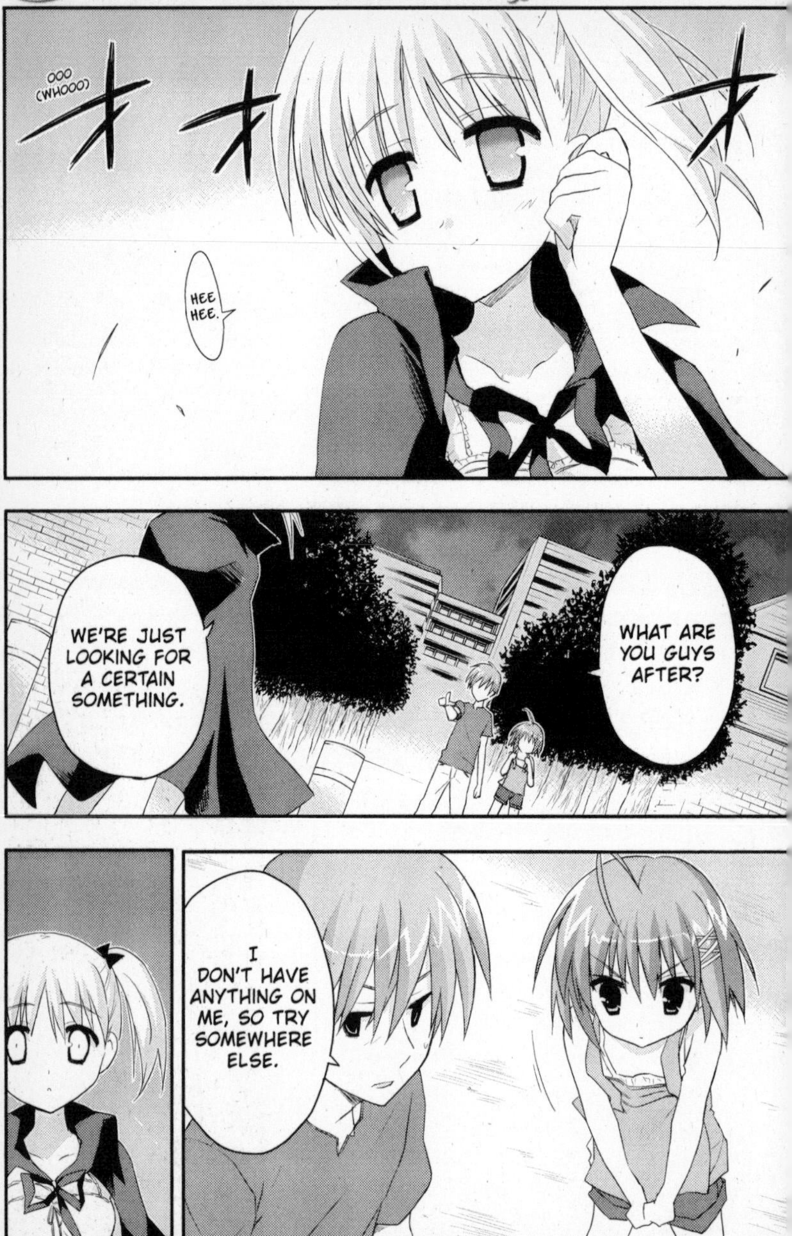
OOO (WHOOO)
HEE HEE.
WHAT ARE YOU GUYS AFTER?
WE'RE JUST LOOKING FOR A CERTAIN SOMETHING.
I DON'T HAVE ANYTHING ON ME, SO TRY SOMEWHERE ELSE.

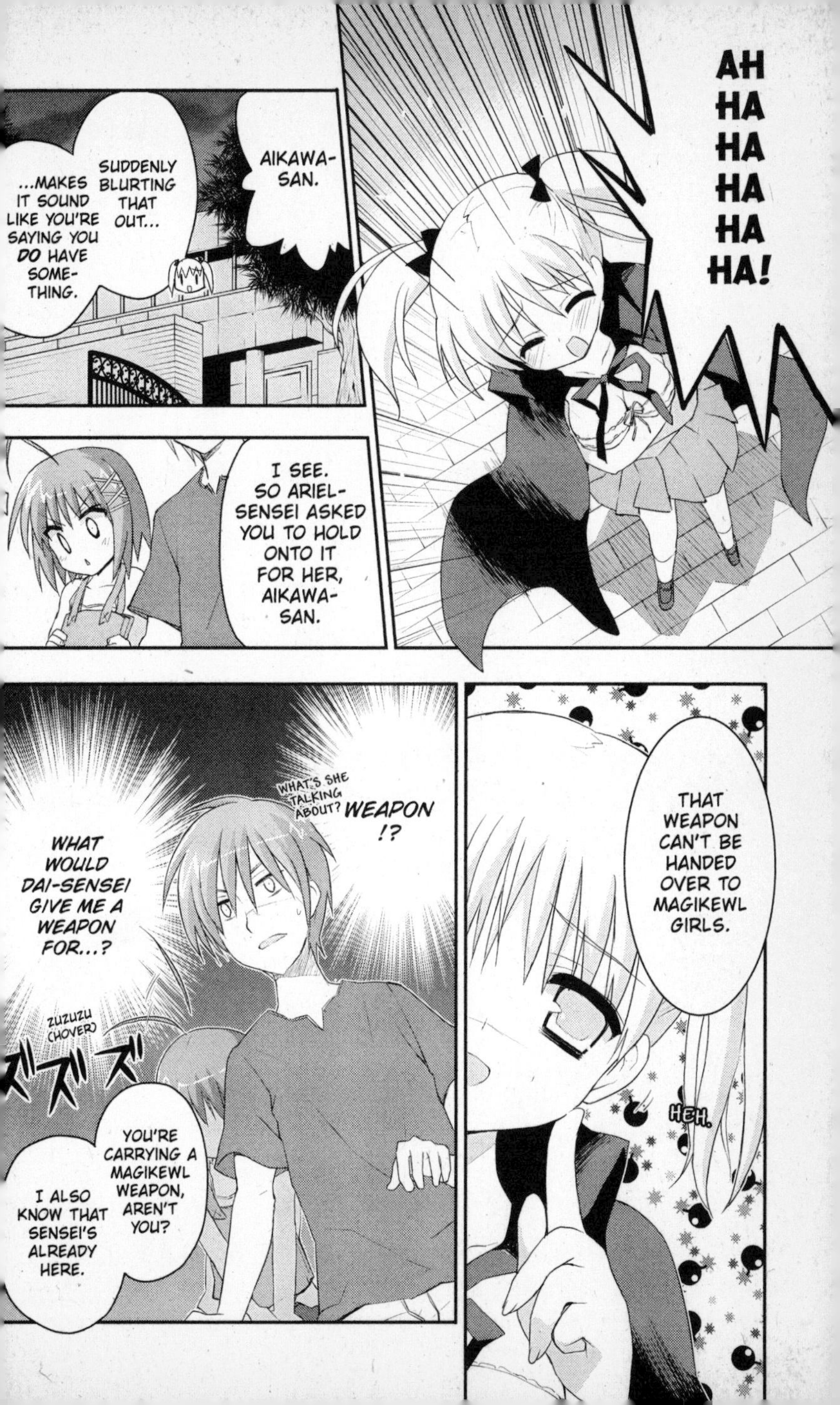
AH HA HA HA HA HA!
AIKAWA-SAN.
SUDDENLY BLURTING THAT OUT...
...MAKES IT SOUND LIKE YOU'RE SAYING YOU *DO* HAVE SOMETHING.
I SEE. SO ARIEL-SENSEI ASKED YOU TO HOLD ONTO IT FOR HER, AIKAWA-SAN.
THAT WEAPON CAN'T BE HANDED OVER TO MAGIKEWL GIRLS.
HEH.
WEAPON!?
WHAT'S SHE TALKING ABOUT?
WHAT WOULD DAI-SENSEI GIVE ME A WEAPON FOR...?
ZUZUZU (HOVER)
YOU'RE CARRYING A MAGIKEWL WEAPON, AREN'T YOU?
I ALSO KNOW THAT SENSEI'S ALREADY HERE.

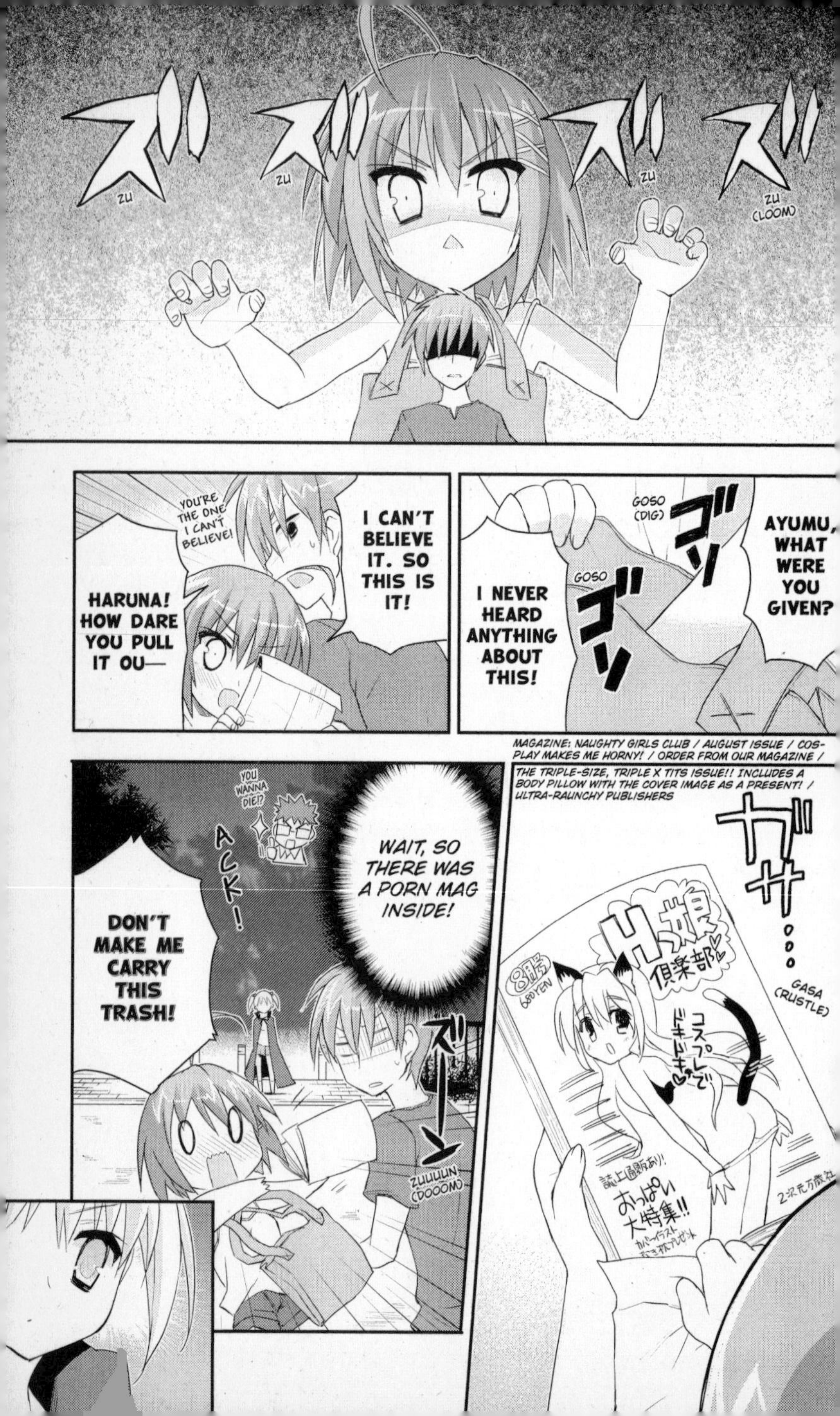
ZU (LOOM)
ZU
ZU
ZU
AYUMU, WHAT WERE YOU GIVEN?
GOSO (DIG)
GOSO
I NEVER HEARD ANYTHING ABOUT THIS!
I CAN'T BELIEVE IT. SO THIS IS IT!
YOU'RE THE ONE I CAN'T BELIEVE!
HARUNA! HOW DARE YOU PULL IT OU—
MAGAZINE: NAUGHTY GIRLS CLUB / AUGUST ISSUE / COSPLAY MAKES ME HORNY! / ORDER FROM OUR MAGAZINE / THE TRIPLE-SIZE, TRIPLE X TITS ISSUE!! INCLUDES A BODY PILLOW WITH THE COVER IMAGE AS A PRESENT! / ULTRA-RAUNCHY PUBLISHERS
GASA (RUSTLE)
Hっ娘倶楽部
8月号
680 YEN
コスプレでドキドキ
おっぱい大特集!!
WAIT, SO THERE WAS A PORN MAG INSIDE!
YOU WANNA DIE!?
ACK!
DON'T MAKE ME CARRY THIS TRASH!
ZUUUUN (DOOOM)

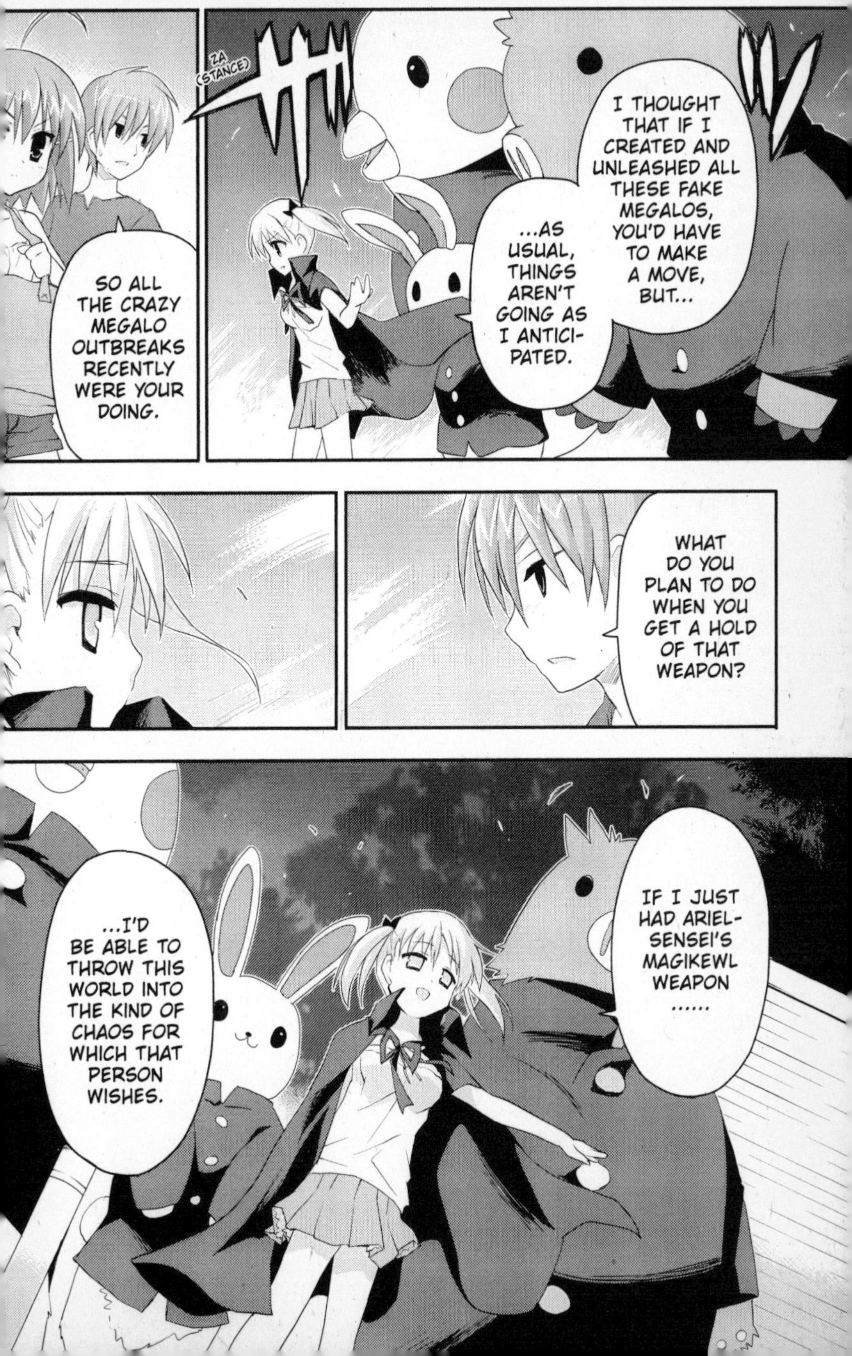
ZA (STANCE)
I THOUGHT THAT IF I CREATED AND UNLEASHED ALL THESE FAKE MEGALOS, YOU'D HAVE TO MAKE A MOVE, BUT...
...AS USUAL, THINGS AREN'T GOING AS I ANTICIPATED.
SO ALL THE CRAZY MEGALO OUTBREAKS RECENTLY WERE YOUR DOING.
WHAT DO YOU PLAN TO DO WHEN YOU GET A HOLD OF THAT WEAPON?
IF I JUST HAD ARIEL-SENSEI'S MAGIKEWL WEAPON ......
...I'D BE ABLE TO THROW THIS WORLD INTO THE KIND OF CHAOS FOR WHICH THAT PERSON WISHES.

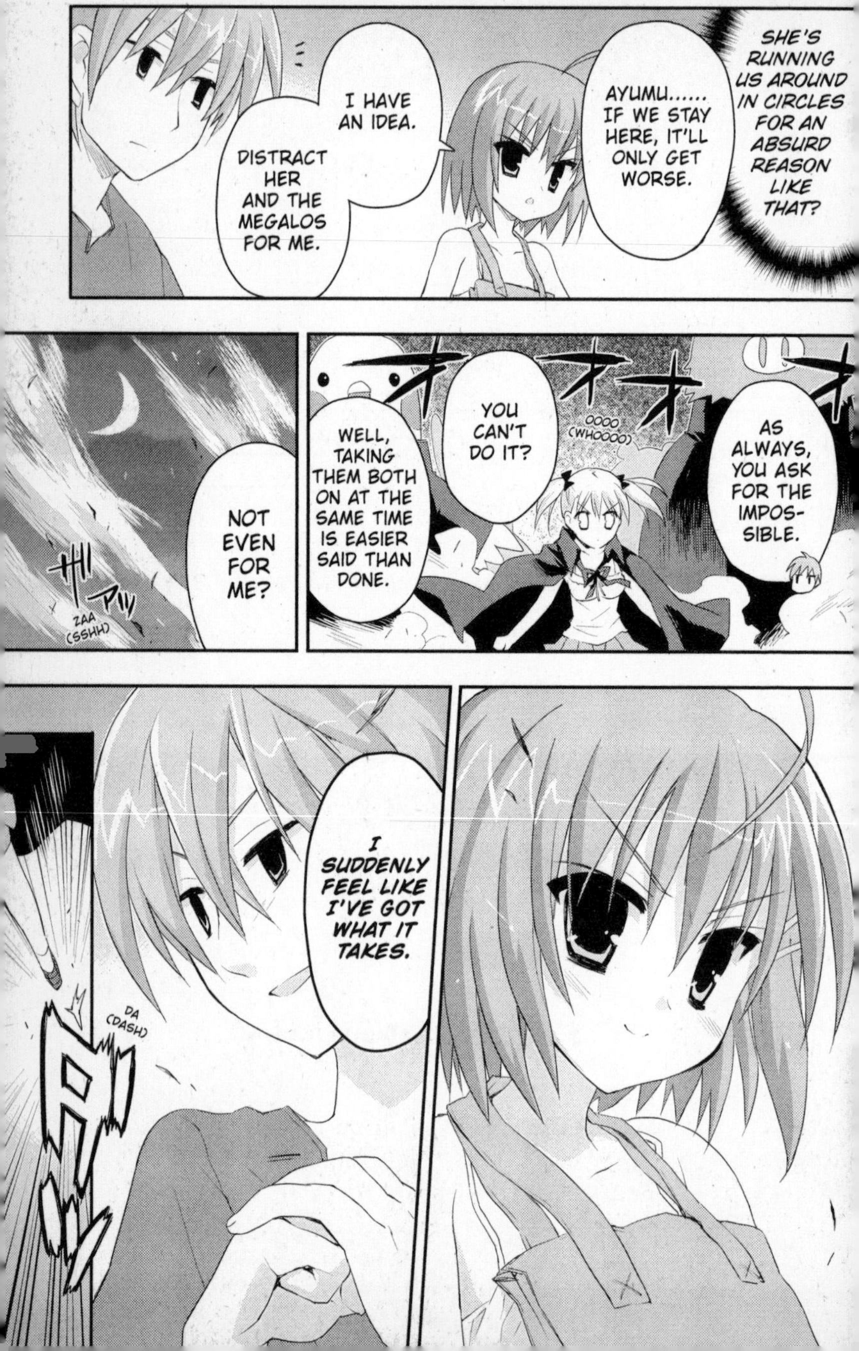
SHE'S RUNNING US AROUND IN CIRCLES FOR AN ABSURD REASON LIKE THAT?
AYUMU...... IF WE STAY HERE, IT'LL ONLY GET WORSE.
I HAVE AN IDEA.
DISTRACT HER AND THE MEGALOS FOR ME.
AS ALWAYS, YOU ASK FOR THE IMPOS-SIBLE.
OOOO (WHOOOO)
YOU CAN'T DO IT?
WELL, TAKING THEM BOTH ON AT THE SAME TIME IS EASIER SAID THAN DONE.
NOT EVEN FOR ME?
ZAA (SSHH)
I SUDDENLY FEEL LIKE I'VE GOT WHAT IT TAKES.
DA (DASH)

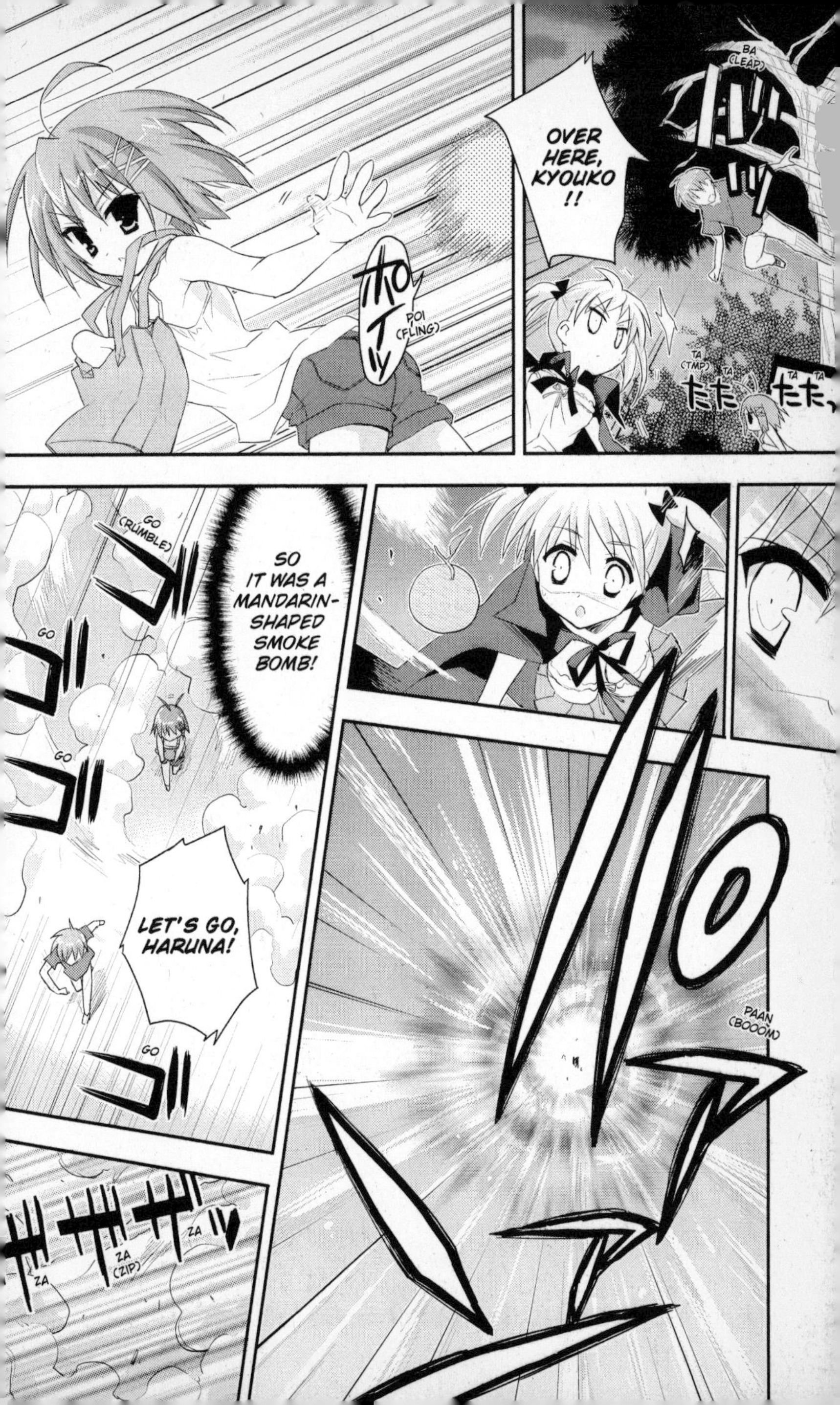
BA (LEAP)
OVER HERE, KYOUKO!!
TA (TMP) TA TA TA
POI (FLING)
SO IT WAS A MANDARIN-SHAPED SMOKE BOMB!
PAAN (BOOOM)
GO (RUMBLE) GO GO
LET'S GO, HARUNA!
GO
ZA ZA (ZIP) ZA

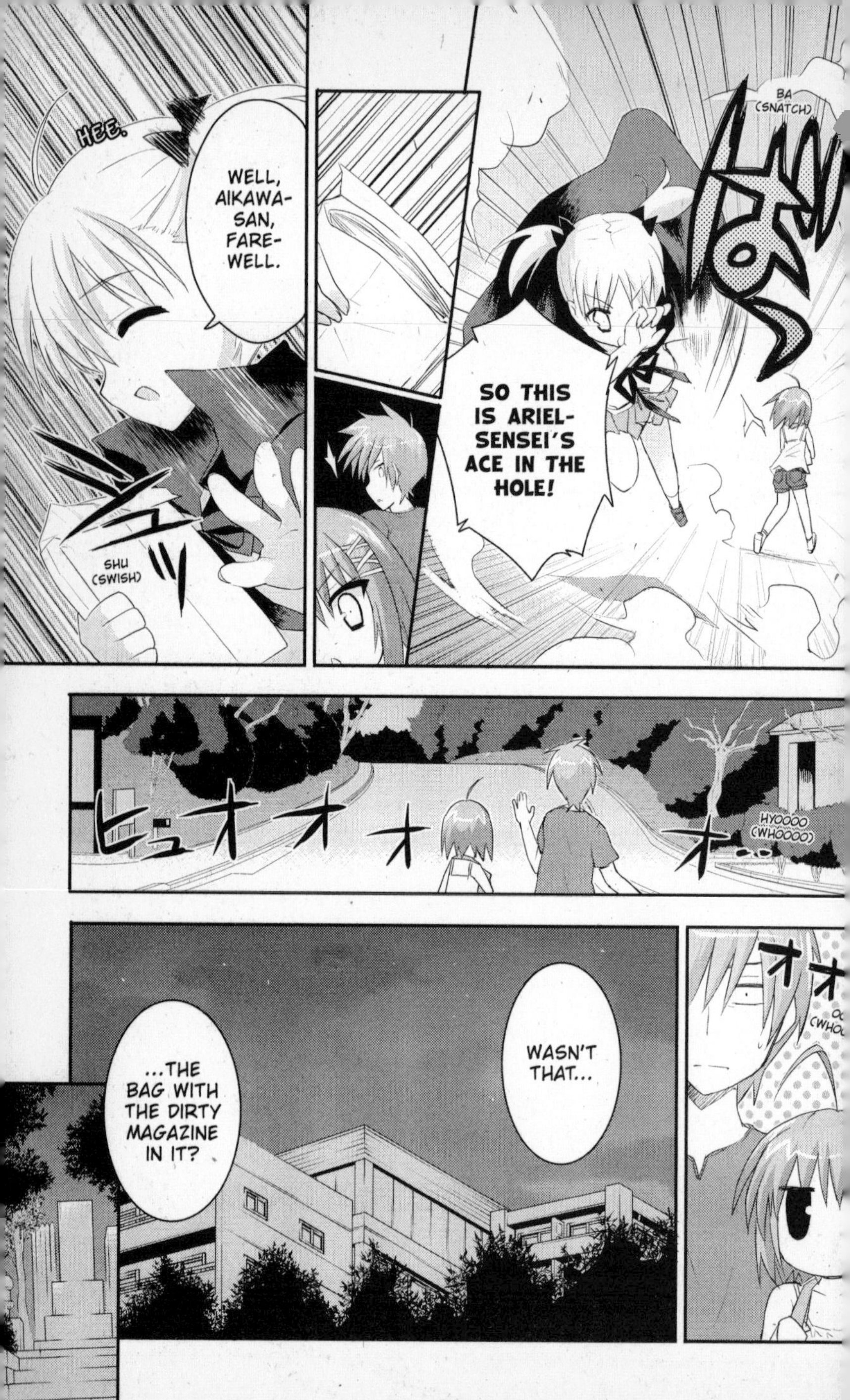
BA (SNATCH)
SO THIS IS ARIEL-SENSEI'S ACE IN THE HOLE!
HEE.
WELL, AIKAWA-SAN, FAREWELL.
SHU (SWISH)
HYOOOO (WHOOOO)
WASN'T THAT...
...THE BAG WITH THE DIRTY MAGAZINE IN IT?

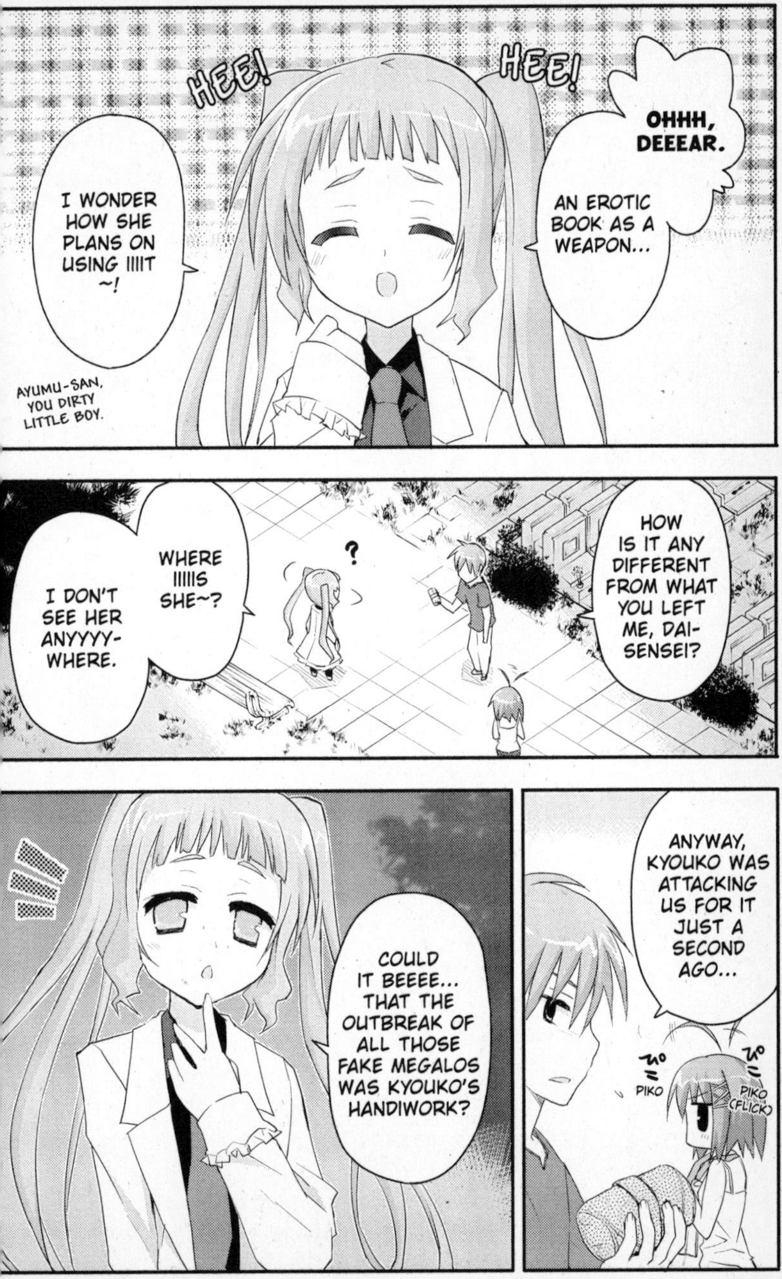
HEE!
OHHH, DEEEAR.
AN EROTIC BOOK AS A WEAPON...
HEE!
I WONDER HOW SHE PLANS ON USING IIIIT ~!
AYUMU-SAN, YOU DIRTY LITTLE BOY.
HOW IS IT ANY DIFFERENT FROM WHAT YOU LEFT ME, DAI-SENSEI?
?
WHERE IIIIIS SHE~?
I DON'T SEE HER ANYYYY-WHERE.
ANYWAY, KYOUKO WAS ATTACKING US FOR IT JUST A SECOND AGO...
ぴこ
PIKO (FLICK)
ぴこ
PIKO
COULD IT BEEEE... THAT THE OUTBREAK OF ALL THOSE FAKE MEGALOS WAS KYOUKO'S HANDIWORK?

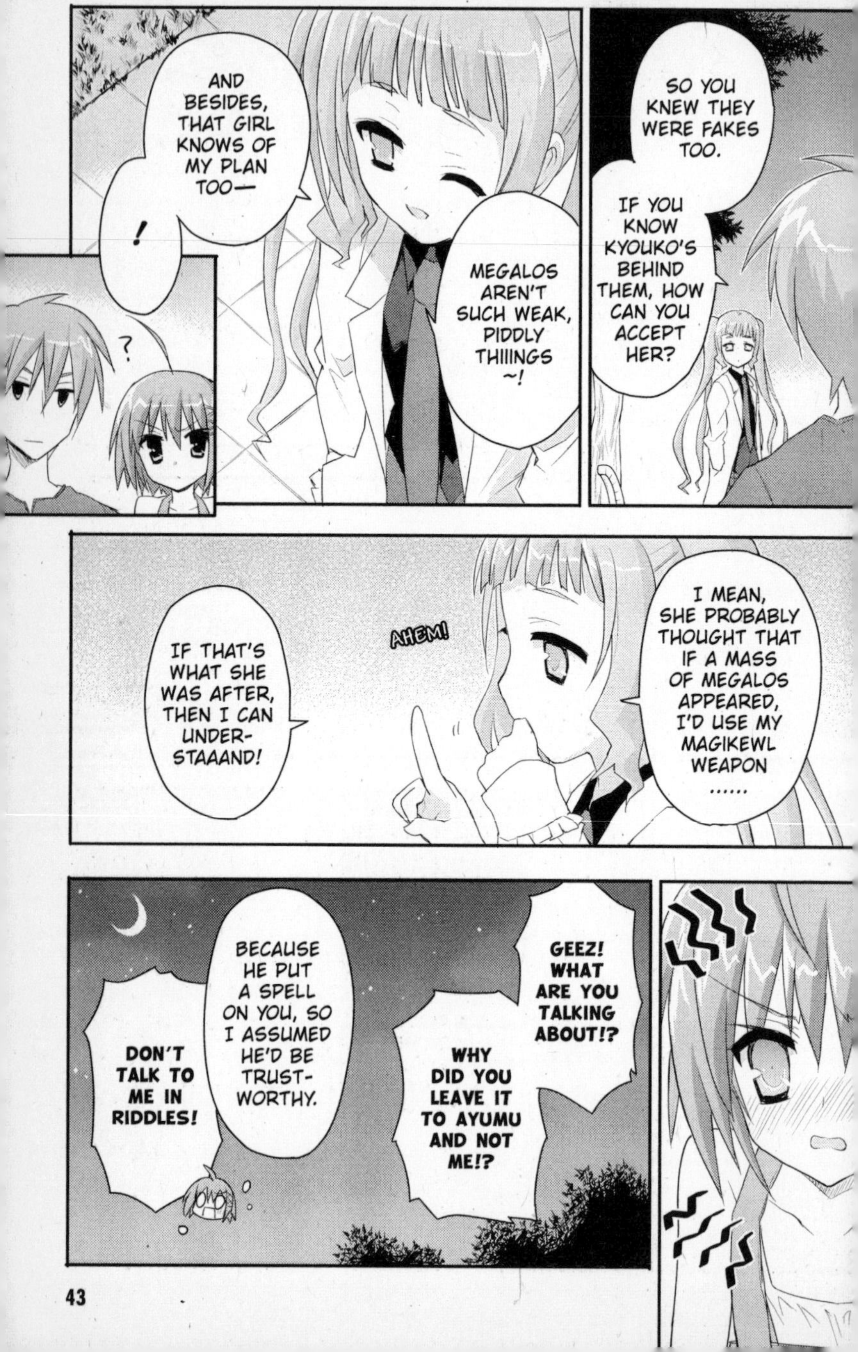

SO YOU KNEW THEY WERE FAKES TOO.
IF YOU KNOW KYOUKO'S BEHIND THEM, HOW CAN YOU ACCEPT HER?
MEGALOS AREN'T SUCH WEAK, PIDDLY THIIINGS ~!
AND BESIDES, THAT GIRL KNOWS OF MY PLAN TOO—
!
?
I MEAN, SHE PROBABLY THOUGHT THAT IF A MASS OF MEGALOS APPEARED, I'D USE MY MAGIKEWL WEAPON ......
AHEM!
IF THAT'S WHAT SHE WAS AFTER, THEN I CAN UNDER-STAAAND!
GEEZ! WHAT ARE YOU TALKING ABOUT!?
WHY DID YOU LEAVE IT TO AYUMU AND NOT ME!?
BECAUSE HE PUT A SPELL ON YOU, SO I ASSUMED HE'D BE TRUST-WORTHY.
DON'T TALK TO ME IN RIDDLES!

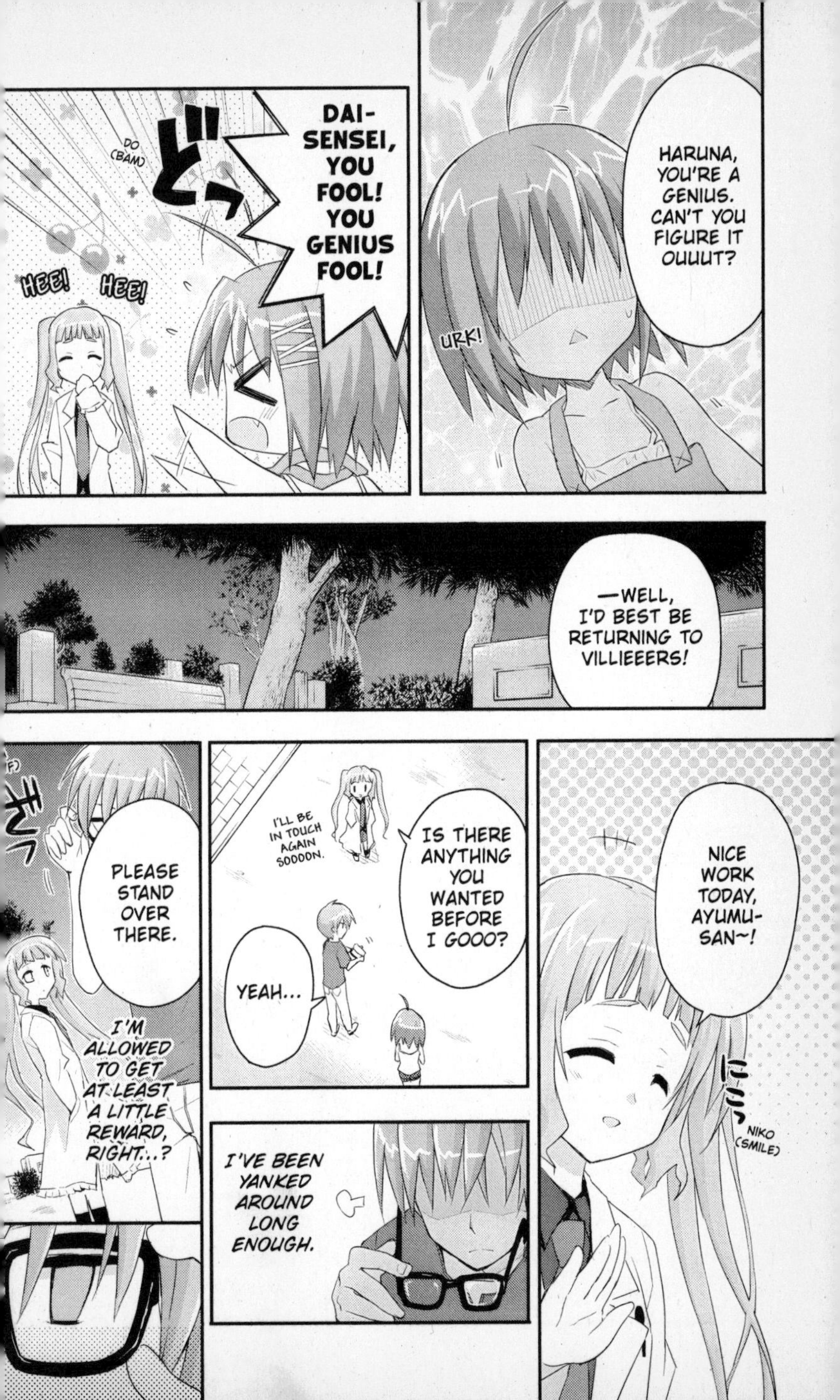
HARUNA, YOU'RE A GENIUS. CAN'T YOU FIGURE IT OUUUT?
URK!
DAI-SENSEI, YOU FOOL! YOU GENIUS FOOL!
DO (BAM)
HEE! HEE!
—WELL, I'D BEST BE RETURNING TO VILLIEEERS!
NICE WORK TODAY, AYUMU-SAN~!
NIKO (SMILE)
IS THERE ANYTHING YOU WANTED BEFORE I GOOO?
I'LL BE IN TOUCH AGAIN SOOOON.
YEAH...
I'VE BEEN YANKED AROUND LONG ENOUGH.
PLEASE STAND OVER THERE.
I'M ALLOWED TO GET AT LEAST A LITTLE REWARD, RIGHT...?

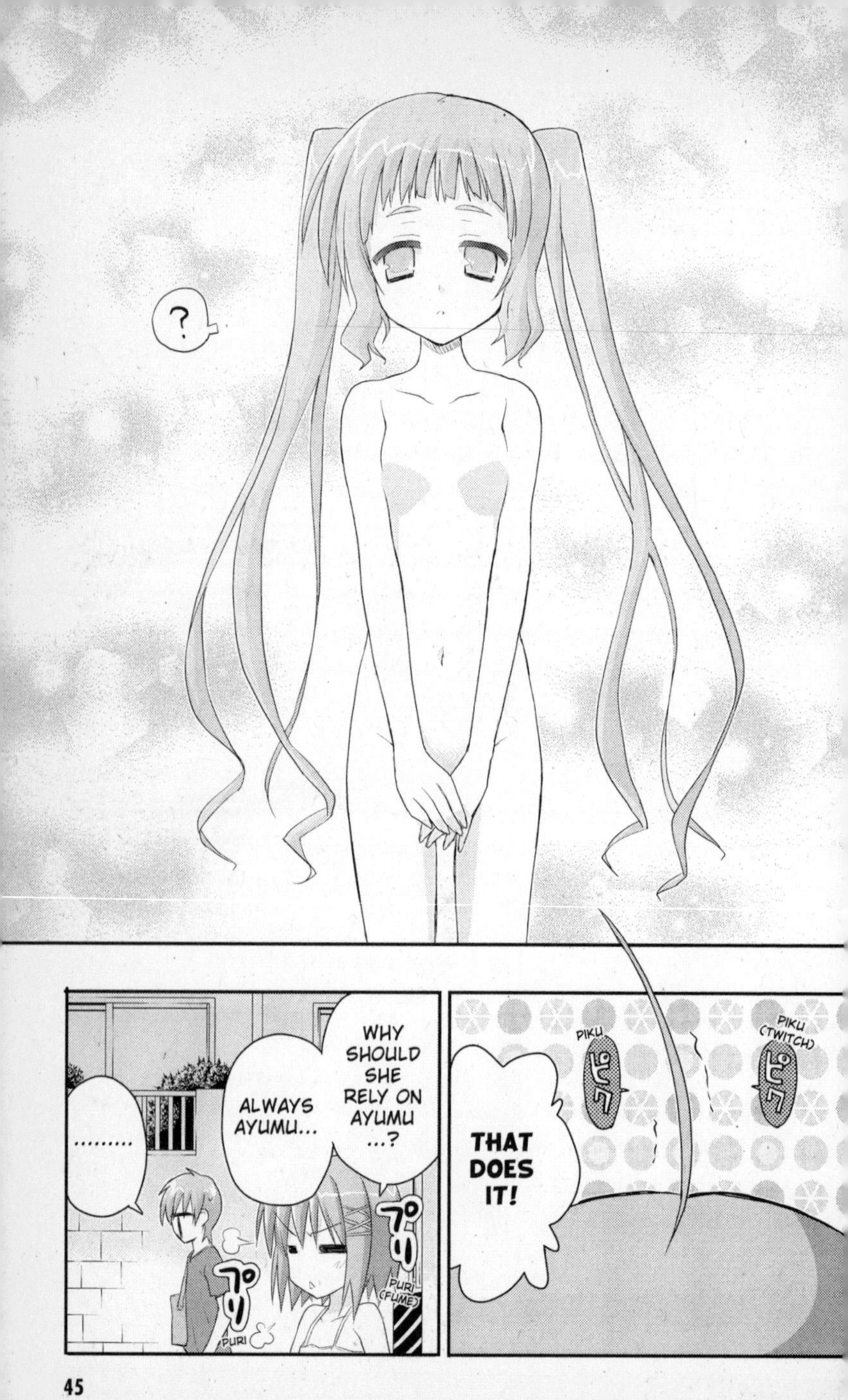
?
ピク
PIKU (TWITCH)
ピク
PIKU
THAT DOES IT!
WHY SHOULD SHE RELY ON AYUMU ...?
ALWAYS AYUMU...
プリ
PURI (FUME)
....
プリ
PURI

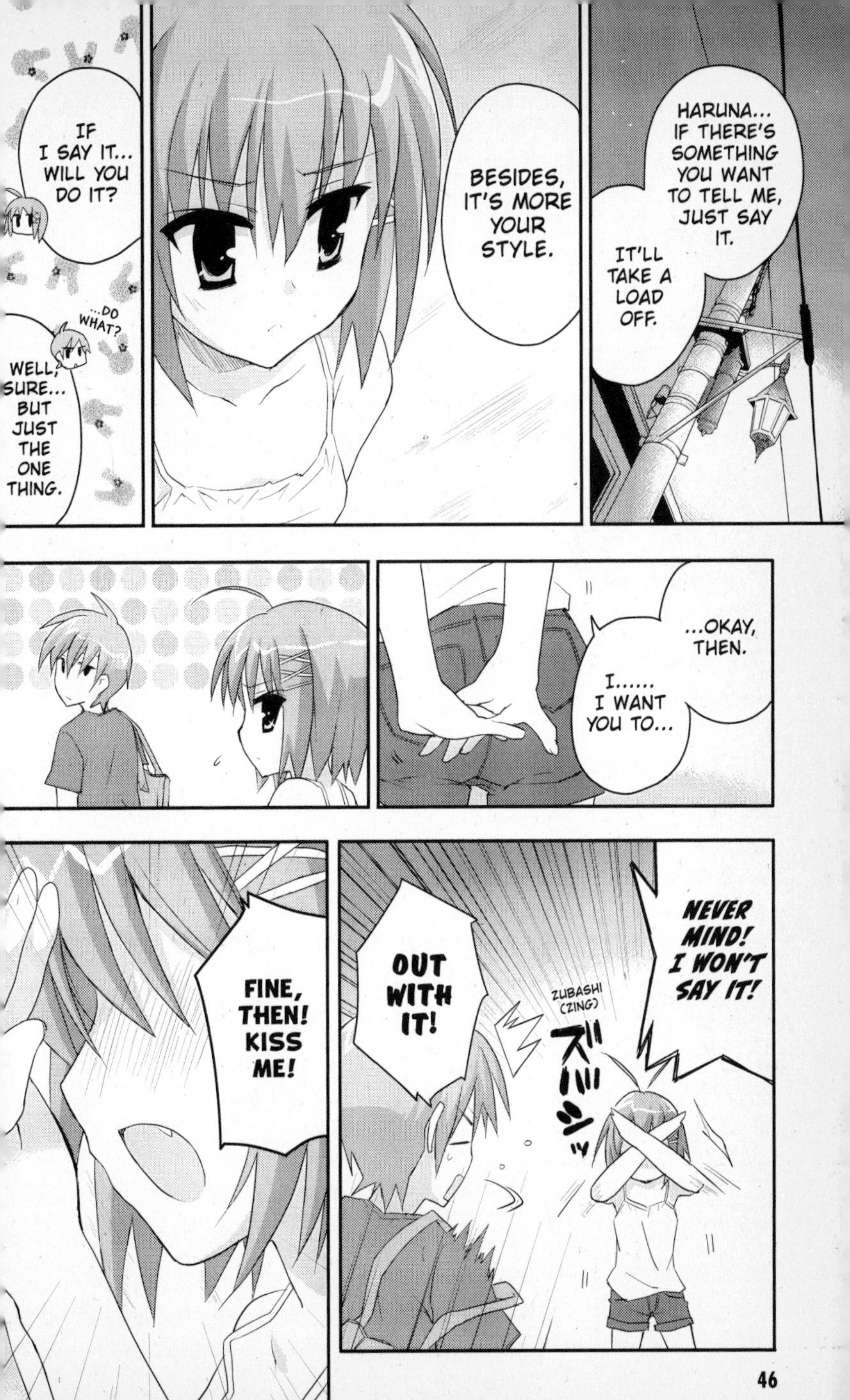
HARUNA... IF THERE'S SOMETHING YOU WANT TO TELL ME, JUST SAY IT.
IT'LL TAKE A LOAD OFF.
BESIDES, IT'S MORE YOUR STYLE.
IF I SAY IT... WILL YOU DO IT?
...DO WHAT?
WELL, SURE... BUT JUST THE ONE THING.
...OKAY, THEN.
I...... I WANT YOU TO...
NEVER MIND! I WON'T SAY IT!
ZUBASHI (ZING)
OUT WITH IT!
FINE, THEN! KISS ME!

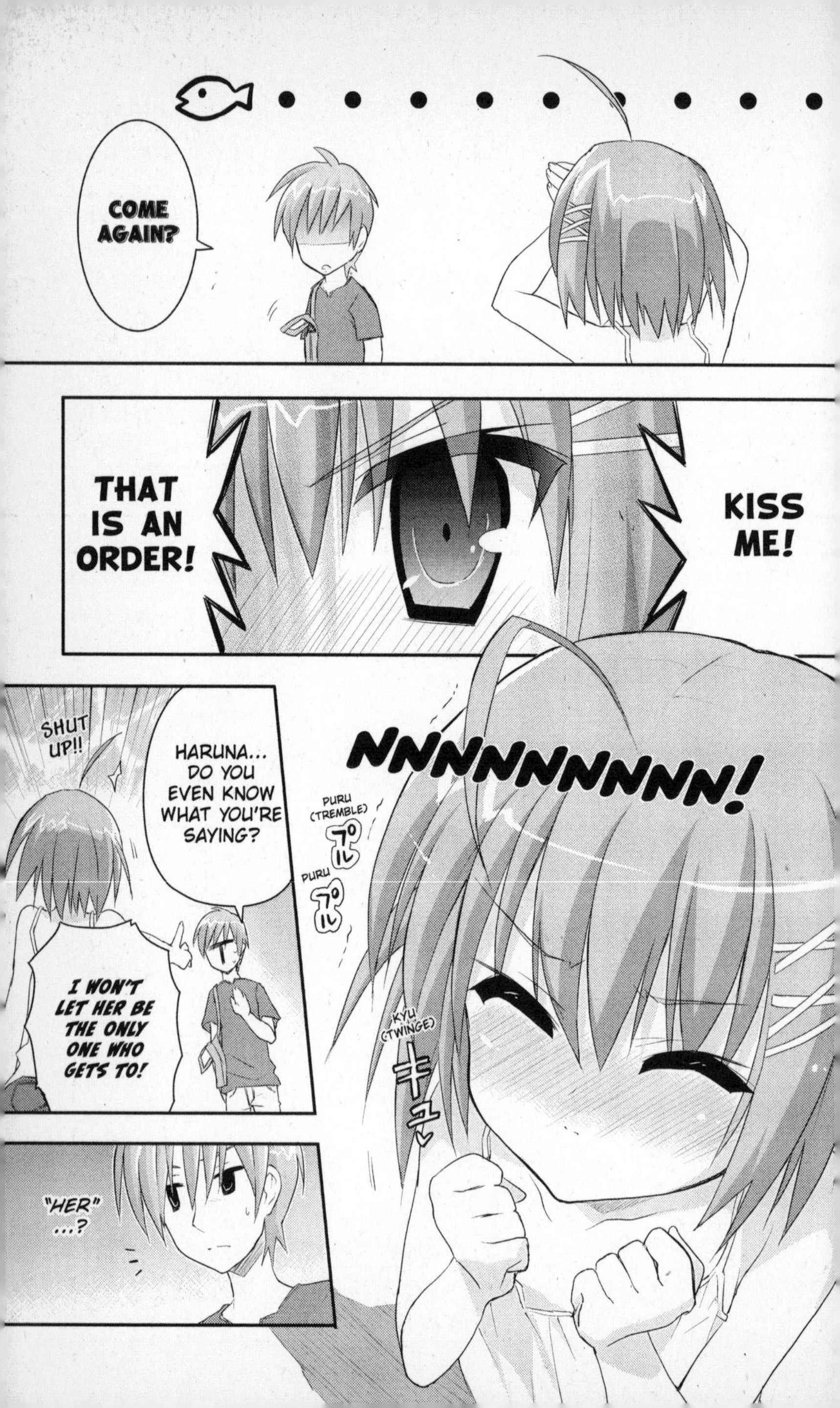
COME AGAIN?
KISS ME!
THAT IS AN ORDER!
NNNNNNNNNN!
PURU (TREMBLE)
プル
PURU
プル
KYU (TWINGE)
キュ
HARUNA... DO YOU EVEN KNOW WHAT YOU'RE SAYING?
SHUT UP!!
I WON'T LET HER BE THE ONLY ONE WHO GETS TO!
"HER" ...?

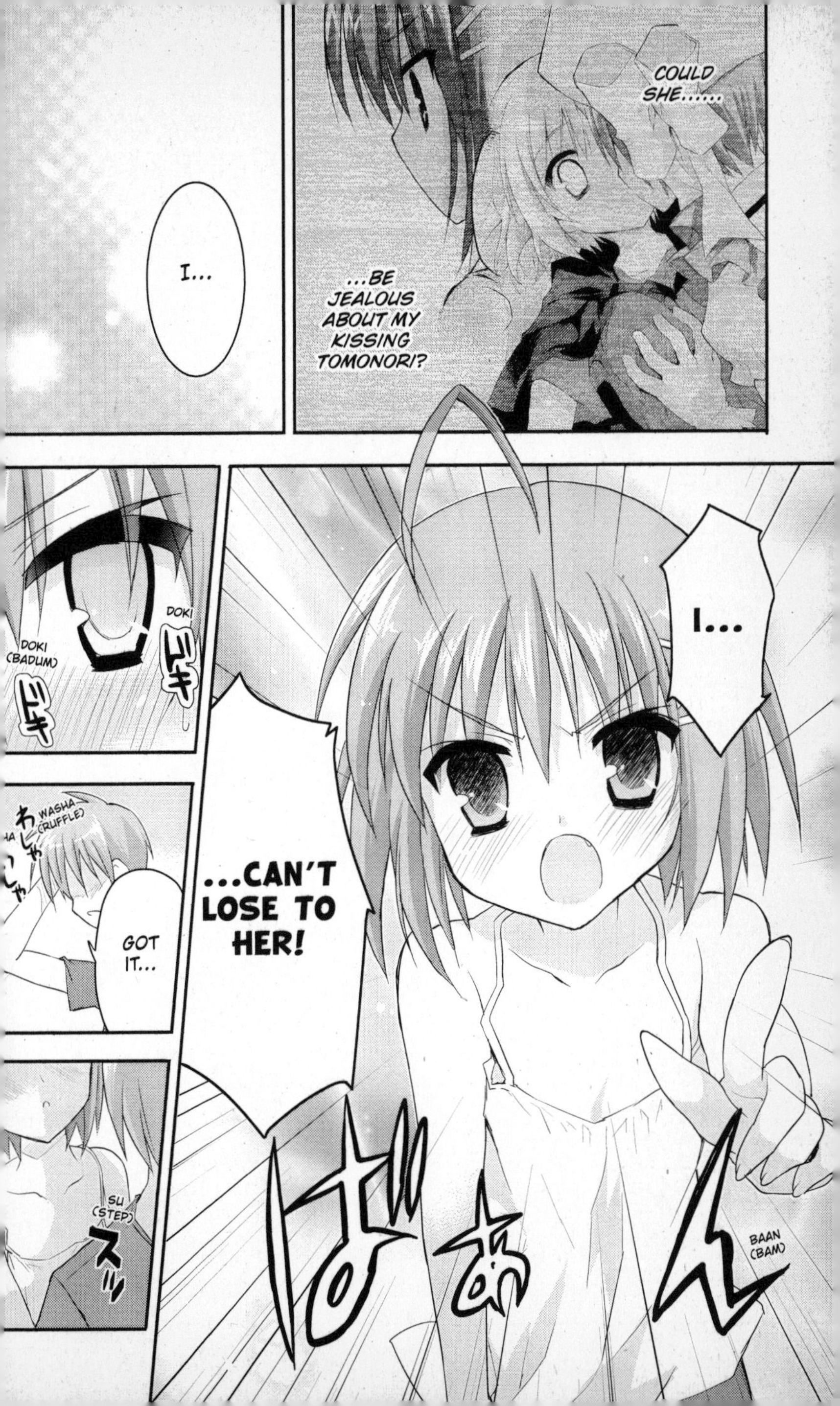
COULD SHE......
...BE JEALOUS ABOUT MY KISSING TOMONORI!?
I...
I...
...CAN'T LOSE TO HER!
BAAN (BAM)
DOKI
DOKI (BADUM)
WASHA (RUFFLE)
GOT IT...
SU (STEP)

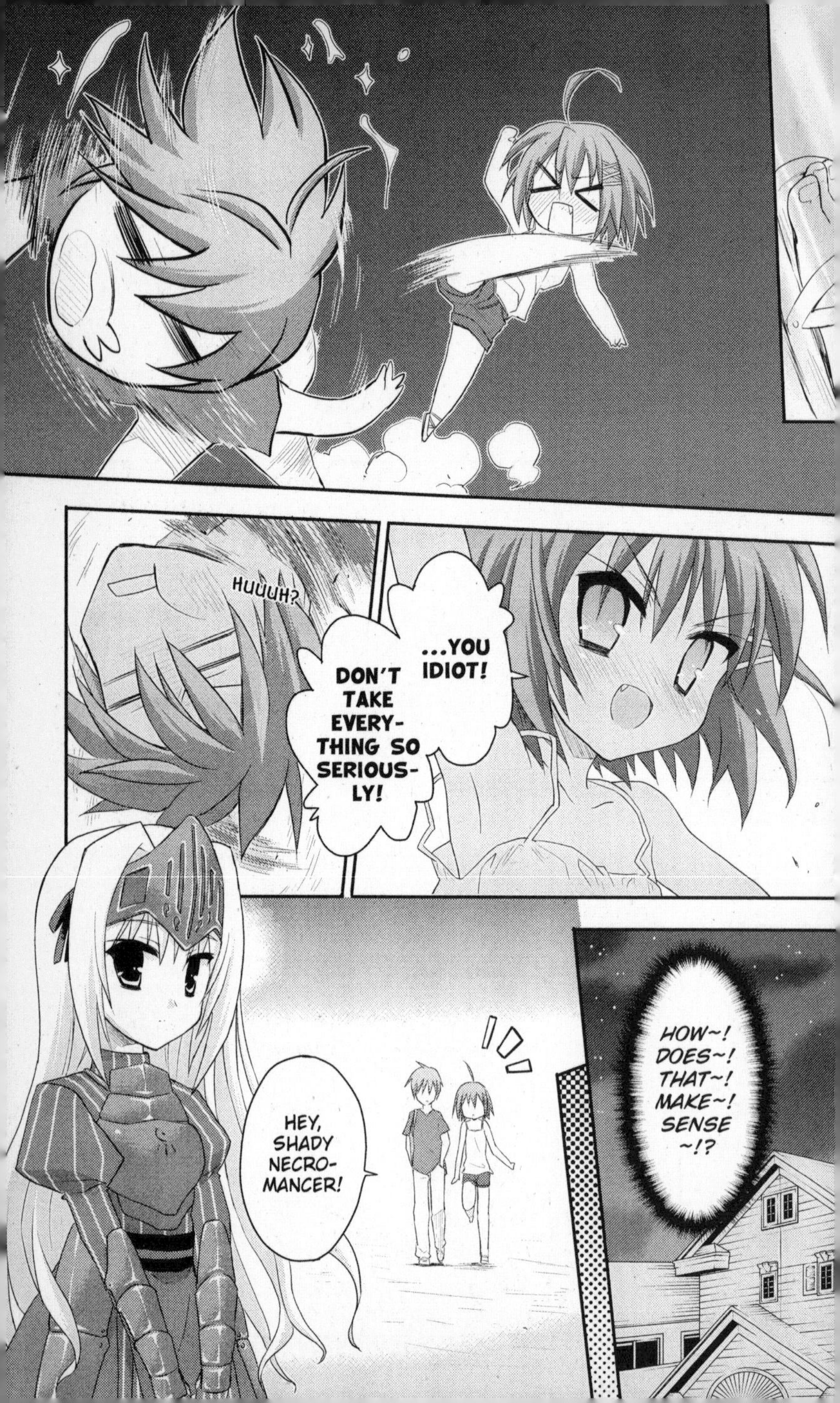
...YOU IDIOT! DON'T TAKE EVERY-THING SO SERIOUS-LY!
HUUUH?
HOW~! DOES~! THAT~! MAKE~! SENSE~!?
HEY, SHADY NECRO-MANCER!

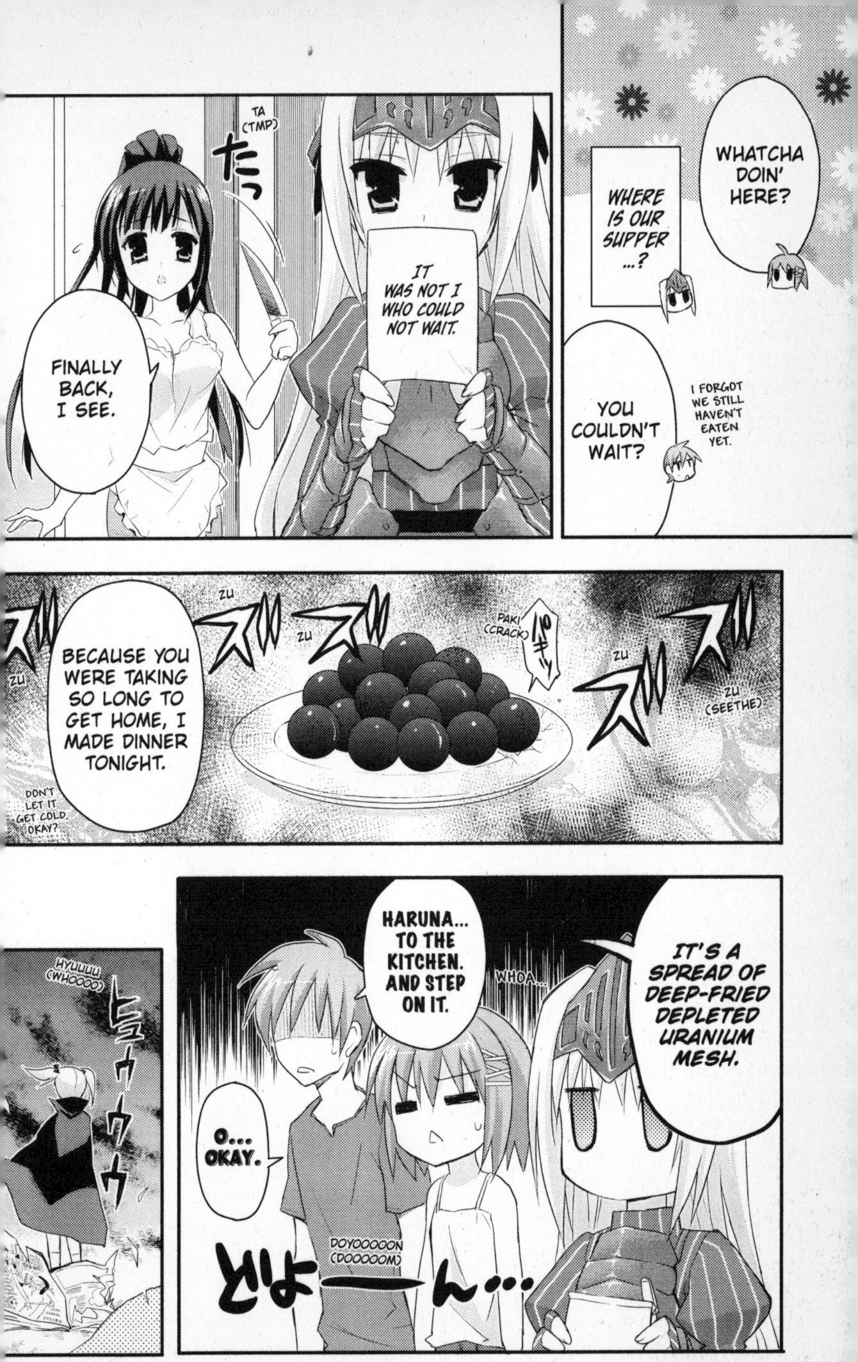
WHATCHA DOIN' HERE?
WHERE IS OUR SUPPER ...?
YOU COULDN'T WAIT?
I FORGOT WE STILL HAVEN'T EATEN YET.
TA (TMP)
たっ
IT WAS NOT I WHO COULD NOT WAIT.
FINALLY BACK, I SEE.
ZU
ズ
ZU (SEETHE)
PAKI (CRACK)
パキッ
ZU
ZU
BECAUSE YOU WERE TAKING SO LONG TO GET HOME, I MADE DINNER TONIGHT.
DON'T LET IT GET COLD OKAY?
IT'S A SPREAD OF DEEP-FRIED DEPLETED URANIUM MESH.
HARUNA... TO THE KITCHEN. AND STEP ON IT.
WHOA...
O... OKAY.
DOYOOOOON (DOOOOOM)
どよーーん…
HYUUUUU (WHOOOO)
ヒュウウウ

IS THIS A ZOMBIE?

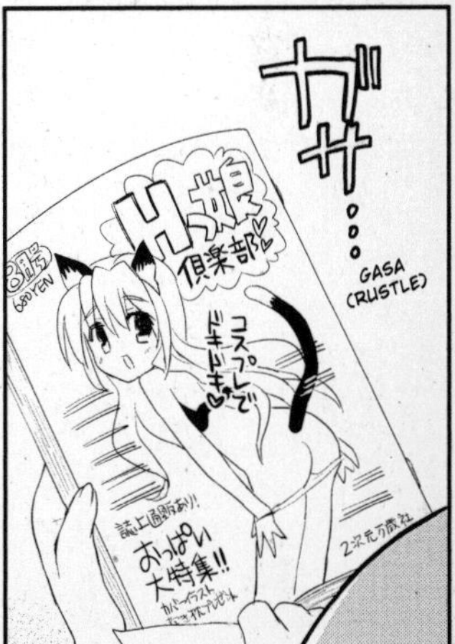

ガサ…
GASA (RUSTLE)
Hっ娘倶楽部
8月号
680YEN
コスプレでドキドキ
誌上通販あり!!
おっぱい大特集!!
2次元万歳社

MAGAZINE: NAUGHTY GIRLS CLUB / AUGUST ISSUE / COSPLAY MAKES ME HORNY! / ORDER FROM OUR MAGAZINE / THE TRIPLE-SIZE, TRIPLE X TITS ISSUE!! INCLUDING A BODY PILLOW WITH THE COVER IMAGE AS A PRESENT! / ULTRA-RAUNCHY PUBLISHERS

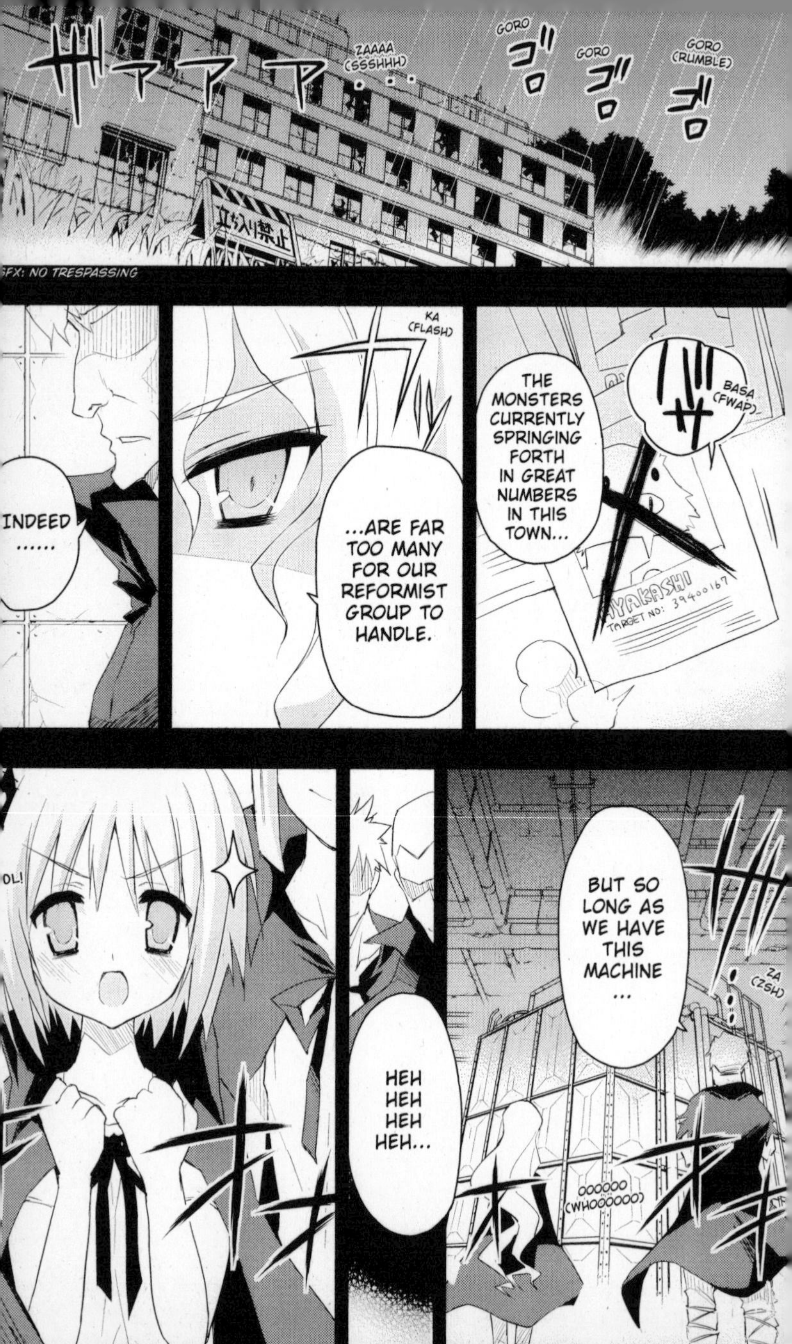
GORO (RUMBLE)
GORO
GORO
ZAAAA (SSSHHH)
SFX: NO TRESPASSING
BASA (FWAP)
AYAKASHI TARGET NO: 39400167
THE MONSTERS CURRENTLY SPRINGING FORTH IN GREAT NUMBERS IN THIS TOWN...
KA (FLASH)
...ARE FAR TOO MANY FOR OUR REFORMIST GROUP TO HANDLE.
INDEED ......
ZA (ZSH)
BUT SO LONG AS WE HAVE THIS MACHINE ...
OOOOOO (WHOOOOOO)
HEH HEH HEH HEH...

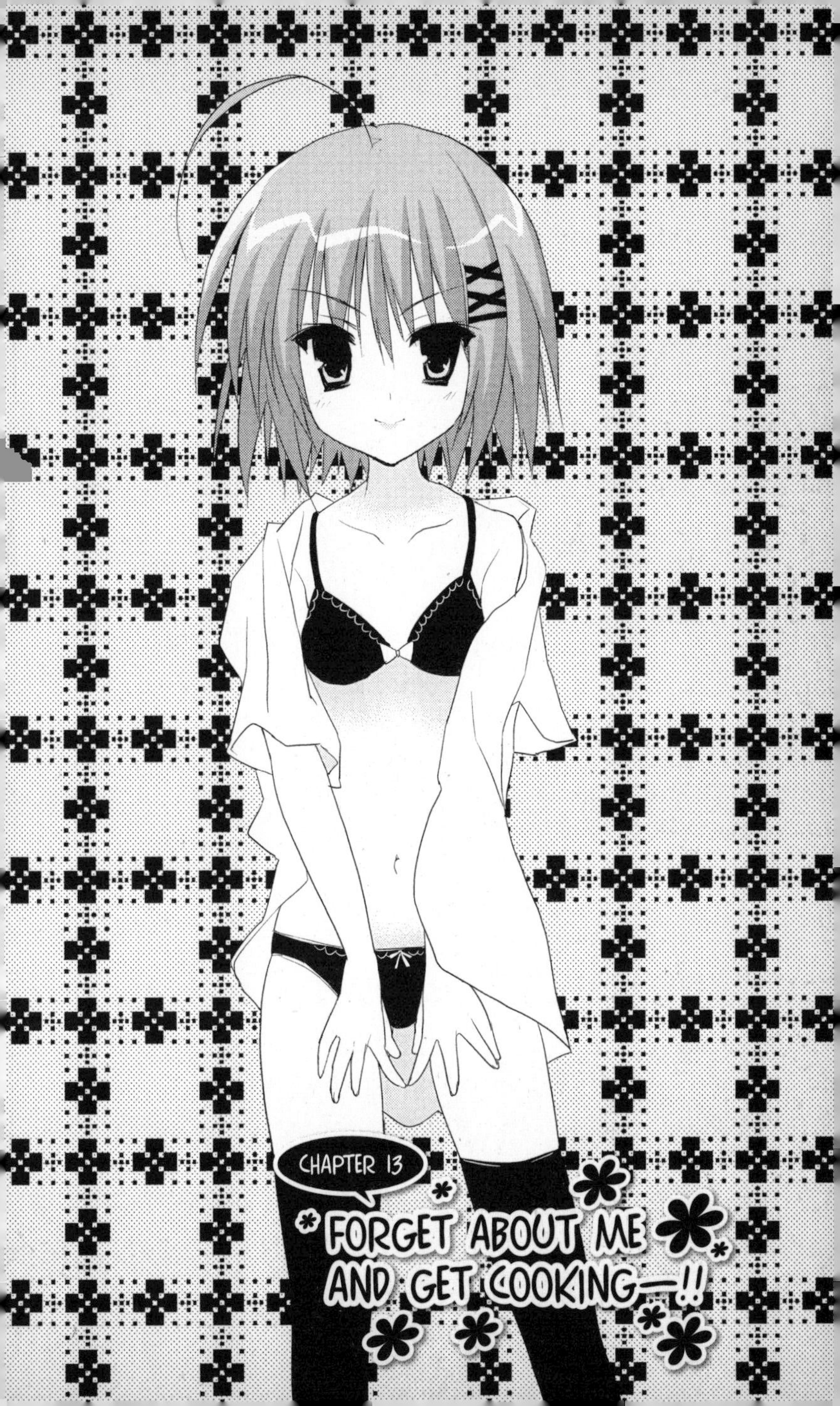
CHAPTER 13
FORGET ABOUT ME AND GET COOKING—!!

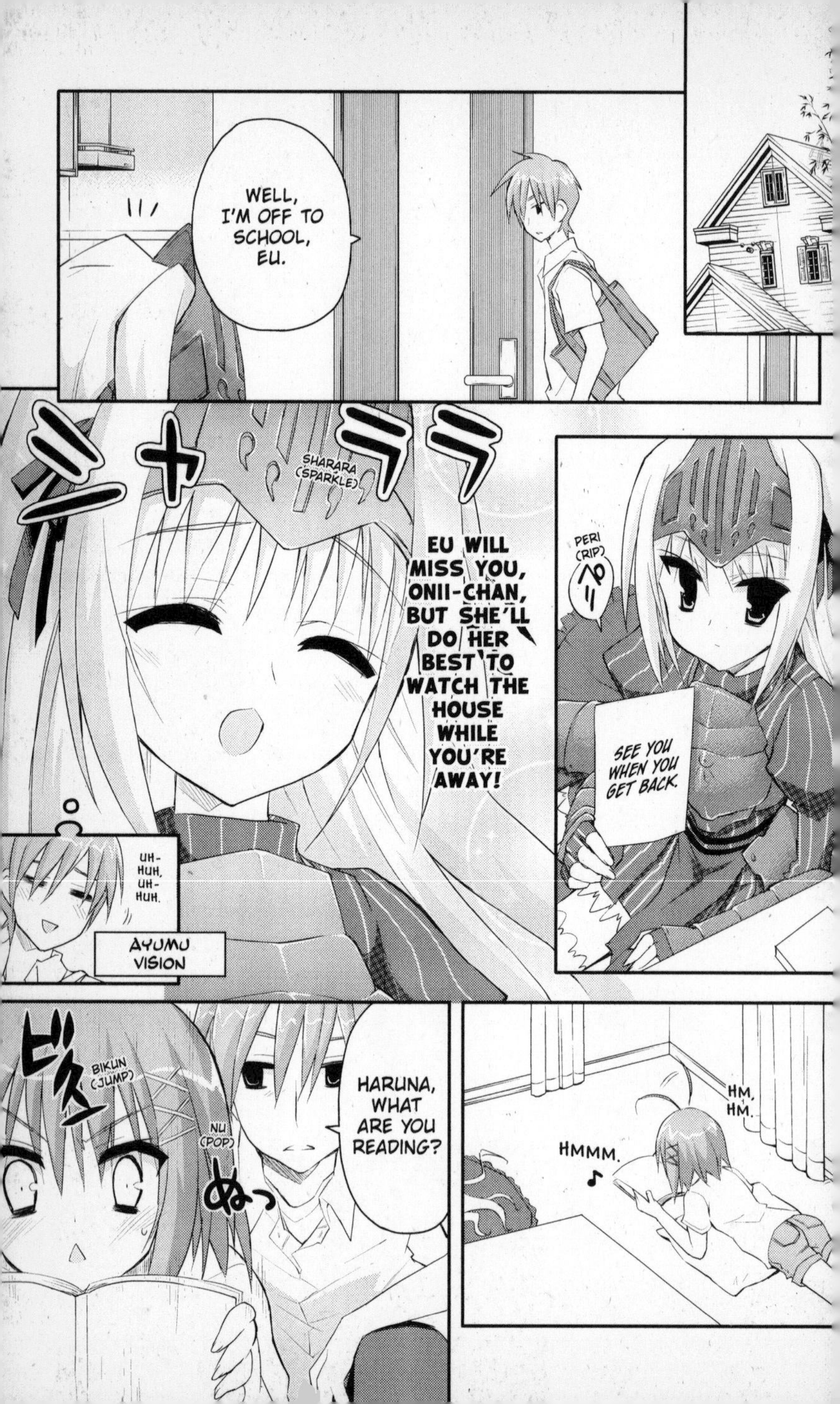
WELL, I'M OFF TO SCHOOL, EU.
PERI (RIP)
SEE YOU WHEN YOU GET BACK.
SHARARA (SPARKLE)
EU WILL MISS YOU, ONII-CHAN, BUT SHE'LL DO HER BEST TO WATCH THE HOUSE WHILE YOU'RE AWAY!
UH-HUH, UH-HUH.
AYUMU VISION
HM, HM.
HMMM. ♪
BIKUN (JUMP)
HARUNA, WHAT ARE YOU READING?
NU (POP)
ぬっ

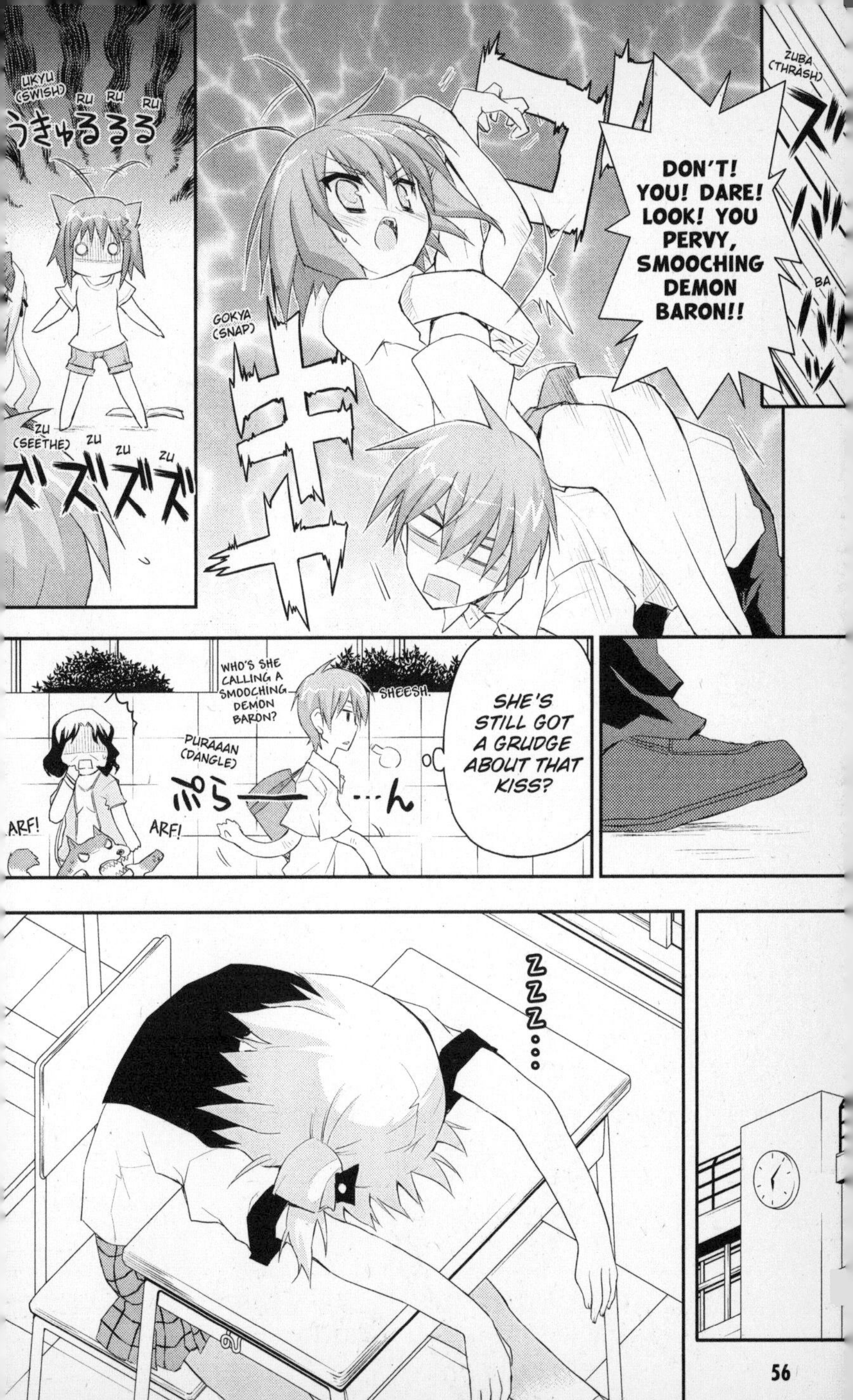
ZUBA (THRASH)
DON'T! YOU! DARE! LOOK! YOU PERVY, SMOOCHING DEMON BARON!!
BA
GOKYA (SNAP)
UKYU (SWISH) RU RU RU
うきゅるるる
ZU (SEETHE) ZU ZU ZU
ズズズズ
SHE'S STILL GOT A GRUDGE ABOUT THAT KISS?
SHEESH.
WHO'S SHE CALLING A SMOOCHING DEMON BARON?
PURAAAN (DANGLE)
ぷら——…ん
ARF!
ARF!
Z Z Z...

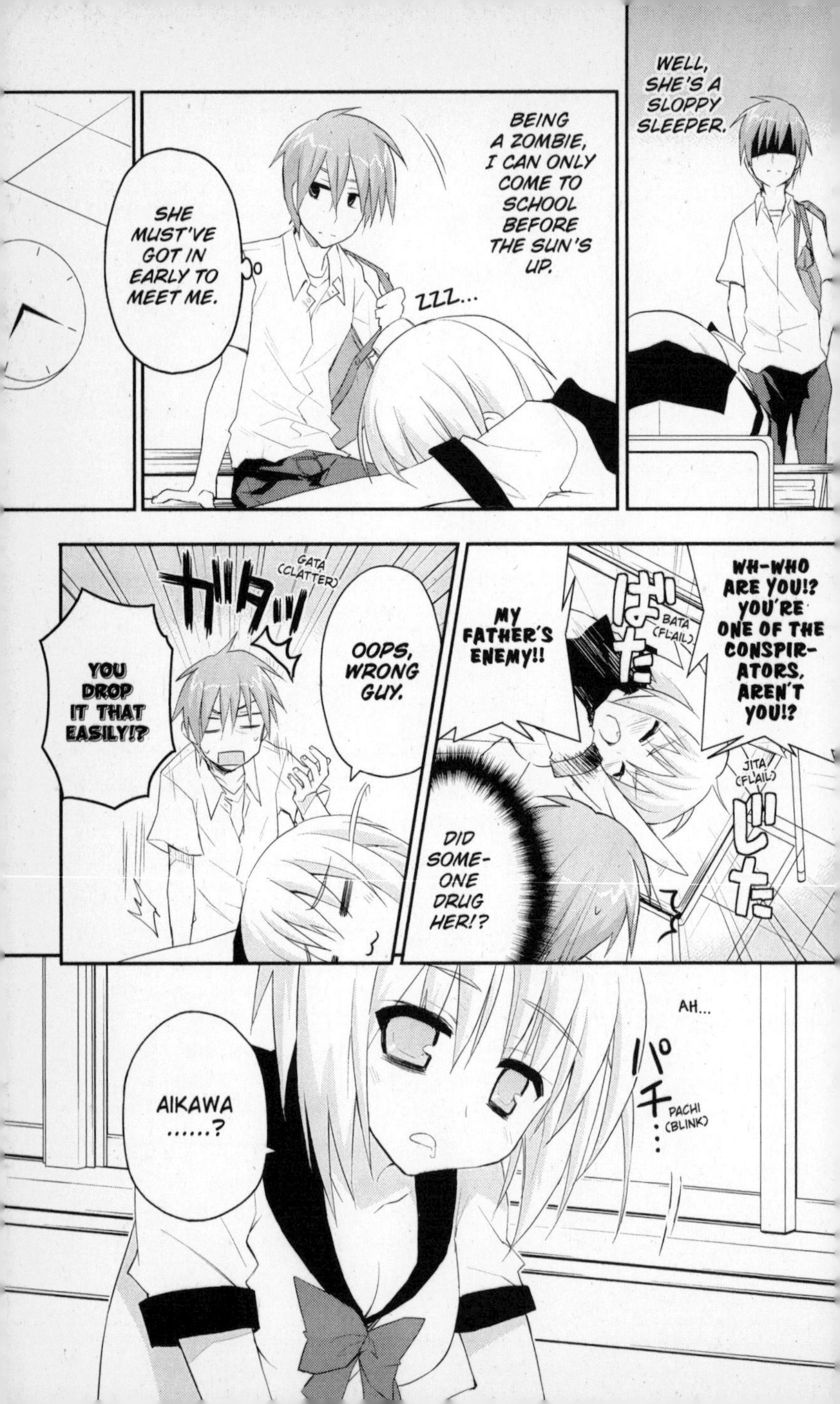
WELL, SHE'S A SLOPPY SLEEPER.
BEING A ZOMBIE, I CAN ONLY COME TO SCHOOL BEFORE THE SUN'S UP.
ZZZ...
SHE MUST'VE GOT IN EARLY TO MEET ME.
WH-WHO ARE YOU!? YOU'RE ONE OF THE CONSPIR-ATORS, AREN'T YOU!?
ばた
BATA (FLAIL)
MY FATHER'S ENEMY!!
じた
JITA (FLAIL)
DID SOME-ONE DRUG HER!?
ガタッ
GATA (CLATTER)
OOPS, WRONG GUY.
YOU DROP IT THAT EASILY!?
AH...
パチ
PACHI (BLINK)
AIKAWA ......?

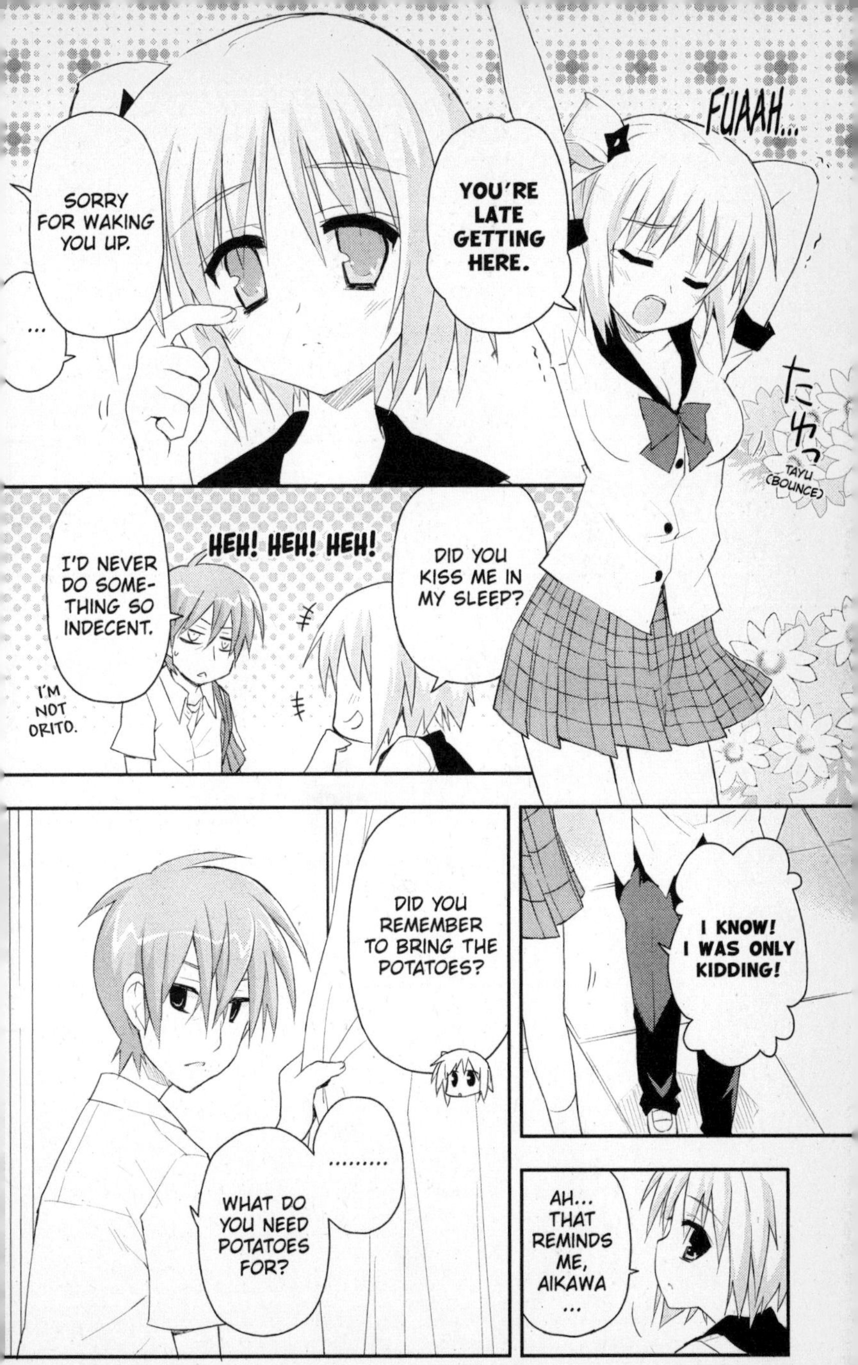
FUAAH...
YOU'RE LATE GETTING HERE.
たゆっ
TAYU (BOUNCE)
SORRY FOR WAKING YOU UP.
...
DID YOU KISS ME IN MY SLEEP?
HEH! HEH! HEH!
I'D NEVER DO SOME-THING SO INDECENT.
I'M NOT ORITO.
I KNOW! I WAS ONLY KIDDING!
AH... THAT REMINDS ME, AIKAWA ...
DID YOU REMEMBER TO BRING THE POTATOES?
....
WHAT DO YOU NEED POTATOES FOR?

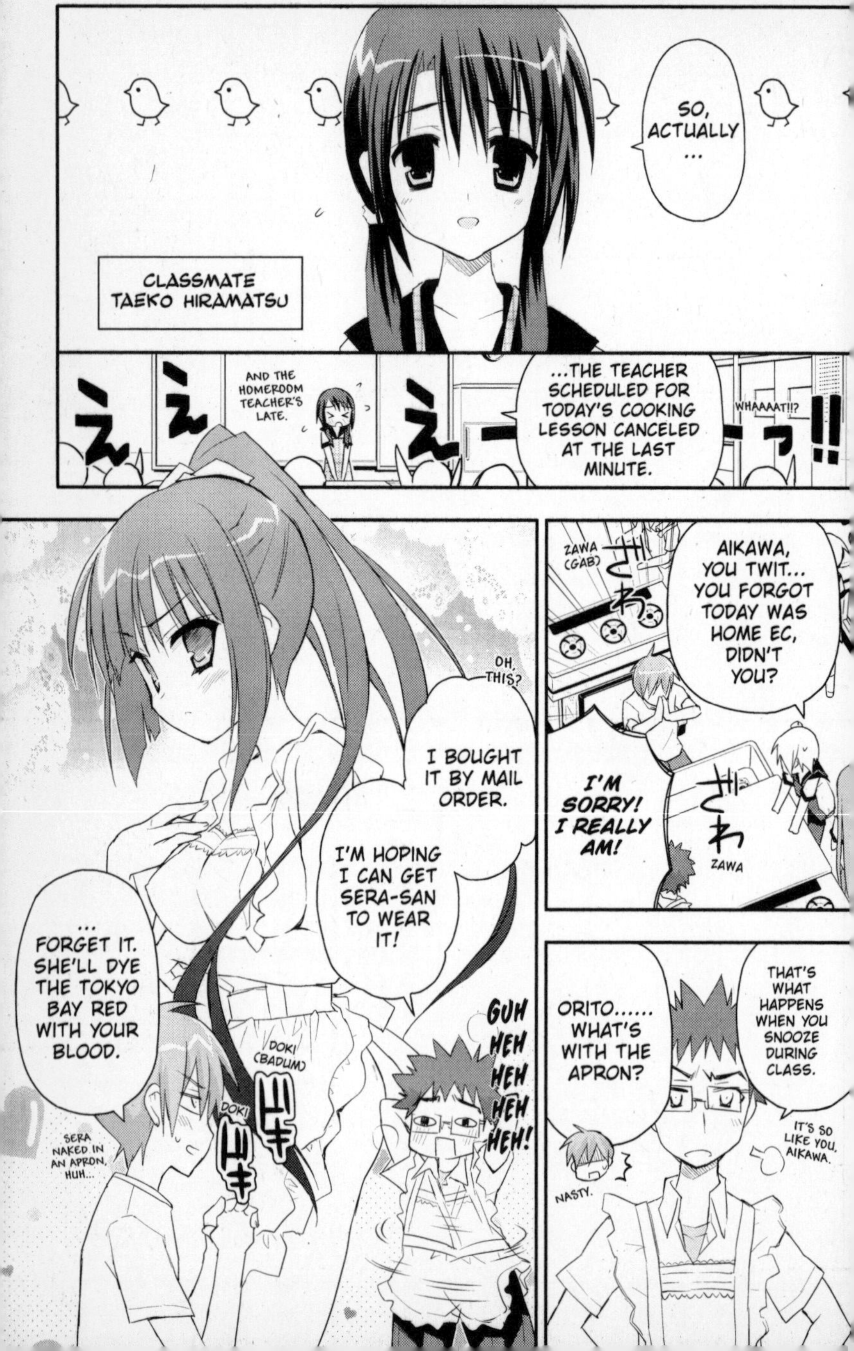
SO, ACTUALLY ...
CLASSMATE TAEKO HIRAMATSU
...THE TEACHER SCHEDULED FOR TODAY'S COOKING LESSON CANCELED AT THE LAST MINUTE.
WHAAAAT!!?
AND THE HOMEROOM TEACHER'S LATE.
ZAWA (GAB)
AIKAWA, YOU TWIT... YOU FORGOT TODAY WAS HOME EC, DIDN'T YOU?
I'M SORRY! I REALLY AM!
ZAWA
THAT'S WHAT HAPPENS WHEN YOU SNOOZE DURING CLASS.
IT'S SO LIKE YOU, AIKAWA.
ORITO...... WHAT'S WITH THE APRON?
NASTY.
OH, THIS?
I BOUGHT IT BY MAIL ORDER.
I'M HOPING I CAN GET SERA-SAN TO WEAR IT!
GUH HEH HEH HEH HEH!
DOKI (BADUMP)
DOKI
... FORGET IT. SHE'LL DYE THE TOKYO BAY RED WITH YOUR BLOOD.
SERA NAKED IN AN APRON, HUH...

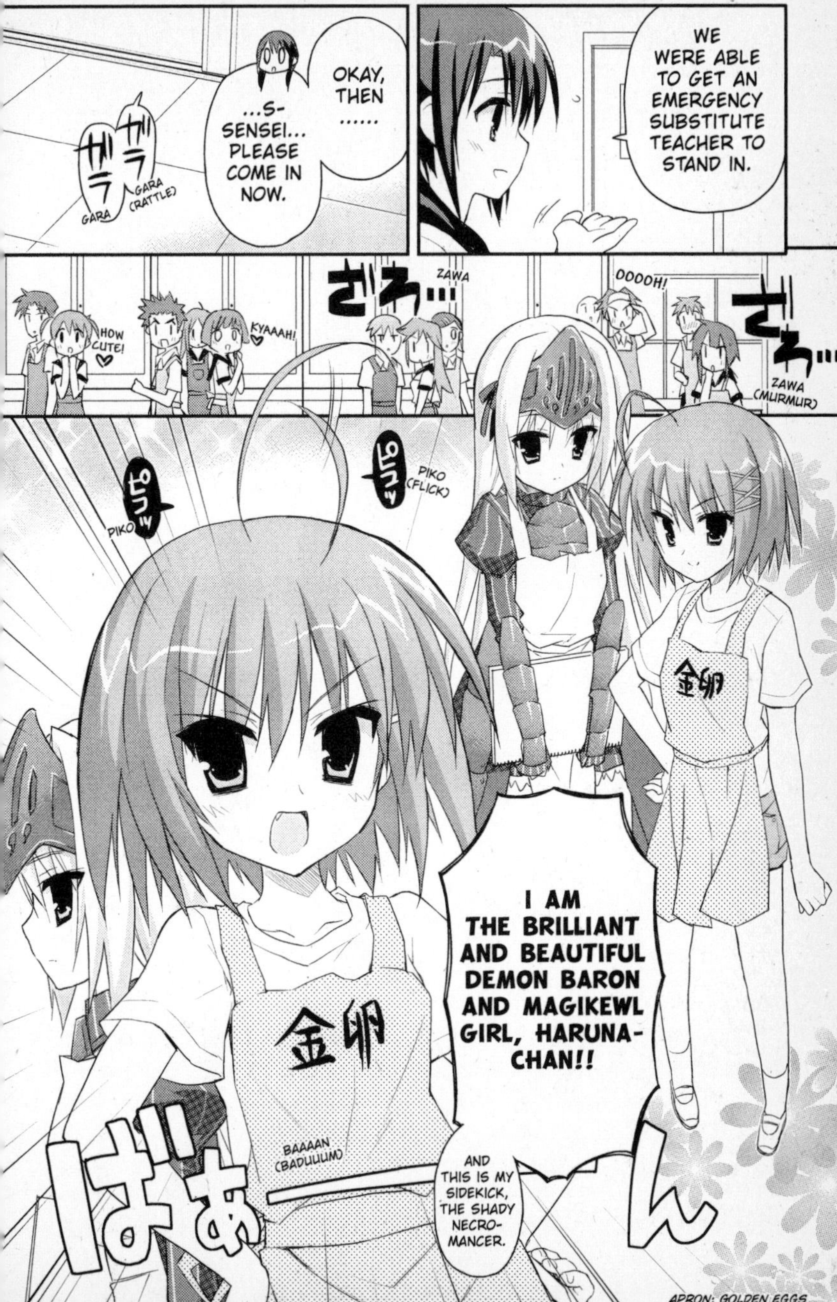
WE WERE ABLE TO GET AN EMERGENCY SUBSTITUTE TEACHER TO STAND IN.
OKAY, THEN ......
...S-SENSEI... PLEASE COME IN NOW.
ガラ
GARA (RATTLE)
ガラ
GARA
ざわ
ZAWA (MURMUR)
OOOOH!
ざわ
ZAWA
KYAAAH!
HOW CUTE!
ピコッ
PIKO (FLICK)
ピコッ
PIKO
金卵
I AM THE BRILLIANT AND BEAUTIFUL DEMON BARON AND MAGIKEWL GIRL, HARUNA-CHAN!!
AND THIS IS MY SIDEKICK, THE SHADY NECRO-MANCER.
金卵
ばぁん
BAAAAN (BADUUUM)
APRON: GOLDEN EGGS

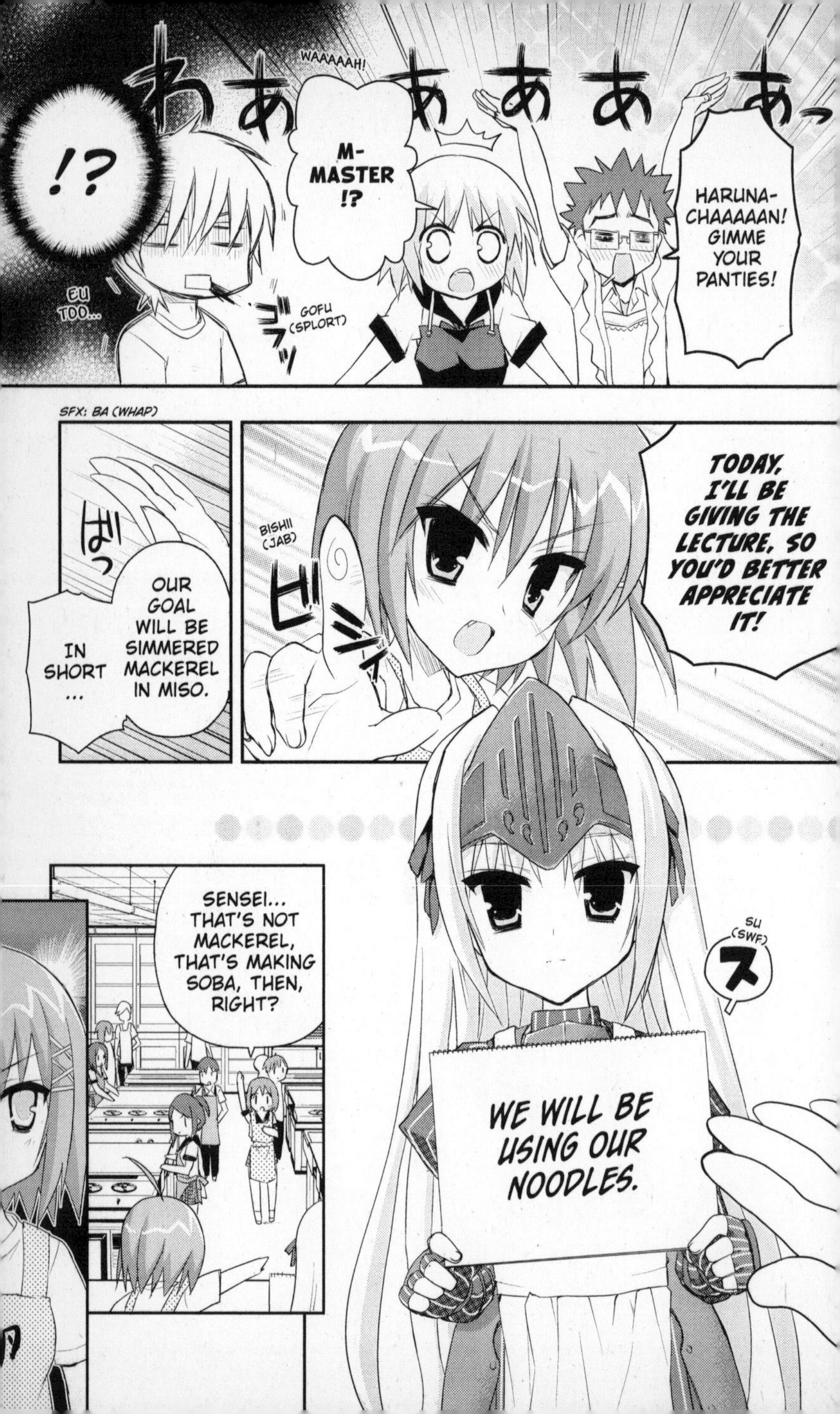
HARUNA-CHAAAAAN! GIMME YOUR PANTIES!
WAAAAAH!
M-MASTER!?
GOFU (SPLORT)
!?
EU TOO...
TODAY, I'LL BE GIVING THE LECTURE, SO YOU'D BETTER APPRECIATE IT!
BISHII (JAB)
SFX: BA (WHAP)
OUR GOAL WILL BE SIMMERED MACKEREL IN MISO.
IN SHORT ...
SU (SWF)
WE WILL BE USING OUR NOODLES.
SENSEI... THAT'S NOT MACKEREL, THAT'S MAKING SOBA, THEN, RIGHT?

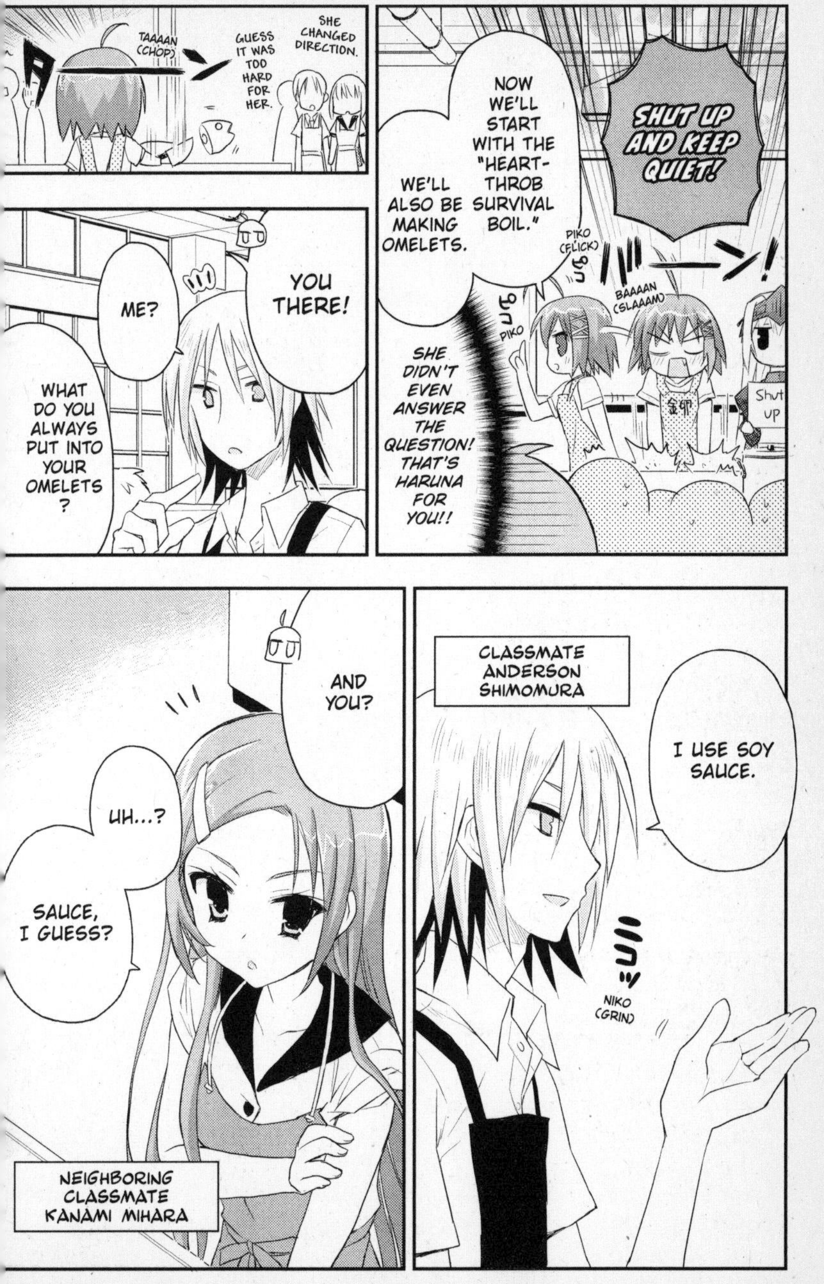
SHUT UP AND KEEP QUIET!
NOW WE'LL START WITH THE "HEART-THROB SURVIVAL BOIL."
WE'LL ALSO BE MAKING OMELETS.
PIKO (FLICK)
PIKO
BAAAAN (SLAAAM)
Shut up
SHE DIDN'T EVEN ANSWER THE QUESTION! THAT'S HARUNA FOR YOU!!
SHE CHANGED DIRECTION.
GUESS IT WAS TOO HARD FOR HER.
TAAAAN (CHOP)
YOU THERE!
ME?
WHAT DO YOU ALWAYS PUT INTO YOUR OMELETS?
CLASSMATE ANDERSON SHIMOMURA
I USE SOY SAUCE.
NIKO (GRIN)
AND YOU?
UH...?
SAUCE, I GUESS?
NEIGHBORING CLASSMATE KANAMI MIHARA

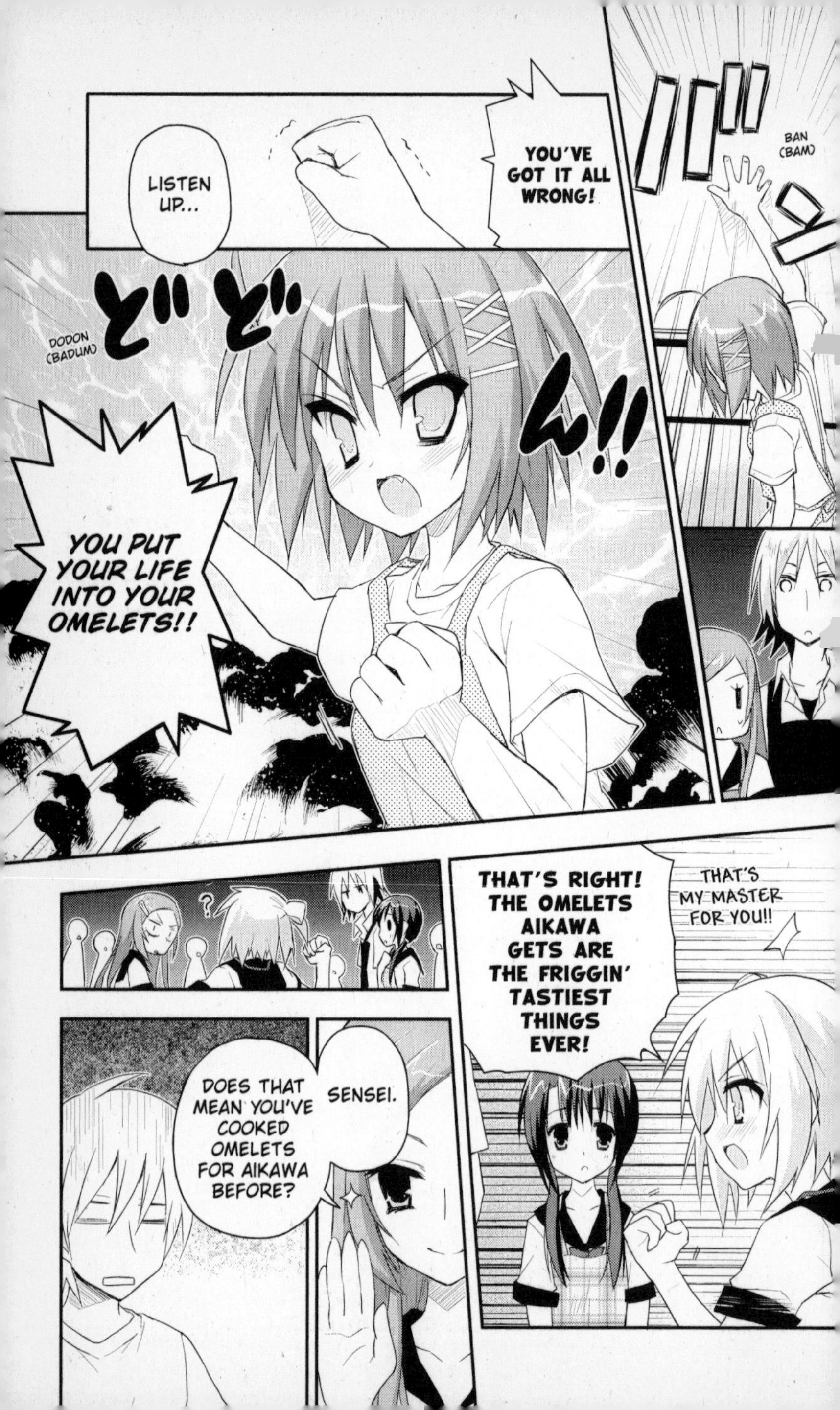
BAN (BAM)
YOU'VE GOT IT ALL WRONG!
LISTEN UP...
DODON (BADUM)
YOU PUT YOUR LIFE INTO YOUR OMELETS!!
THAT'S RIGHT! THE OMELETS AIKAWA GETS ARE THE FRIGGIN' TASTIEST THINGS EVER!
THAT'S MY MASTER FOR YOU!!
?
SENSEI.
DOES THAT MEAN YOU'VE COOKED OMELETS FOR AIKAWA BEFORE?

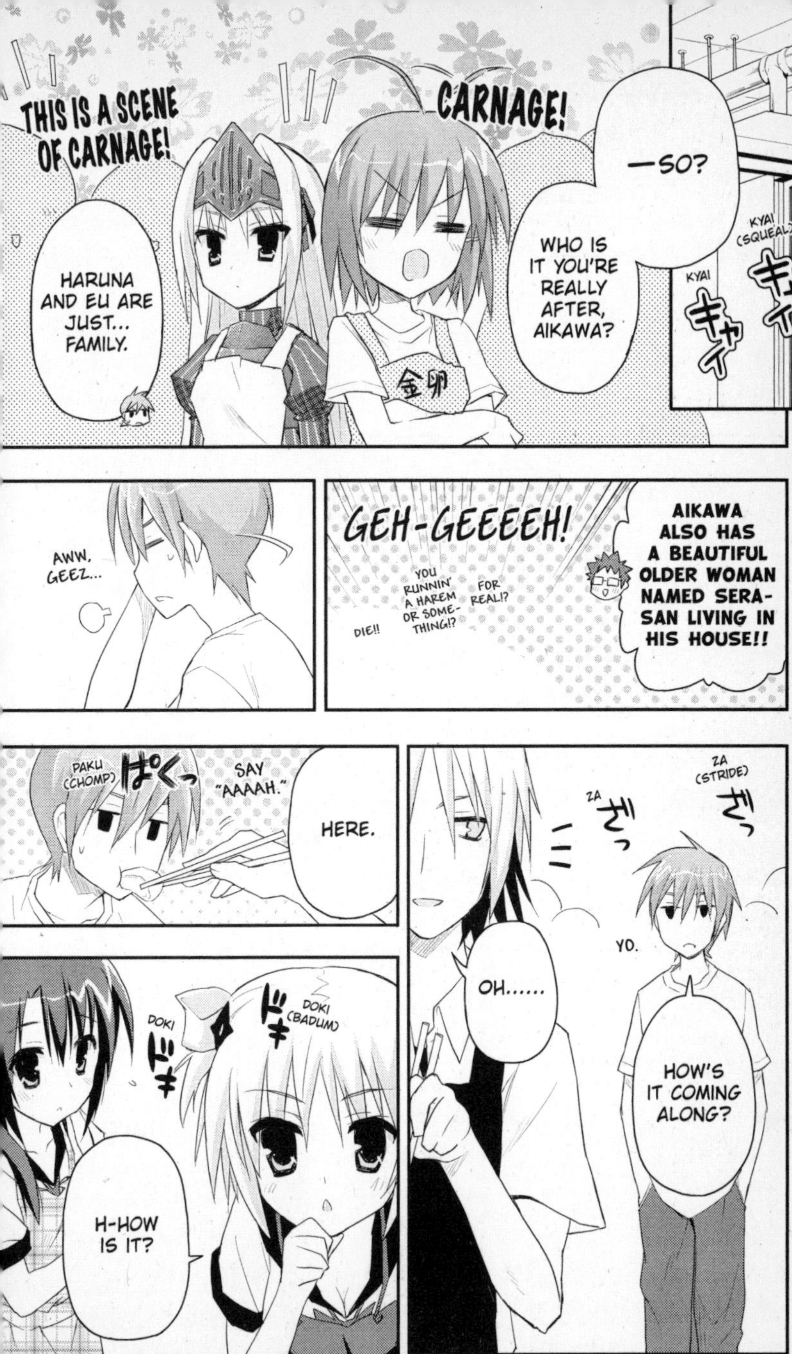
KYAI (SQUEAL) キャイ
KYAI キャイ
—SO?
WHO IS IT YOU'RE REALLY AFTER, AIKAWA?
CARNAGE!
THIS IS A SCENE OF CARNAGE!
HARUNA AND EU ARE JUST... FAMILY.
AIKAWA ALSO HAS A BEAUTIFUL OLDER WOMAN NAMED SERA-SAN LIVING IN HIS HOUSE!!
GEH-GEEEEH!
FOR REAL!?
YOU RUNNIN' A HAREM OR SOME-THING!?
DIE!!
AWW, GEEZ...
ZA (STRIDE)
ZA
YO.
HOW'S IT COMING ALONG?
OH......
HERE.
SAY "AAAAH."
PAKU (CHOMP) ぱくっ
DOKI (BADUM) ドキ
DOKI ドキ
H-HOW IS IT?

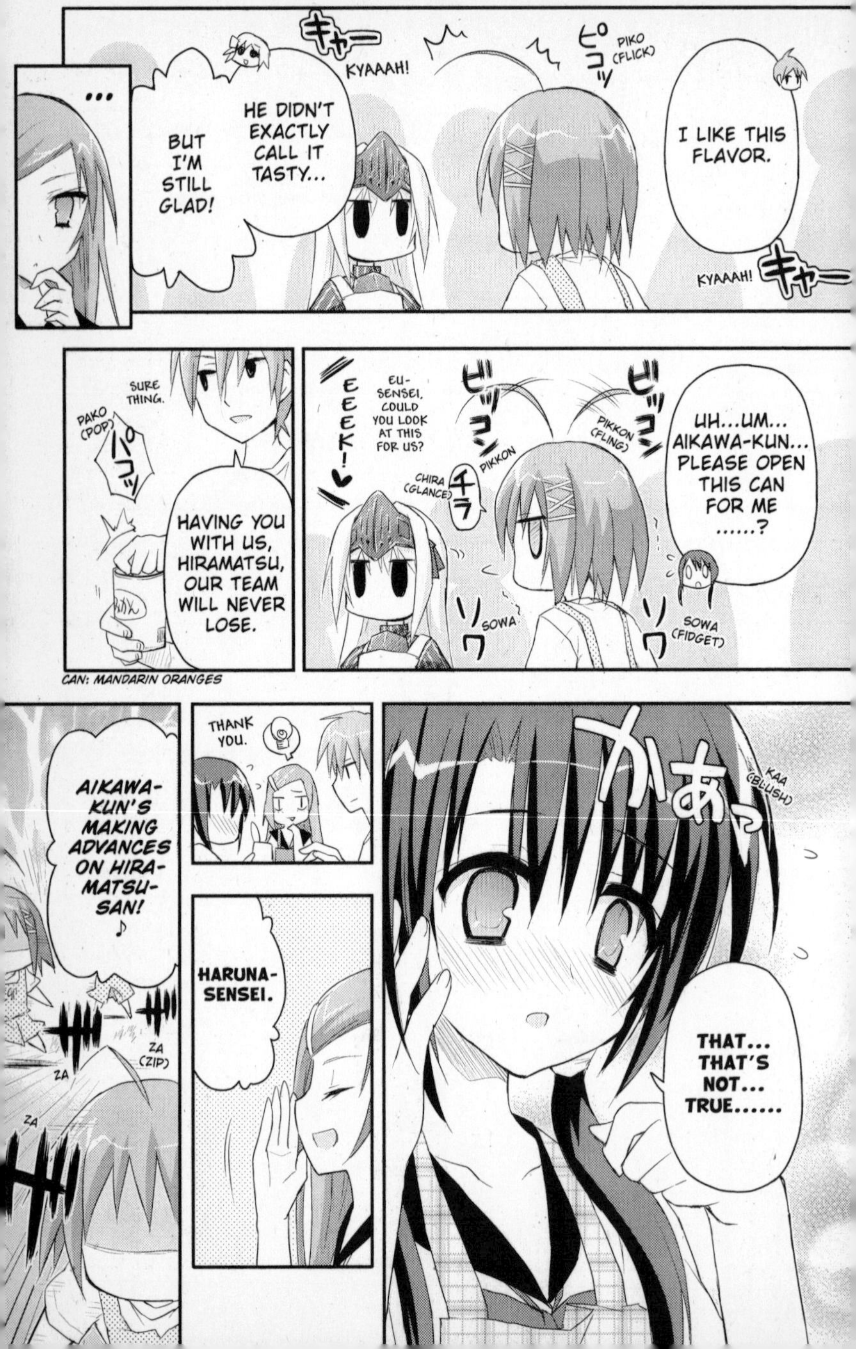
I LIKE THIS FLAVOR.
KYAAAH!
PIKO (FLICK)
KYAAAH!
HE DIDN'T EXACTLY CALL IT TASTY...
BUT I'M STILL GLAD!
...
UH...UM... AIKAWA-KUN... PLEASE OPEN THIS CAN FOR ME ......?
PIKKON (FLING)
PIKKON
SOWA (FIDGET)
CHIRA (GLANCE)
EU-SENSEI, COULD YOU LOOK AT THIS FOR US?
EEEK!♥
SOWA
SURE THING.
PAKO (POP)
HAVING YOU WITH US, HIRAMATSU, OUR TEAM WILL NEVER LOSE.
CAN: MANDARIN ORANGES
KAA (BLUSH)
THAT... THAT'S NOT... TRUE......
THANK YOU.
HARUNA-SENSEI.
AIKAWA-KUN'S MAKING ADVANCES ON HIRAMATSU-SAN! ♪
ZA (ZIP)
ZA
ZA

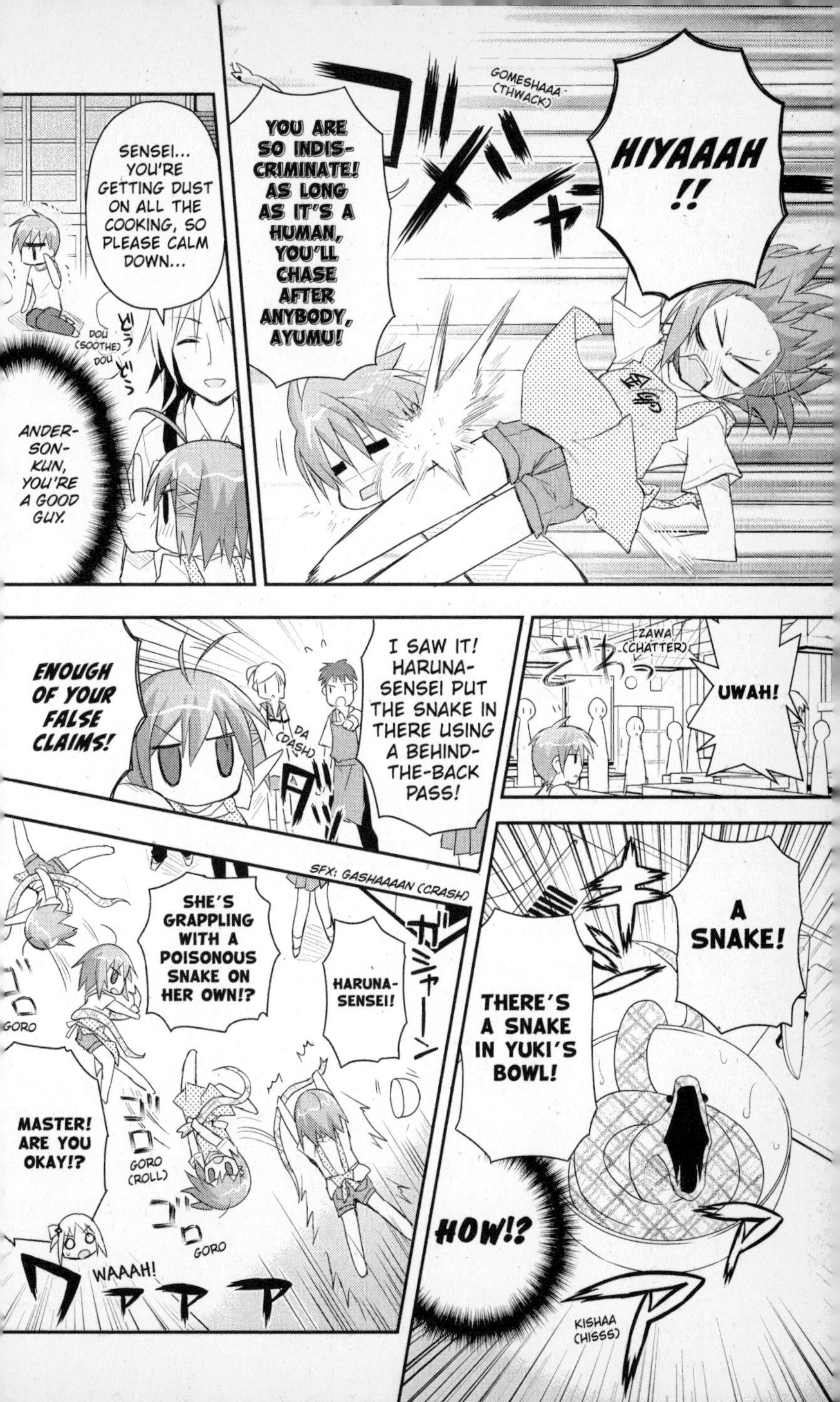
HIYAAAH!!
GOMESHAAA (THWACK)
YOU ARE SO INDIS-CRIMINATE! AS LONG AS IT'S A HUMAN, YOU'LL CHASE AFTER ANYBODY, AYUMU!
SENSEI... YOU'RE GETTING DUST ON ALL THE COOKING, SO PLEASE CALM DOWN...
DOU (SOOTHE) DOU
ANDER-SON-KUN, YOU'RE A GOOD GUY.
ZAWA (CHATTER)
UWAH!
I SAW IT! HARUNA-SENSEI PUT THE SNAKE IN THERE USING A BEHIND-THE-BACK PASS!
DA (DASH)
ENOUGH OF YOUR FALSE CLAIMS!
A SNAKE!
THERE'S A SNAKE IN YUKI'S BOWL!
HOW!?
KISHAA (HISSS)
SFX: GASHAAAAN (CRASH)
HARUNA-SENSEI!
SHE'S GRAPPLING WITH A POISONOUS SNAKE ON HER OWN!?
GORO
MASTER! ARE YOU OKAY!?
GORO (ROLL)
GORO
WAAAH!

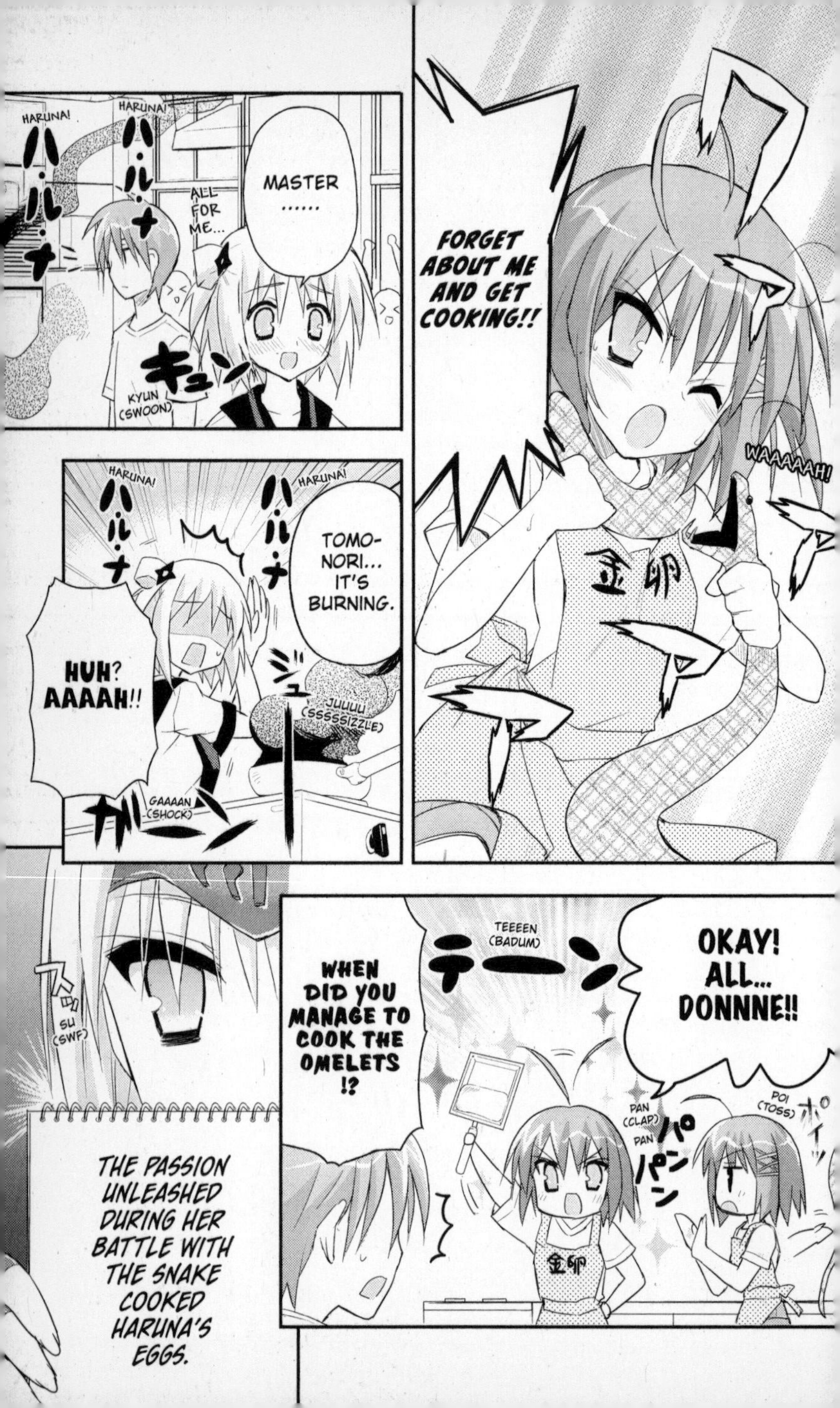
FORGET ABOUT ME AND GET COOKING!!
WAAAAAAH!
MASTER ......
ALL FOR ME...
HARUNA!
HARUNA!
KYUN (SWOON)
HARUNA!
TOMO-NORI... IT'S BURNING.
HARUNA!
HUH? AAAAH!!
JUUUU (SSSSSIZZLE)
GAAAAN (SHOCK)
OKAY! ALL... DONNNE!!
POI (TOSS)
PAN (CLAP) PAN
TEEEEN (BADUM)
WHEN DID YOU MANAGE TO COOK THE OMELETS !?
SU (SWF)
THE PASSION UNLEASHED DURING HER BATTLE WITH THE SNAKE COOKED HARUNA'S EGGS.

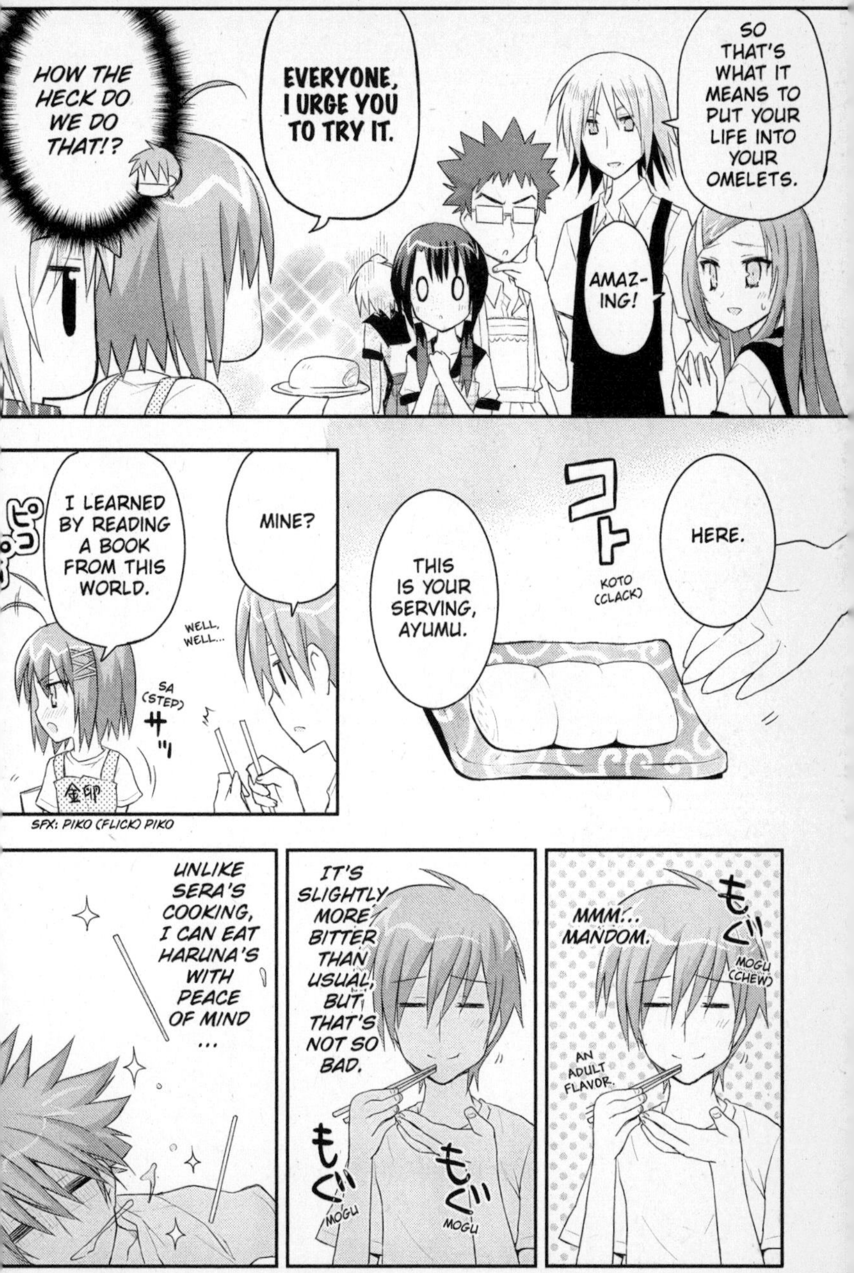

SO THAT'S WHAT IT MEANS TO PUT YOUR LIFE INTO YOUR OMELETS.
AMAZ-ING!
EVERYONE, I URGE YOU TO TRY IT.
HOW THE HECK DO WE DO THAT!?
HERE.
KOTO (CLACK)
THIS IS YOUR SERVING, AYUMU.
MINE?
I LEARNED BY READING A BOOK FROM THIS WORLD.
WELL, WELL...
SA (STEP)
SFX: PIKO (FLICK) PIKO
MMM... MANDOM.
MOGU (CHEW)
AN ADULT FLAVOR.
IT'S SLIGHTLY MORE BITTER THAN USUAL, BUT THAT'S NOT SO BAD.
MOGU
MOGU
UNLIKE SERA'S COOKING, I CAN EAT HARUNA'S WITH PEACE OF MIND...

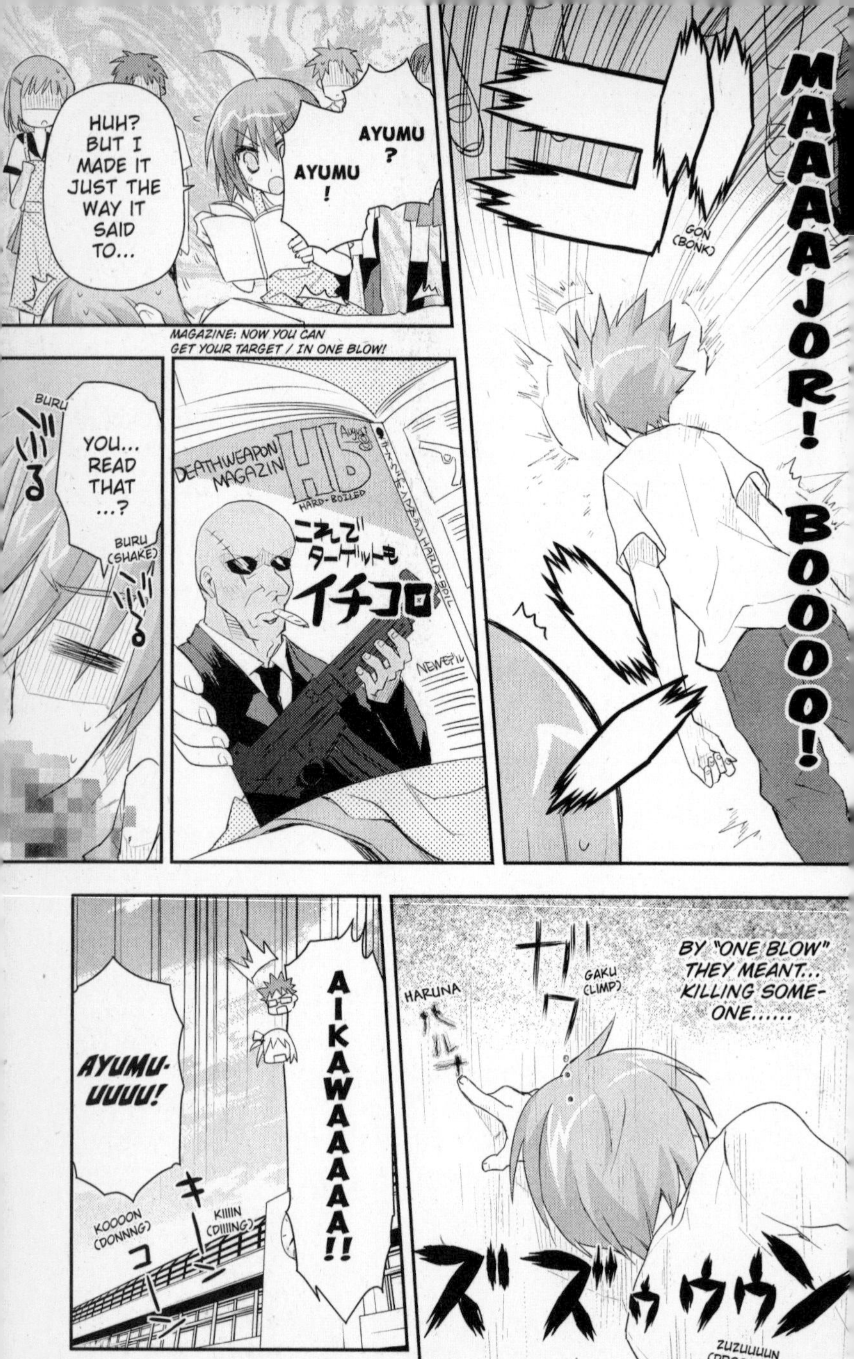
MAAAAJOR! BOOOOOO!
GON (BONK)
AYUMU?
AYUMU!
HUH? BUT I MADE IT JUST THE WAY IT SAID TO...
MAGAZINE: NOW YOU CAN GET YOUR TARGET / IN ONE BLOW!
DEATHWEAPON MAGAZIN
HB
HARD-BOILED
August
これでターゲットもイチコロ
BURU
YOU... READ THAT ...?
BURU (SHAKE)
BY "ONE BLOW" THEY MEANT... KILLING SOME-ONE......
GAKU (LIMP)
HARUNA
ZUZUUUUN (DROOOOOP)
AIKAWAAAAAAA!!
AYUMU-UUUU!
KIIIIN (DIIIING)
KOOOON (DONNNG)

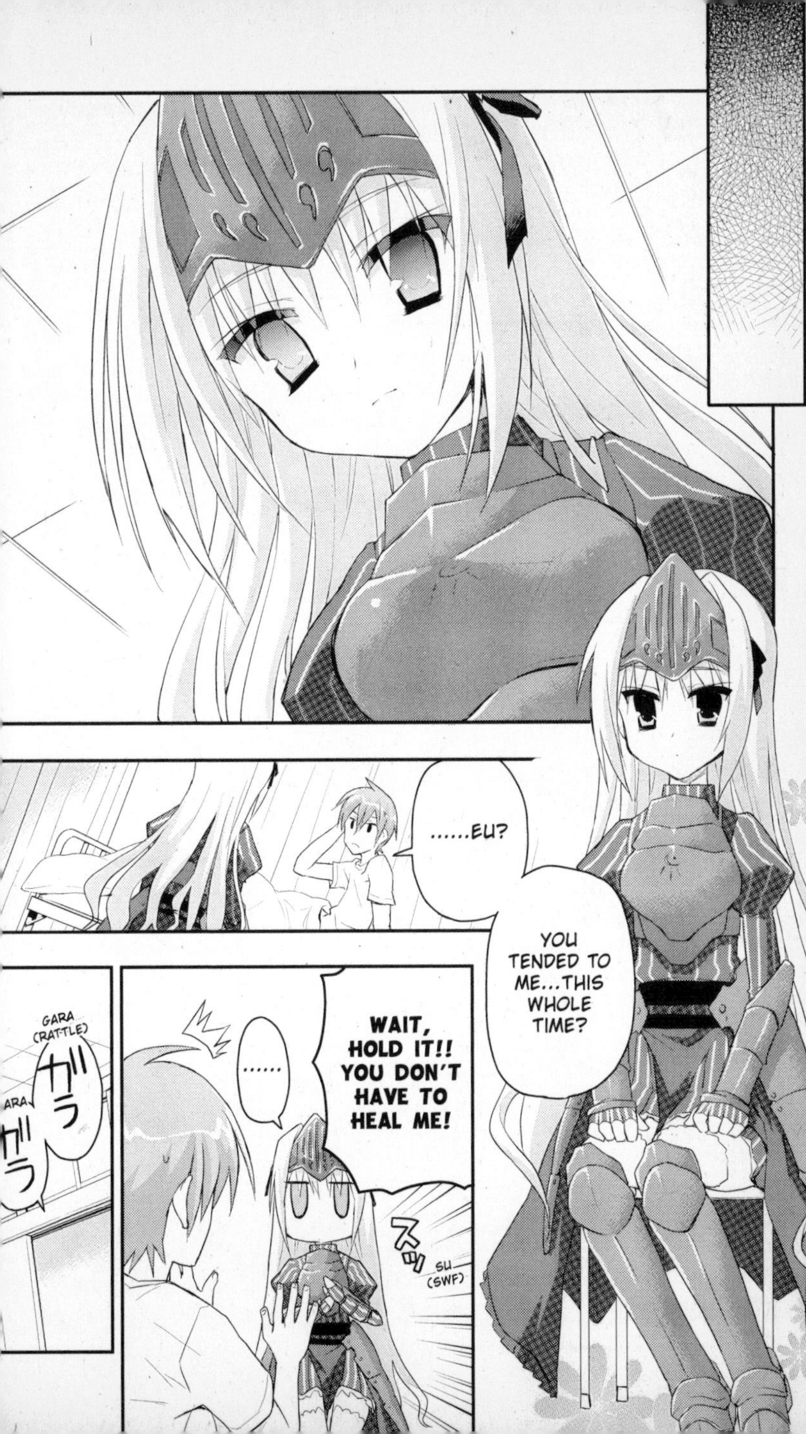
......EU?
YOU TENDED TO ME...THIS WHOLE TIME?
WAIT, HOLD IT!! YOU DON'T HAVE TO HEAL ME!
......
スッ
SU (SWF)
GARA (RATTLE)
ガラ
ARA
ガラ

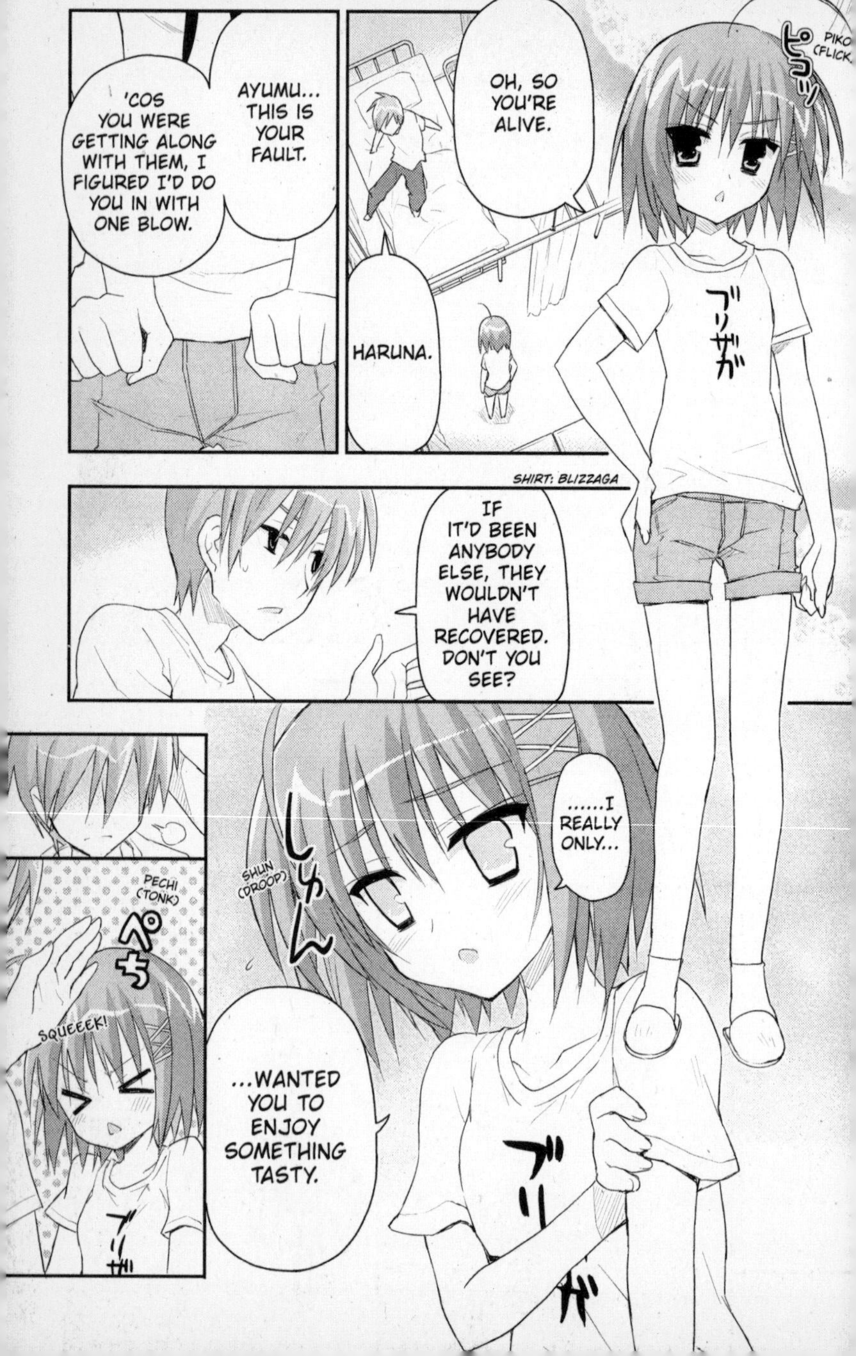
ピコッ
PIKO (FLICK)
ブリザガ
OH, SO YOU'RE ALIVE.
HARUNA.
AYUMU... THIS IS YOUR FAULT.
'COS YOU WERE GETTING ALONG WITH THEM, I FIGURED I'D DO YOU IN WITH ONE BLOW.
SHIRT: BLIZZAGA
IF IT'D BEEN ANYBODY ELSE, THEY WOULDN'T HAVE RECOVERED. DON'T YOU SEE?
......I REALLY ONLY...
しゅん
SHUN (DROOP)
...WANTED YOU TO ENJOY SOMETHING TASTY.
ブリザガ
ぺち
PECHI (TONK)
SQUEEEK!
ブリザガ

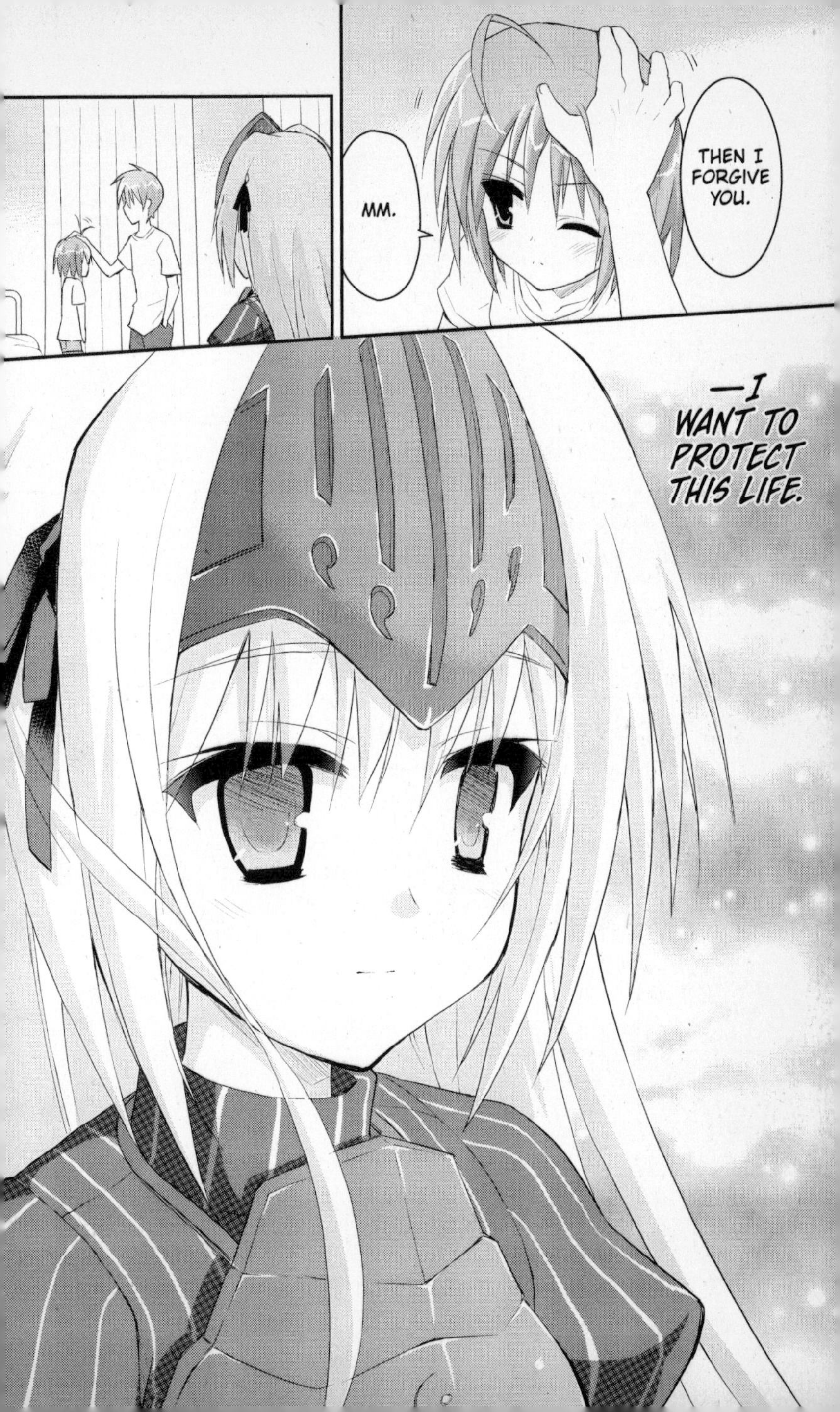
THEN I FORGIVE YOU.
MM.
—I WANT TO PROTECT THIS LIFE.

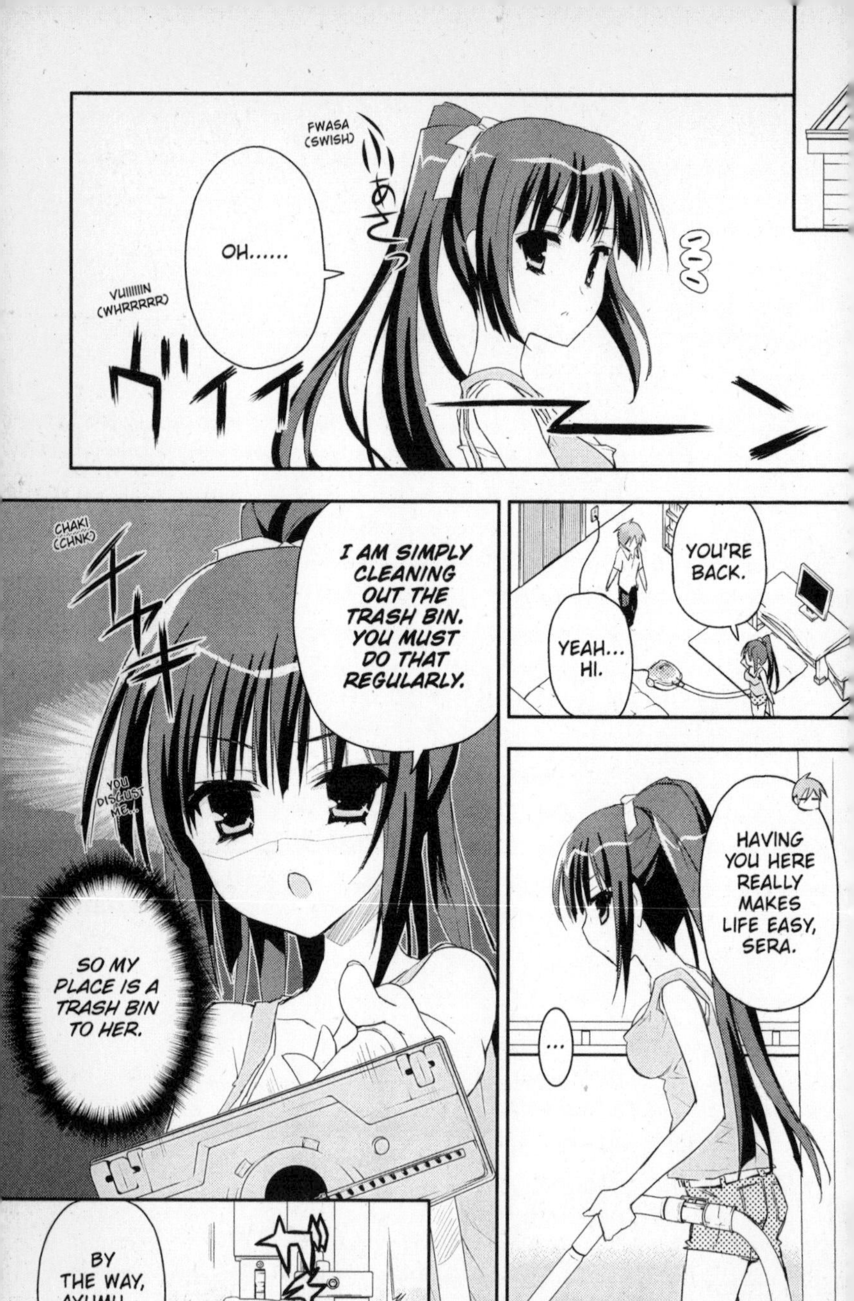
FWASA (SWISH)
OH......
VUIIIIIN (WHRRRRR)
YOU'RE BACK.
YEAH... HI.
HAVING YOU HERE REALLY MAKES LIFE EASY, SERA.
...
CHAKI (CHNK)
I AM SIMPLY CLEANING OUT THE TRASH BIN. YOU MUST DO THAT REGULARLY.
YOU DISGUST ME...
SO MY PLACE IS A TRASH BIN TO HER.
BY THE WAY, AYUMU...
GACHA (CLICK)

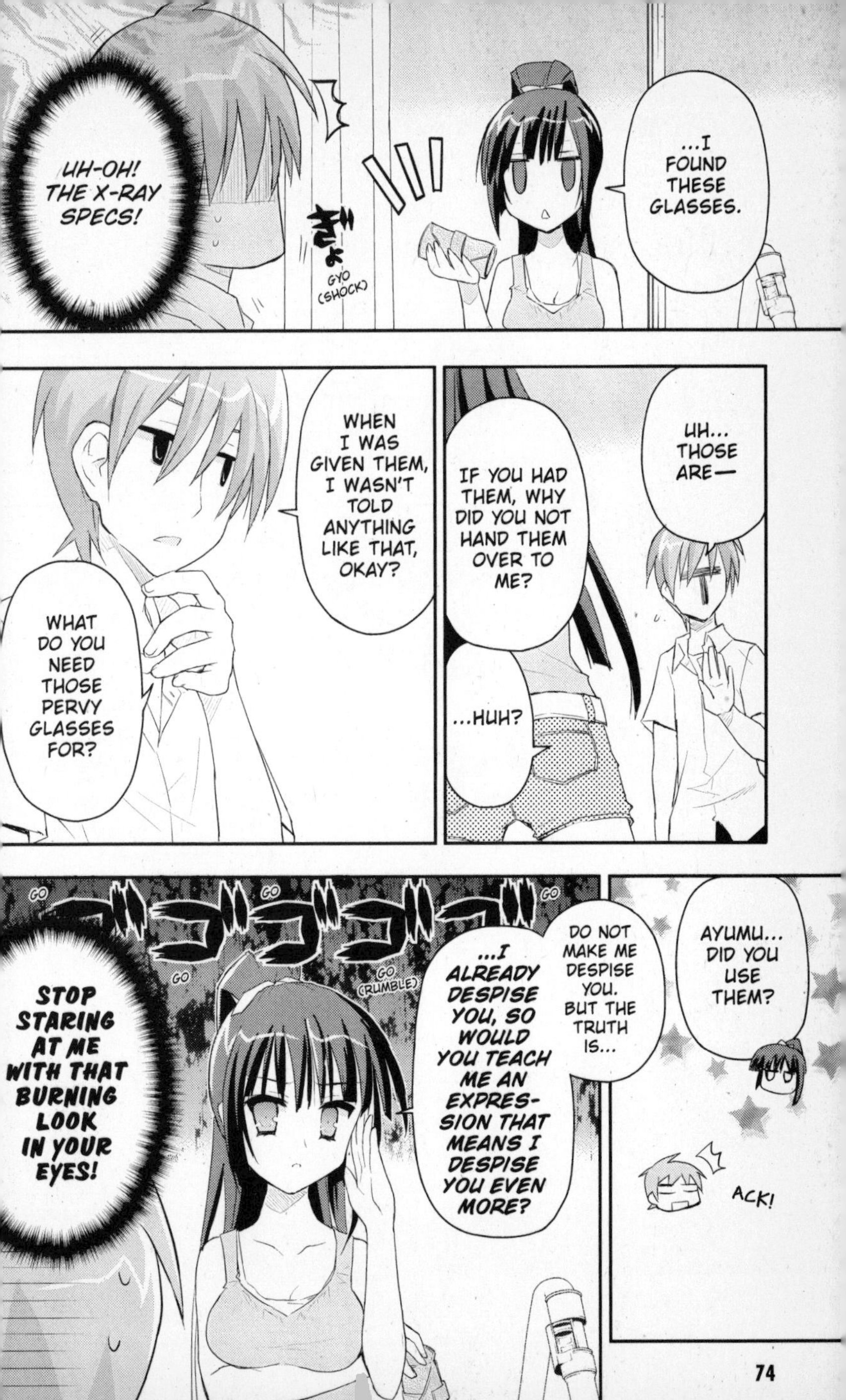
...I FOUND THESE GLASSES.
GYO (SHOCK)
UH-OH! THE X-RAY SPECS!
UH... THOSE ARE—
IF YOU HAD THEM, WHY DID YOU NOT HAND THEM OVER TO ME?
...HUH?
WHEN I WAS GIVEN THEM, I WASN'T TOLD ANYTHING LIKE THAT, OKAY?
WHAT DO YOU NEED THOSE PERVY GLASSES FOR?
AYUMU... DID YOU USE THEM?
ACK!
DO NOT MAKE ME DESPISE YOU. BUT THE TRUTH IS...
...I ALREADY DESPISE YOU, SO WOULD YOU TEACH ME AN EXPRESSION THAT MEANS I DESPISE YOU EVEN MORE?
GO GO GO GO GO (RUMBLE)
STOP STARING AT ME WITH THAT BURNING LOOK IN YOUR EYES!

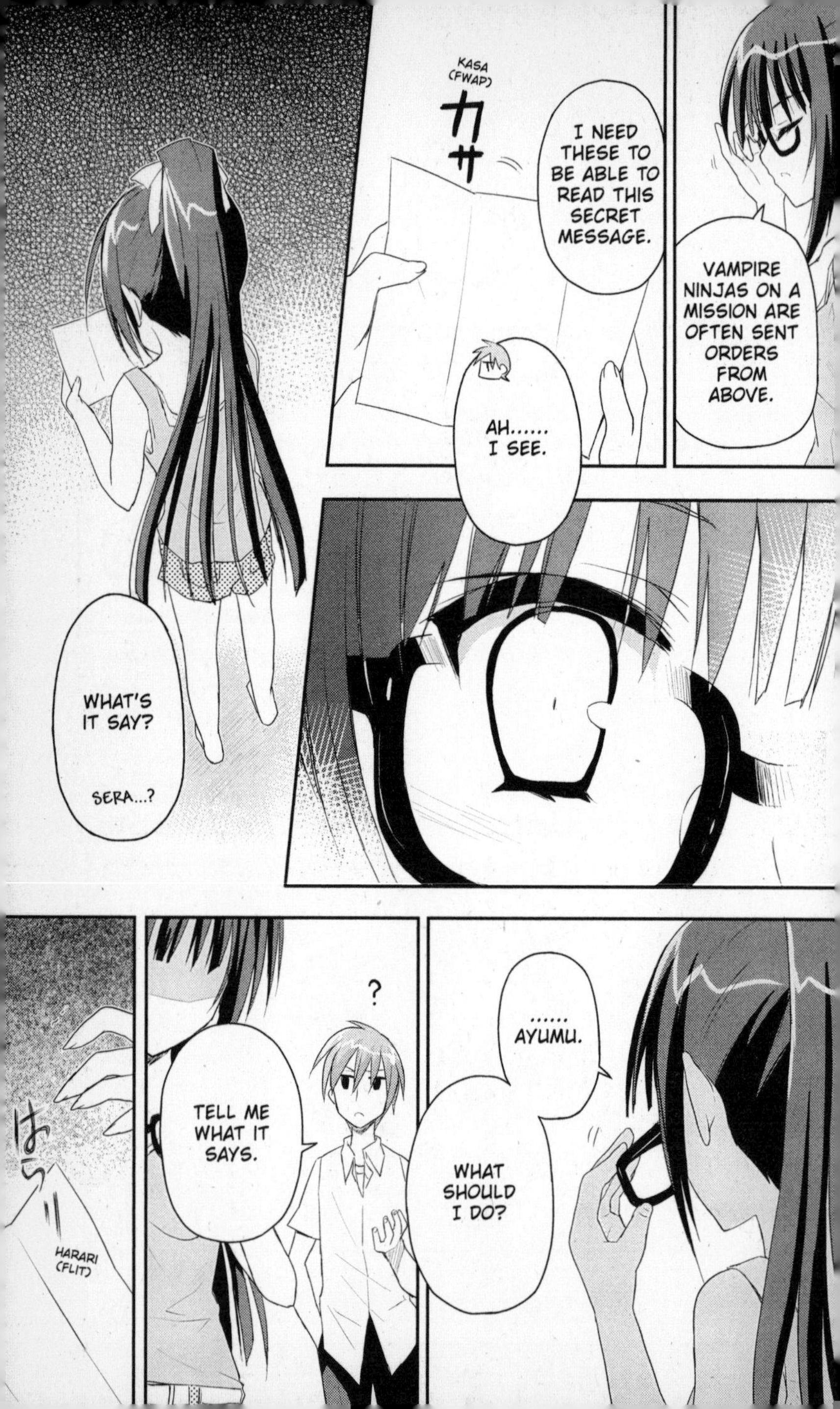
VAMPIRE NINJAS ON A MISSION ARE OFTEN SENT ORDERS FROM ABOVE.
KASA (FWAP)
カサ
I NEED THESE TO BE ABLE TO READ THIS SECRET MESSAGE.
AH...... I SEE.
WHAT'S IT SAY?
SERA...?
...... AYUMU.
WHAT SHOULD I DO?
?
TELL ME WHAT IT SAYS.
はらり
HARARI (FLIT)

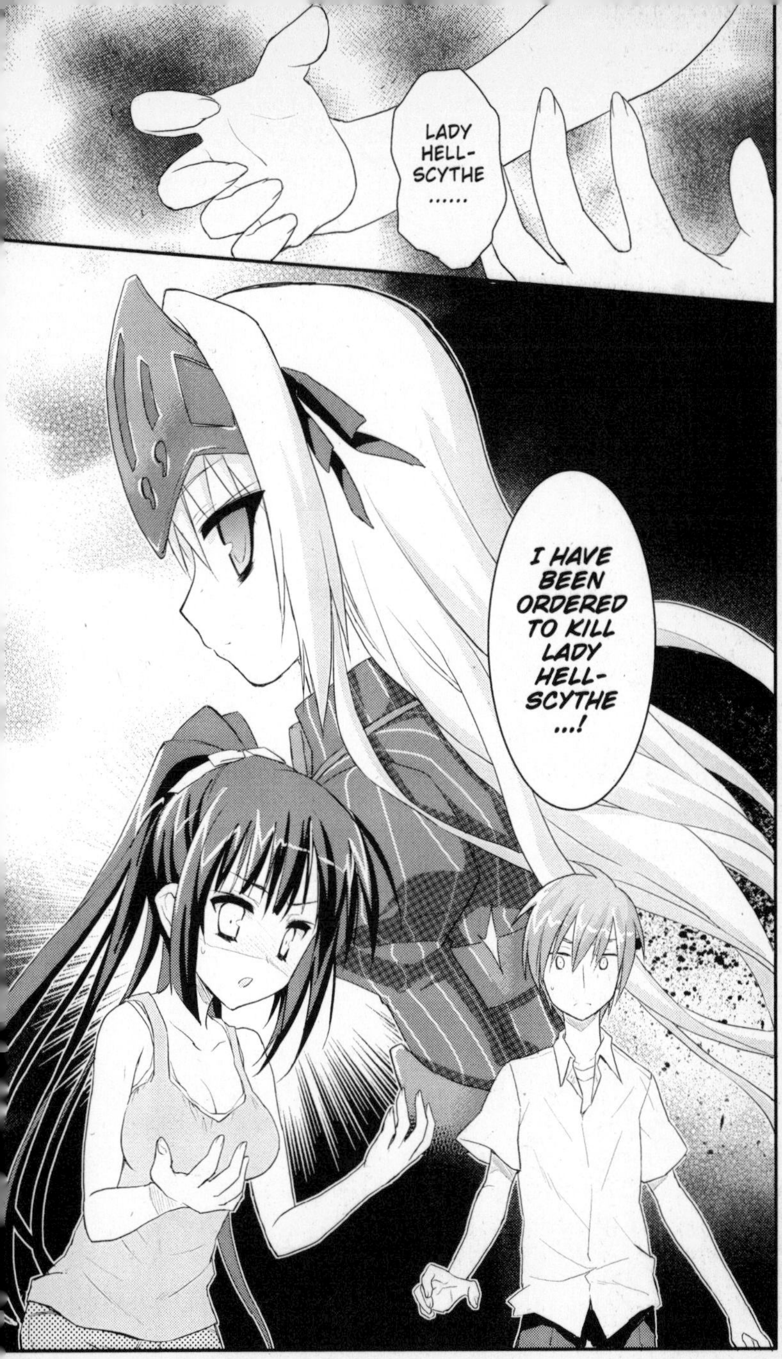
LADY HELL-SCYTHE ......
I HAVE BEEN ORDERED TO KILL LADY HELL-SCYTHE ...!

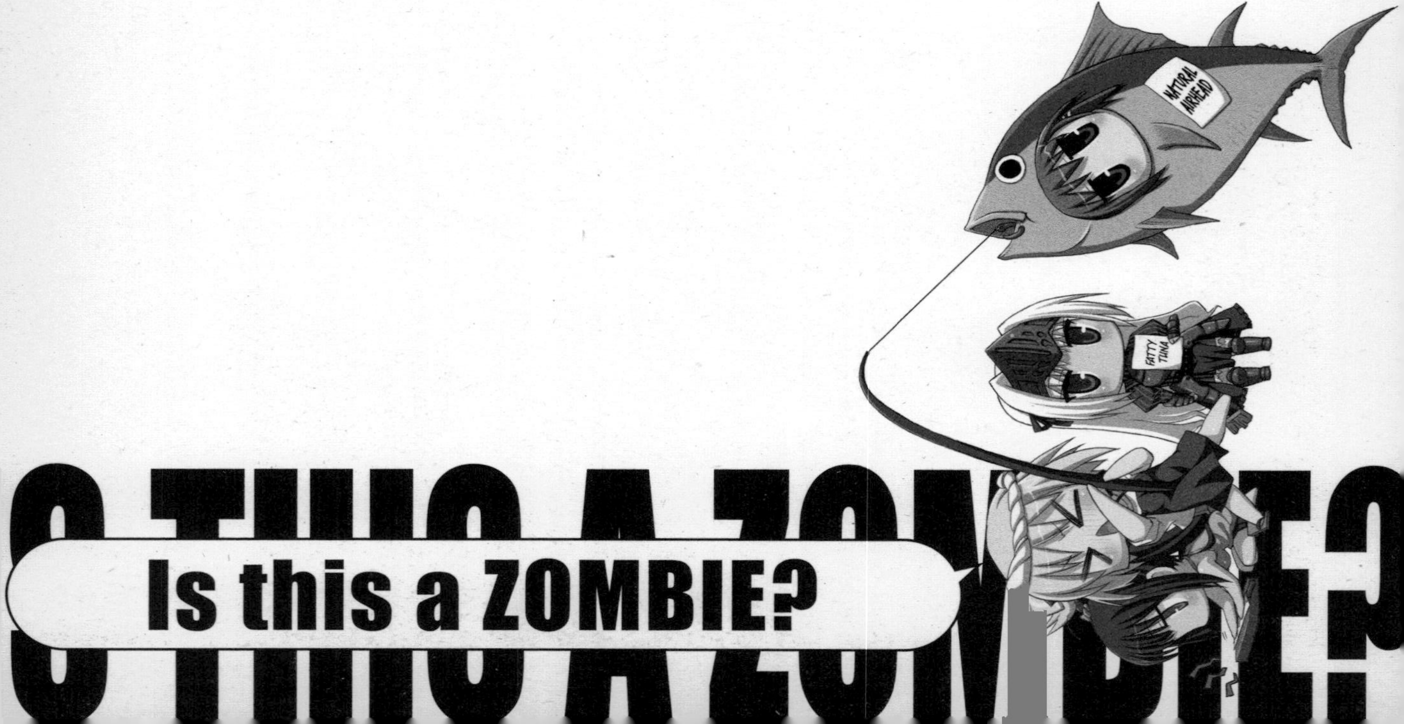
Is this a ZOMBIE?
NATURAL AIRHEAD
FATTY TUNA

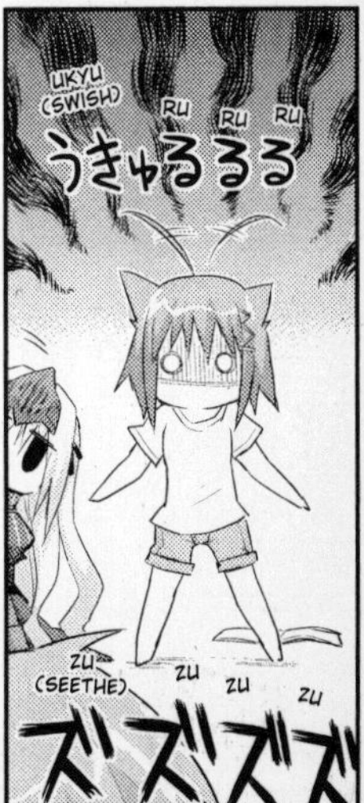

UKYU (SWISH) RU RU RU
うきゅるるる
ZU (SEETHE) ZU ZU ZU
ズズズズ

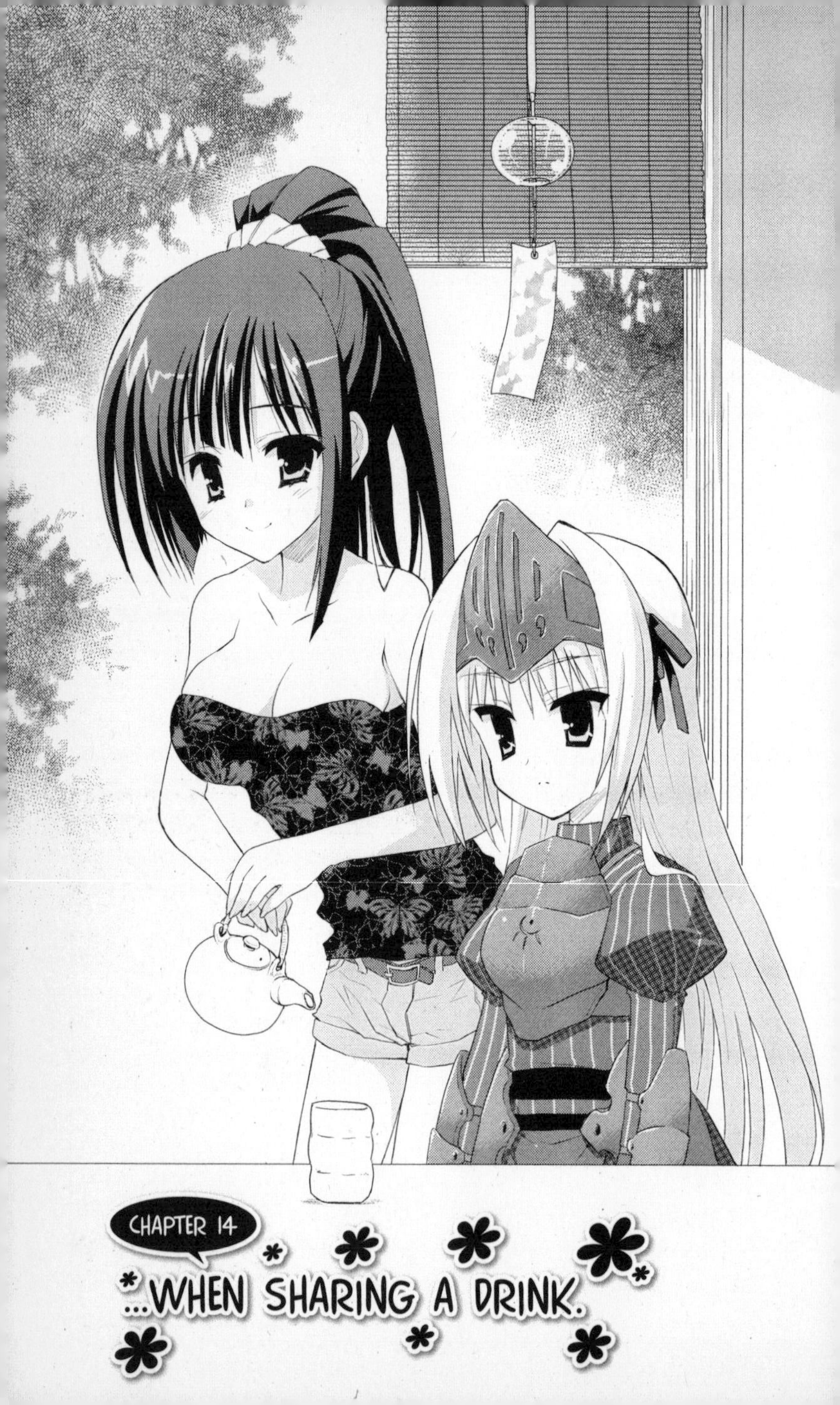
CHAPTER 14
...WHEN SHARING A DRINK.

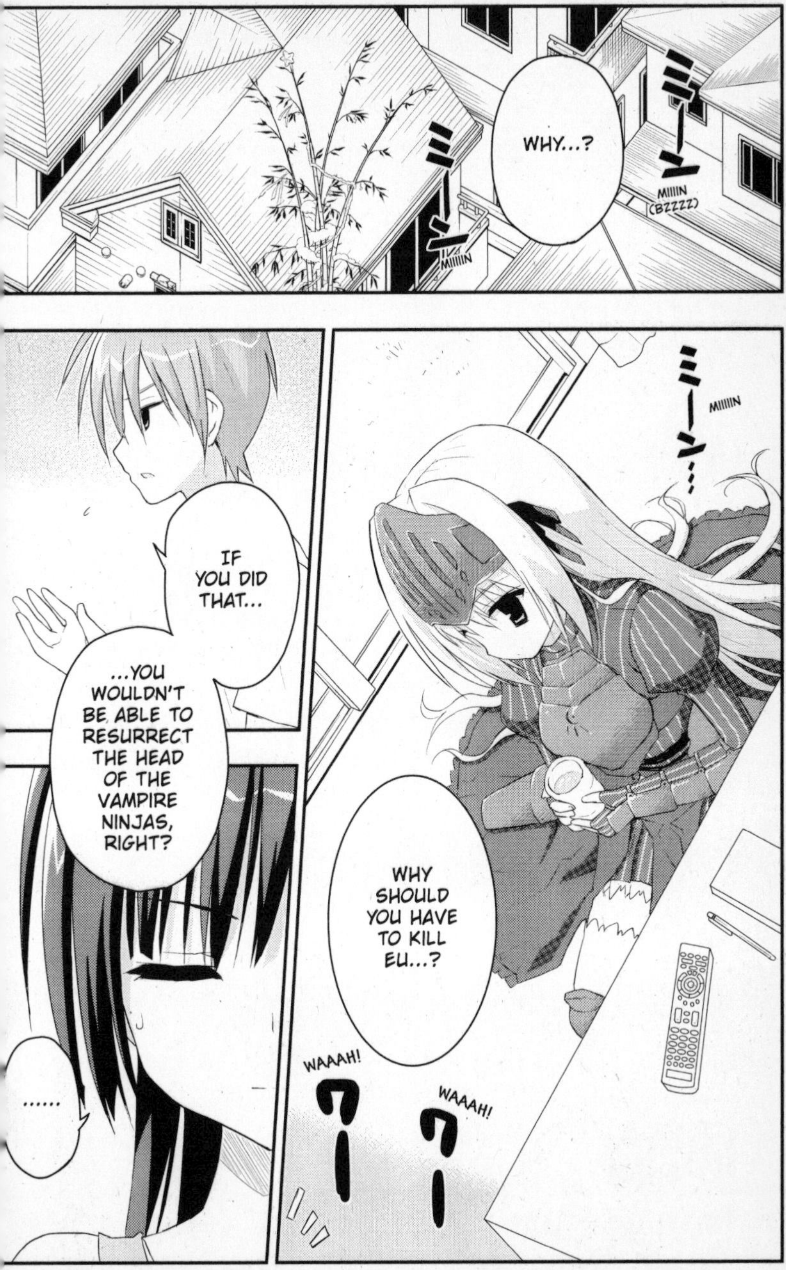
MIIIIN (BZZZZ)
WHY...?
MIIIIN
MIIIIN
WHY SHOULD YOU HAVE TO KILL EU...?
WAAAH!
WAAAH!
IF YOU DID THAT...
...YOU WOULDN'T BE ABLE TO RESURRECT THE HEAD OF THE VAMPIRE NINJAS, RIGHT?
......

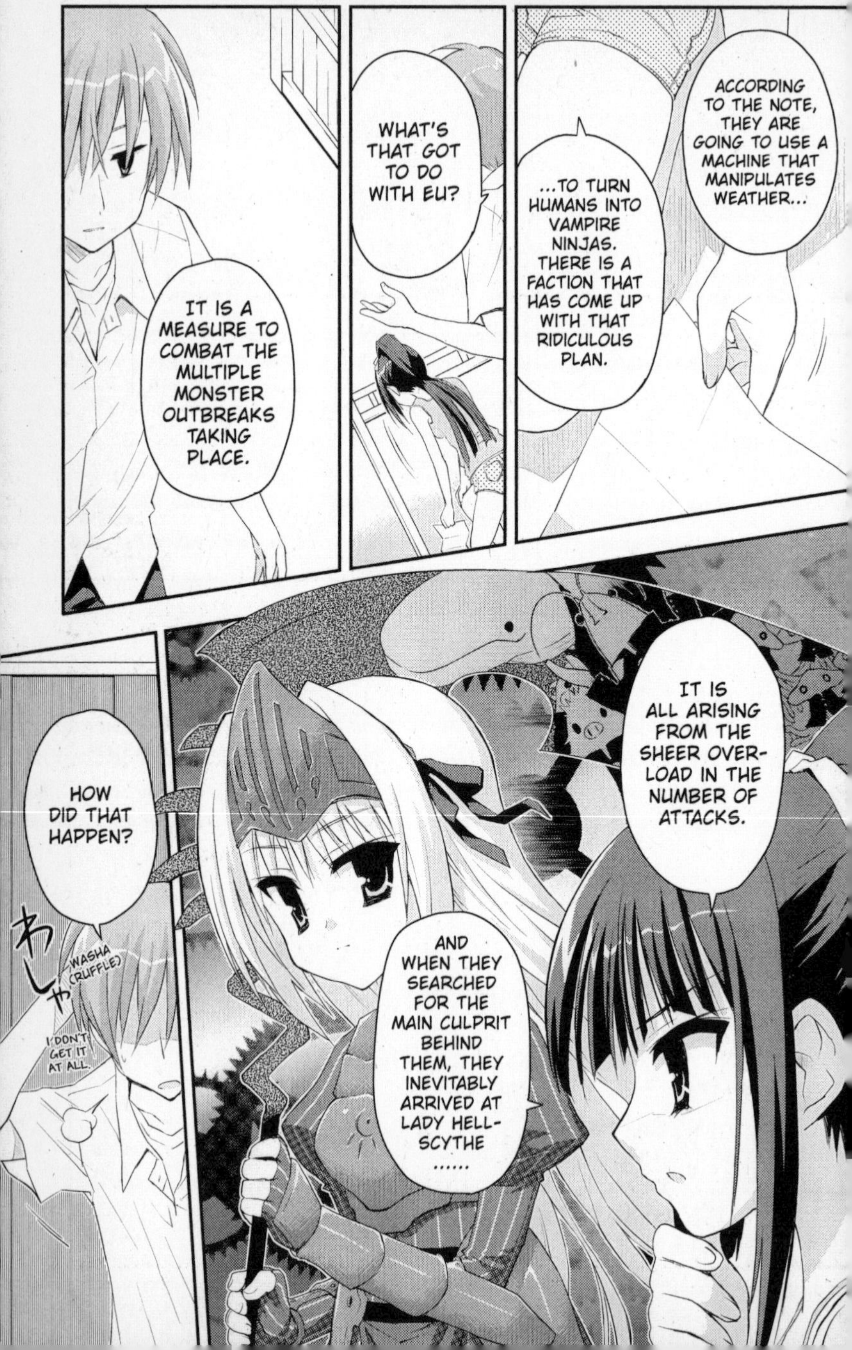
ACCORDING TO THE NOTE, THEY ARE GOING TO USE A MACHINE THAT MANIPULATES WEATHER...
...TO TURN HUMANS INTO VAMPIRE NINJAS. THERE IS A FACTION THAT HAS COME UP WITH THAT RIDICULOUS PLAN.
WHAT'S THAT GOT TO DO WITH EU?
IT IS A MEASURE TO COMBAT THE MULTIPLE MONSTER OUTBREAKS TAKING PLACE.
IT IS ALL ARISING FROM THE SHEER OVER-LOAD IN THE NUMBER OF ATTACKS.
AND WHEN THEY SEARCHED FOR THE MAIN CULPRIT BEHIND THEM, THEY INEVITABLY ARRIVED AT LADY HELL-SCYTHE ......
HOW DID THAT HAPPEN?
わしゃ
WASHA (RUFFLE)
I DON'T GET IT AT ALL.

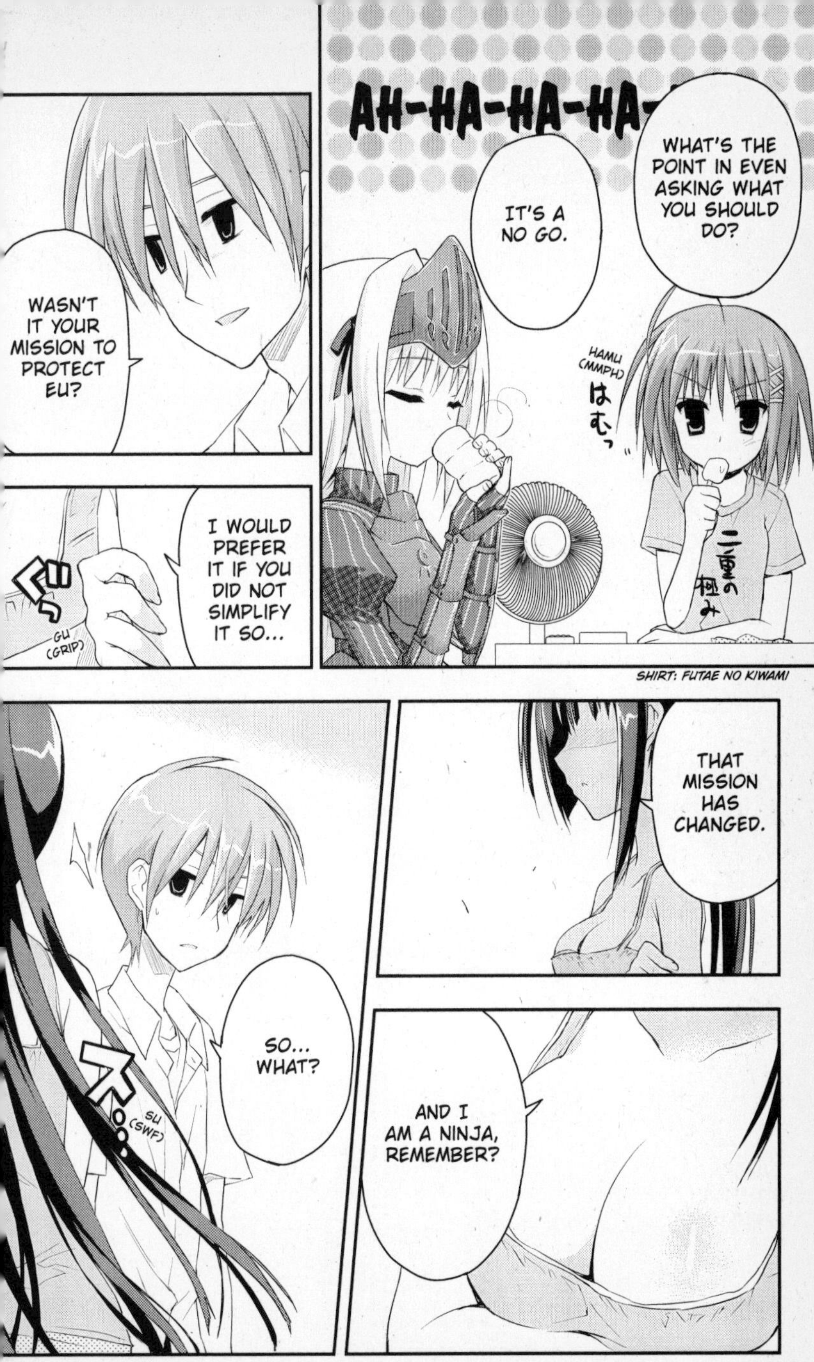
AH-HA-HA-HA-
WHAT'S THE POINT IN EVEN ASKING WHAT YOU SHOULD DO?
IT'S A NO GO.
HAMU (MMPH)
はむっ
WASN'T IT YOUR MISSION TO PROTECT EU?
I WOULD PREFER IT IF YOU DID NOT SIMPLIFY IT SO...
GU (GRIP)
SHIRT: FUTAE NO KIWAMI
THAT MISSION HAS CHANGED.
AND I AM A NINJA, REMEMBER?
SO... WHAT?
SU (SWF)

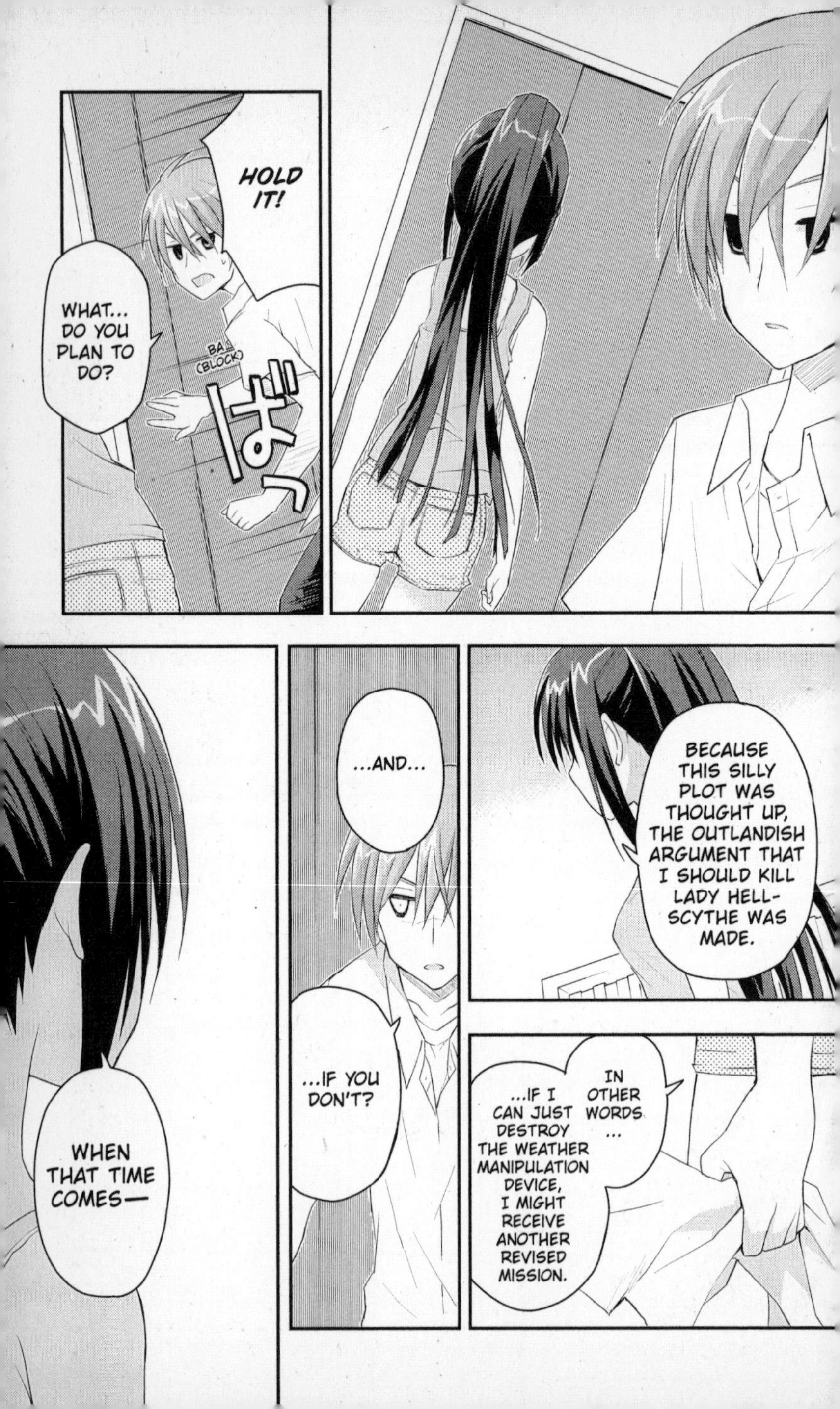
HOLD IT!
WHAT... DO YOU PLAN TO DO?
BA (BLOCK)
ばっ
BECAUSE THIS SILLY PLOT WAS THOUGHT UP, THE OUTLANDISH ARGUMENT THAT I SHOULD KILL LADY HELL-SCYTHE WAS MADE.
IN OTHER WORDS...
...IF I CAN JUST DESTROY THE WEATHER MANIPULATION DEVICE, I MIGHT RECEIVE ANOTHER REVISED MISSION.
...AND...
...IF YOU DON'T?
WHEN THAT TIME COMES—

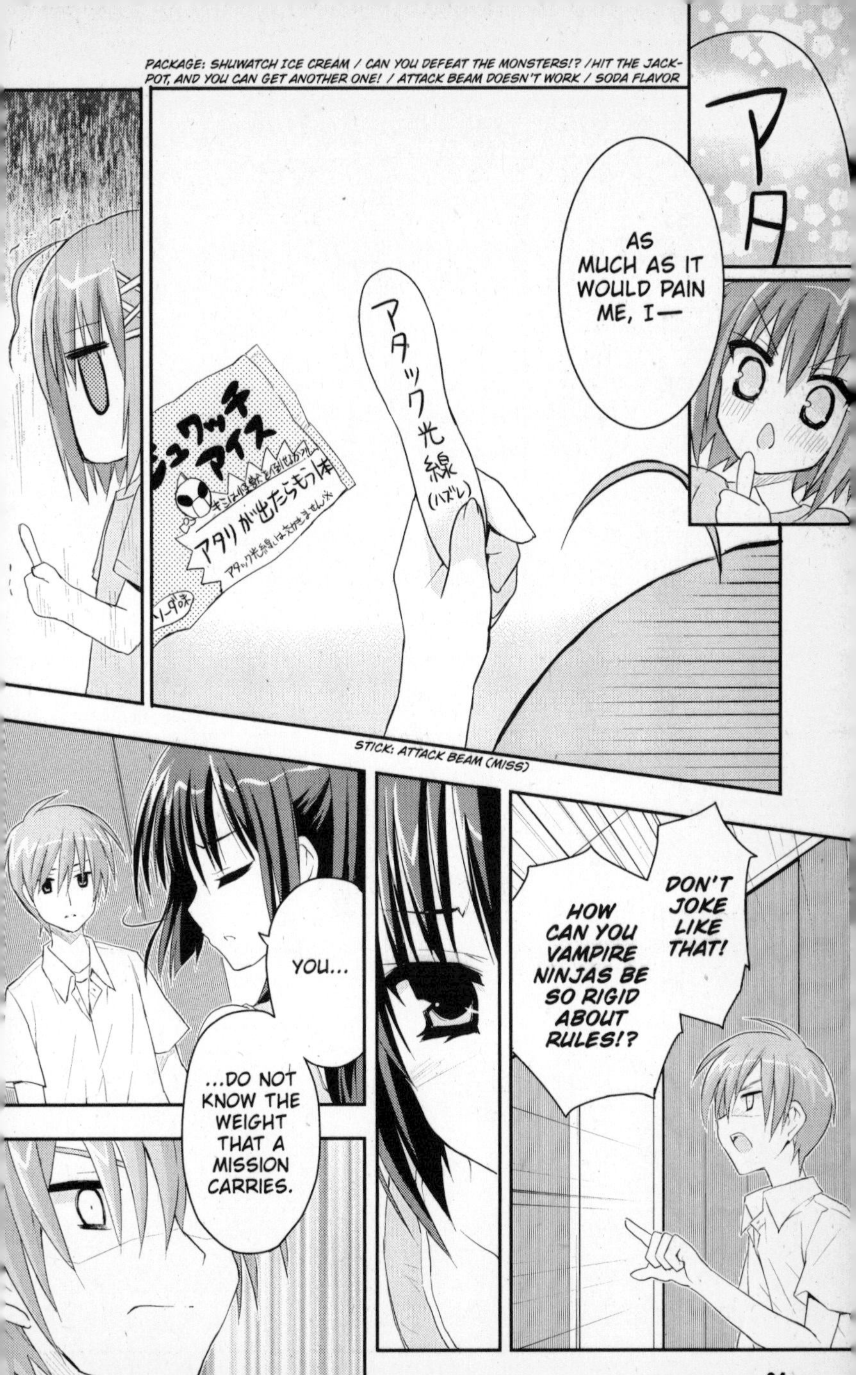
アタ
AS MUCH AS IT WOULD PAIN ME, I—
PACKAGE: SHUWATCH ICE CREAM / CAN YOU DEFEAT THE MONSTERS!? / HIT THE JACKPOT, AND YOU CAN GET ANOTHER ONE! / ATTACK BEAM DOESN'T WORK / SODA FLAVOR
アタック光線 (ハズレ)
シュワッチ アイス
アタリが出たらもう1本
ソーダ味
STICK: ATTACK BEAM (MISS)
DON'T JOKE LIKE THAT!
HOW CAN YOU VAMPIRE NINJAS BE SO RIGID ABOUT RULES!?
YOU...
...DO NOT KNOW THE WEIGHT THAT A MISSION CARRIES.

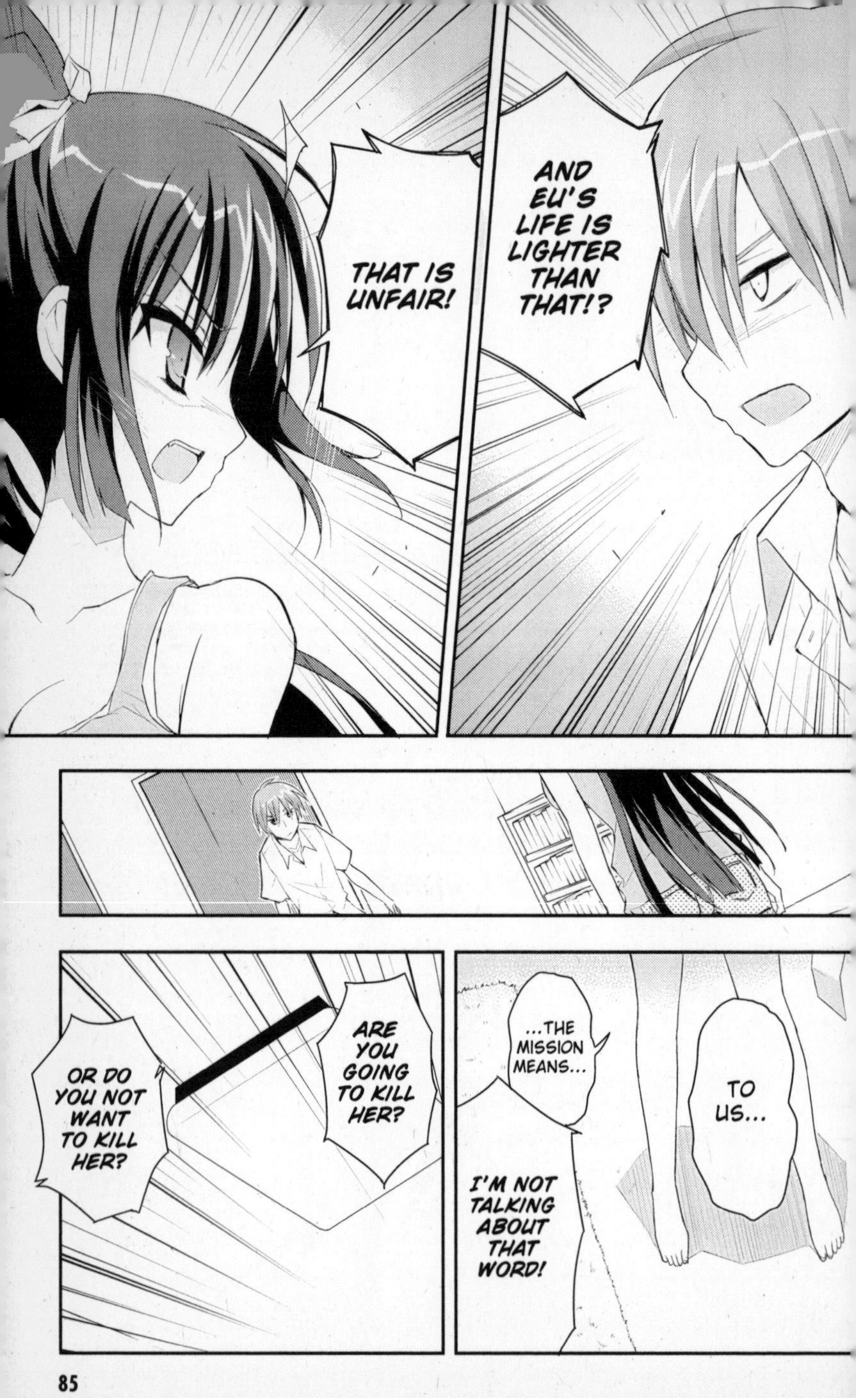
AND EU'S LIFE IS LIGHTER THAN THAT!?
THAT IS UNFAIR!
...THE MISSION MEANS...
TO US...
I'M NOT TALKING ABOUT THAT WORD!
ARE YOU GOING TO KILL HER?
OR DO YOU NOT WANT TO KILL HER?

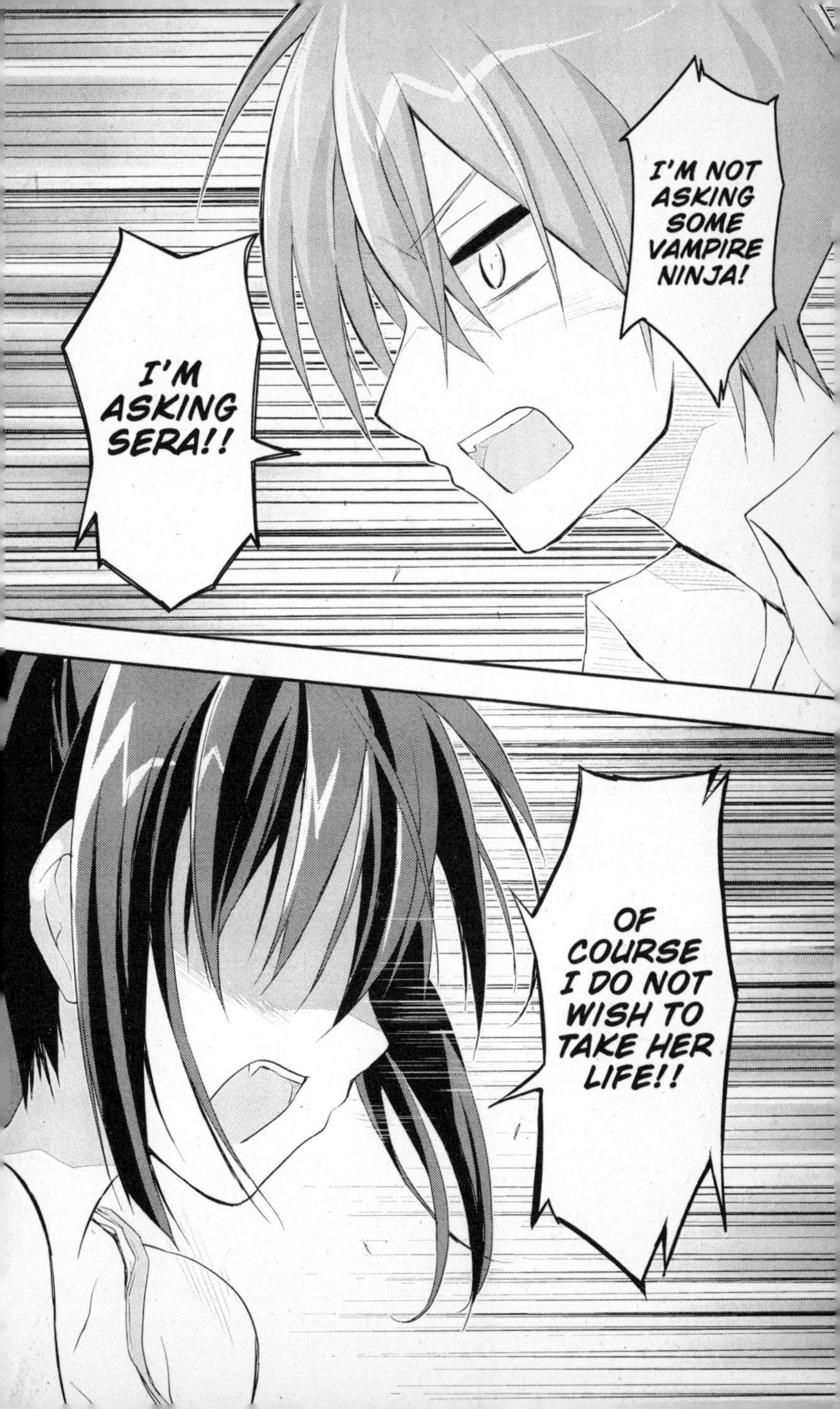
I'M NOT ASKING SOME VAMPIRE NINJA!
I'M ASKING SERA!!
OF COURSE I DO NOT WISH TO TAKE HER LIFE!!

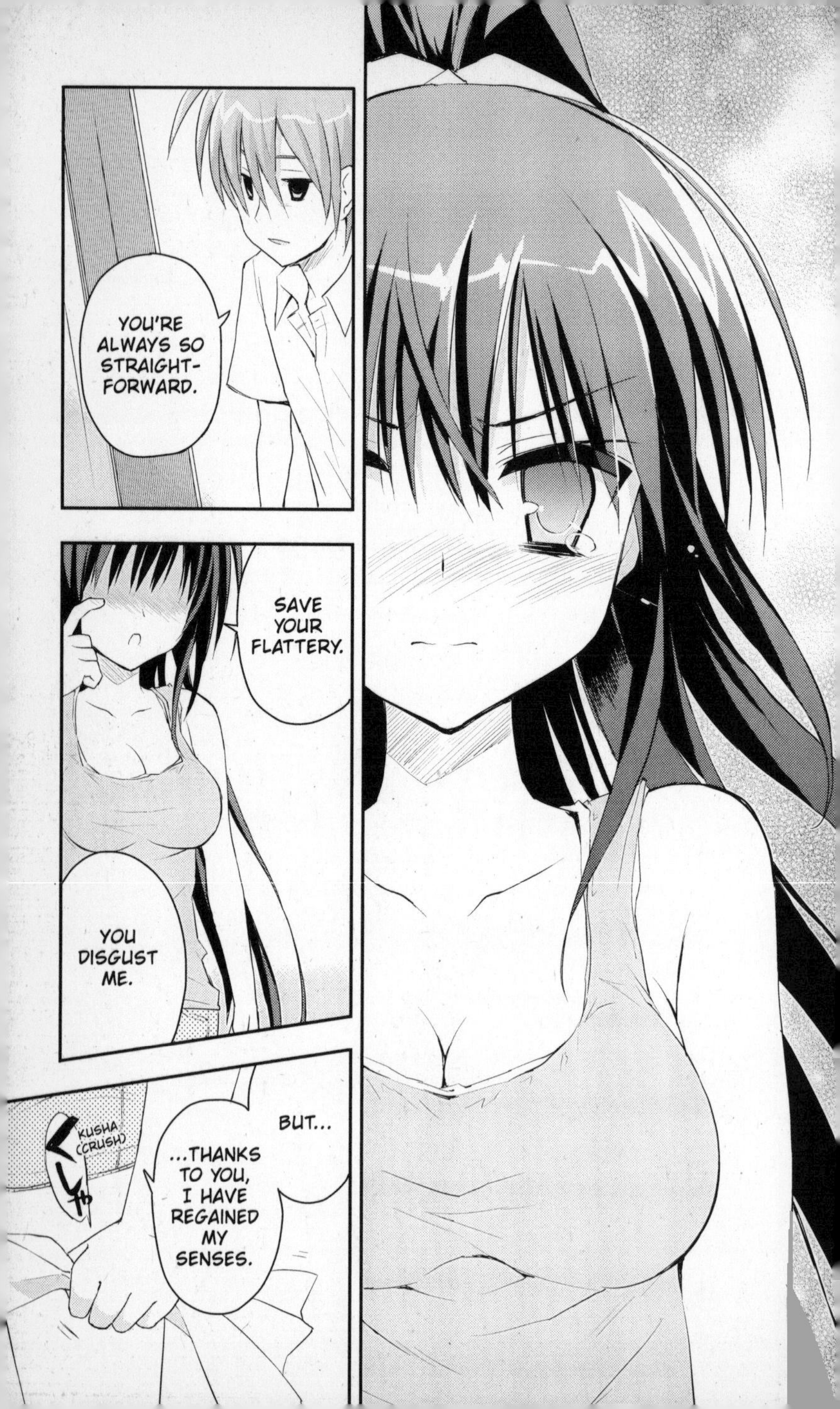
YOU'RE ALWAYS SO STRAIGHT-FORWARD.
SAVE YOUR FLATTERY.
YOU DISGUST ME.
BUT...
...THANKS TO YOU, I HAVE REGAINED MY SENSES.
KUSHA (CRUSH)

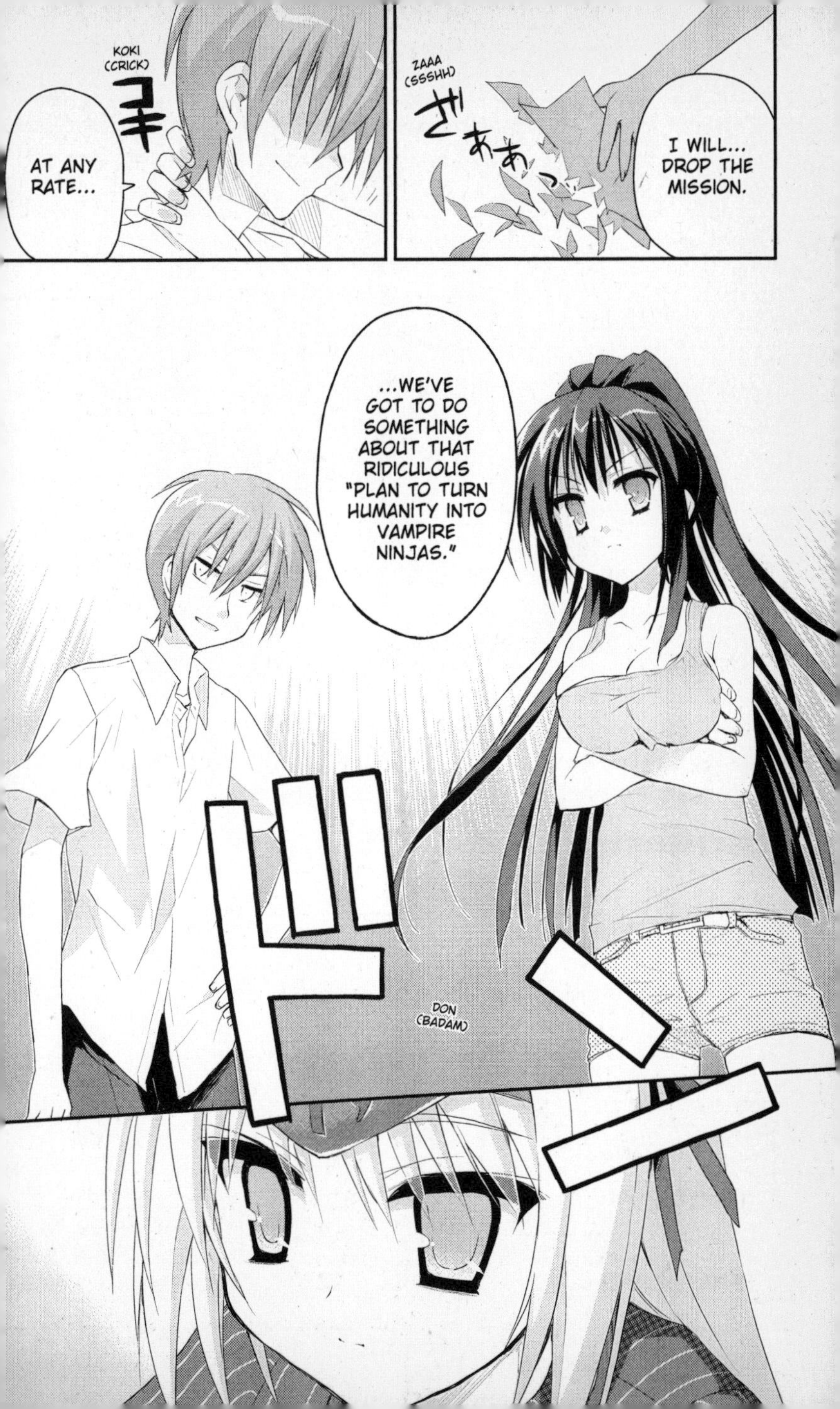
I WILL... DROP THE MISSION.
ZAAA (SSSHH)
ざあぁっ
KOKI (CRICK)
コキ
AT ANY RATE...
...WE'VE GOT TO DO SOMETHING ABOUT THAT RIDICULOUS "PLAN TO TURN HUMANITY INTO VAMPIRE NINJAS."
ドン
DON (BADAM)

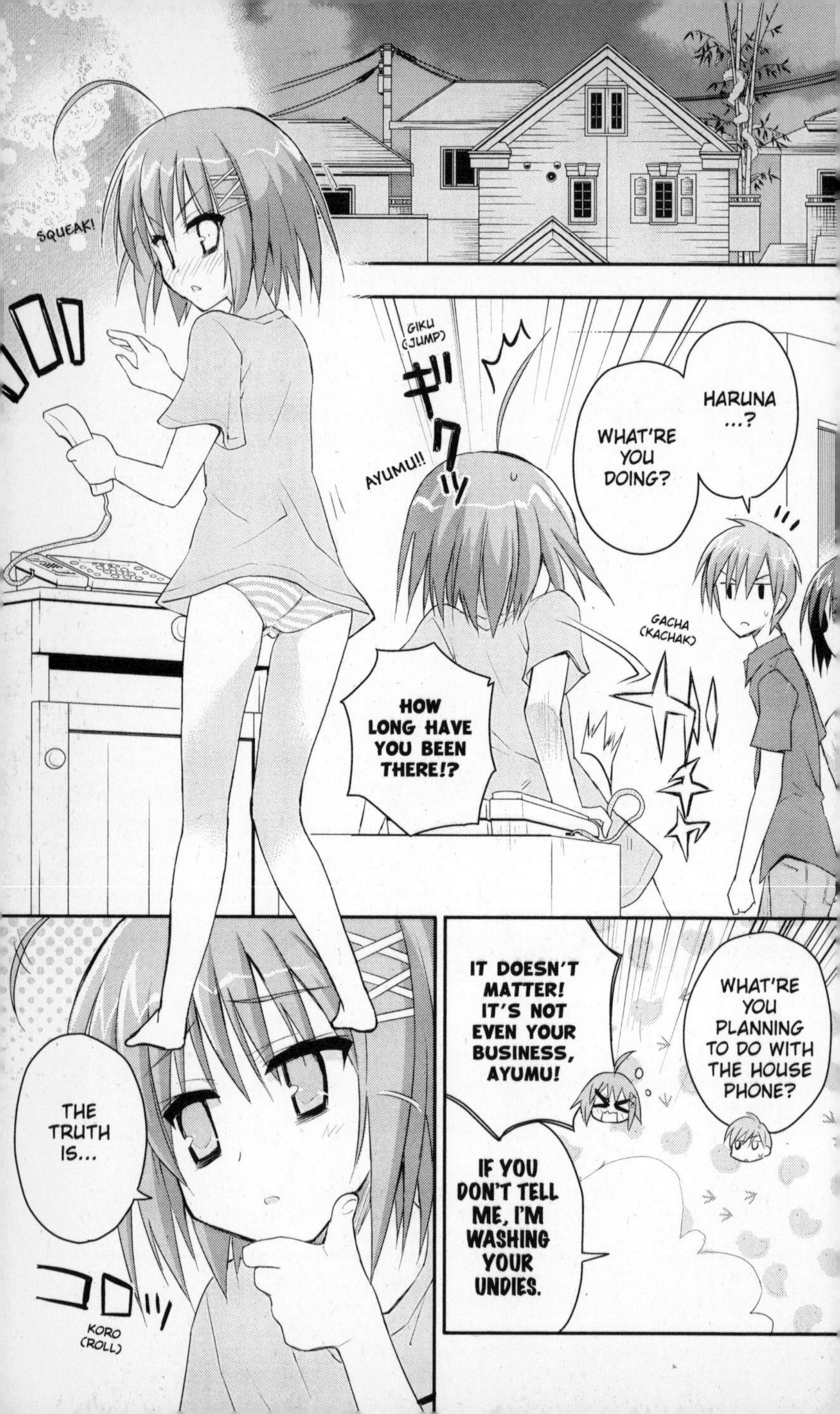
SQUEAK!
HARUNA ...?
WHAT'RE YOU DOING?
GIKU (JUMP)
AYUMU!!
GACHA (KACHAK)
HOW LONG HAVE YOU BEEN THERE!?
WHAT'RE YOU PLANNING TO DO WITH THE HOUSE PHONE?
IT DOESN'T MATTER! IT'S NOT EVEN YOUR BUSINESS, AYUMU!
IF YOU DON'T TELL ME, I'M WASHING YOUR UNDIES.
THE TRUTH IS...
KORO (ROLL)

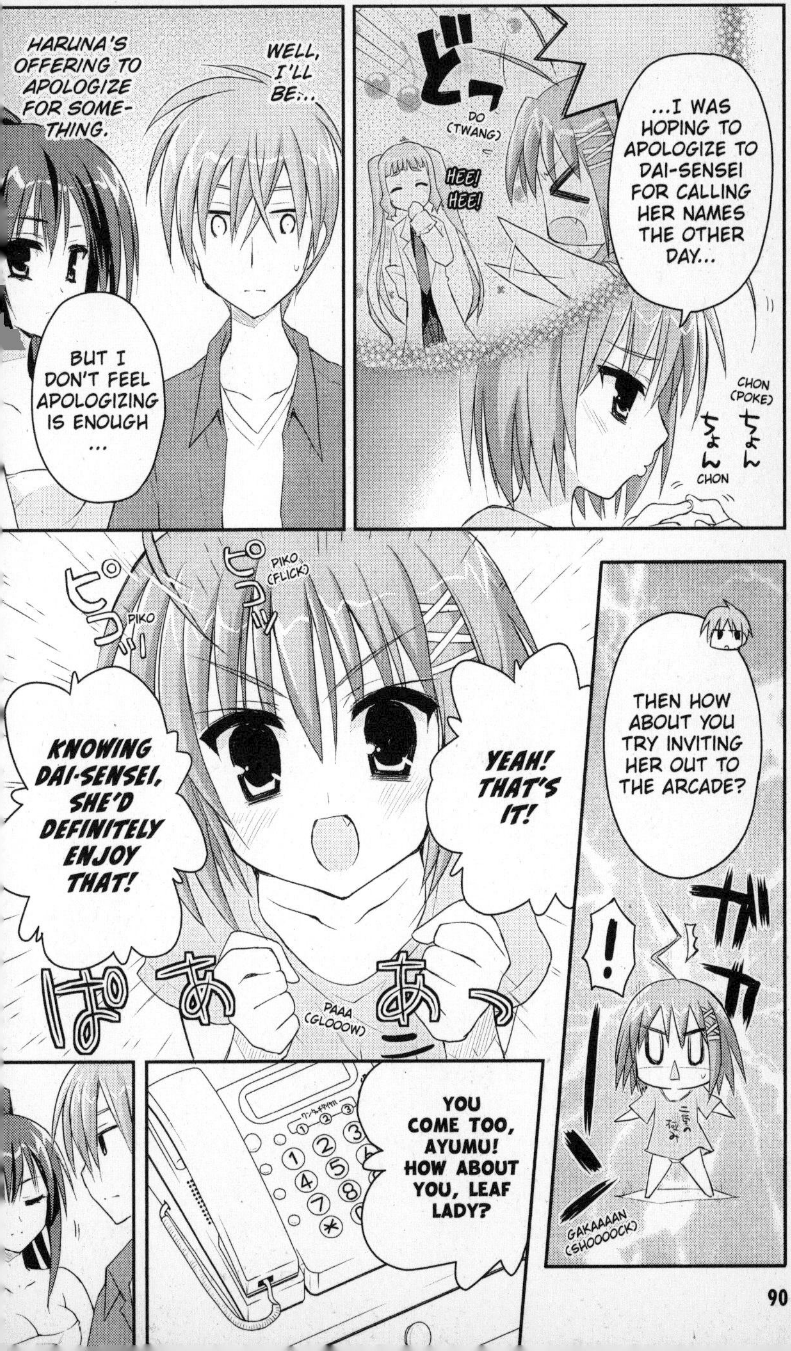

...I WAS HOPING TO APOLOGIZE TO DAI-SENSEI FOR CALLING HER NAMES THE OTHER DAY...
DO (TWANG)
HEE! HEE!
CHON (POKE)
CHON
WELL, I'LL BE...
HARUNA'S OFFERING TO APOLOGIZE FOR SOME-THING.
BUT I DON'T FEEL APOLOGIZING IS ENOUGH ...
THEN HOW ABOUT YOU TRY INVITING HER OUT TO THE ARCADE?
!
GAKAAAAN (SHOOOOCK)
PIKO (FLICK)
PIKO
YEAH! THAT'S IT!
KNOWING DAI-SENSEI, SHE'D DEFINITELY ENJOY THAT!
PAAA (GLOOOW)
YOU COME TOO, AYUMU! HOW ABOUT YOU, LEAF LADY?

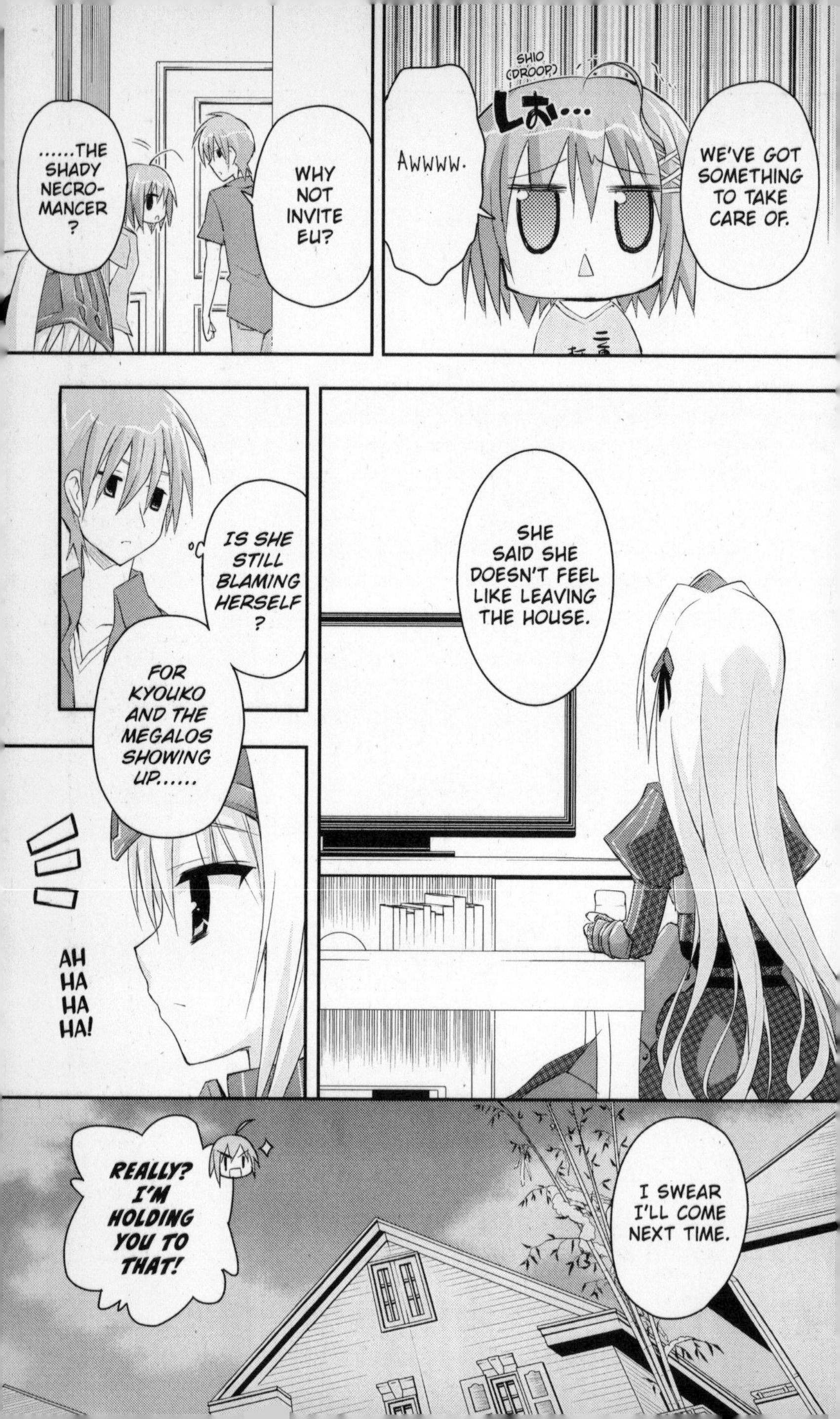
WE'VE GOT SOMETHING TO TAKE CARE OF.
SHIO (DROOP)
しお…
AWWWW.
WHY NOT INVITE EU?
......THE SHADY NECRO-MANCER ?
SHE SAID SHE DOESN'T FEEL LIKE LEAVING THE HOUSE.
IS SHE STILL BLAMING HERSELF ?
FOR KYOUKO AND THE MEGALOS SHOWING UP......
AH HA HA HA!
I SWEAR I'LL COME NEXT TIME.
REALLY? I'M HOLDING YOU TO THAT!

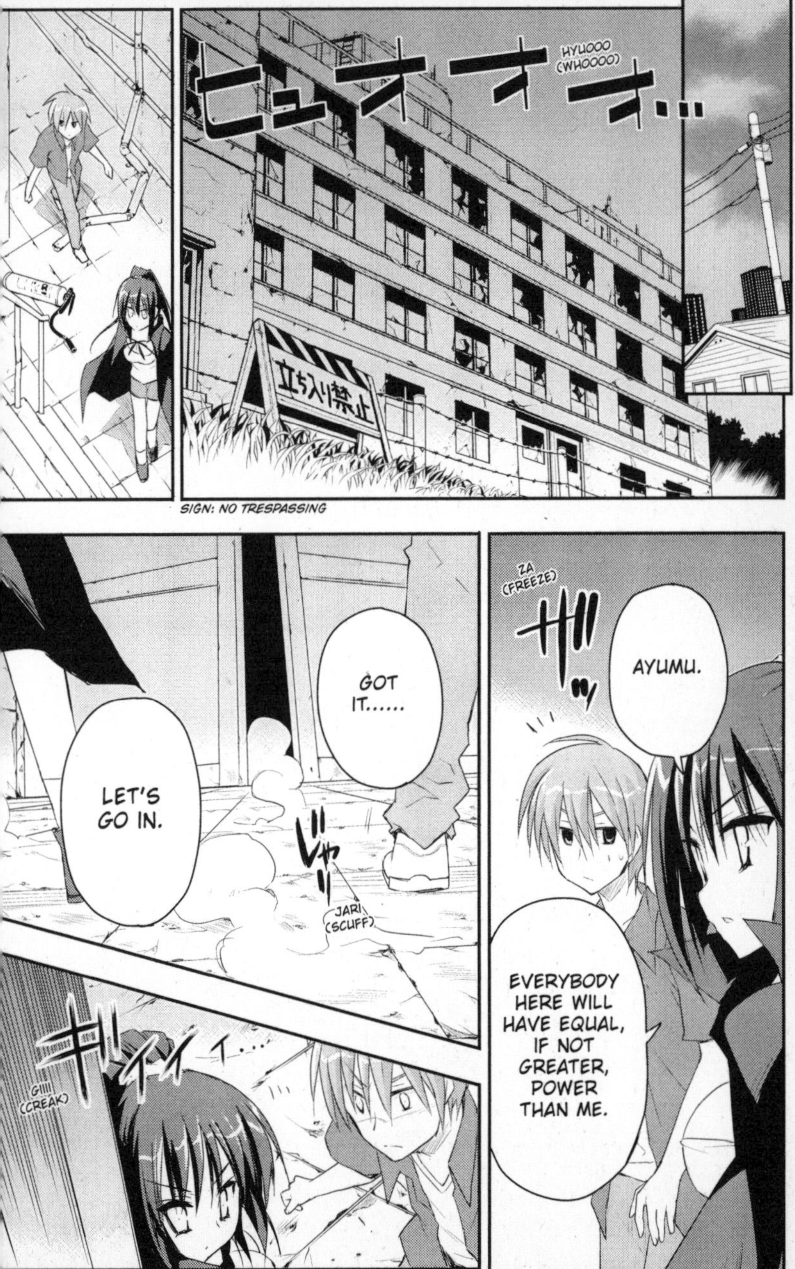
HYUOOO (WHOOOO)
立ち入り禁止
SIGN: NO TRESPASSING
ZA (FREEZE)
AYUMU.
EVERYBODY HERE WILL HAVE EQUAL, IF NOT GREATER, POWER THAN ME.
GOT IT......
LET'S GO IN.
JARI (SCUFF)
GIII (CREAK)

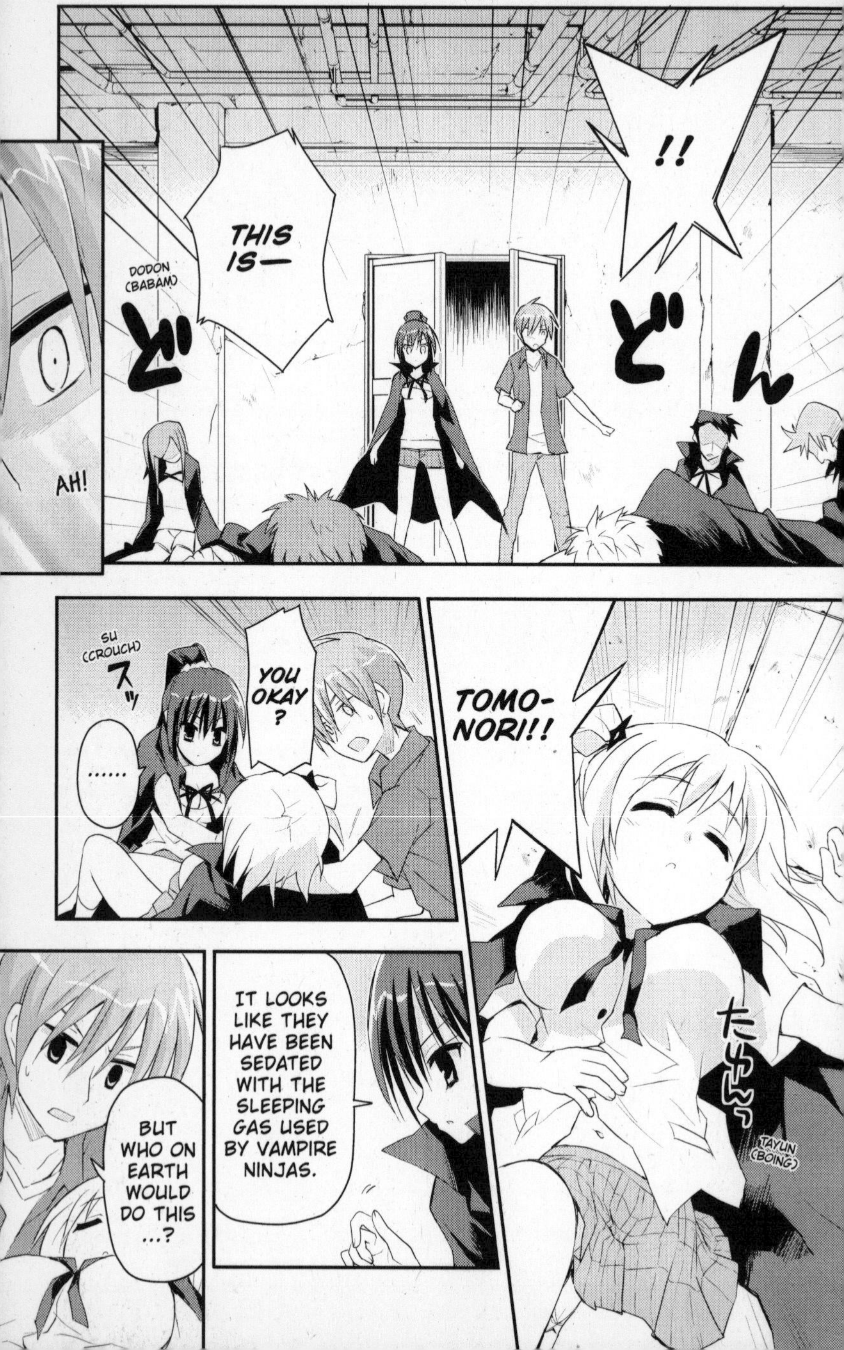
!!
どん
THIS IS—
ど
DODON (BABAM)
AH!
TOMO-NORI!!
たゆんっ
TAYUN (BOING)
YOU OKAY?
SU (CROUCH)
スッ
......
IT LOOKS LIKE THEY HAVE BEEN SEDATED WITH THE SLEEPING GAS USED BY VAMPIRE NINJAS.
BUT WHO ON EARTH WOULD DO THIS ...?

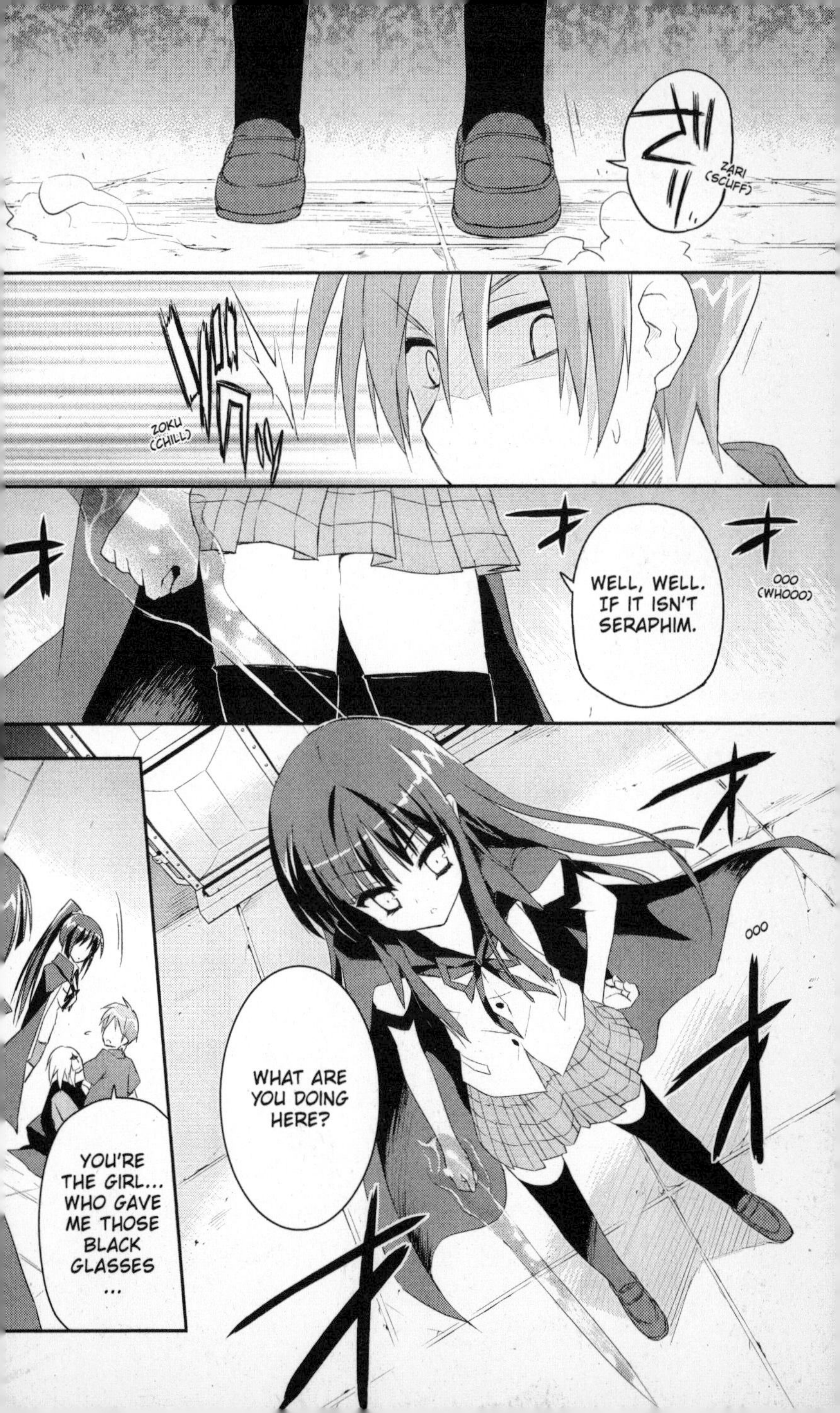
ZARI (SCUFF)
ZOKU (CHILL)
OOO (WHOOO)
WELL, WELL. IF IT ISN'T SERAPHIM.
OOO
WHAT ARE YOU DOING HERE?
YOU'RE THE GIRL... WHO GAVE ME THOSE BLACK GLASSES ...

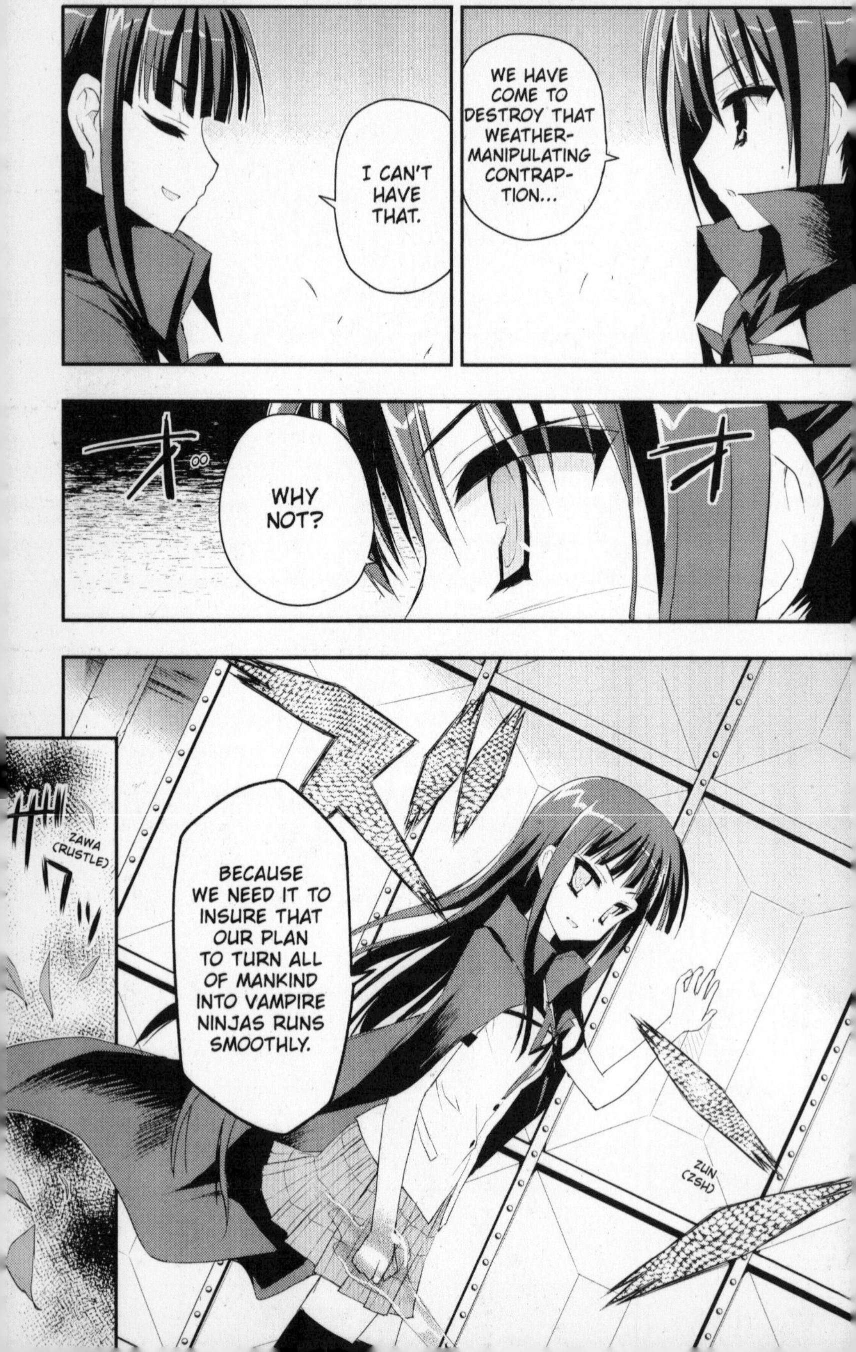
WE HAVE COME TO DESTROY THAT WEATHER-MANIPULATING CONTRAP-TION...
I CAN'T HAVE THAT.
WHY NOT?
ZAWA (RUSTLE)
BECAUSE WE NEED IT TO INSURE THAT OUR PLAN TO TURN ALL OF MANKIND INTO VAMPIRE NINJAS RUNS SMOOTHLY.
ZUN (ZSH)

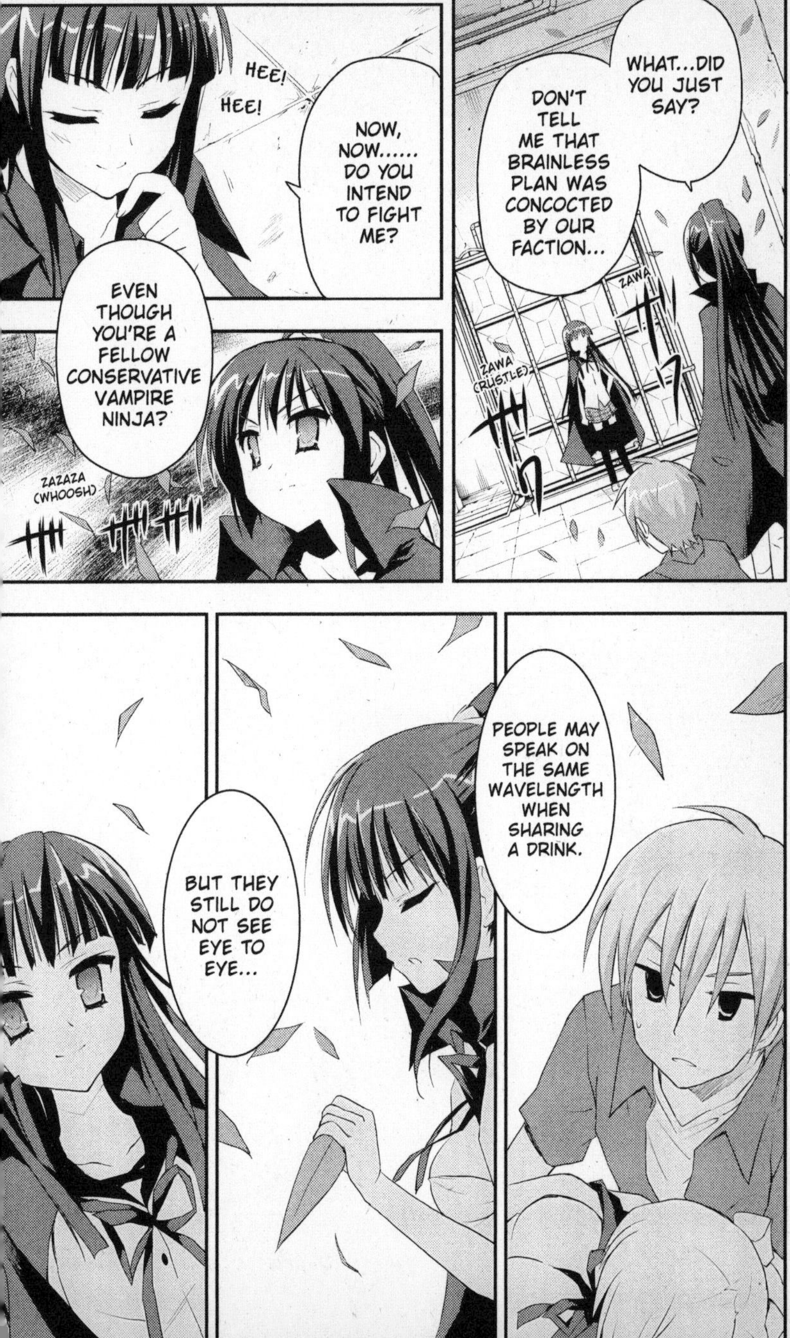
WHAT...DID YOU JUST SAY?
DON'T TELL ME THAT BRAINLESS PLAN WAS CONCOCTED BY OUR FACTION...
ZAWA
ZAWA (RUSTLE)
HEE!
HEE!
NOW, NOW...... DO YOU INTEND TO FIGHT ME?
EVEN THOUGH YOU'RE A FELLOW CONSERVATIVE VAMPIRE NINJA?
ZAZAZA (WHOOSH)
PEOPLE MAY SPEAK ON THE SAME WAVELENGTH WHEN SHARING A DRINK.
BUT THEY STILL DO NOT SEE EYE TO EYE...

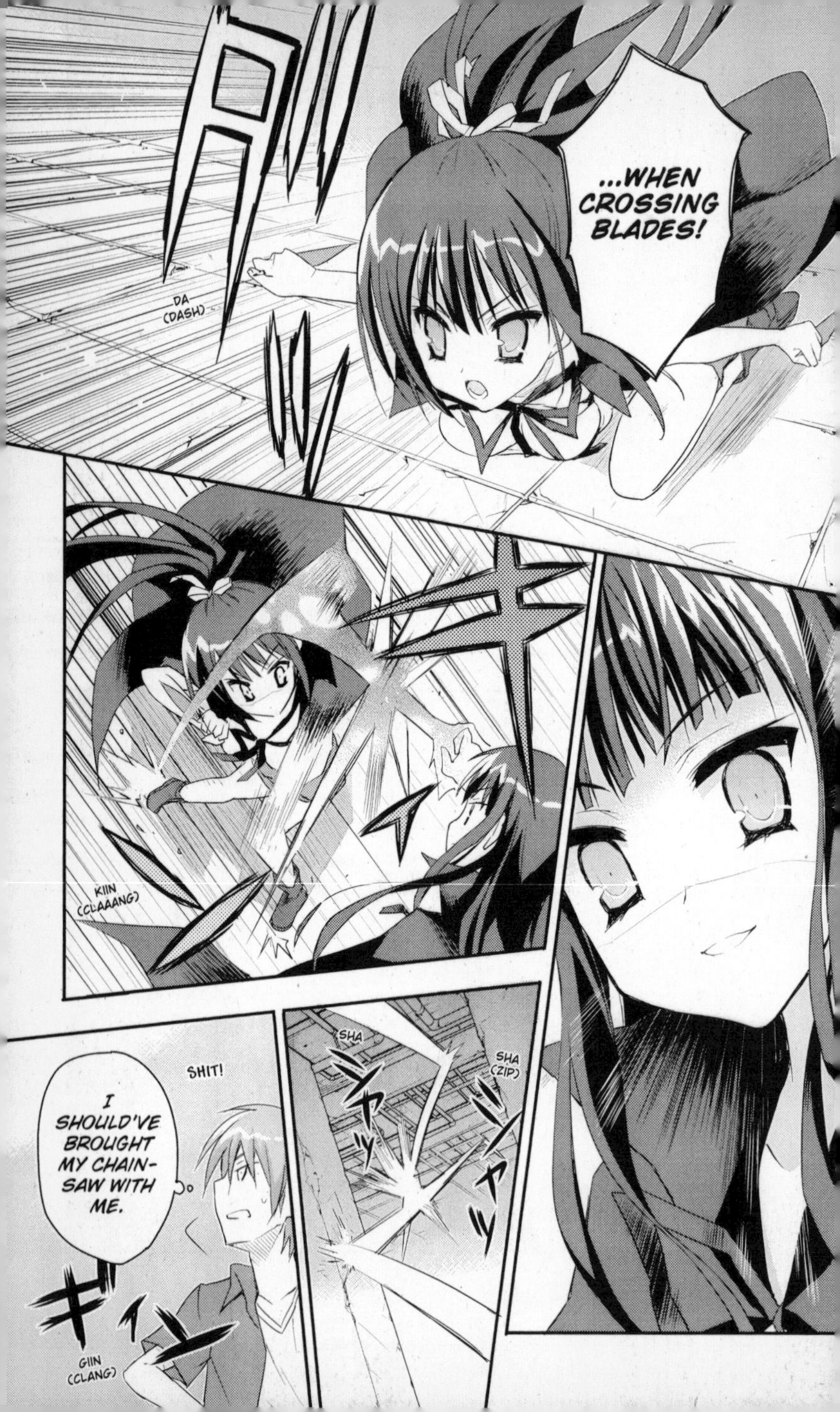
...WHEN CROSSING BLADES!
DA (DASH)
KIIN (CLAAANG)
SHA
SHA (ZIP)
SHIT!
I SHOULD'VE BROUGHT MY CHAIN-SAW WITH ME.
GIIN (CLANG)

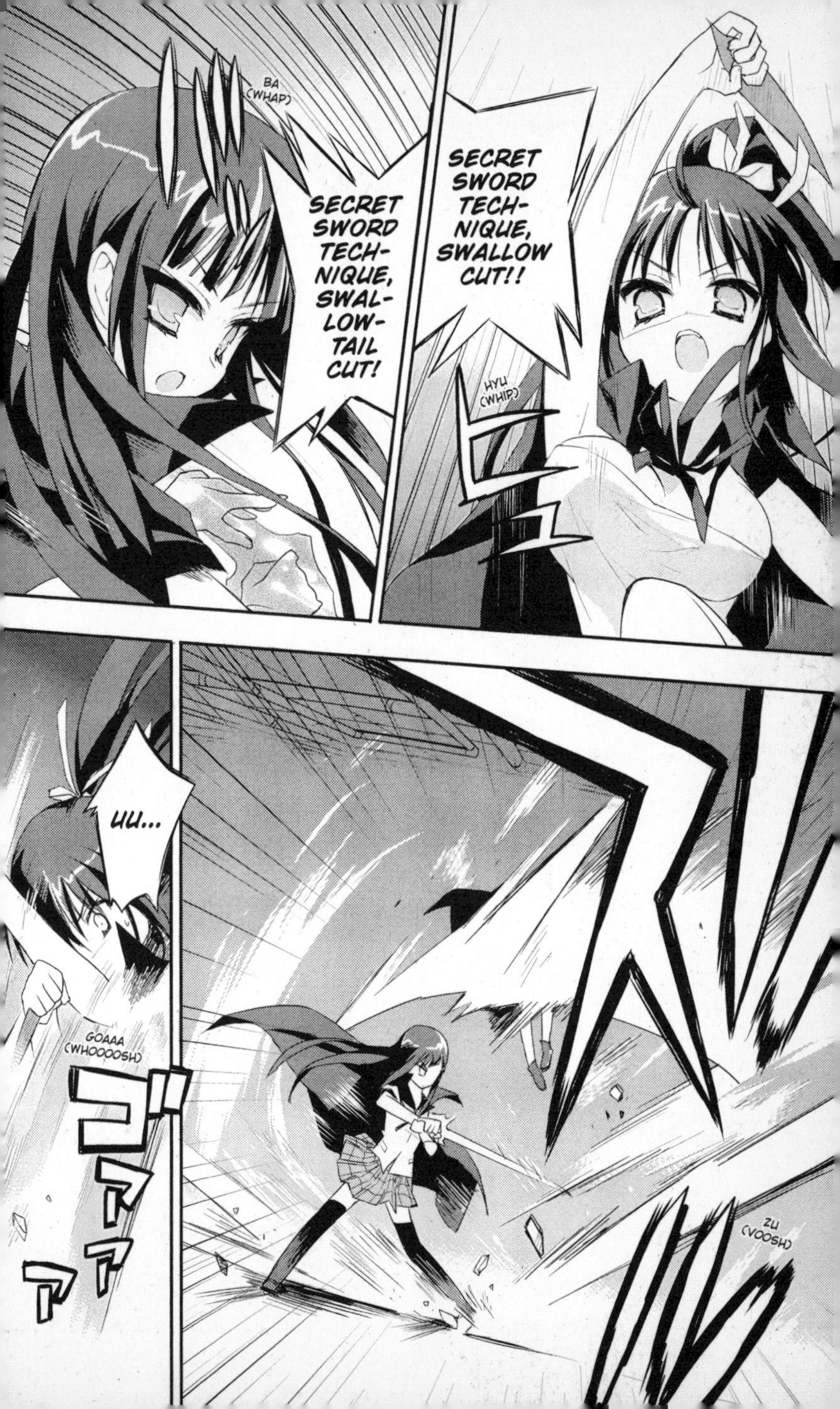
HYU (WHIP)
SECRET SWORD TECHNIQUE, SWALLOW CUT!!
BA (WHAP)
SECRET SWORD TECH-NIQUE, SWAL-LOW-TAIL CUT!
ZU (VOOSH)
UU...
GOAAA (WHOOOSH)

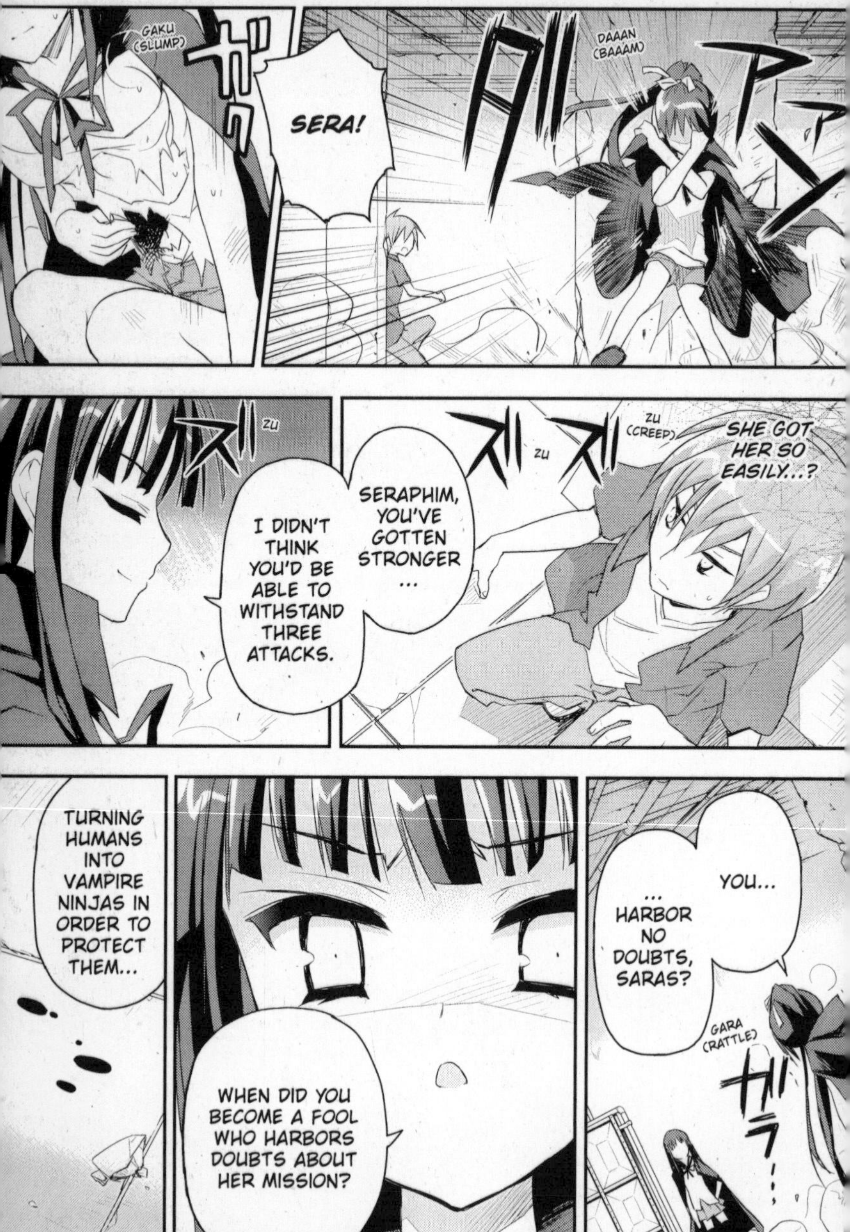
DAAAN (BAAAM)
SERA!
GAKU (SLUMP)
ZU (CREEP)
ZU
SHE GOT HER SO EASILY...?
SERAPHIM, YOU'VE GOTTEN STRONGER...
I DIDN'T THINK YOU'D BE ABLE TO WITHSTAND THREE ATTACKS.
ZU
YOU...
...HARBOR NO DOUBTS, SARAS?
GARA (RATTLE)
WHEN DID YOU BECOME A FOOL WHO HARBORS DOUBTS ABOUT HER MISSION?
TURNING HUMANS INTO VAMPIRE NINJAS IN ORDER TO PROTECT THEM...

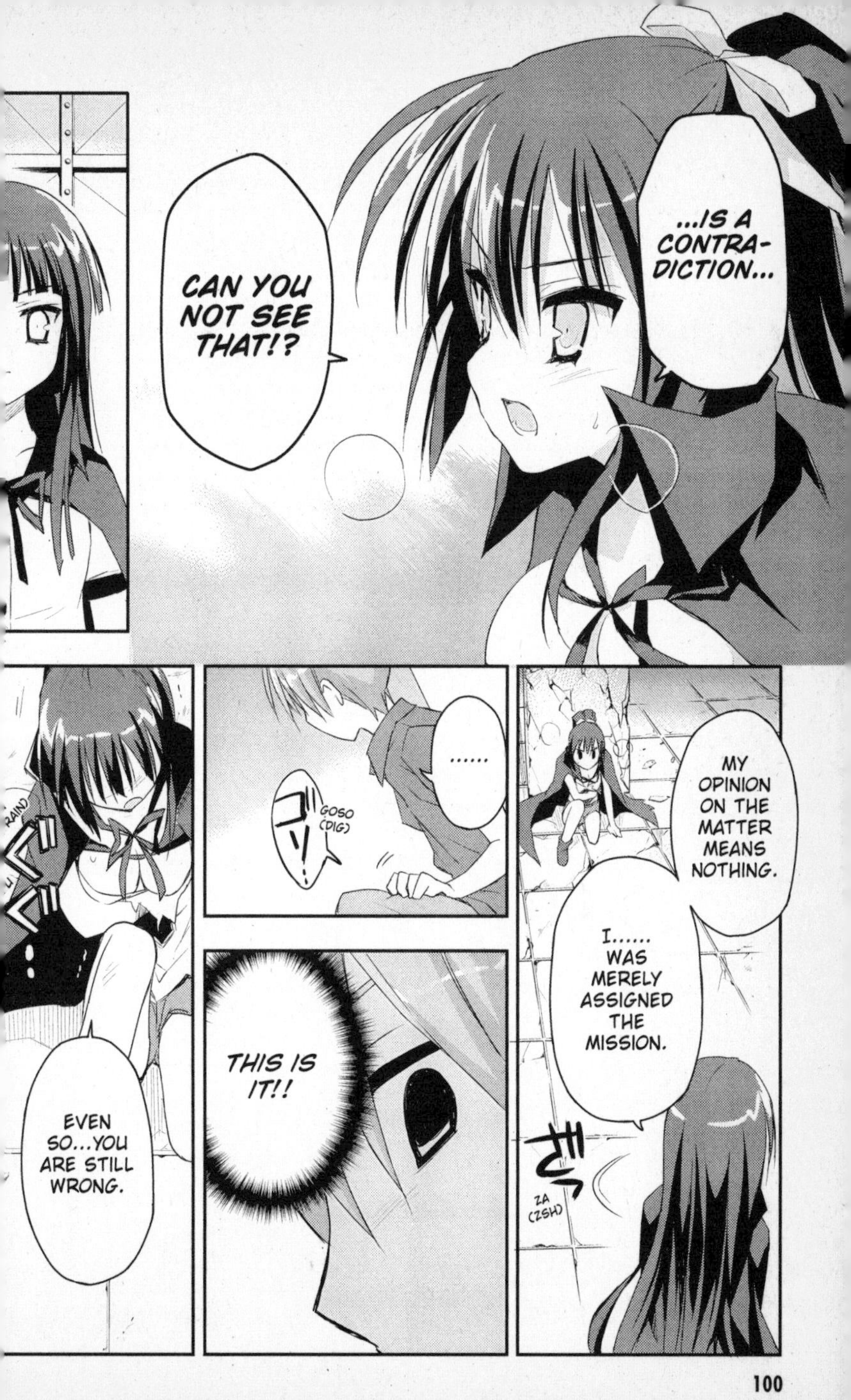
...IS A CONTRA-DICTION...
CAN YOU NOT SEE THAT!?
MY OPINION ON THE MATTER MEANS NOTHING.
I...... WAS MERELY ASSIGNED THE MISSION.
ZA (ZSH)
......
GOSO (DIG)
THIS IS IT!!
EVEN SO...YOU ARE STILL WRONG.

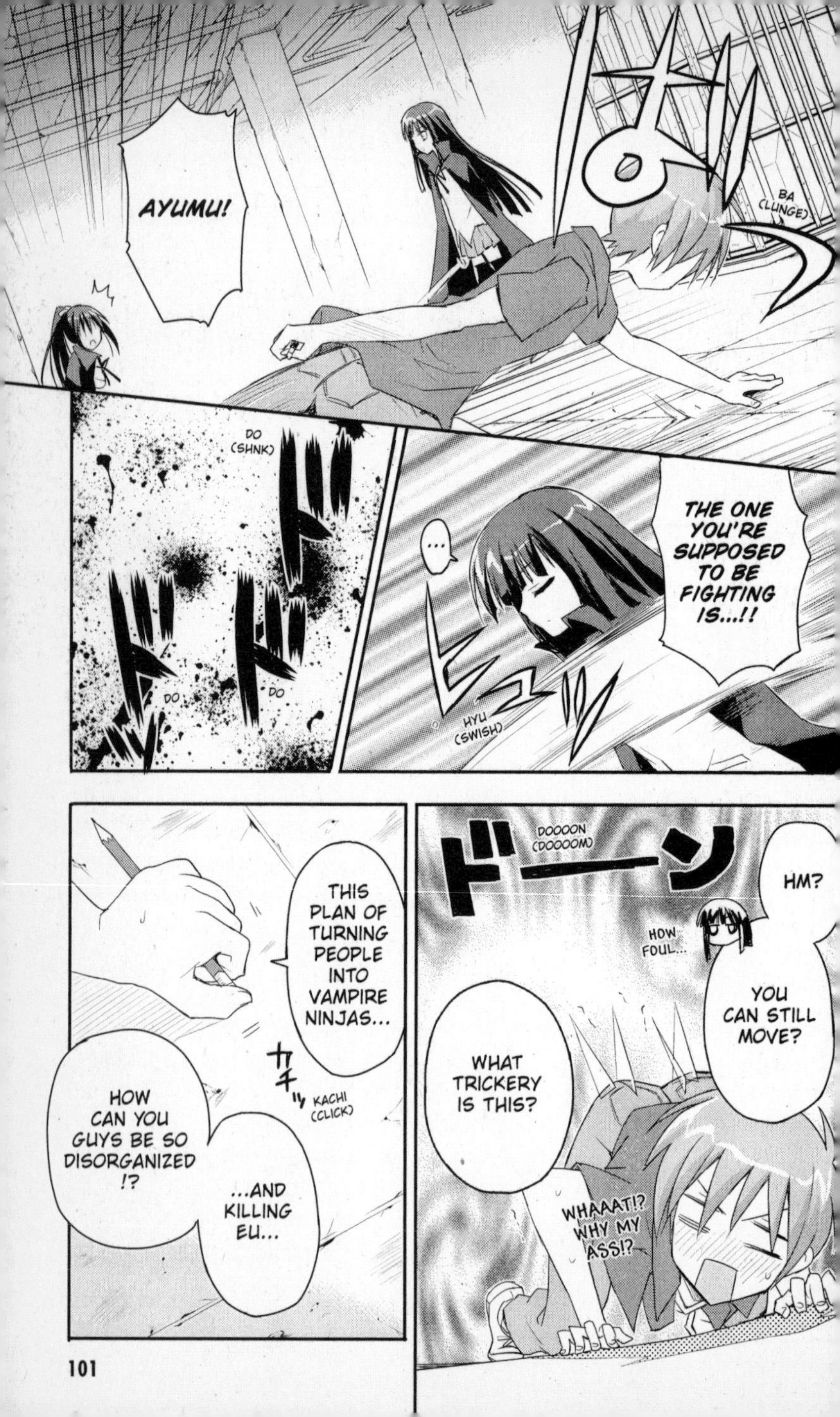

AYUMU!
BA (LUNGE)
THE ONE YOU'RE SUPPOSED TO BE FIGHTING IS...!!
...
HYU (SWISH)
DO (SHNK)
DO
DO
DOOOON (DOOOOM)
HM?
HOW FOUL...
YOU CAN STILL MOVE?
WHAT TRICKERY IS THIS?
WHAAAT!? WHY MY ASS!?
THIS PLAN OF TURNING PEOPLE INTO VAMPIRE NINJAS...
KACHI (CLICK)
...AND KILLING EU...
HOW CAN YOU GUYS BE SO DISORGANIZED!?

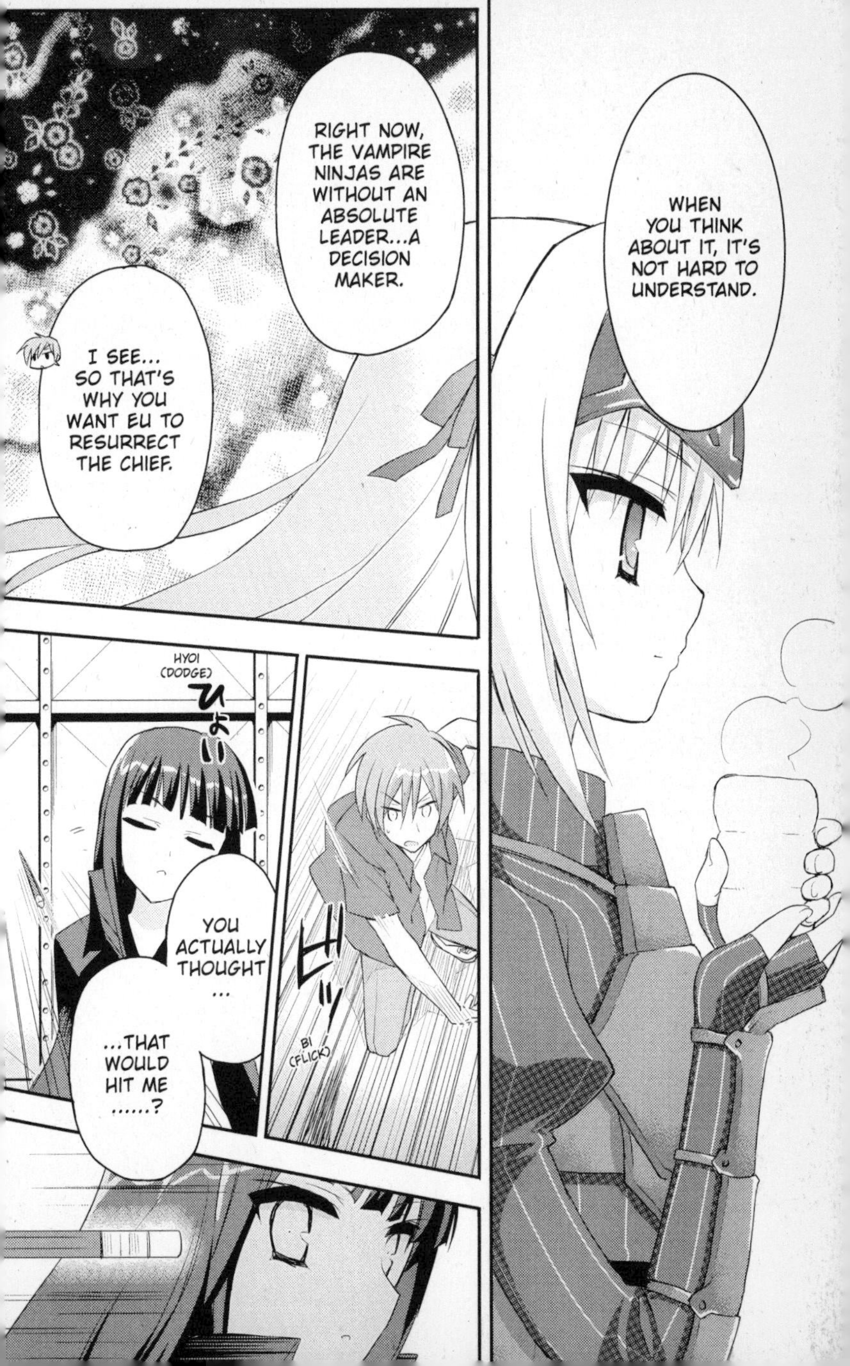
WHEN YOU THINK ABOUT IT, IT'S NOT HARD TO UNDERSTAND.
RIGHT NOW, THE VAMPIRE NINJAS ARE WITHOUT AN ABSOLUTE LEADER...A DECISION MAKER.
I SEE... SO THAT'S WHY YOU WANT EU TO RESURRECT THE CHIEF.
ビッ
BI (FLICK)
ひょい
HYOI (DODGE)
YOU ACTUALLY THOUGHT ...
...THAT WOULD HIT ME ......?

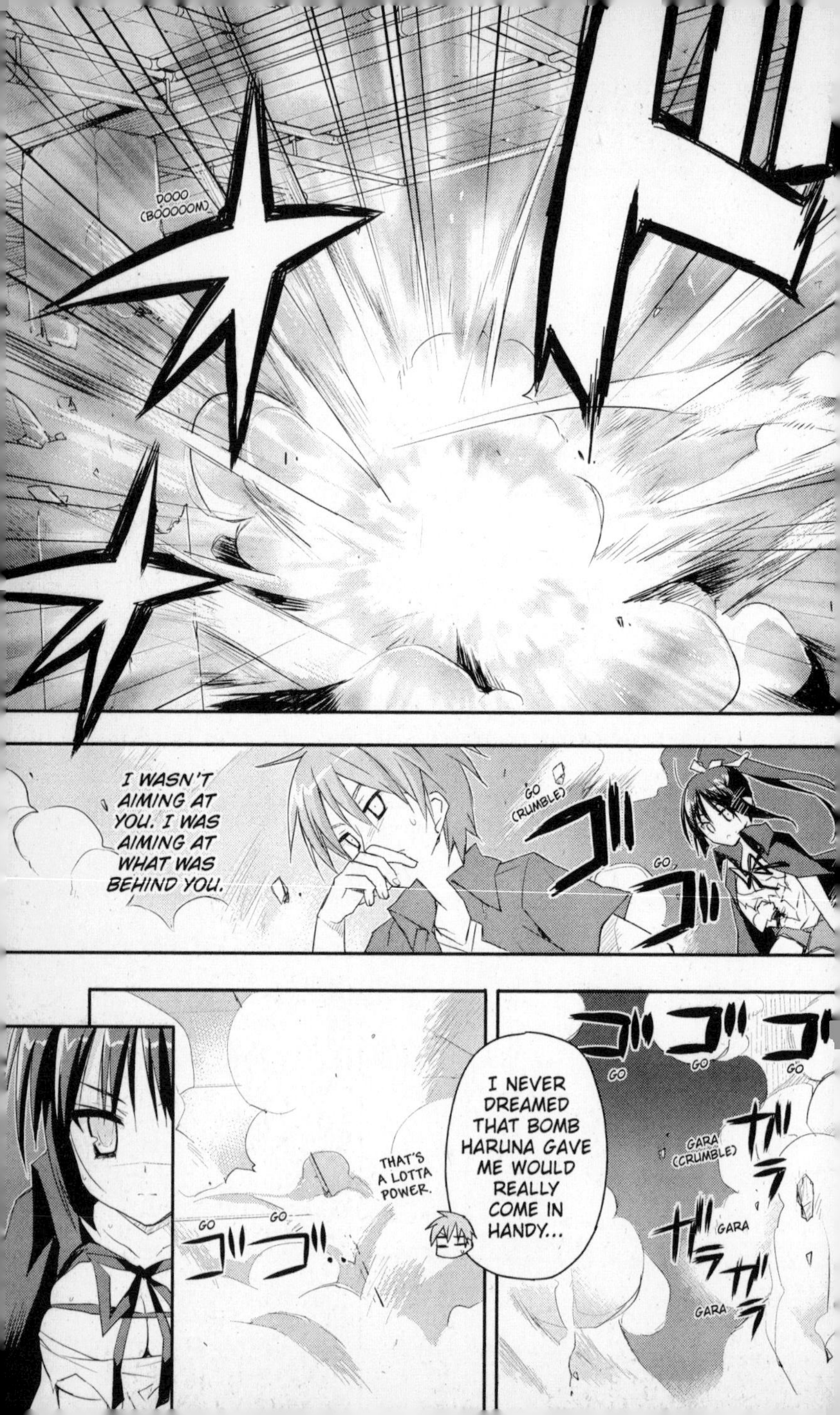
DOOO (BOOOOOM)
GO (CRUMBLE)
GO
I WASN'T AIMING AT YOU. I WAS AIMING AT WHAT WAS BEHIND YOU.
GO
GO
GO
GARA (CRUMBLE)
GARA
GARA
I NEVER DREAMED THAT BOMB HARUNA GAVE ME WOULD REALLY COME IN HANDY...
THAT'S A LOTTA POWER.
GO
GO

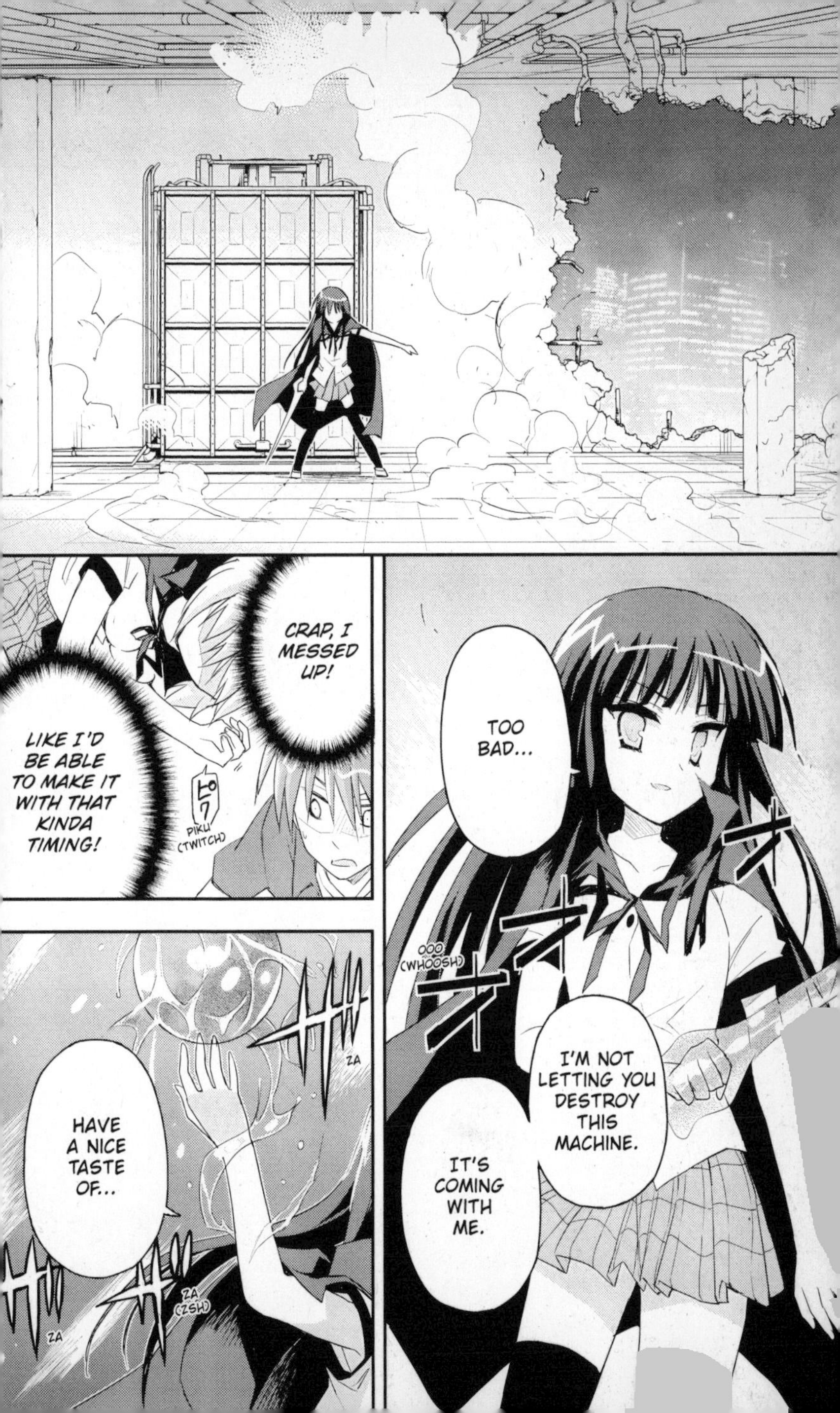
TOO BAD...
OOO (WHOOSH)
I'M NOT LETTING YOU DESTROY THIS MACHINE.
IT'S COMING WITH ME.
CRAP, I MESSED UP!
PIKU (TWITCH)
LIKE I'D BE ABLE TO MAKE IT WITH THAT KINDA TIMING!
ZA
HAVE A NICE TASTE OF...
ZA (ZSH)
ZA

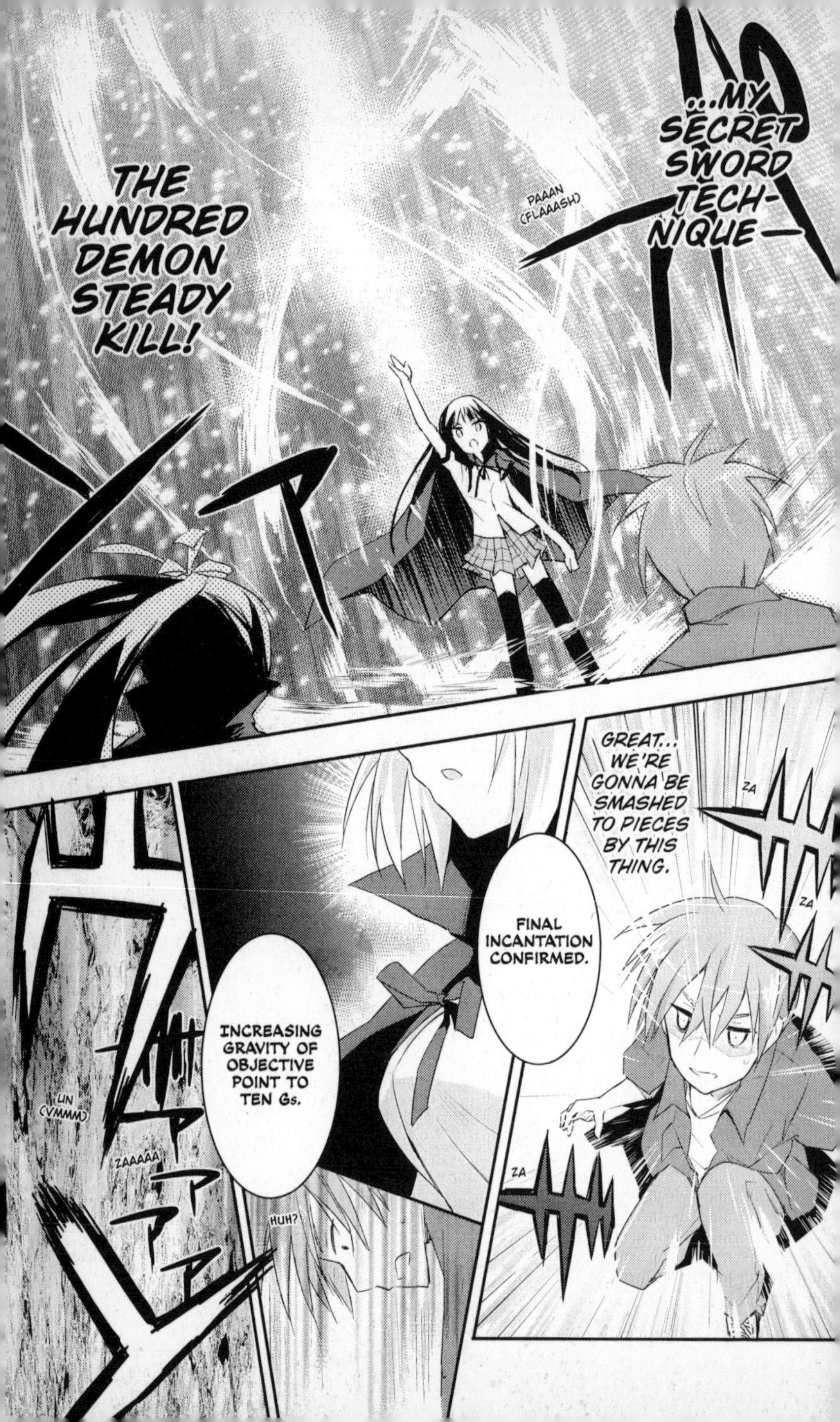
...MY SECRET SWORD TECH-NIQUE—
PAAAN (FLAAASH)
THE HUNDRED DEMON STEADY KILL!
GREAT... WE'RE GONNA BE SMASHED TO PIECES BY THIS THING.
ZA
ZA
ZA
FINAL INCANTATION CONFIRMED.
INCREASING GRAVITY OF OBJECTIVE POINT TO TEN Gs.
HUH?
UN (VMMM)
ZAAAAA

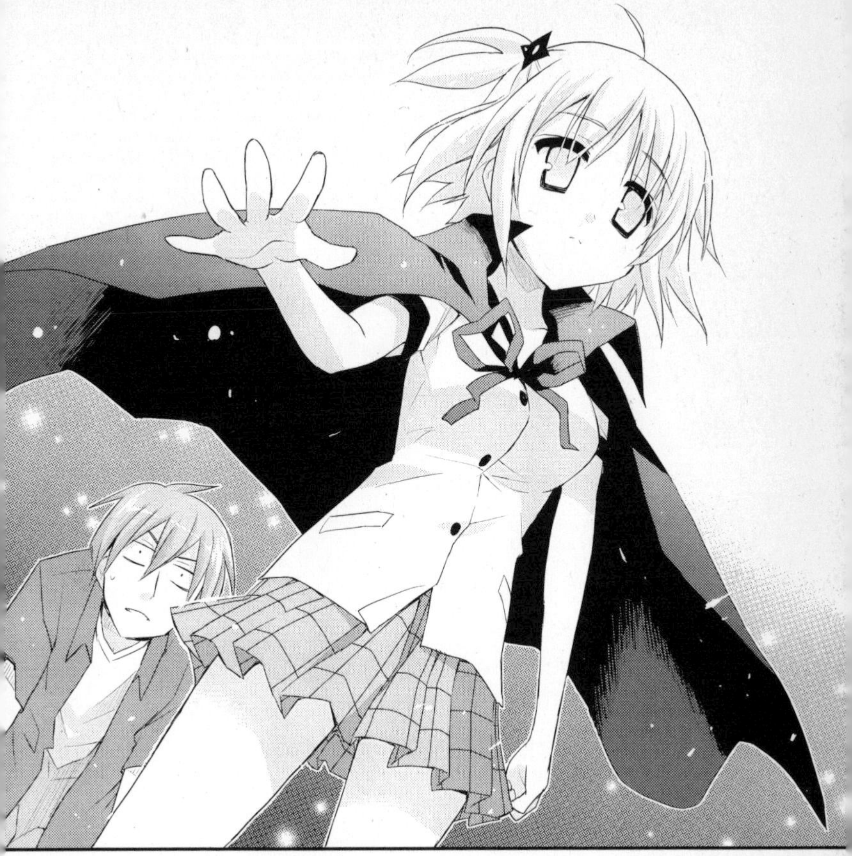

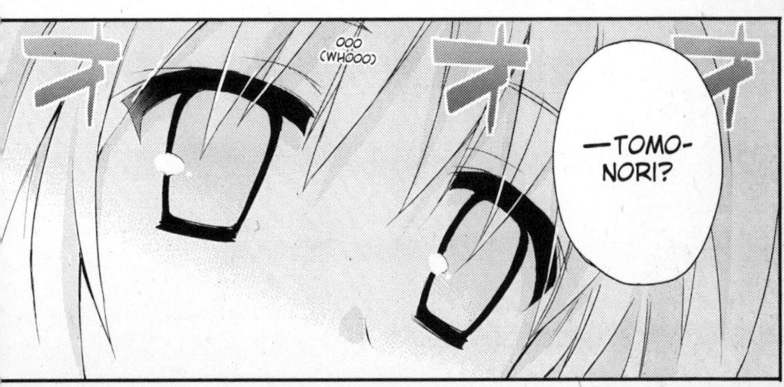
—TOMO-
NORI?
OOO
(WHOOO)

IS THIS A ZOMBIE?

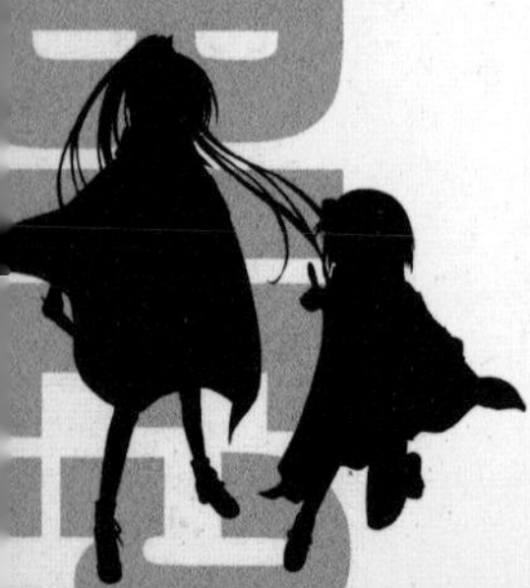

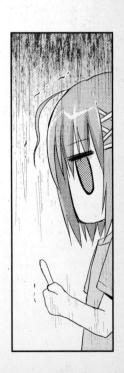

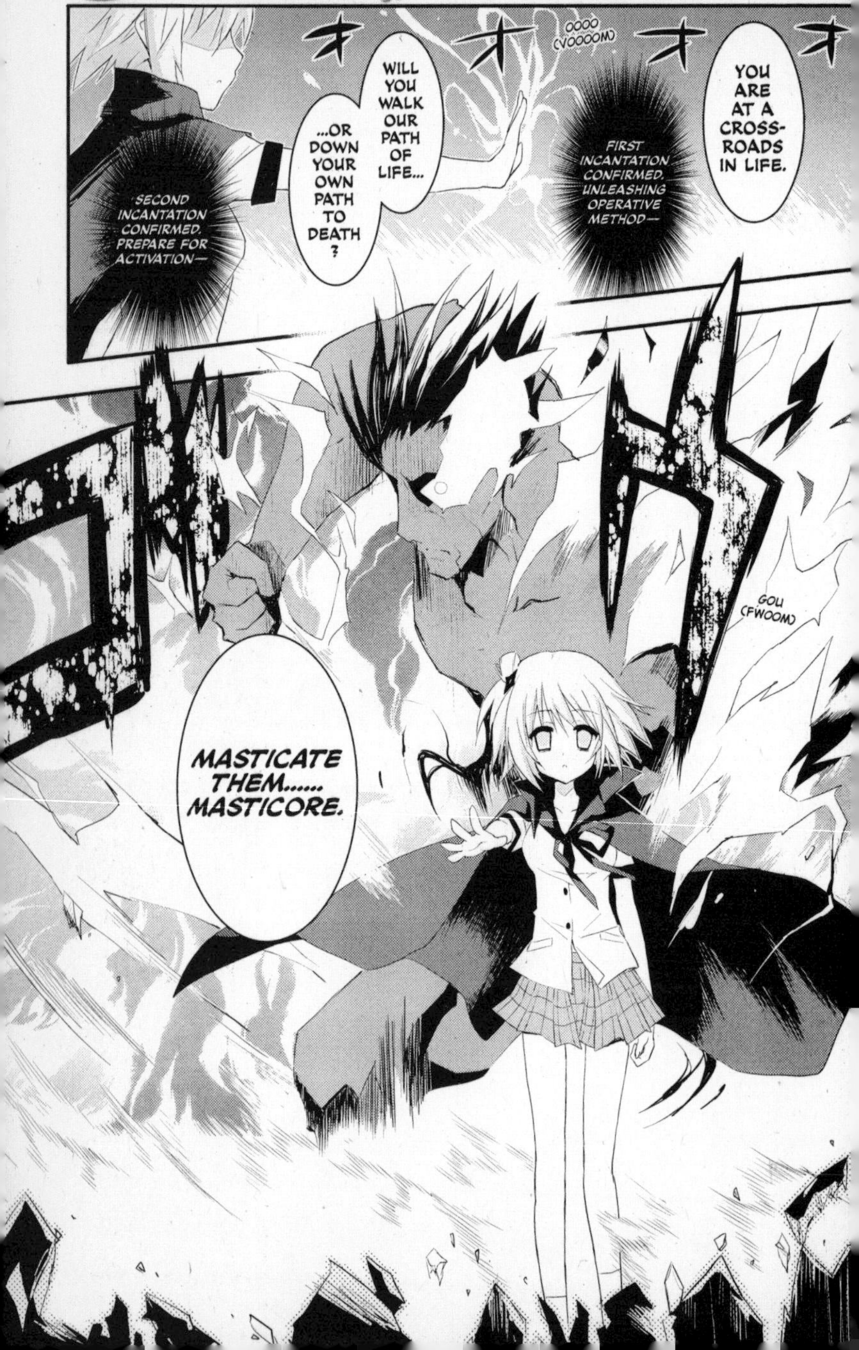
YOU ARE AT A CROSS-ROADS IN LIFE.
OOOO (VOOOOM)
FIRST INCANTATION CONFIRMED. UNLEASHING OPERATIVE METHOD—
WILL YOU WALK OUR PATH OF LIFE...
...OR DOWN YOUR OWN PATH TO DEATH?
SECOND INCANTATION CONFIRMED. PREPARE FOR ACTIVATION—
GOU (FWOOM)
MASTICATE THEM...... MASTICORE.

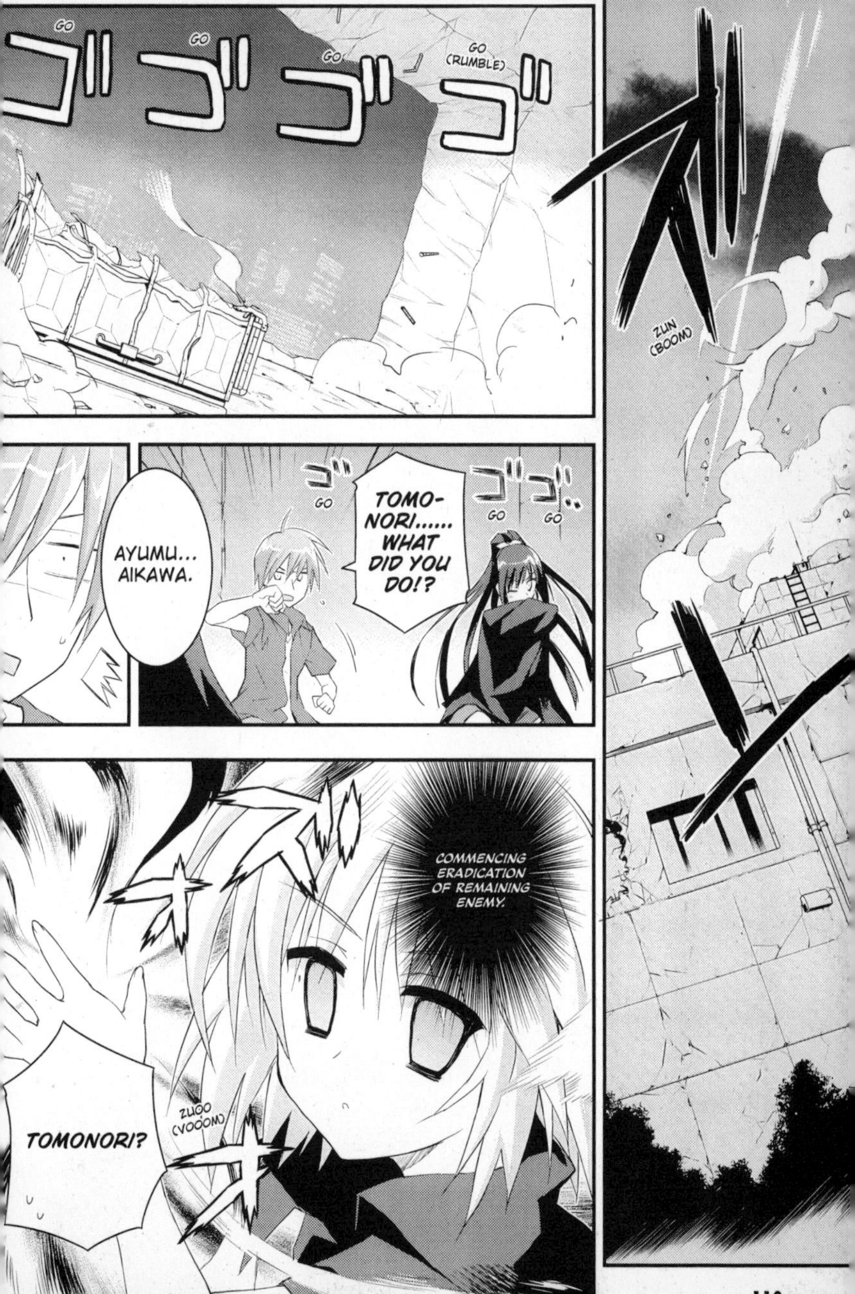
ZUN (BOOM)
GO GO GO GO (RUMBLE)
GO GO
TOMO-NORI...... WHAT DID YOU DO!?
GO
AYUMU... AIKAWA.
COMMENCING ERADICATION OF REMAINING ENEMY.
ZUOO (VOOOM)
TOMONORI?

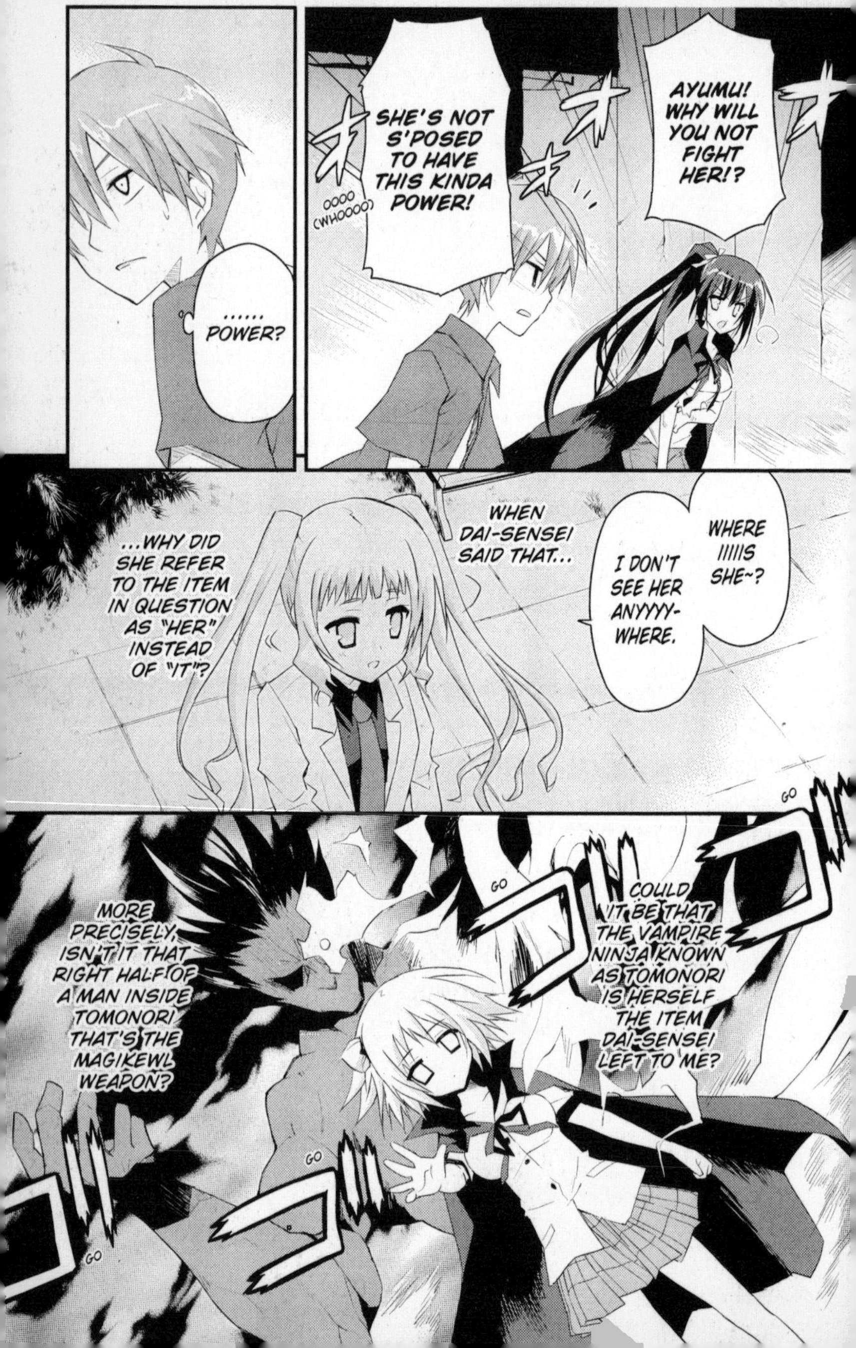
AYUMU! WHY WILL YOU NOT FIGHT HER!?
SHE'S NOT S'POSED TO HAVE THIS KINDA POWER!
OOOO (WHOOOO)
......POWER?
WHERE IIIIIS SHE~?
I DON'T SEE HER ANYYYY-WHERE.
WHEN DAI-SENSEI SAID THAT...
...WHY DID SHE REFER TO THE ITEM IN QUESTION AS "HER" INSTEAD OF "IT"?
GO
COULD IT BE THAT THE VAMPIRE NINJA KNOWN AS TOMONORI IS HERSELF THE ITEM DAI-SENSEI LEFT TO ME?
GO
MORE PRECISELY, ISN'T IT THAT RIGHT HALF OF A MAN INSIDE TOMONORI THAT'S THE MAGIKEWL WEAPON?
GO
GO

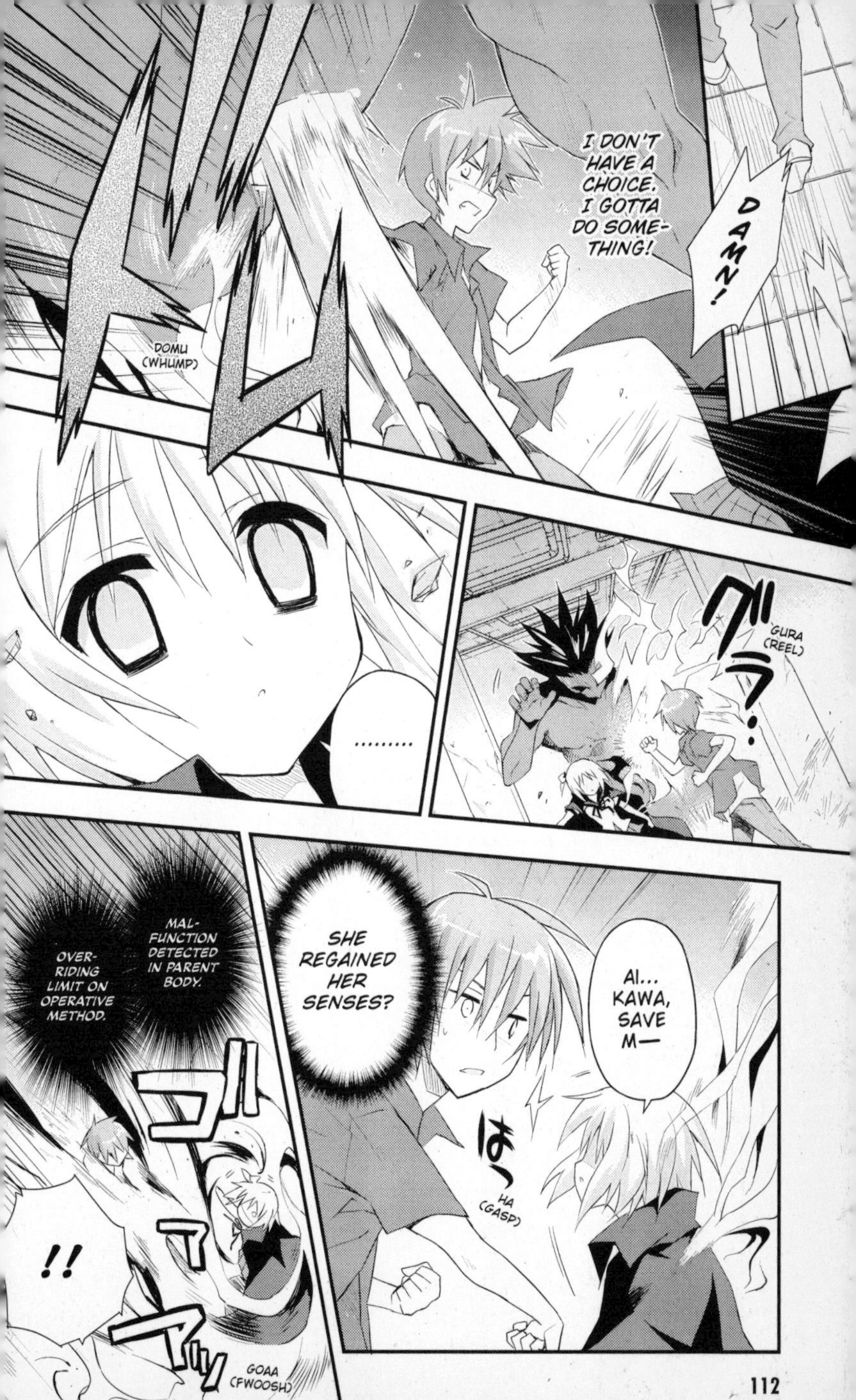
DAMN!
I DON'T HAVE A CHOICE. I GOTTA DO SOME-THING!
DOMU (WHUMP)
GURA (REEL)
....
AI... KAWA, SAVE M—
SHE REGAINED HER SENSES?
HA (GASP)
MAL-FUNCTION DETECTED IN PARENT BODY.
OVER-RIDING LIMIT ON OPERATIVE METHOD.
!!
GOAA (FWOOSH)

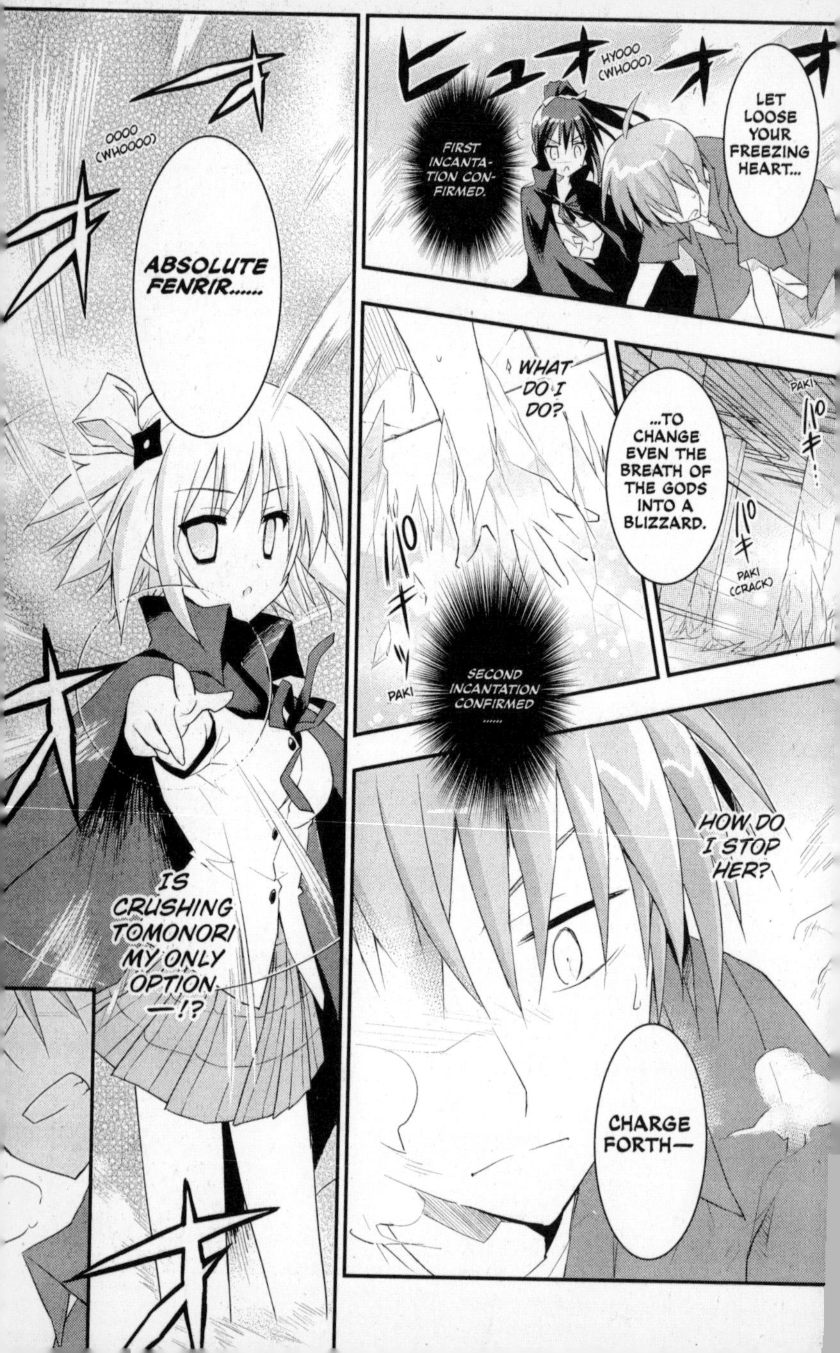
LET LOOSE YOUR FREEZING HEART...
HYOOO (WHOOO)
FIRST INCANTATION CONFIRMED.
PAKI
...TO CHANGE EVEN THE BREATH OF THE GODS INTO A BLIZZARD.
PAKI (CRACK)
WHAT DO I DO?
PAKI
SECOND INCANTATION CONFIRMED ......
HOW DO I STOP HER?
CHARGE FORTH—
OOOO (WHOOOO)
ABSOLUTE FENRIR......
IS CRUSHING TOMONORI MY ONLY OPTION—!?

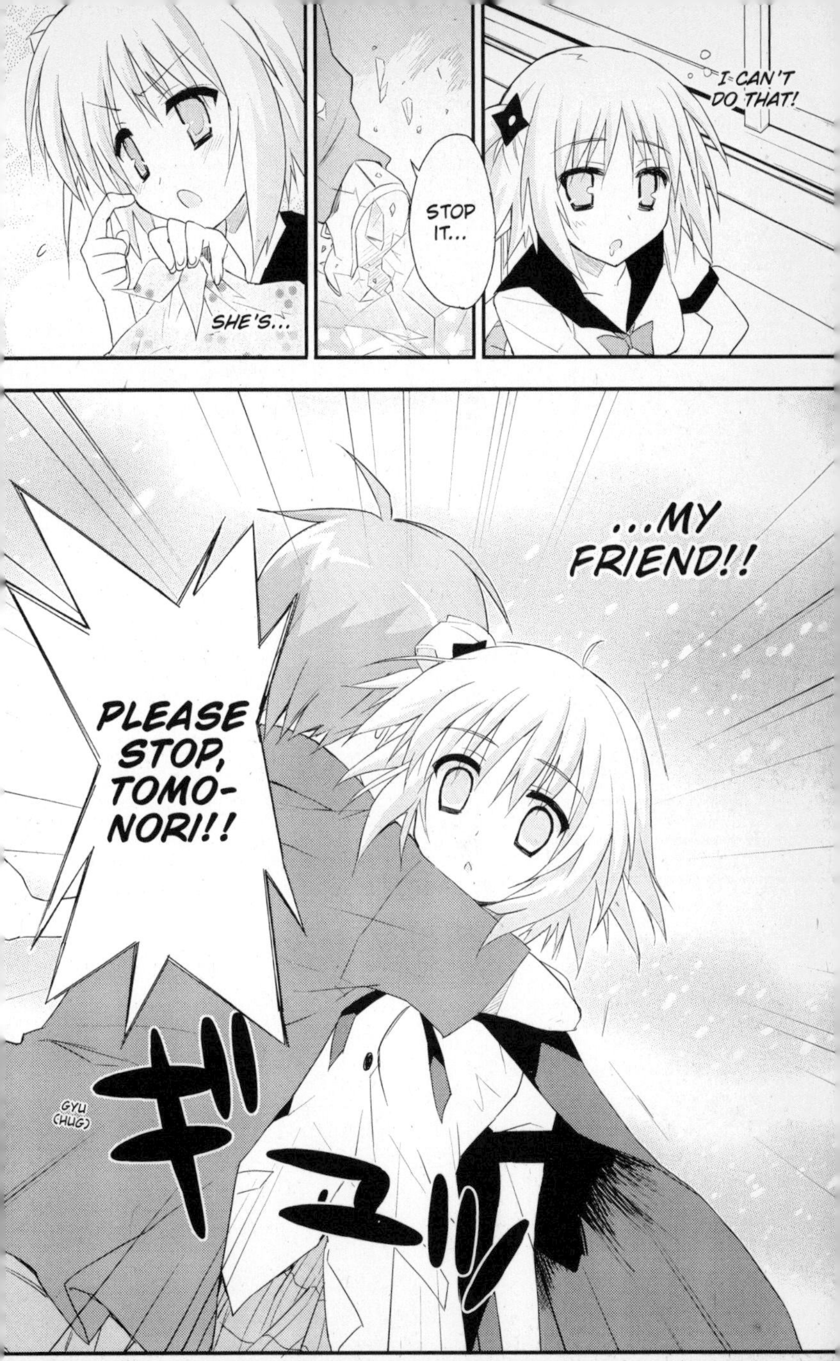
I CAN'T DO THAT!
STOP IT...
SHE'S...
...MY FRIEND!!
PLEASE STOP, TOMO-NORI!!
GYU (HUG)

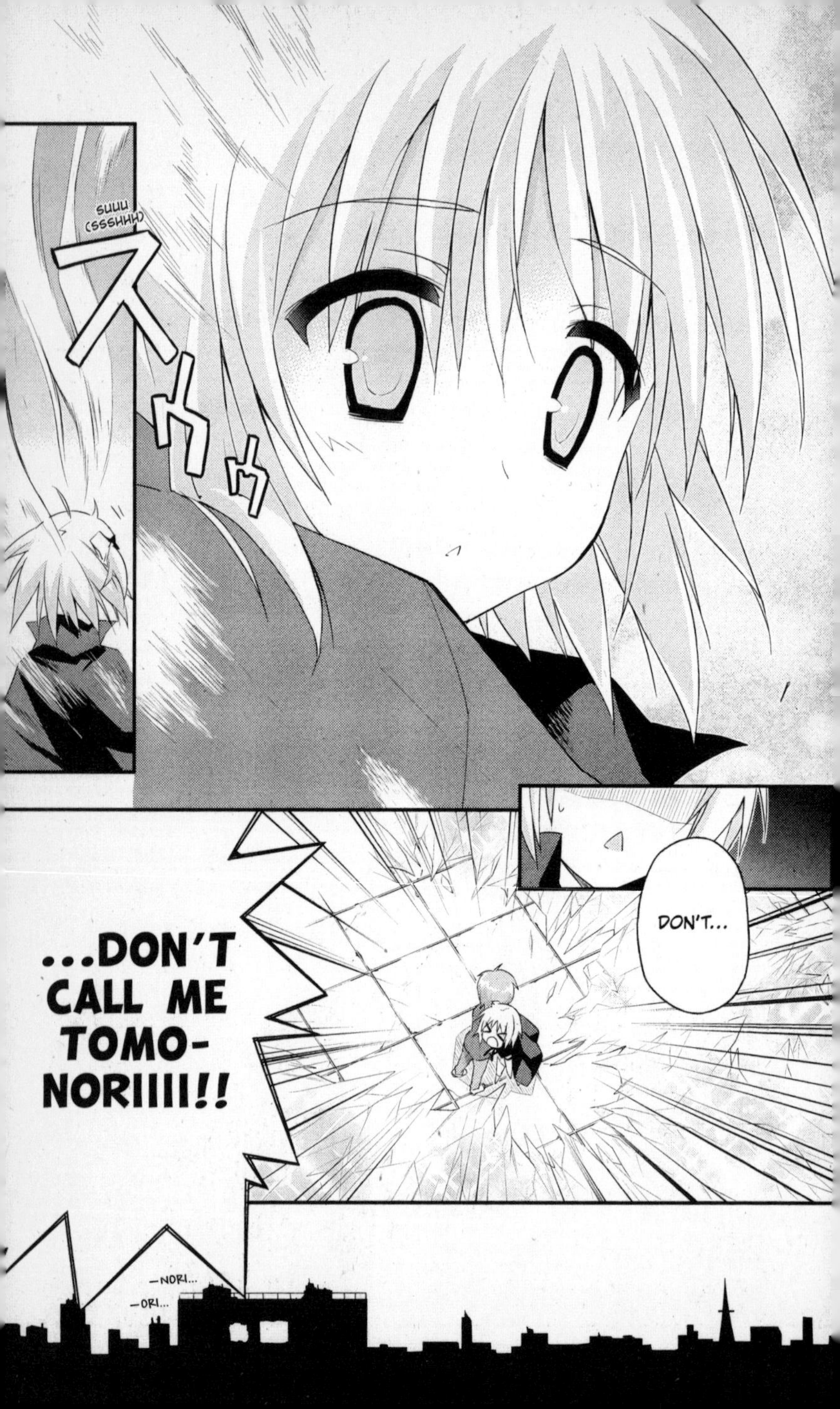

スゥゥ
SUUU (SSSHHH)
DON'T...
...DON'T CALL ME TOMO-NORIIIII!!
—NORI...
—ORI...

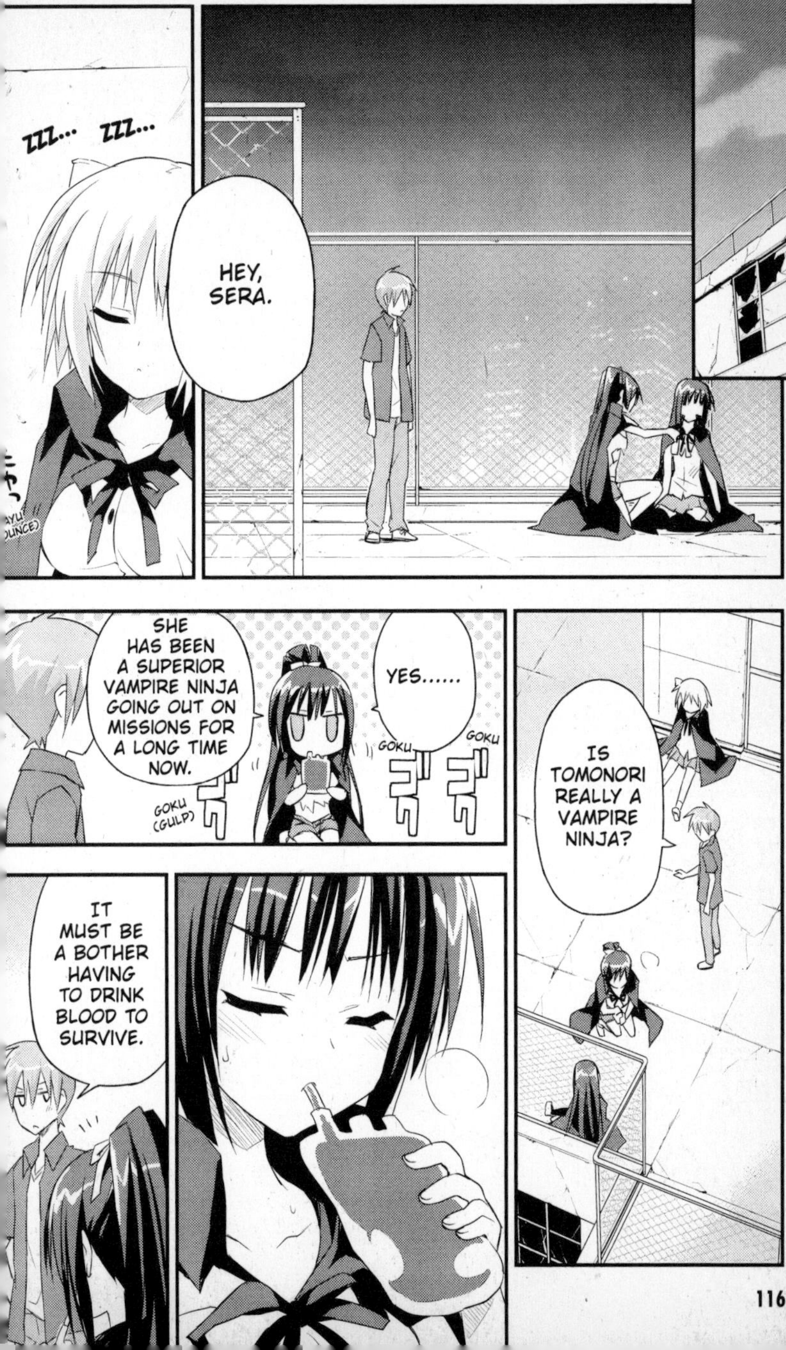
HEY, SERA.
ZZZ... ZZZ...
にゃっ
AYU
OUNCE)
IS TOMONORI REALLY A VAMPIRE NINJA?
YES......
GOKU
GOKU
SHE HAS BEEN A SUPERIOR VAMPIRE NINJA GOING OUT ON MISSIONS FOR A LONG TIME NOW.
GOKU (GULP)
IT MUST BE A BOTHER HAVING TO DRINK BLOOD TO SURVIVE.

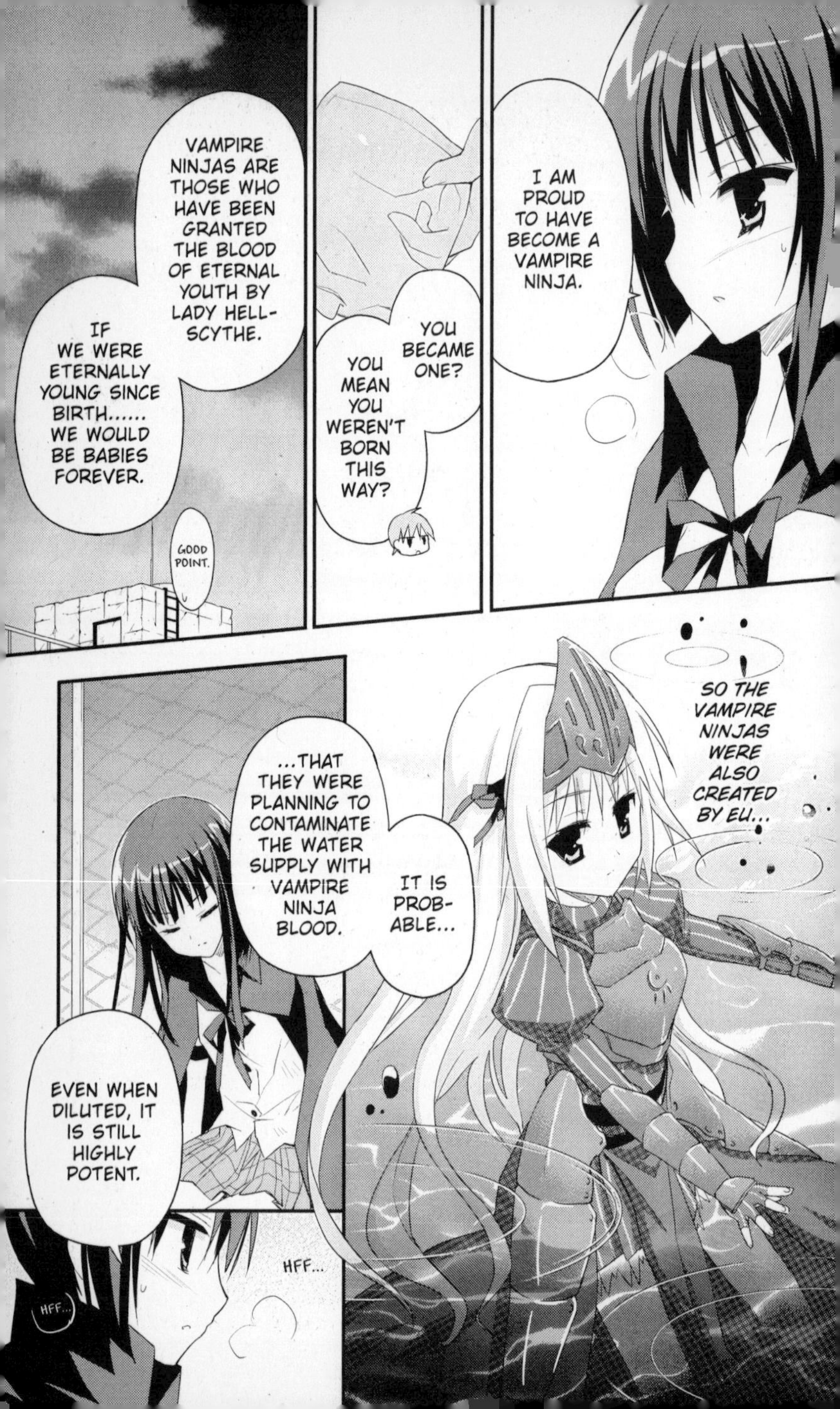
I AM PROUD TO HAVE BECOME A VAMPIRE NINJA.
YOU BECAME ONE?
YOU MEAN YOU WEREN'T BORN THIS WAY?
VAMPIRE NINJAS ARE THOSE WHO HAVE BEEN GRANTED THE BLOOD OF ETERNAL YOUTH BY LADY HELL-SCYTHE.
IF WE WERE ETERNALLY YOUNG SINCE BIRTH...... WE WOULD BE BABIES FOREVER.
GOOD POINT.
SO THE VAMPIRE NINJAS WERE ALSO CREATED BY EU...
IT IS PROBABLE...
...THAT THEY WERE PLANNING TO CONTAMINATE THE WATER SUPPLY WITH VAMPIRE NINJA BLOOD.
EVEN WHEN DILUTED, IT IS STILL HIGHLY POTENT.
HFF...
HFF...

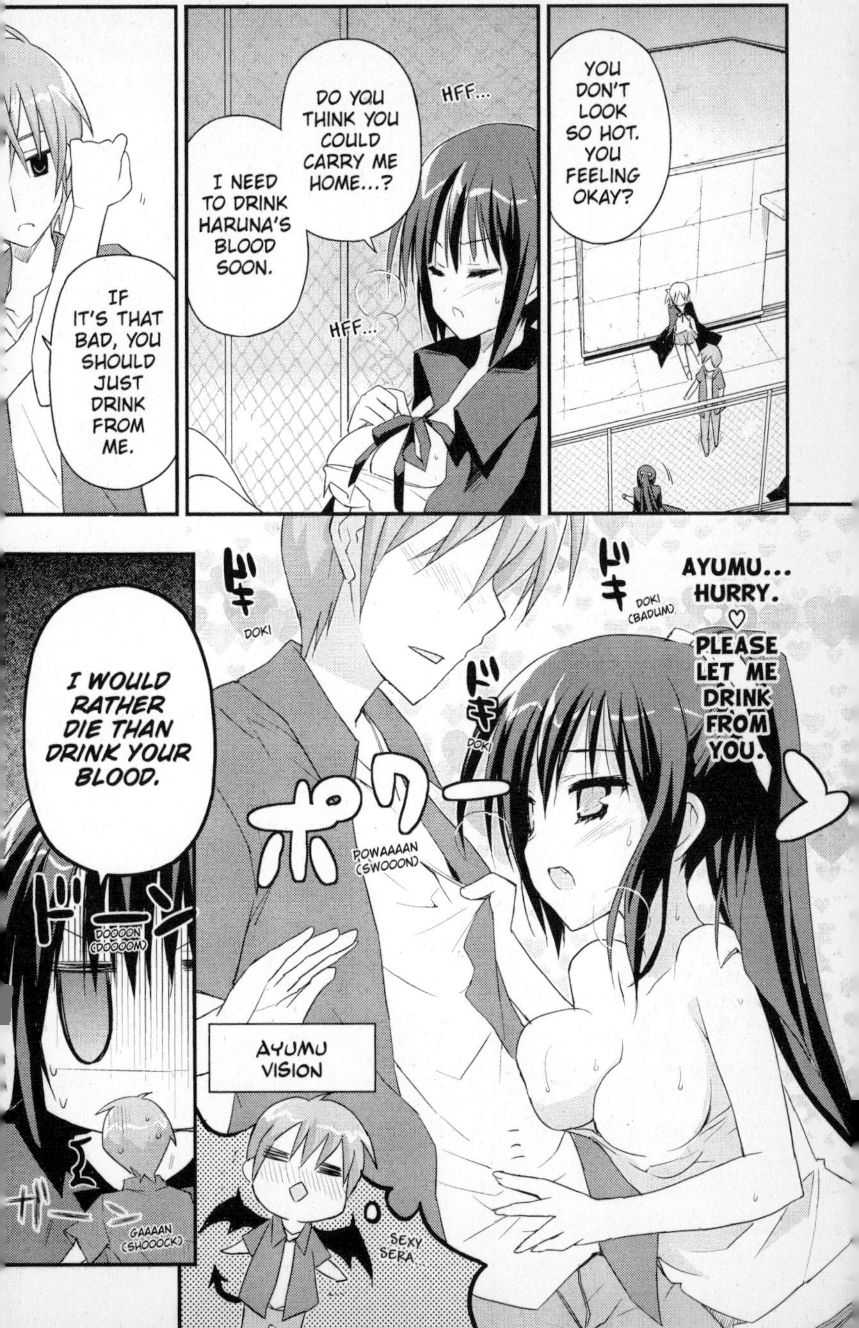

YOU DON'T LOOK SO HOT. YOU FEELING OKAY?
HFF...
DO YOU THINK YOU COULD CARRY ME HOME...?
I NEED TO DRINK HARUNA'S BLOOD SOON.
HFF...
IF IT'S THAT BAD, YOU SHOULD JUST DRINK FROM ME.
AYUMU... HURRY. ♡ PLEASE LET ME DRINK FROM YOU.
DOKI (BADUM)
DOKI
DOKI
POWAAAAN (SWOOON)
AYUMU VISION
SEXY SERA
I WOULD RATHER DIE THAN DRINK YOUR BLOOD.
DOOOON (DOOOOM)
GAAAAN (SHOOOCK)

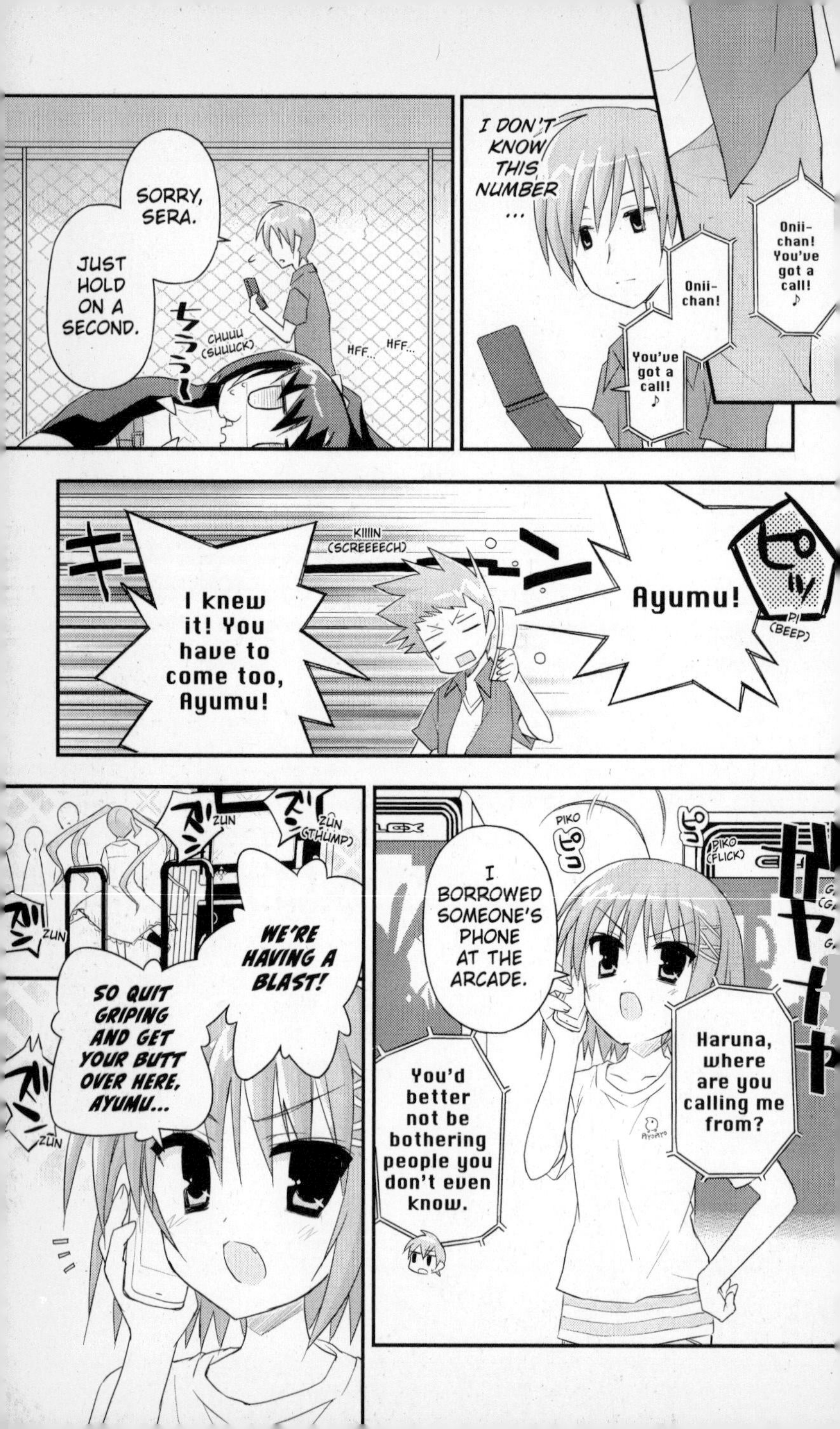
Onii-chan! You've got a call! ♪
Onii-chan!
You've got a call! ♪
I DON'T KNOW THIS NUMBER...
SORRY, SERA.
JUST HOLD ON A SECOND.
CHUUU (SUUUCK)
HFF... HFF...
PI (BEEP)
Ayumu!
KIIIN (SCREEEECH)
I knew it! You have to come too, Ayumu!
PIKO (FLICK)
PIKO
I BORROWED SOMEONE'S PHONE AT THE ARCADE.
Haruna, where are you calling me from?
You'd better not be bothering people you don't even know.
ZUN (THUMP)
ZUN
WE'RE HAVING A BLAST!
ZUN
SO QUIT GRIPING AND GET YOUR BUTT OVER HERE, AYUMU...
ZUN

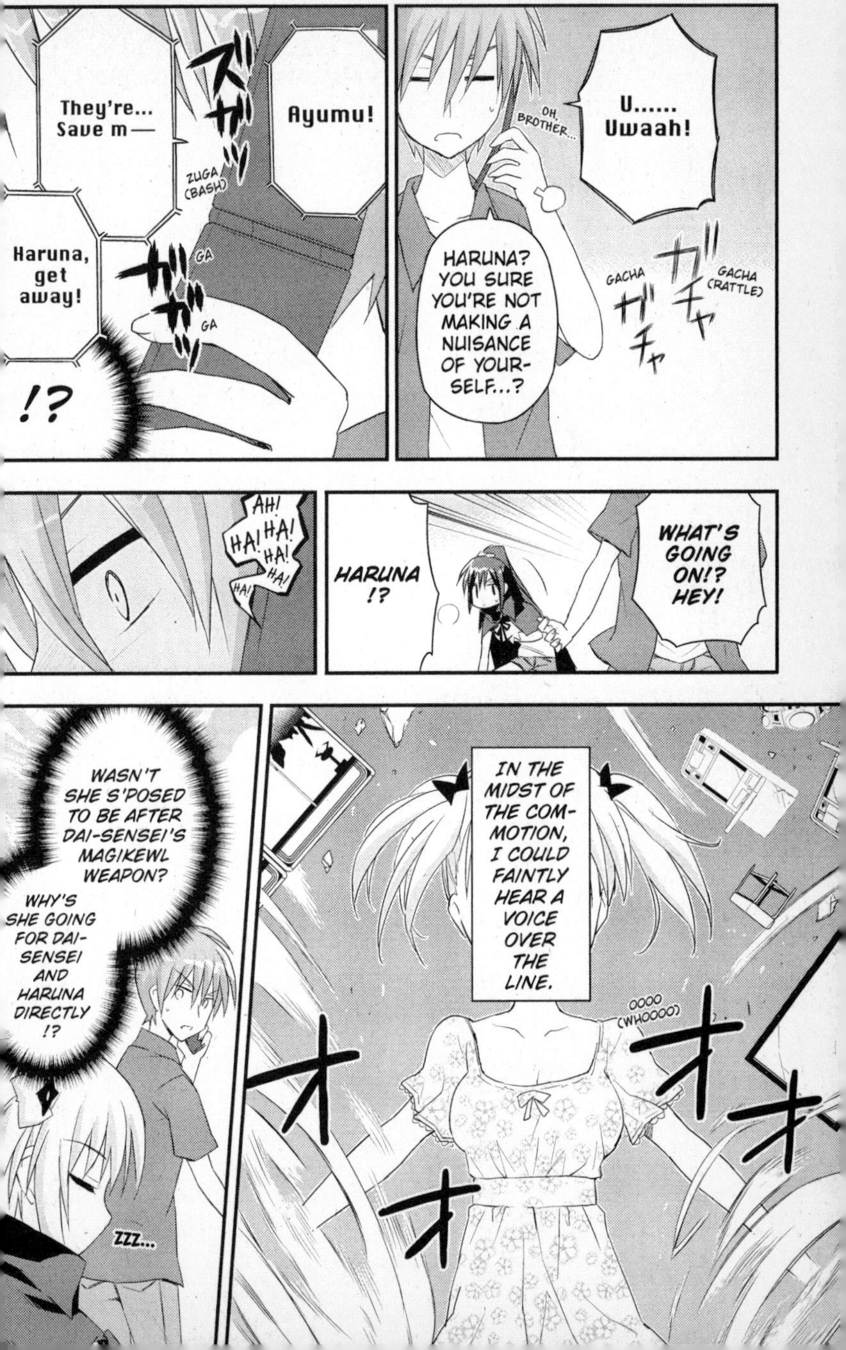

U...... Uwaah!
OH, BROTHER...
HARUNA? YOU SURE YOU'RE NOT MAKING A NUISANCE OF YOUR-SELF...?
GACHA
GACHA (RATTLE)
Ayumu!
ZUGA (BASH)
They're... Save m—
GA
GA
Haruna, get away!
!?
WHAT'S GOING ON!? HEY!
HARUNA !?
AH! HA! HA! HA! HA! HA!
IN THE MIDST OF THE COM-MOTION, I COULD FAINTLY HEAR A VOICE OVER THE LINE.
OOOO (WHOOOO)
WASN'T SHE S'POSED TO BE AFTER DAI-SENSEI'S MAGIKEWL WEAPON?
WHY'S SHE GOING FOR DAI-SENSEI AND HARUNA DIRECTLY !?
ZZZ...

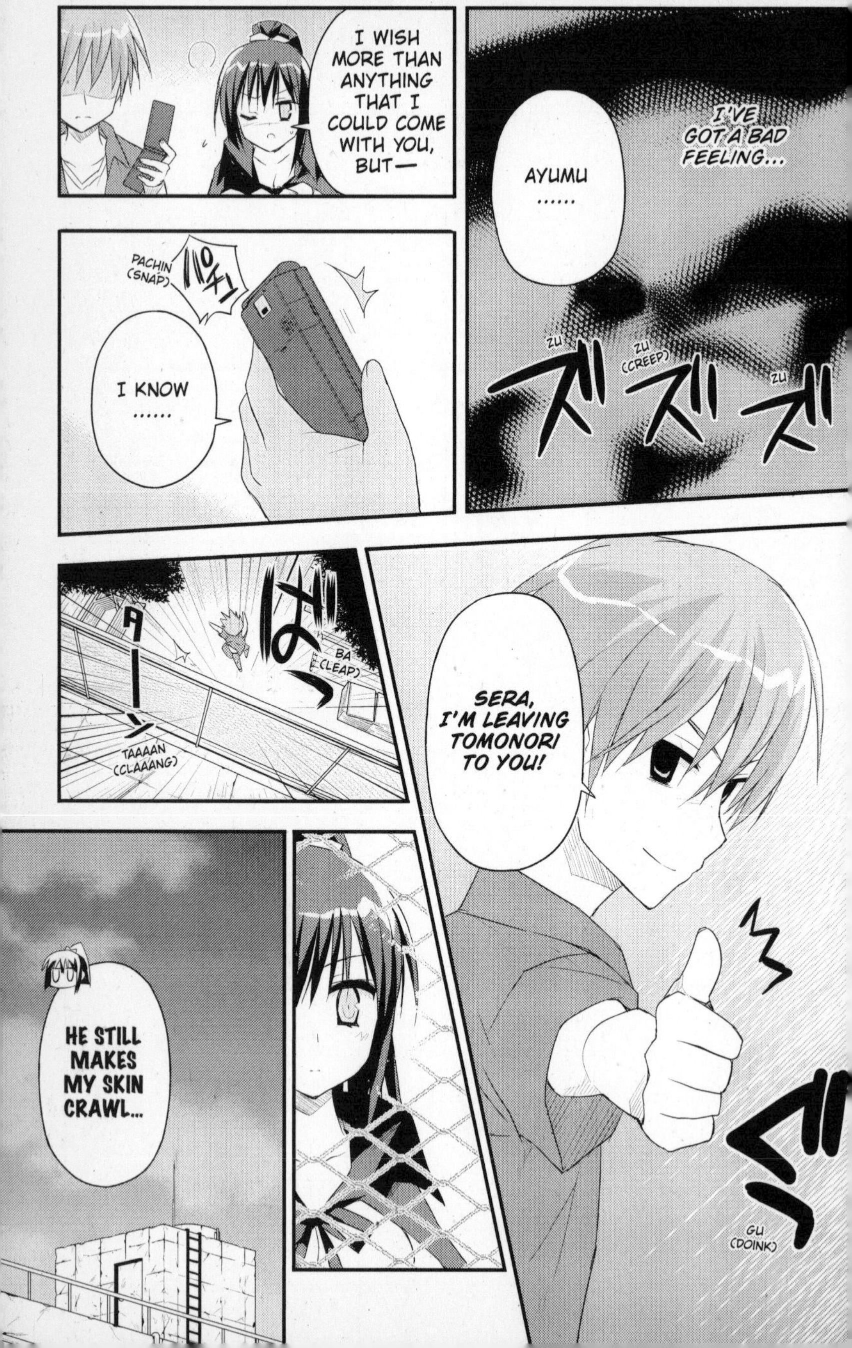
I'VE GOT A BAD FEELING...
AYUMU ......
ZU
ZU (CREEP)
ZU
I WISH MORE THAN ANYTHING THAT I COULD COME WITH YOU, BUT—
PACHIN (SNAP)
I KNOW ......
SERA, I'M LEAVING TOMONORI TO YOU!
GU (DOINK)
BA (LEAP)
TAAAAN (CLAAANG)
HE STILL MAKES MY SKIN CRAWL...

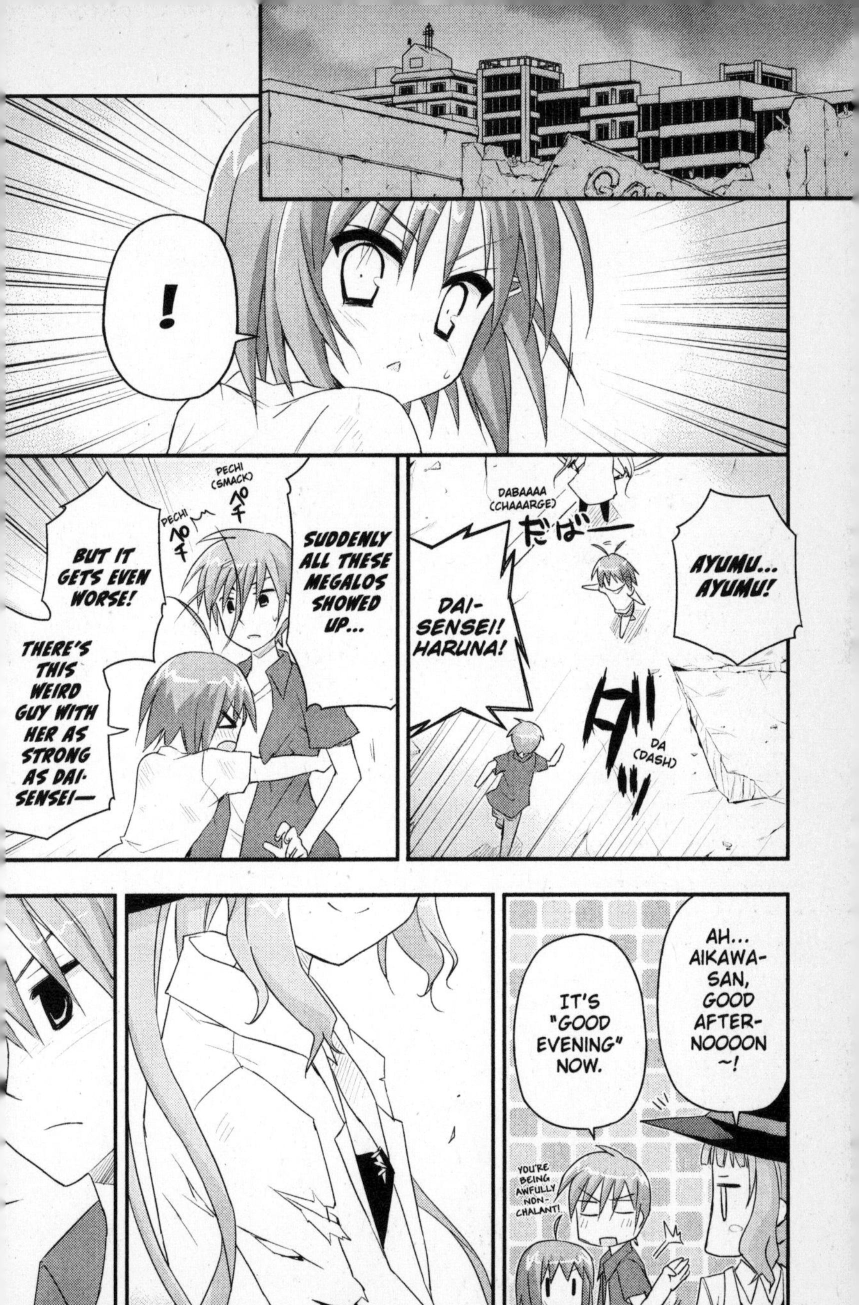
!
AYUMU... AYUMU!
DABAAAA (CHAAARGE)
だばー
DAI-SENSEI! HARUNA!
ダッ
DA (DASH)
SUDDENLY ALL THESE MEGALOS SHOWED UP...
PECHI (SMACK)
ペチ
PECHI
ペチ
BUT IT GETS EVEN WORSE!
THERE'S THIS WEIRD GUY WITH HER AS STRONG AS DAI-SENSEI—
AH... AIKAWA-SAN, GOOD AFTER-NOOOON ~!
IT'S "GOOD EVENING" NOW.
YOU'RE BEING AWFULLY NON-CHALANT!

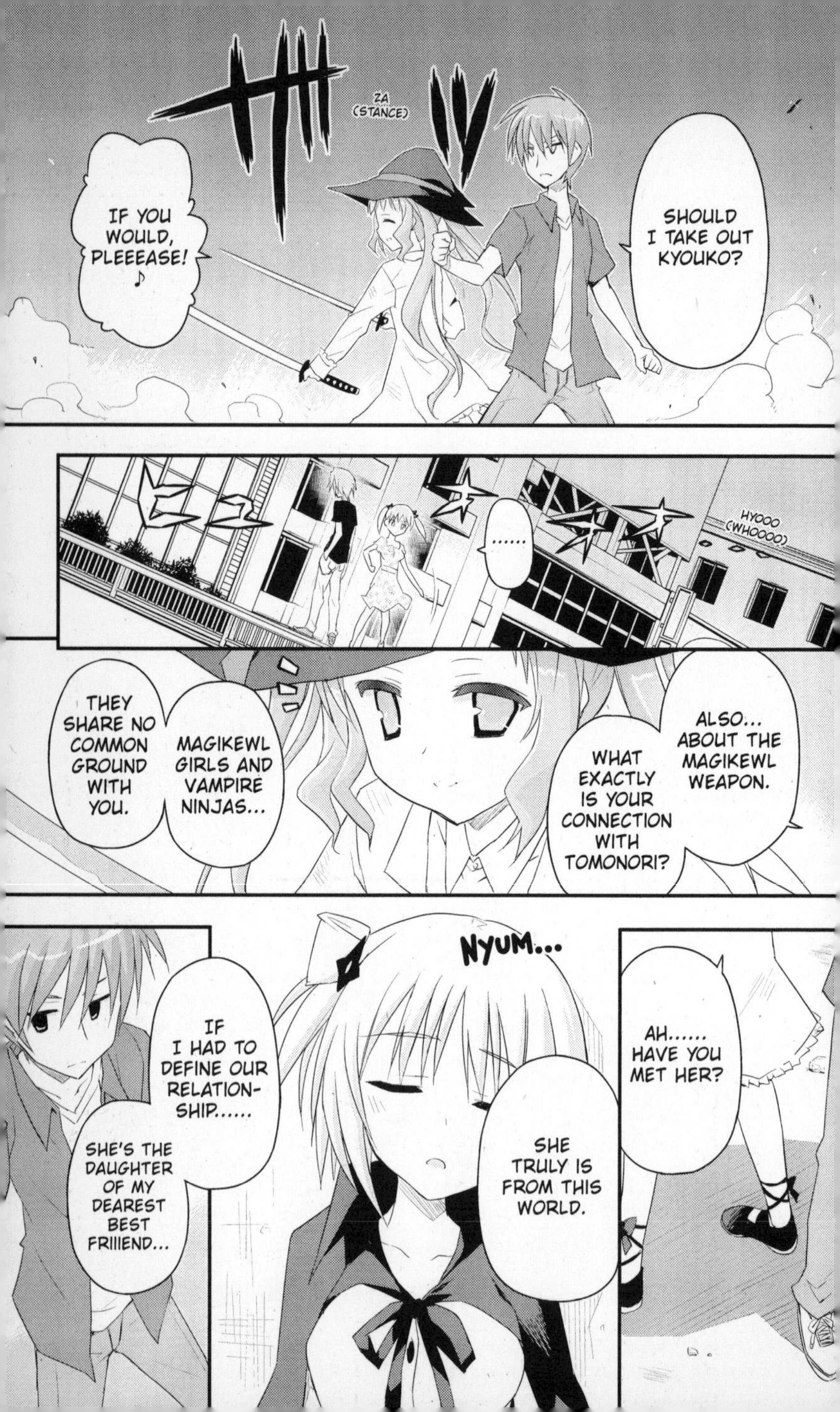
SHOULD I TAKE OUT KYOUKO?
ZA (STANCE)
IF YOU WOULD, PLEEEASE! ♪
HYOOO (WHOOOO)
......
ALSO... ABOUT THE MAGIKEWL WEAPON.
WHAT EXACTLY IS YOUR CONNECTION WITH TOMONORI?
MAGIKEWL GIRLS AND VAMPIRE NINJAS...
THEY SHARE NO COMMON GROUND WITH YOU.
AH...... HAVE YOU MET HER?
NYUM...
SHE TRULY IS FROM THIS WORLD.
IF I HAD TO DEFINE OUR RELATION-SHIP......
SHE'S THE DAUGHTER OF MY DEAREST BEST FRIIIEND...

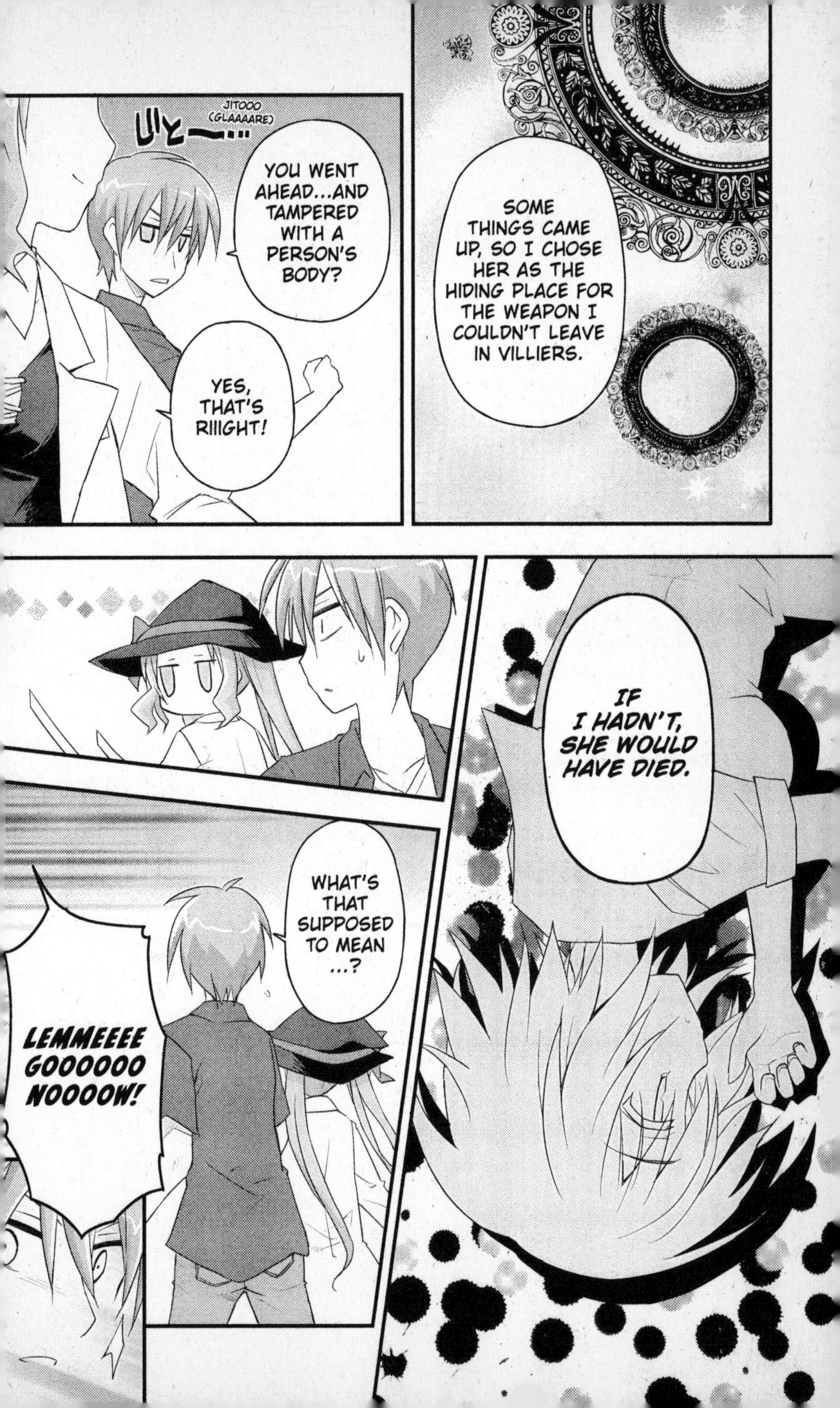
SOME THINGS CAME UP, SO I CHOSE HER AS THE HIDING PLACE FOR THE WEAPON I COULDN'T LEAVE IN VILLIERS.
JITOOO (GLAAAARE)
YOU WENT AHEAD...AND TAMPERED WITH A PERSON'S BODY?
YES, THAT'S RIIIGHT!
IF I HADN'T, SHE WOULD HAVE DIED.
WHAT'S THAT SUPPOSED TO MEAN ...?
LEMMEEEE GOOOOOO NOOOOW!

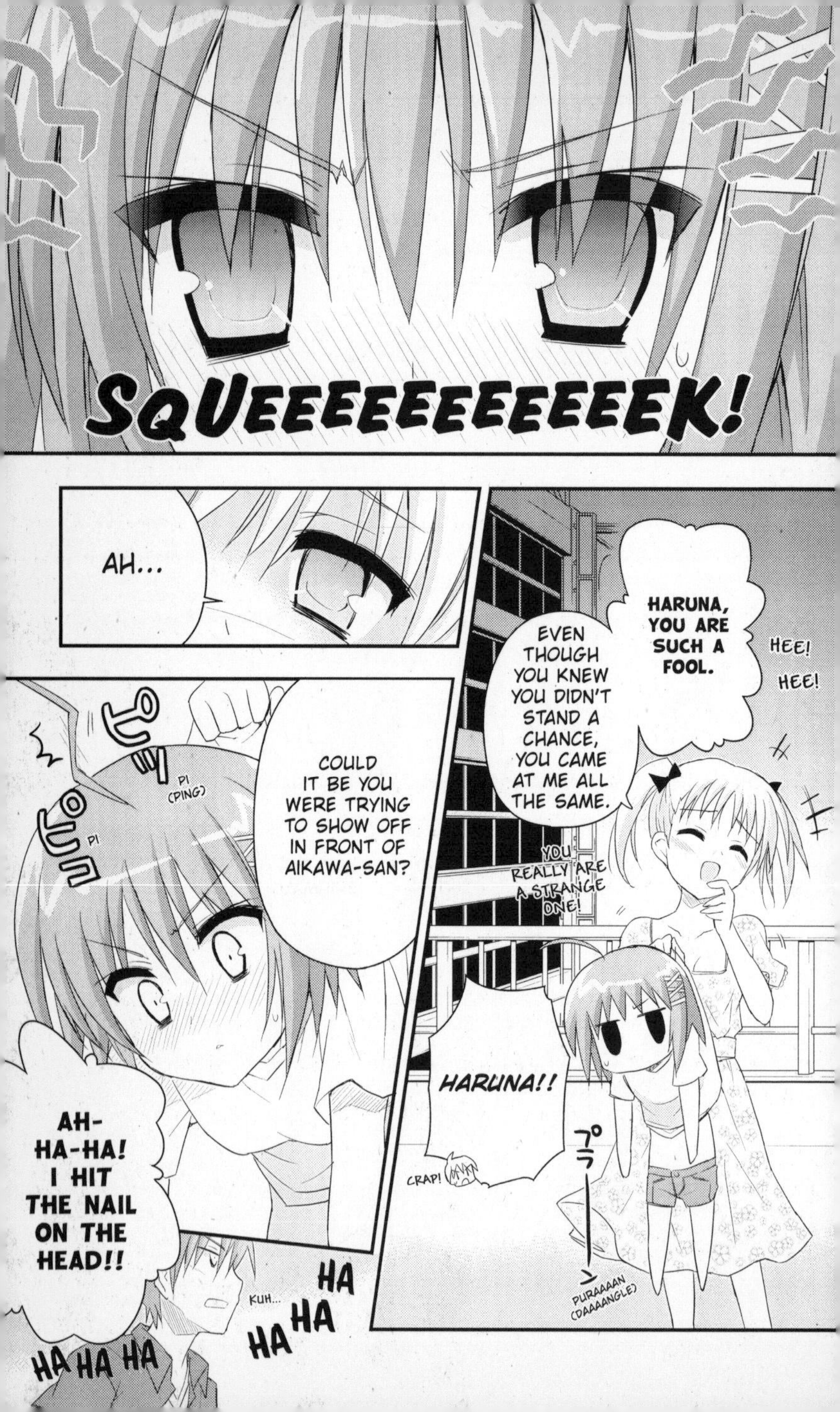
SQUEEEEEEEEEEEEK!
HARUNA, YOU ARE SUCH A FOOL.
HEE! HEE!
EVEN THOUGH YOU KNEW YOU DIDN'T STAND A CHANCE, YOU CAME AT ME ALL THE SAME.
YOU REALLY ARE A STRANGE ONE!
HARUNA!!
CRAP!
プラーン
PURAAAAN (DAAAANGLE)
AH...
PI (PING)
PI
COULD IT BE YOU WERE TRYING TO SHOW OFF IN FRONT OF AIKAWA-SAN?
AH-HA-HA! I HIT THE NAIL ON THE HEAD!!
HA HA HA
KUH...
HA HA HA HA HA

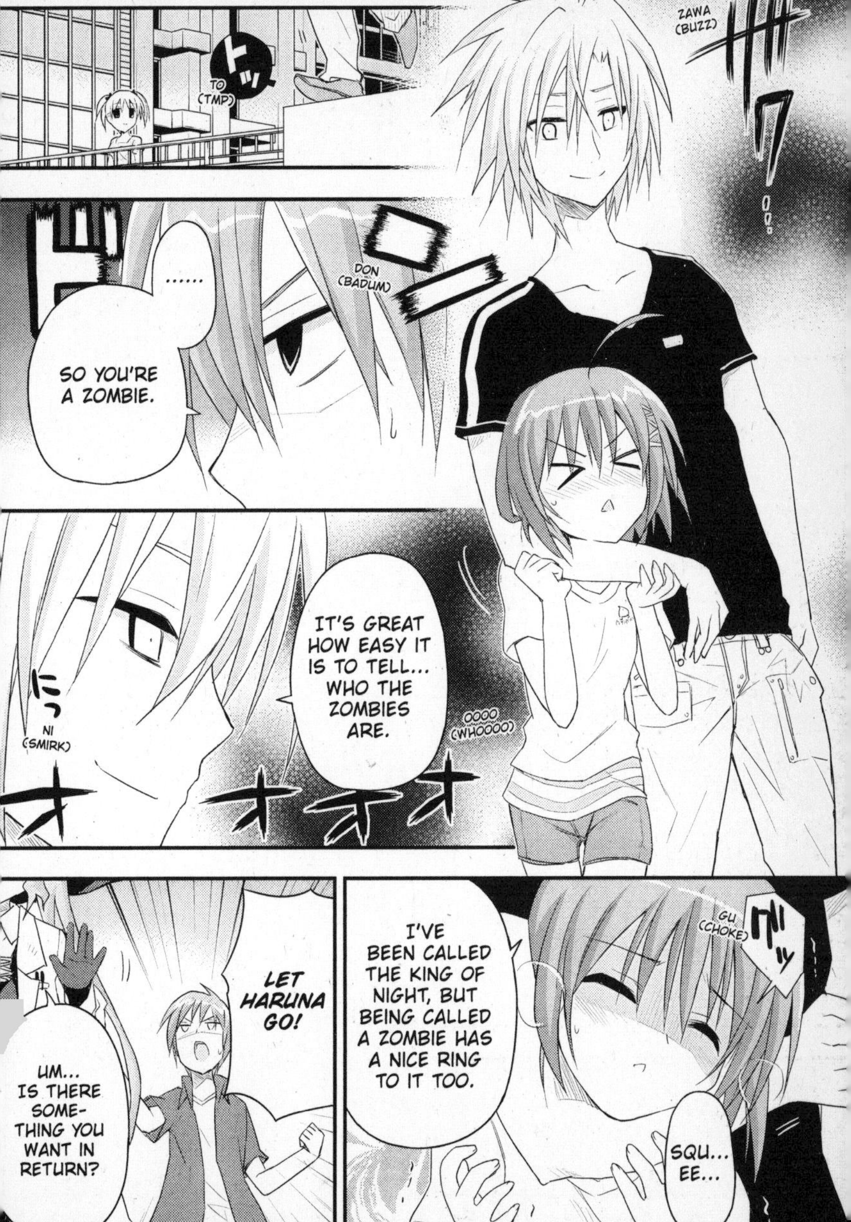
ZAWA (BUZZ)
OOOO (WHOOOO)
TO (TMP)
DON (BADUM)
......
SO YOU'RE A ZOMBIE.
NI (SMIRK)
IT'S GREAT HOW EASY IT IS TO TELL... WHO THE ZOMBIES ARE.
GU (CHOKE)
I'VE BEEN CALLED THE KING OF NIGHT, BUT BEING CALLED A ZOMBIE HAS A NICE RING TO IT TOO.
SQU... EE...
PIYOPIYO
LET HARUNA GO!
UM... IS THERE SOME-THING YOU WANT IN RETURN?

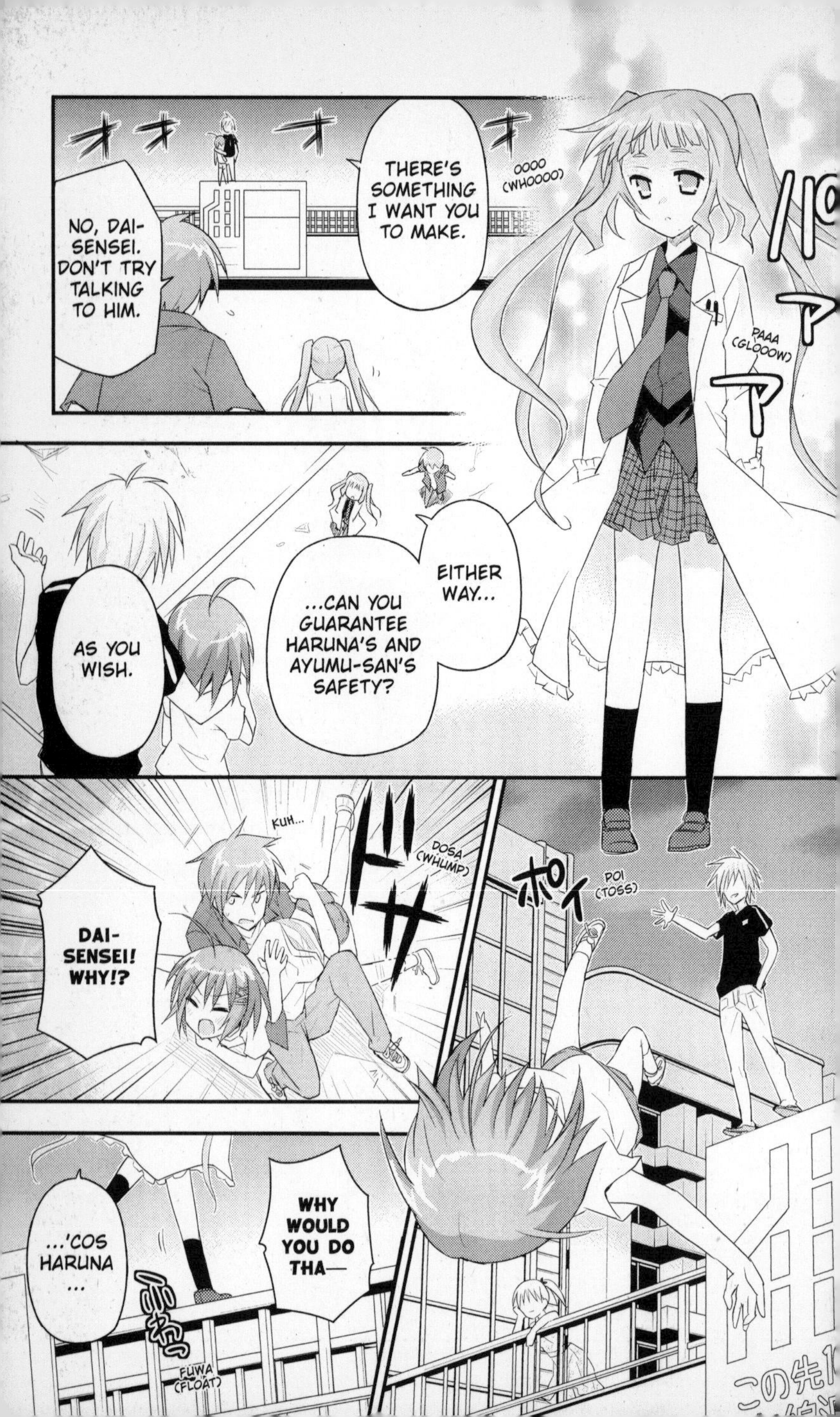
PAAA (GLOOOW)
OOOO (WHOOOO)
THERE'S SOMETHING I WANT YOU TO MAKE.
NO, DAI-SENSEI. DON'T TRY TALKING TO HIM.
EITHER WAY...
...CAN YOU GUARANTEE HARUNA'S AND AYUMU-SAN'S SAFETY?
AS YOU WISH.
POI (TOSS)
KUH...
DOSA (WHUMP)
DAI-SENSEI! WHY!?
WHY WOULD YOU DO THA—
...'COS HARUNA ...
FUWA (FLOAT)

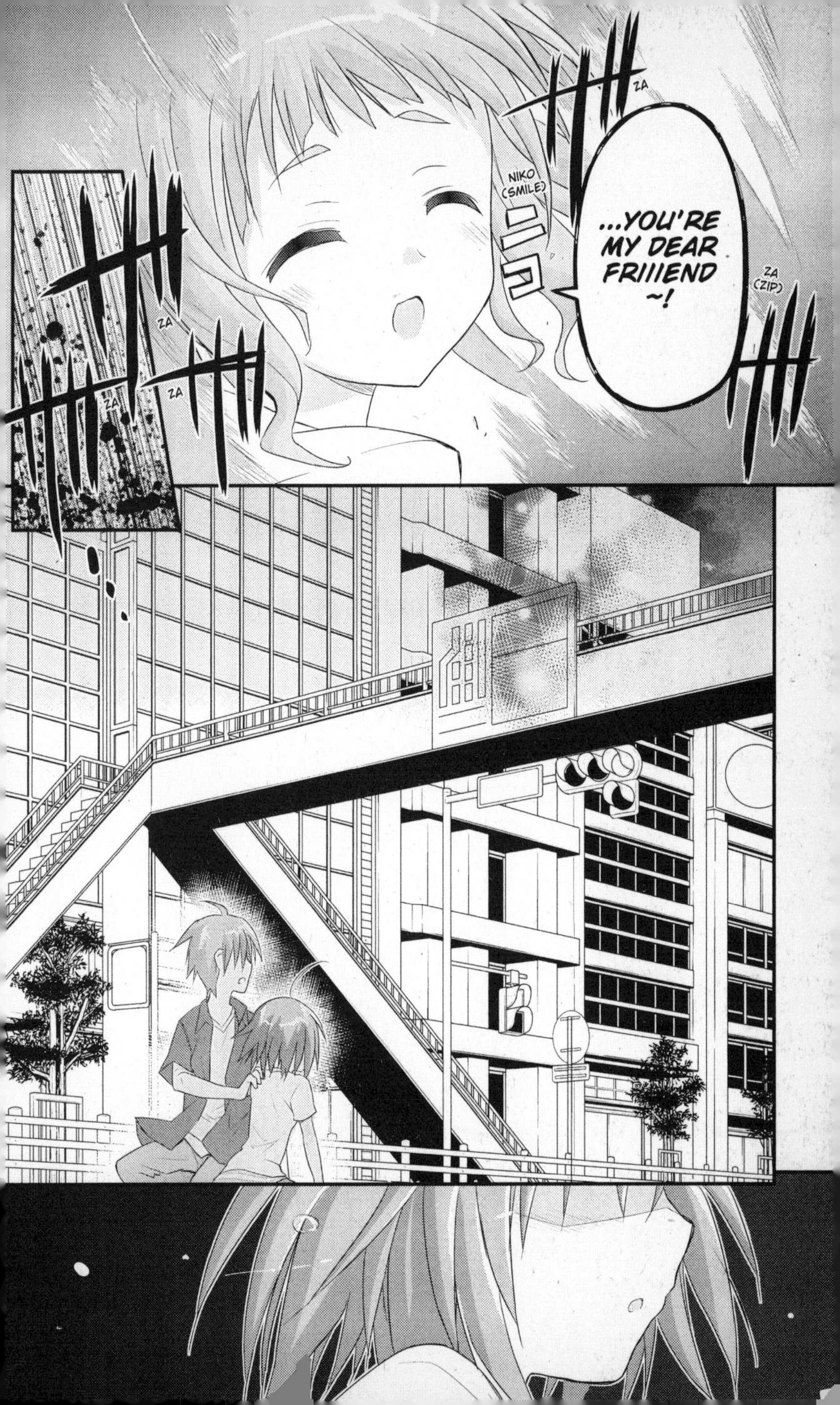
ZA
ZA (ZIP)
...YOU'RE MY DEAR FRIIIEND ~!
NIKO (SMILE)
ZA
ZA
ZA

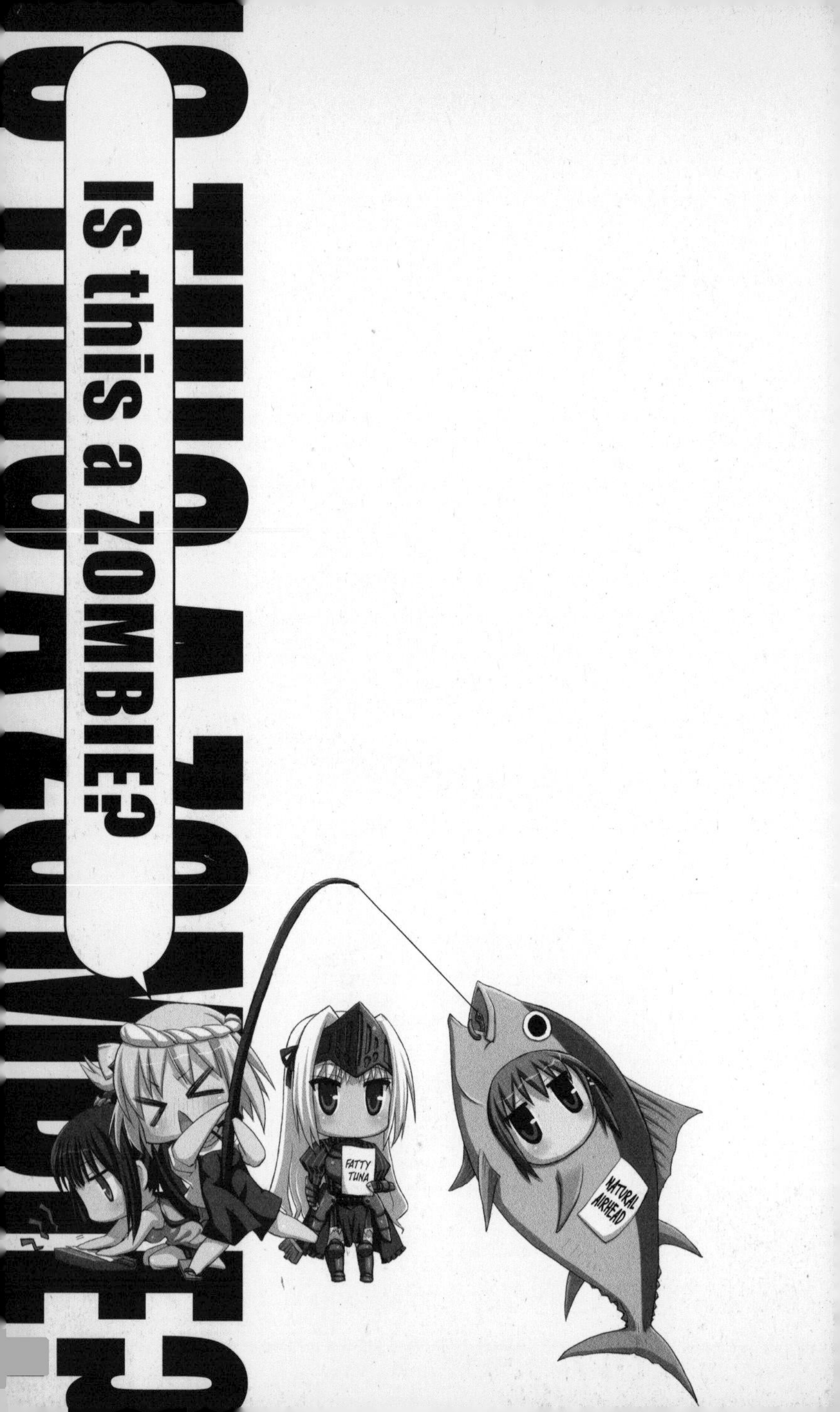
Is this a ZOMBIE?
FATTY TUNA
NATURAL AIRHEAD

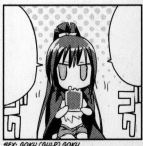

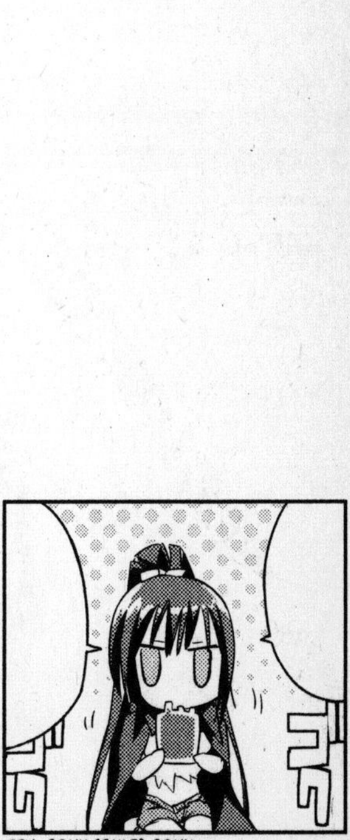

SFX: GOKU (GULP) GOKU

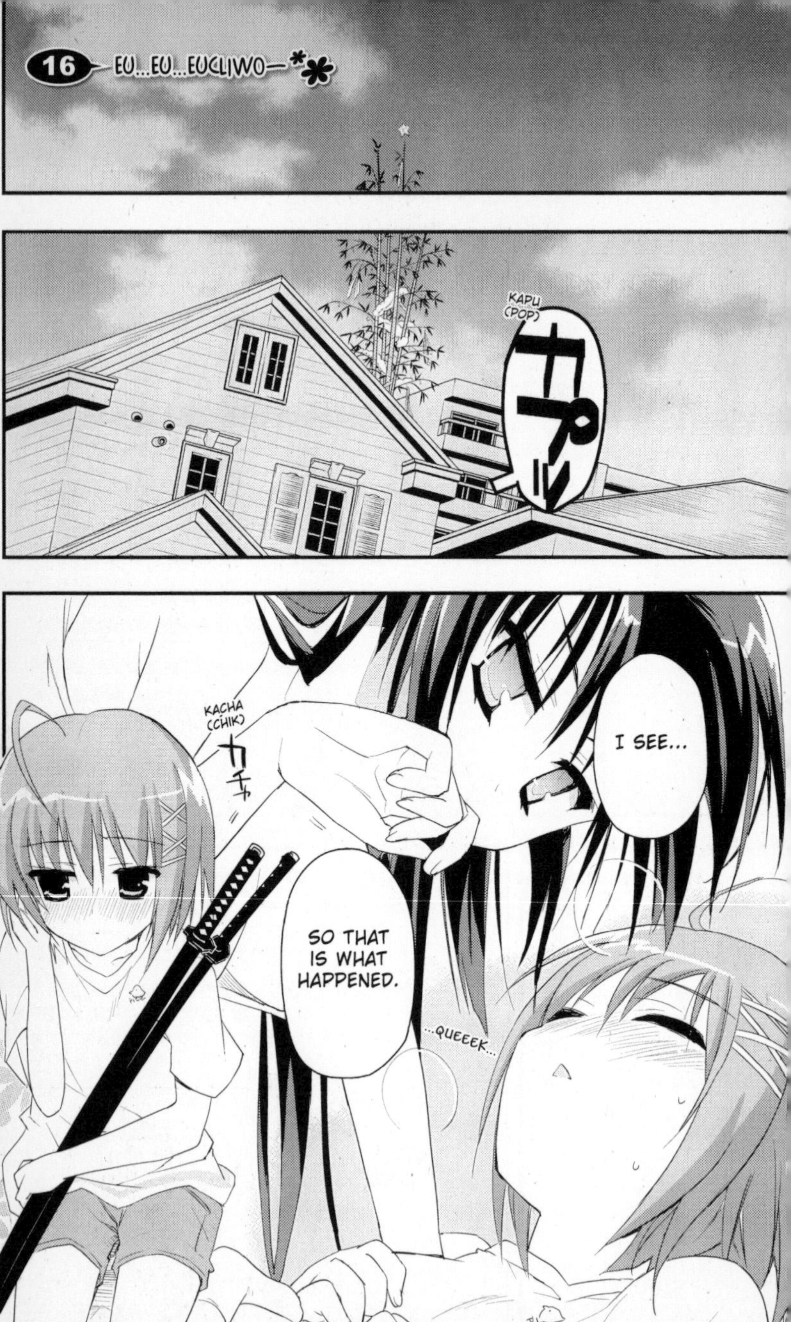

16
EU...EU...EUCLIWO—
KAPU (POP)
I SEE...
SO THAT IS WHAT HAPPENED.
KACHA (CHIK)
...QUEEEK...

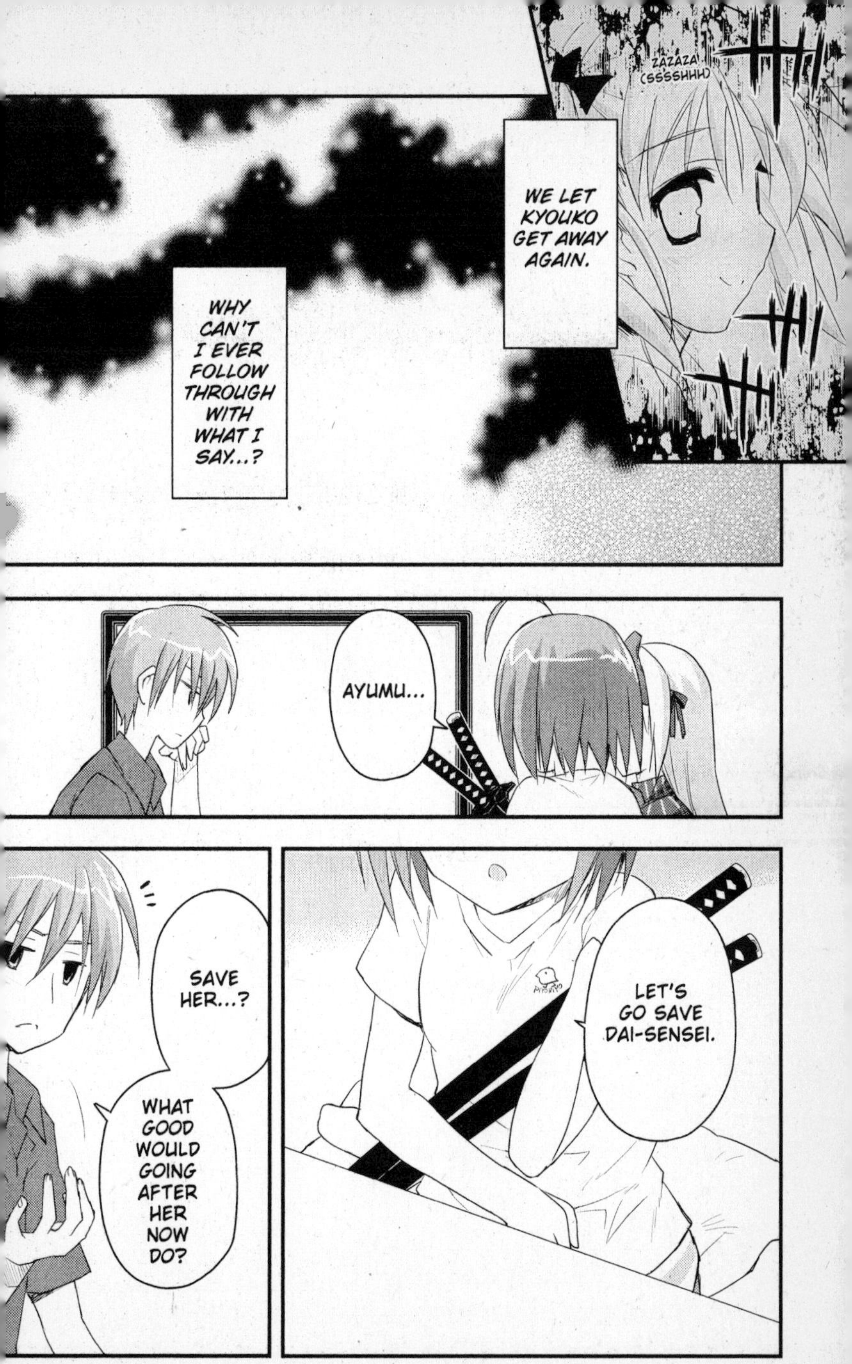
ZAZAZA (SSSSHHH)
WE LET KYOUKO GET AWAY AGAIN.
WHY CAN'T I EVER FOLLOW THROUGH WITH WHAT I SAY...?
AYUMU...
LET'S GO SAVE DAI-SENSEI.
SAVE HER...?
WHAT GOOD WOULD GOING AFTER HER NOW DO?

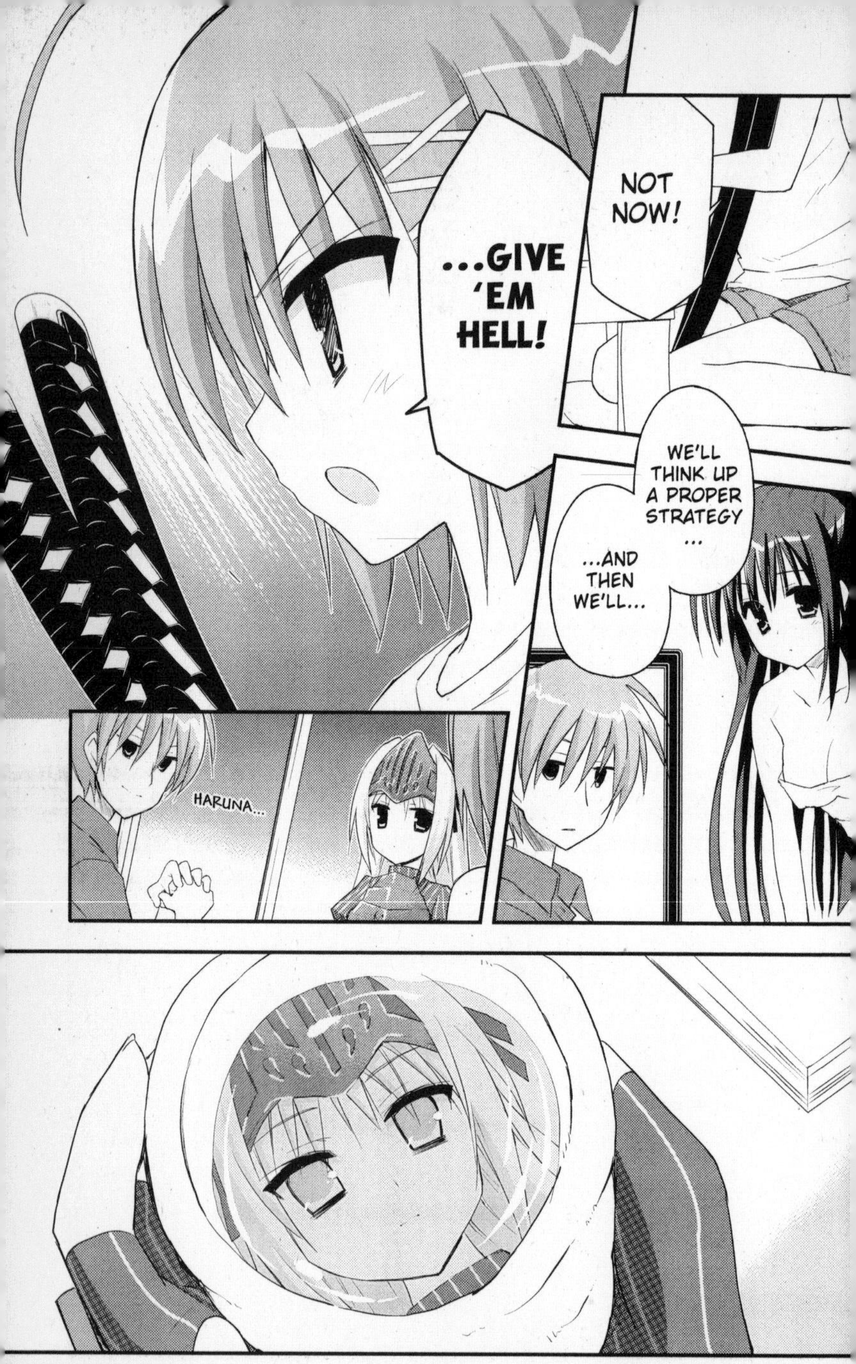
NOT NOW!
WE'LL THINK UP A PROPER STRATEGY ...
...AND THEN WE'LL...
...GIVE 'EM HELL!
HARUNA...

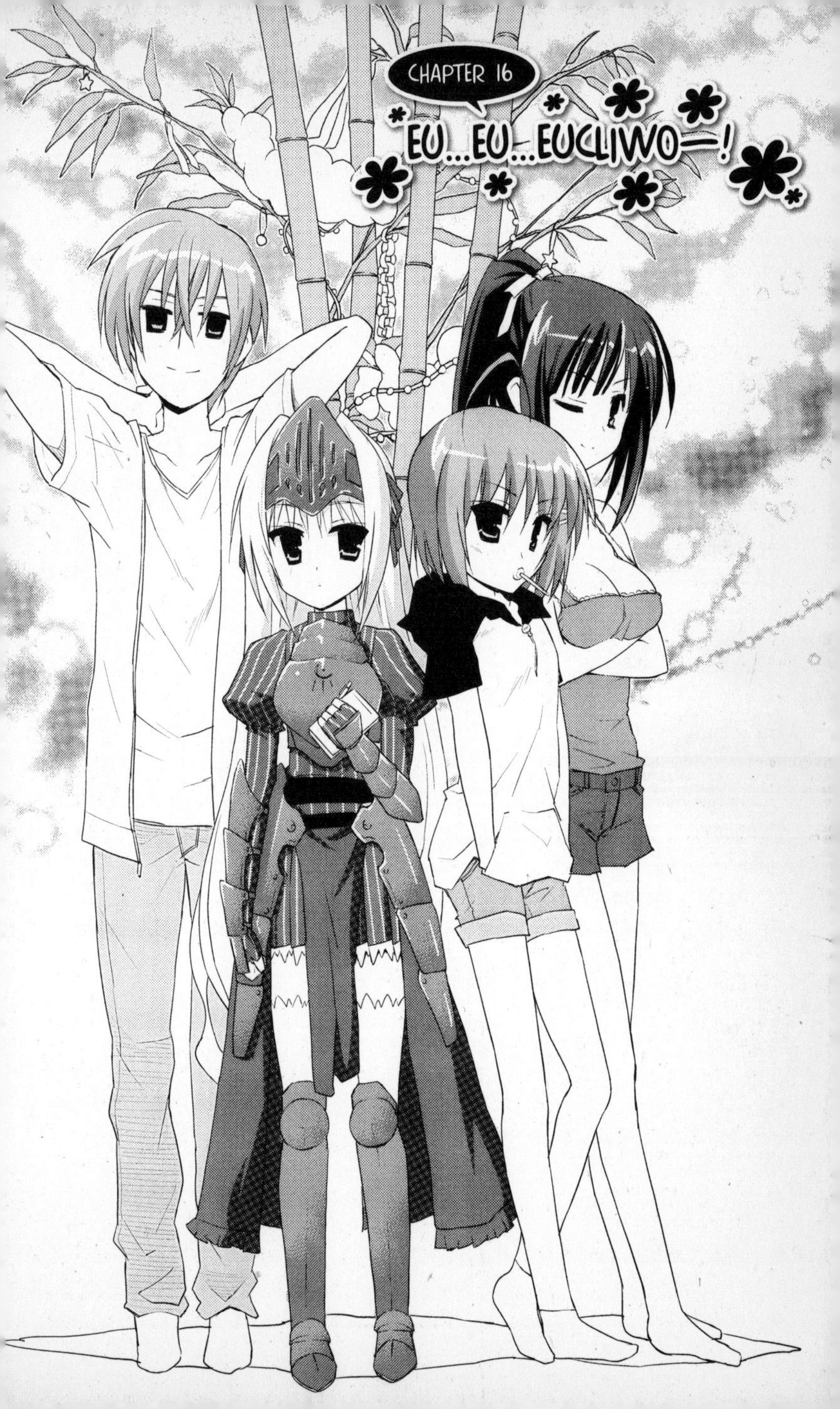
CHAPTER 16
EU...EU...EUCLIWO—!

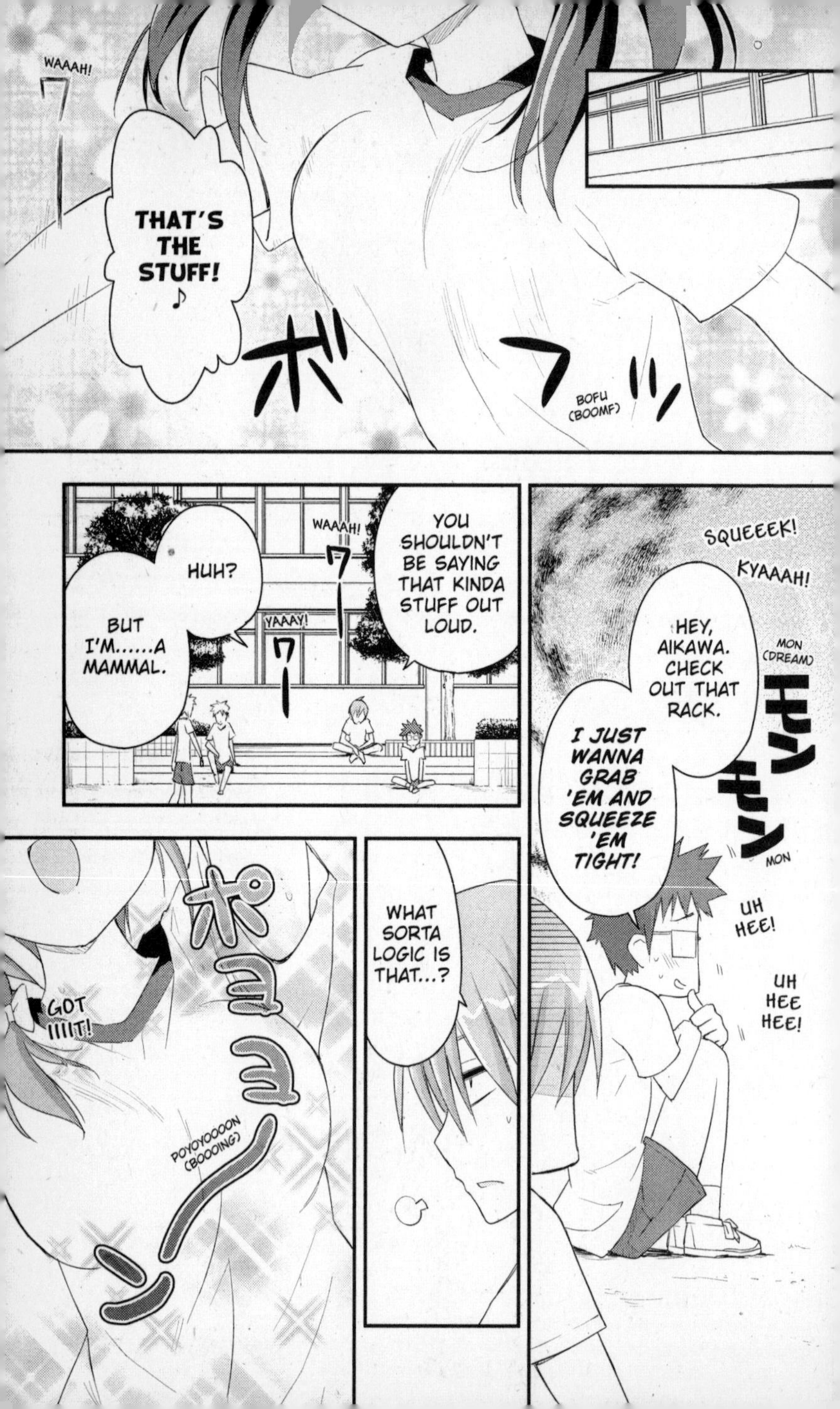

WAAAH!
THAT'S THE STUFF! ♪
ボフッ
BOFU (BOOMF)
SQUEEEK!
KYAAAH!
HEY, AIKAWA. CHECK OUT THAT RACK.
I JUST WANNA GRAB 'EM AND SQUEEZE 'EM TIGHT!
モンモン
MON (DREAM) MON
UH HEE!
UH HEE HEE!
YOU SHOULDN'T BE SAYING THAT KINDA STUFF OUT LOUD.
WAAAH!
YAAAY!
HUH?
BUT I'M......A MAMMAL.
WHAT SORTA LOGIC IS THAT...?
GOT IIIIT!
POYOYOOOON (BOOOING)

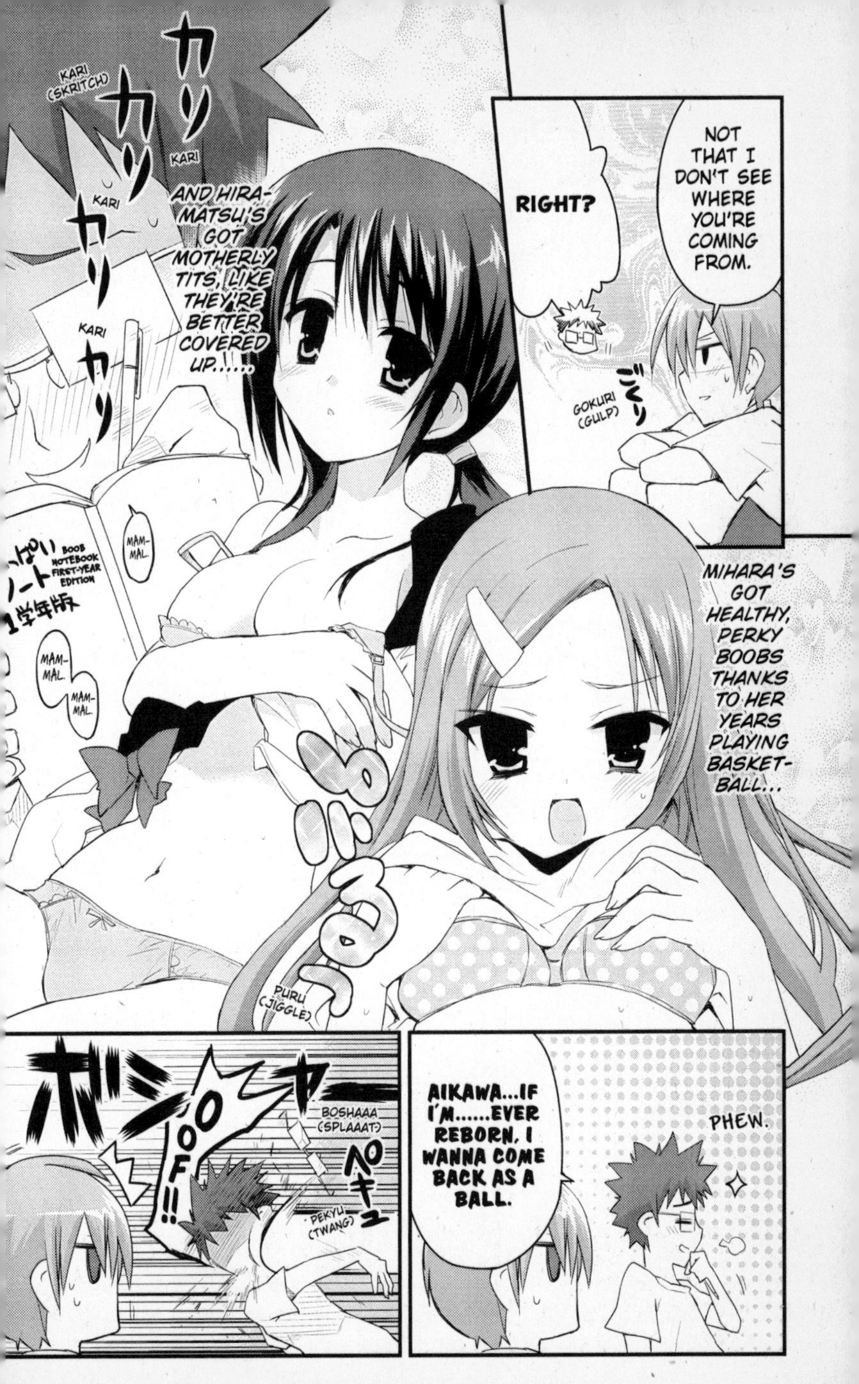
NOT THAT I DON'T SEE WHERE YOU'RE COMING FROM.
RIGHT?
GOKURI (GULP)
KARI (SKRITCH)
KARI
KARI
KARI
AND HIRA-MATSU'S GOT MOTHERLY TITS, LIKE THEY'RE BETTER COVERED UP......
BOOB NOTEBOOK FIRST-YEAR EDITION
MAM-MAL.
MAM-MAL.
MAM-MAL.
MIHARA'S GOT HEALTHY, PERKY BOOBS THANKS TO HER YEARS PLAYING BASKET-BALL...
PURU (JIGGLE)
PHEW.
AIKAWA...IF I'M......EVER REBORN, I WANNA COME BACK AS A BALL.
BOSHAAA (SPLAAAT)
OOF!!
PEKYU (TWANG)

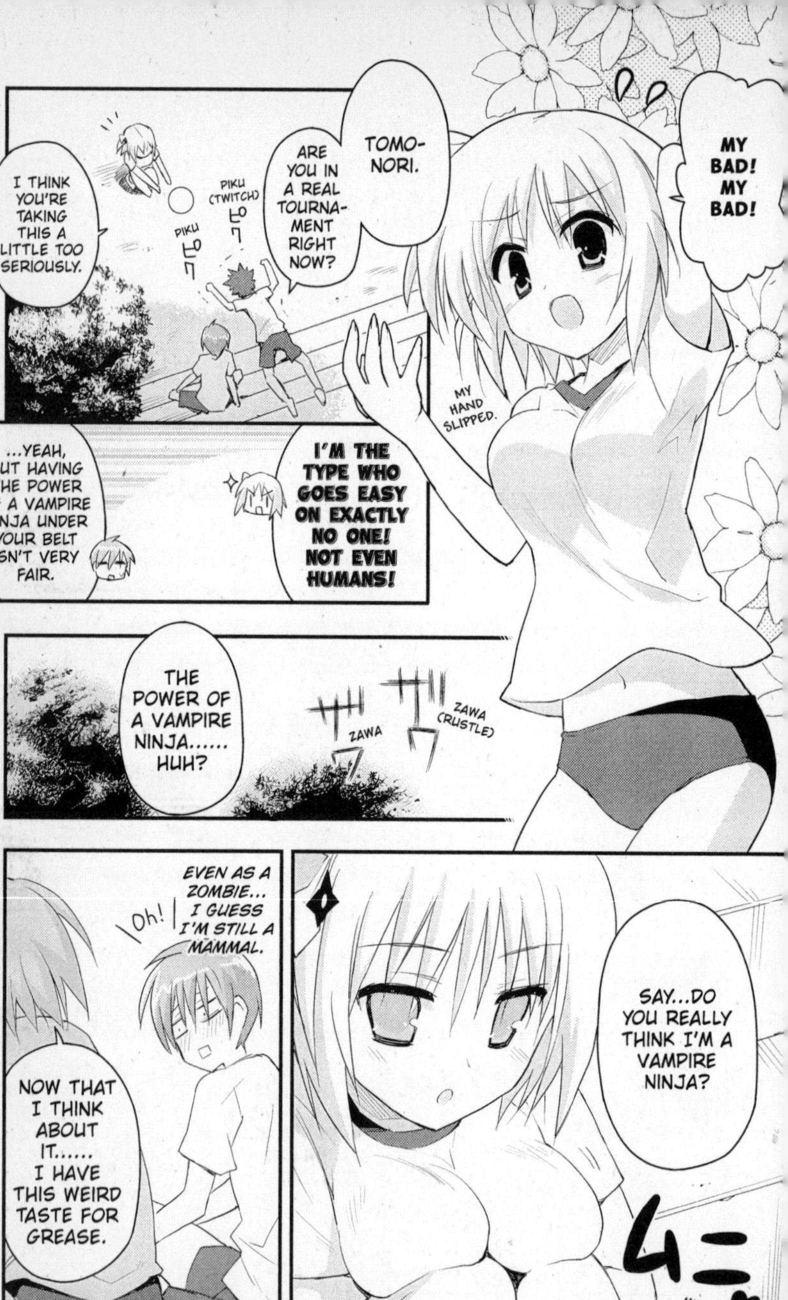
MY BAD! MY BAD!
MY HAND SLIPPED.
TOMO-NORI.
ARE YOU IN A REAL TOURNA-MENT RIGHT NOW?
PIKU (TWITCH)
PIKU
I THINK YOU'RE TAKING THIS A LITTLE TOO SERIOUSLY.
I'M THE TYPE WHO GOES EASY ON EXACTLY NO ONE! NOT EVEN HUMANS!
...YEAH, BUT HAVING THE POWER OF A VAMPIRE NINJA UNDER YOUR BELT ISN'T VERY FAIR.
ZAWA (RUSTLE)
ZAWA
THE POWER OF A VAMPIRE NINJA...... HUH?
SAY...DO YOU REALLY THINK I'M A VAMPIRE NINJA?
MUNI (SQUISH)
EVEN AS A ZOMBIE... I GUESS I'M STILL A MAMMAL.
Oh!
NOW THAT I THINK ABOUT IT...... I HAVE THIS WEIRD TASTE FOR GREASE.

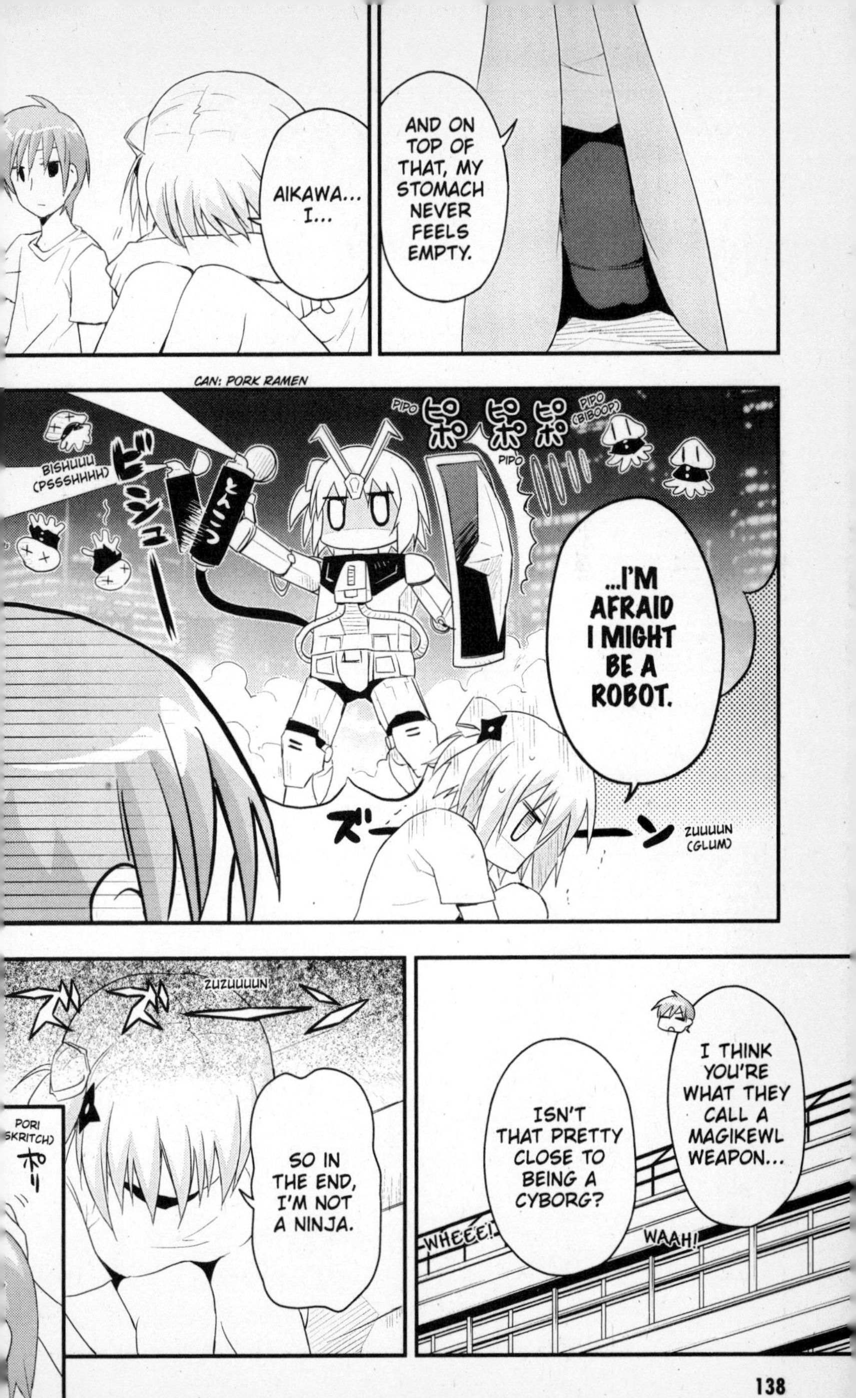
AND ON TOP OF THAT, MY STOMACH NEVER FEELS EMPTY.
AIKAWA... I...
CAN: PORK RAMEN
PIPO PIPO (BIBOOP)
PIPO
PIPO
BISHUUU (PSSSHHHH)
...I'M AFRAID I MIGHT BE A ROBOT.
ZUUUUN (GLUM)
I THINK YOU'RE WHAT THEY CALL A MAGIKEWL WEAPON...
ISN'T THAT PRETTY CLOSE TO BEING A CYBORG?
WHEEE!
WAAH!
ZUZUUUUN
SO IN THE END, I'M NOT A NINJA.
PORI (SKRITCH)

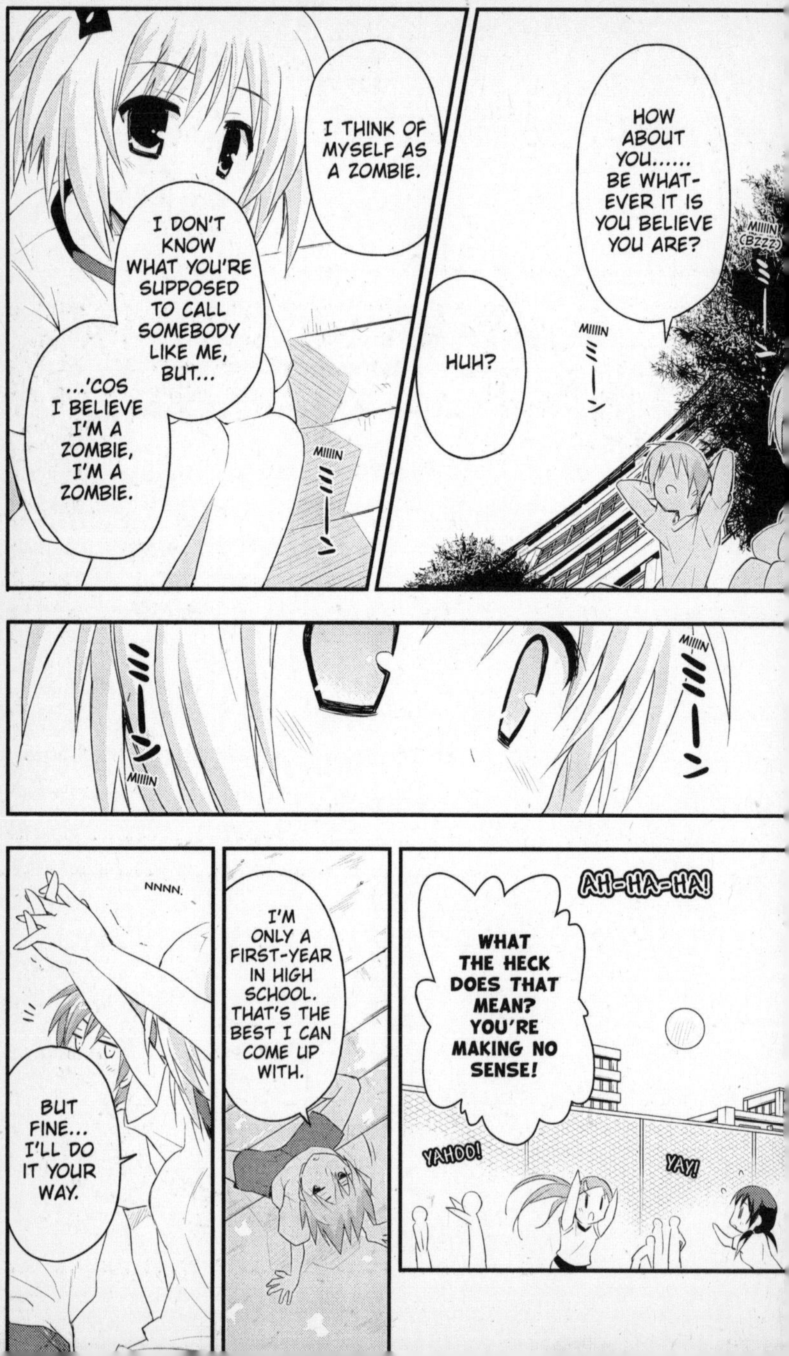
HOW ABOUT YOU...... BE WHAT-EVER IT IS YOU BELIEVE YOU ARE?
MIIIN (BZZZ)
HUH?
MIIIN
I THINK OF MYSELF AS A ZOMBIE.
I DON'T KNOW WHAT YOU'RE SUPPOSED TO CALL SOMEBODY LIKE ME, BUT...
...'COS I BELIEVE I'M A ZOMBIE, I'M A ZOMBIE.
MIIIN
MIIIN
MIIIN
AH-HA-HA!
WHAT THE HECK DOES THAT MEAN? YOU'RE MAKING NO SENSE!
YAY!
YAHOO!
I'M ONLY A FIRST-YEAR IN HIGH SCHOOL. THAT'S THE BEST I CAN COME UP WITH.
NNNN.
BUT FINE... I'LL DO IT YOUR WAY.

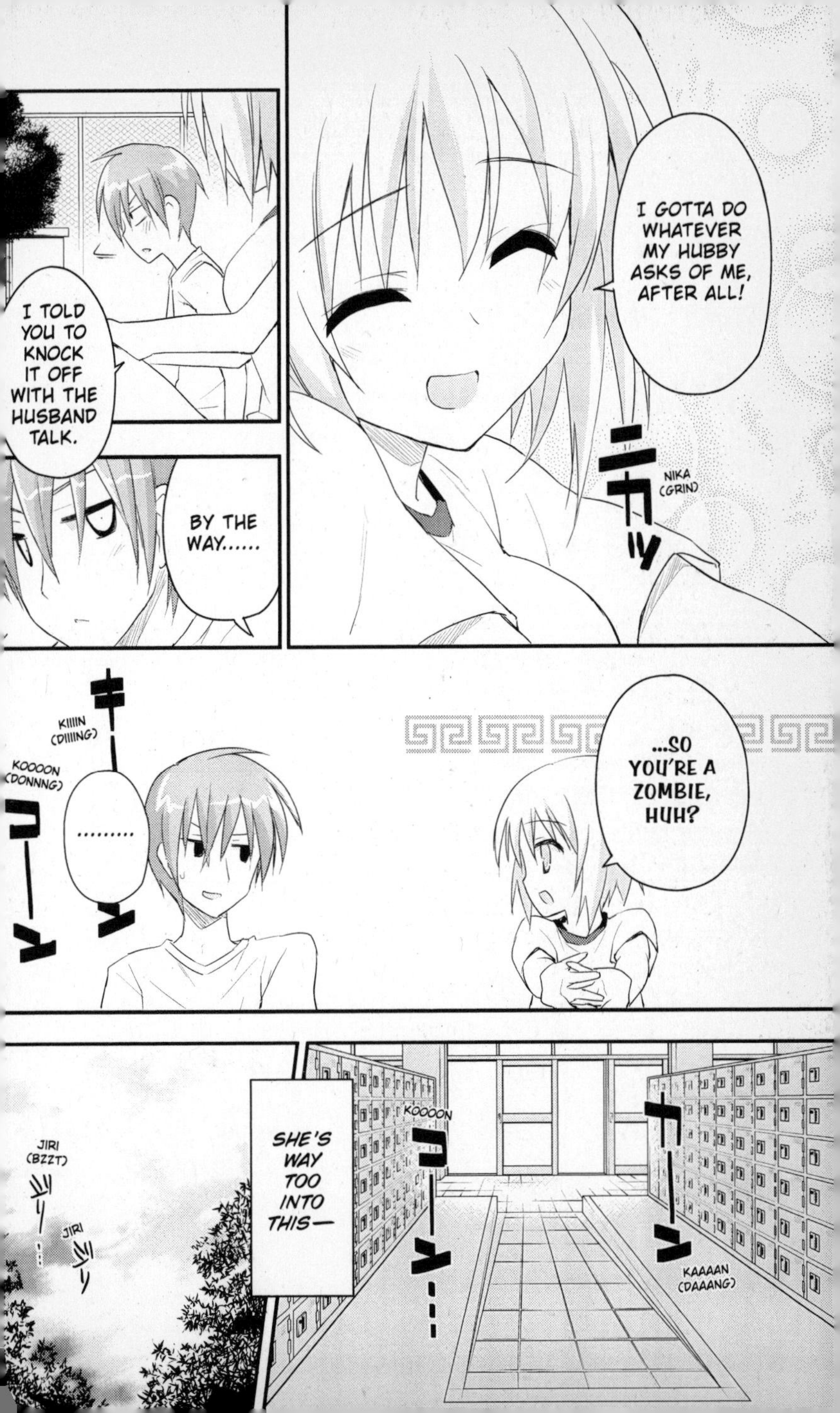
I GOTTA DO WHATEVER MY HUBBY ASKS OF ME, AFTER ALL!
ニカッ
NIKA (GRIN)
I TOLD YOU TO KNOCK IT OFF WITH THE HUSBAND TALK.
BY THE WAY......
...SO YOU'RE A ZOMBIE, HUH?
キーン
KIIIIN (DIIIING)
コーン
KOOOON (DONNNG)
....
カーン
KAAAAN (DAAANG)
コーン...
KOOOON
SHE'S WAY TOO INTO THIS—
ジリ...
JIRI (BZZT)
ジリ
JIRI

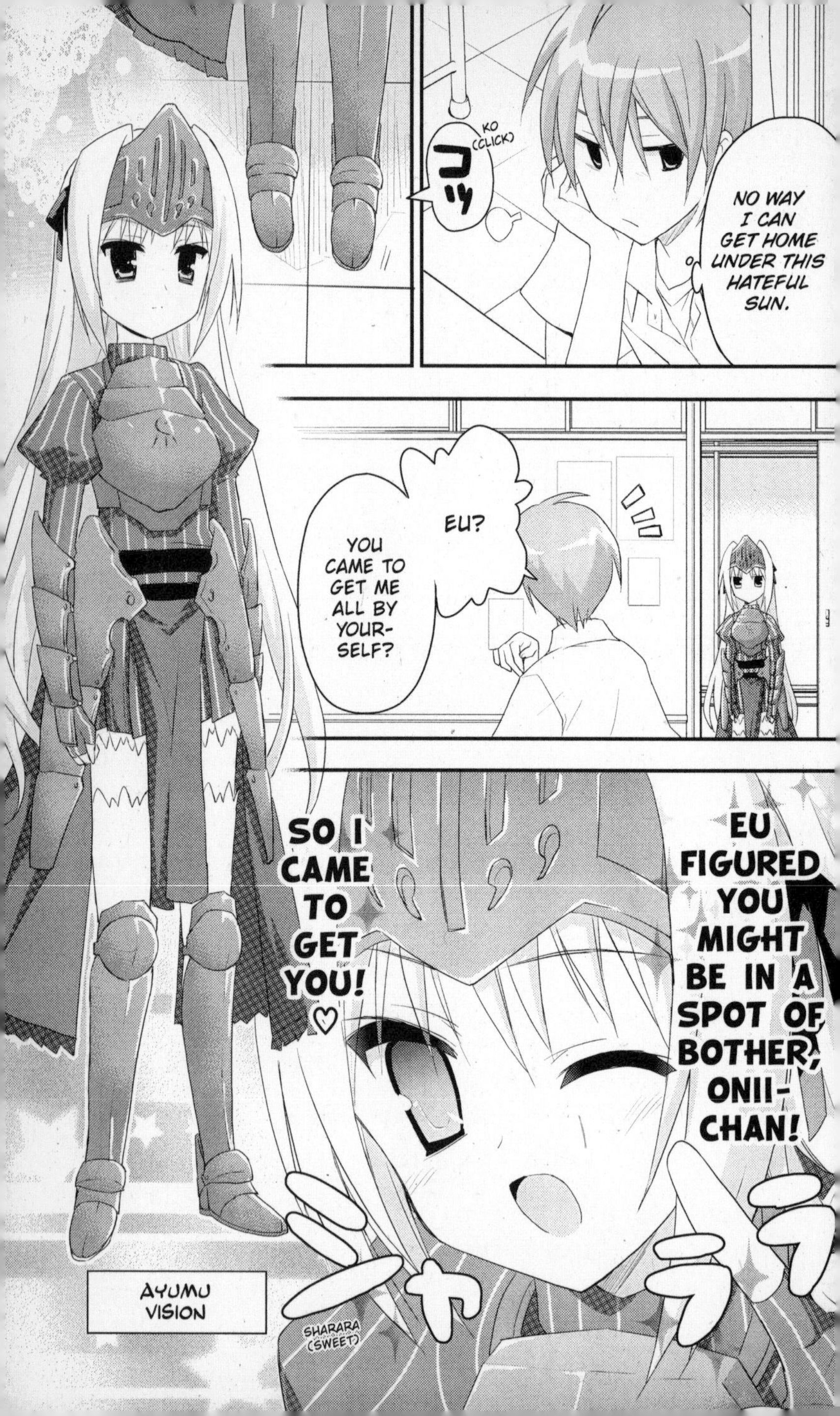
NO WAY I CAN GET HOME UNDER THIS HATEFUL SUN.
コッ
KO (CLICK)
EU?
YOU CAME TO GET ME ALL BY YOUR-SELF?
EU FIGURED YOU MIGHT BE IN A SPOT OF BOTHER, ONII-CHAN!
SO I CAME TO GET YOU! ♡
SHARARA (SWEET)
AYUMU VISION

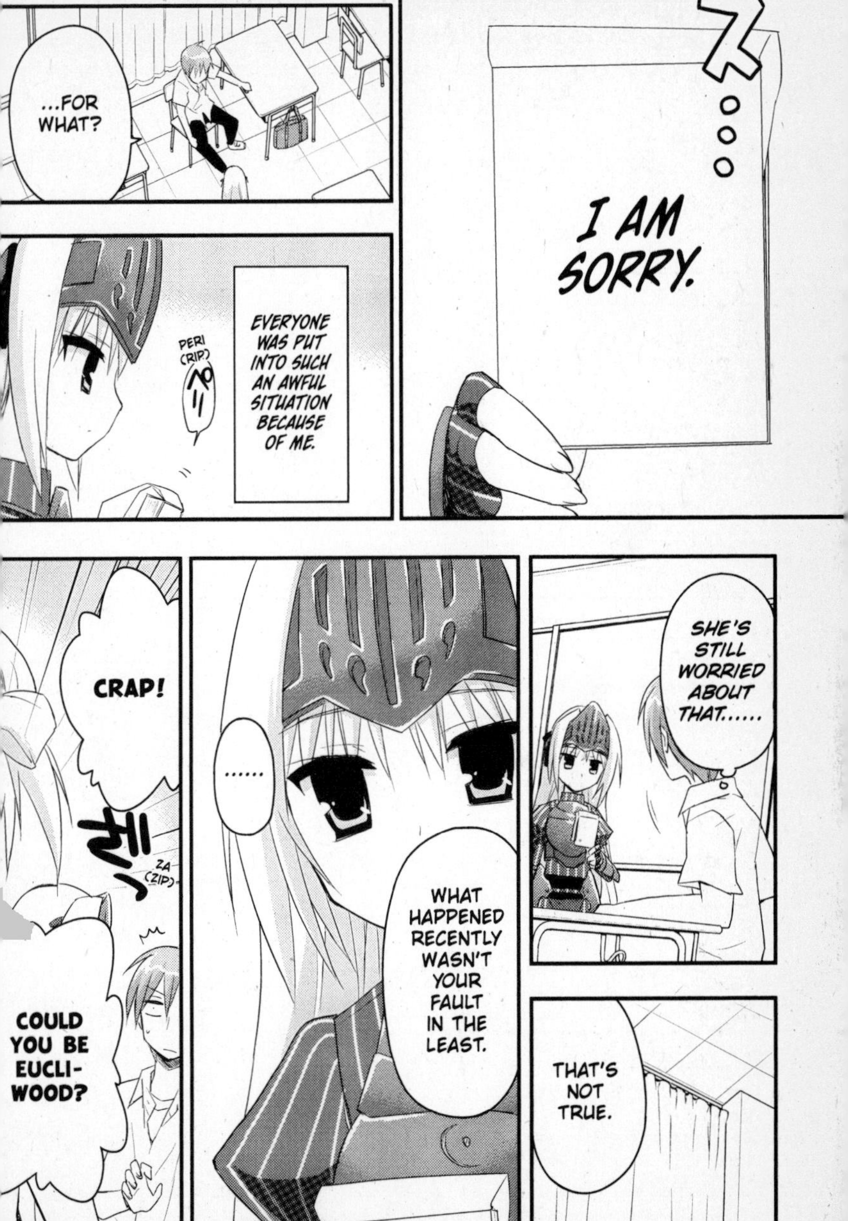
SU (SWF)
I AM SORRY.
...FOR WHAT?
EVERYONE WAS PUT INTO SUCH AN AWFUL SITUATION BECAUSE OF ME.
PERI (RIP)
SHE'S STILL WORRIED ABOUT THAT......
THAT'S NOT TRUE.
......
WHAT HAPPENED RECENTLY WASN'T YOUR FAULT IN THE LEAST.
CRAP!
ZA (ZIP)
COULD YOU BE EUCLI-WOOD?

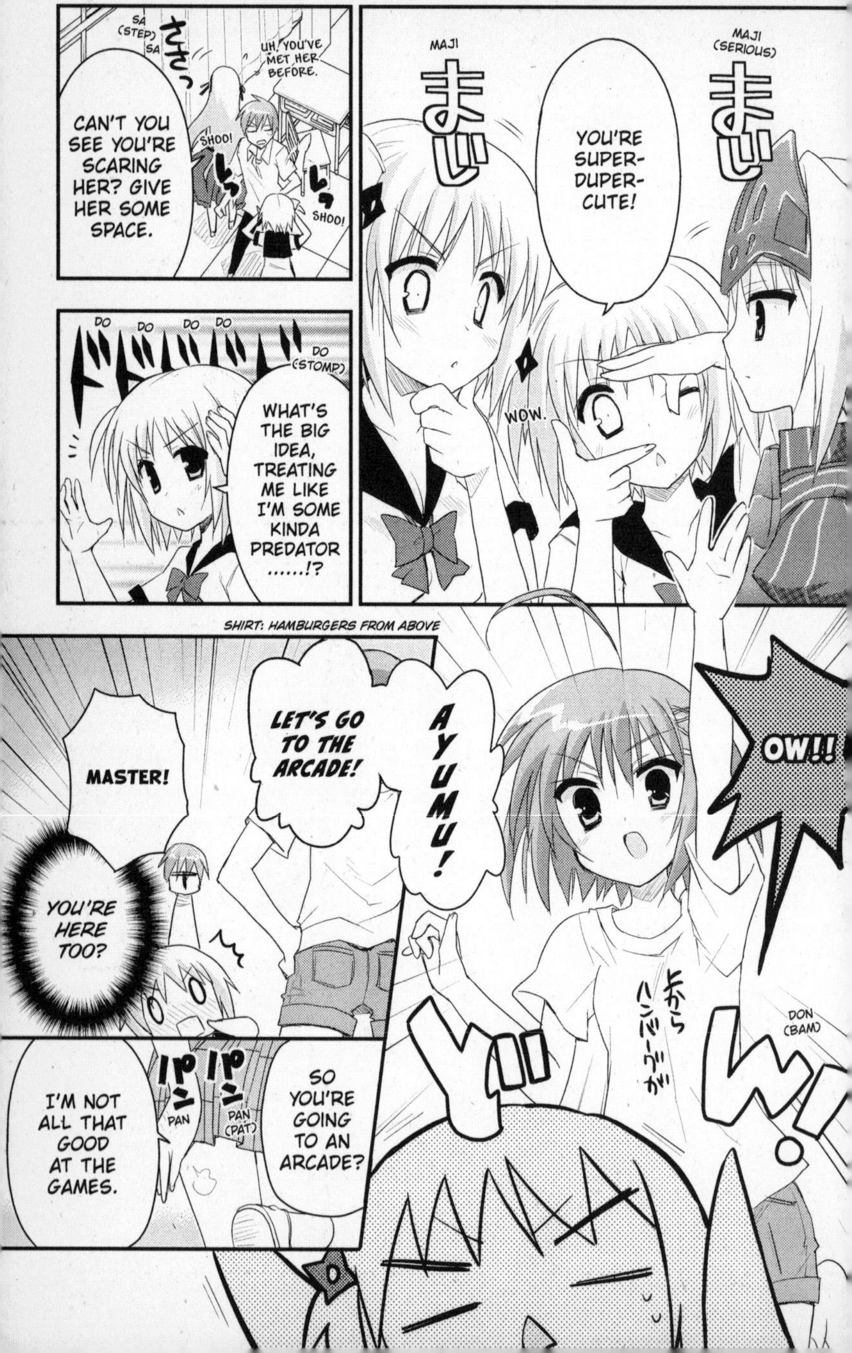
MAJI
まじ
YOU'RE SUPER-DUPER-CUTE!
MAJI (SERIOUS)
まじ
WOW.
SA (STEP) SA
UH, YOU'VE MET HER BEFORE.
SHOO!
SHOO!
CAN'T YOU SEE YOU'RE SCARING HER? GIVE HER SOME SPACE.
DO DO DO DO DO (STOMP)
WHAT'S THE BIG IDEA, TREATING ME LIKE I'M SOME KINDA PREDATOR ......!?
SHIRT: HAMBURGERS FROM ABOVE
OW!!
DON (BAM)
AYUMU!
LET'S GO TO THE ARCADE!
上からハンバーグが
MASTER!
YOU'RE HERE TOO?
SO YOU'RE GOING TO AN ARCADE?
PAN PAN (PAT)
I'M NOT ALL THAT GOOD AT THE GAMES.

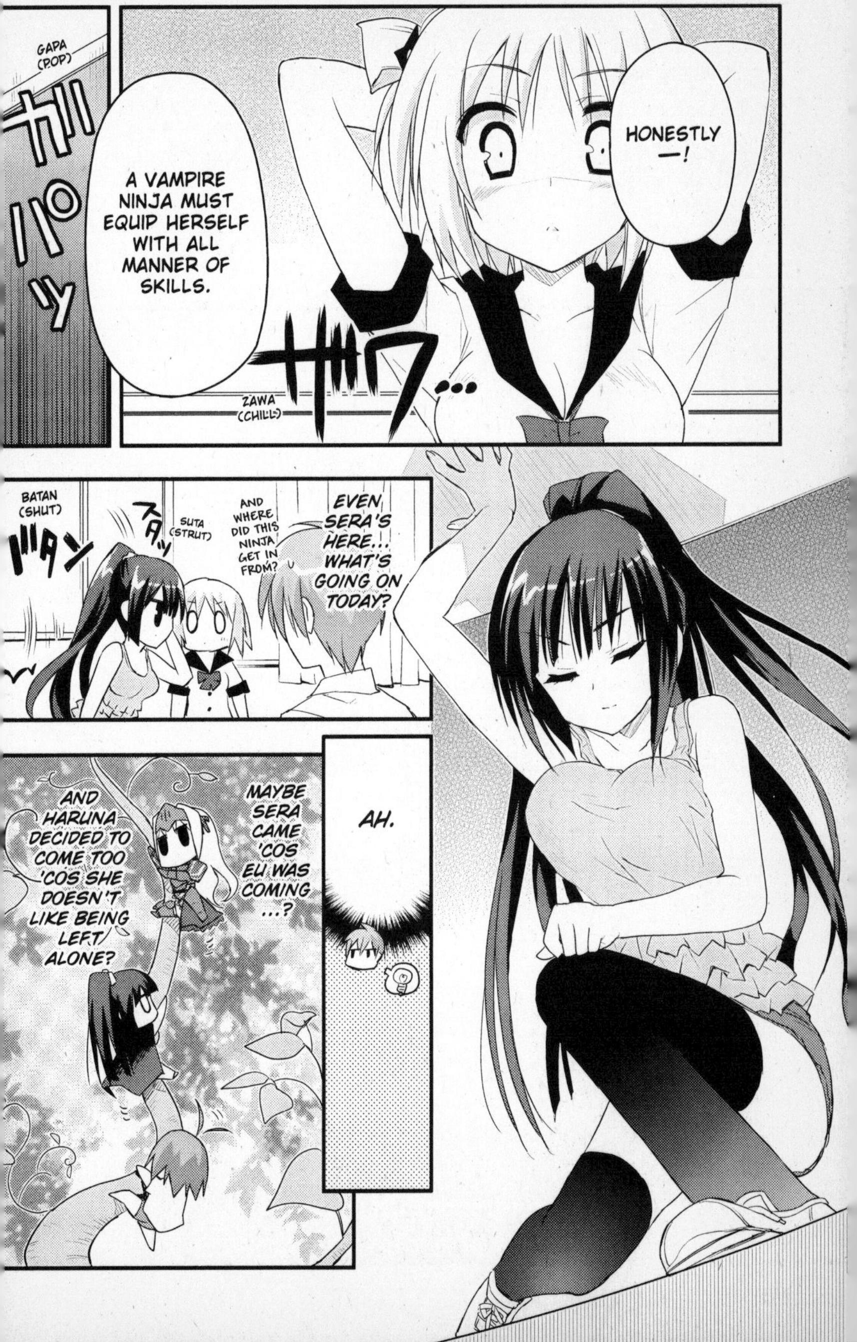

HONESTLY—!
A VAMPIRE NINJA MUST EQUIP HERSELF WITH ALL MANNER OF SKILLS.
ZAWA (CHILL)
GAPA (POP)
EVEN SERA'S HERE... WHAT'S GOING ON TODAY?
AND WHERE DID THIS NINJA GET IN FROM?
SUTA (STRUT)
BATAN (SHUT)
AH.
MAYBE SERA CAME 'COS EU WAS COMING ...?
AND HARUNA DECIDED TO COME TOO 'COS SHE DOESN'T LIKE BEING LEFT ALONE?

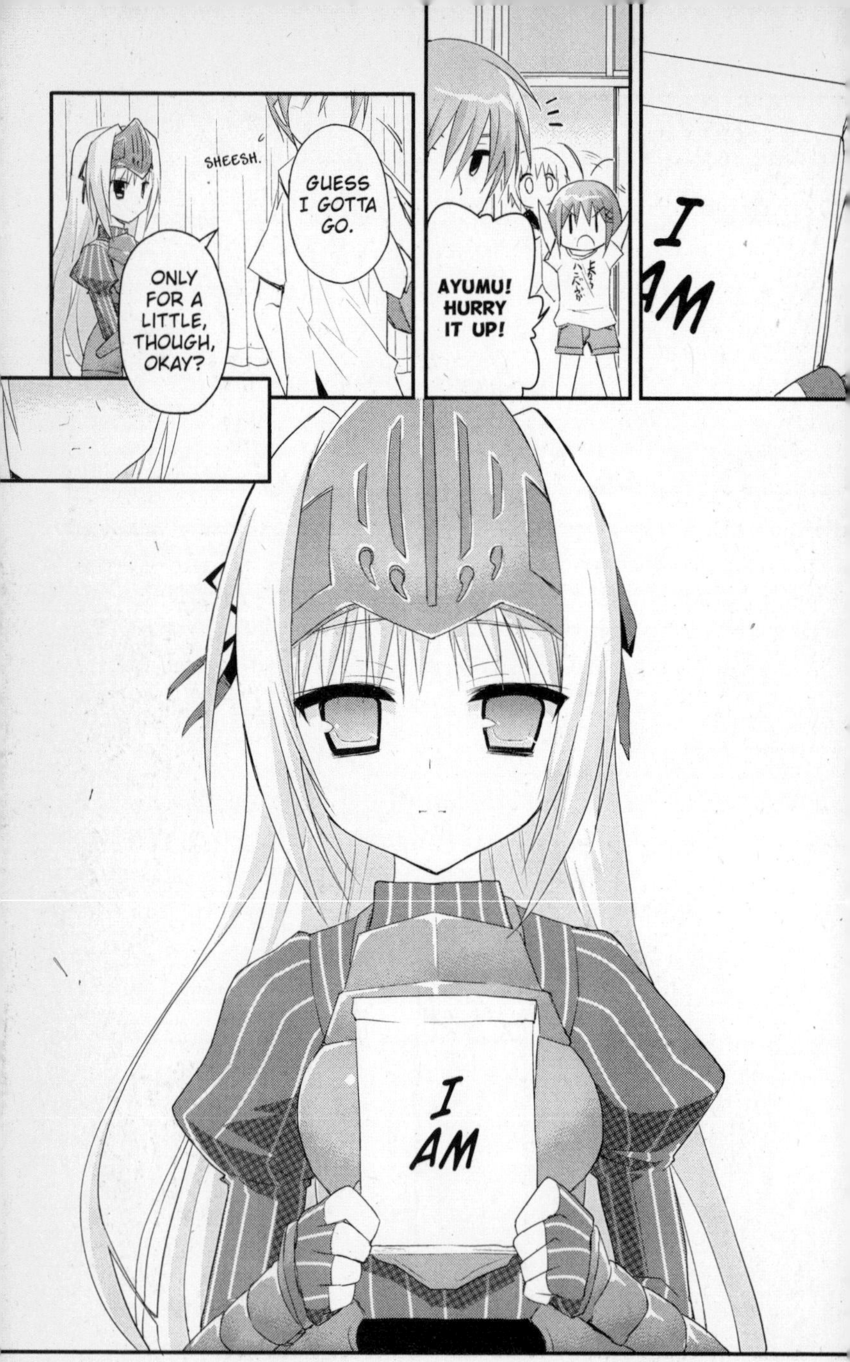
I AM
AYUMU! HURRY IT UP!
GUESS I GOTTA GO.
SHEESH.
ONLY FOR A LITTLE, THOUGH, OKAY?
I AM

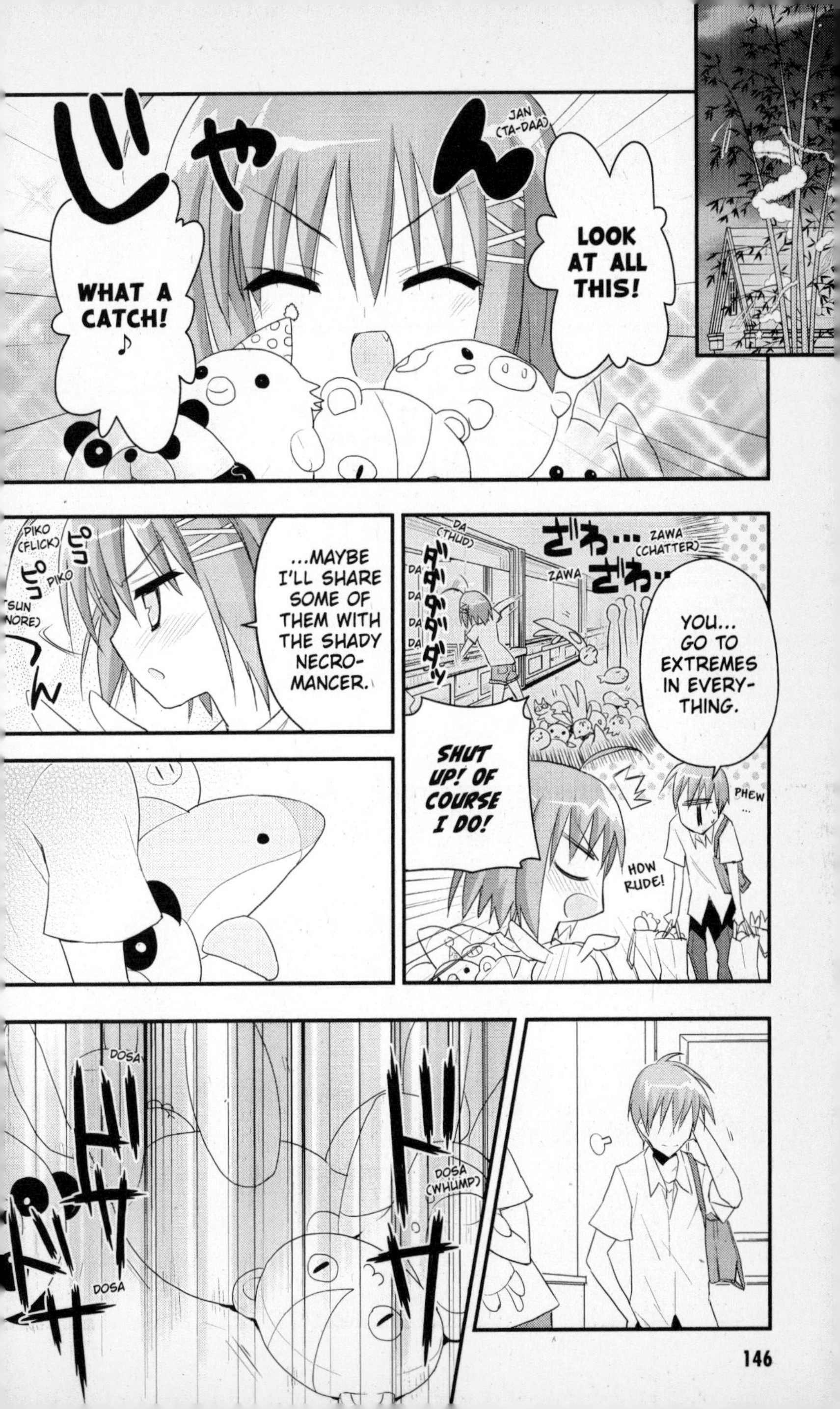

じゃん
JAN (TA-DAA)
LOOK AT ALL THIS!
WHAT A CATCH! ♪
ざわ… ざわ…
ZAWA (CHATTER)
ZAWA
DA (THUD)
DA
DA
DA
DA
YOU... GO TO EXTREMES IN EVERY-THING.
SHUT UP! OF COURSE I DO!
PHEW...
HOW RUDE!
PIKO (FLICK)
PIKO
...MAYBE I'LL SHARE SOME OF THEM WITH THE SHADY NECRO-MANCER.
DOSA
DOSA (WHUMP)
DOSA

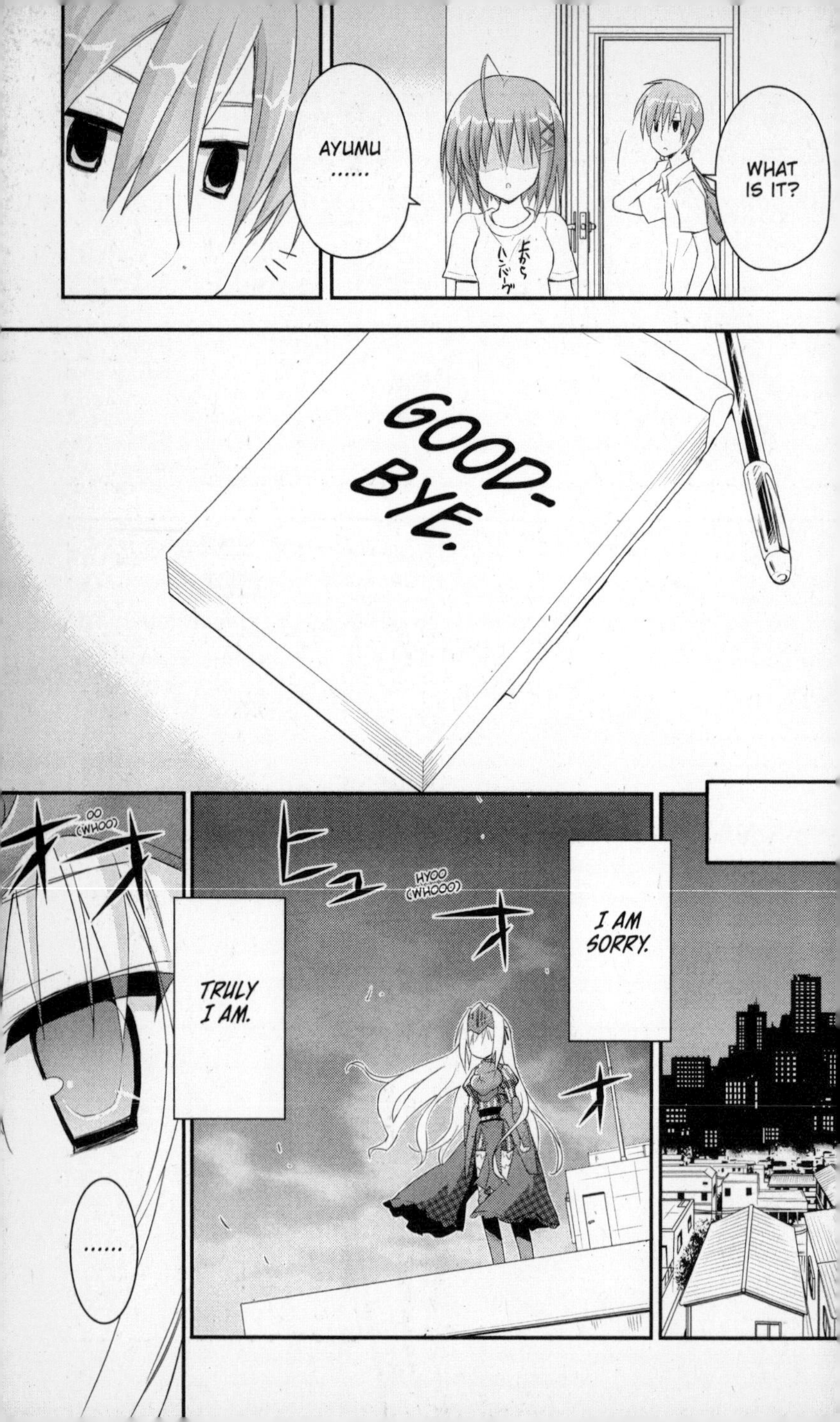

WHAT IS IT?
AYUMU ......
GOOD-BYE.
I AM SORRY.
HYOO (WHOOO)
TRULY I AM.
OO (WHOO)
......

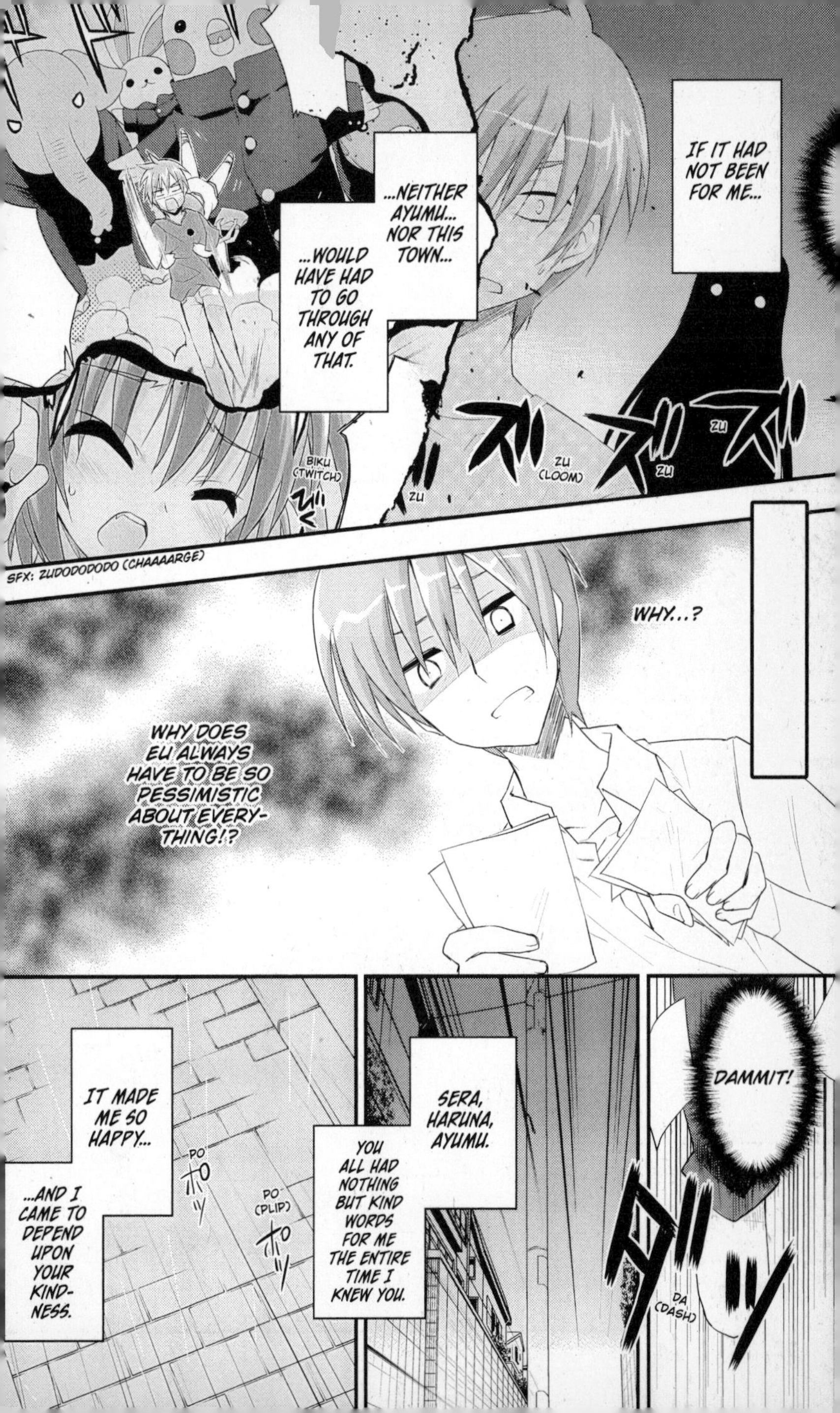
IF IT HAD NOT BEEN FOR ME...
...NEITHER AYUMU... NOR THIS TOWN...
...WOULD HAVE HAD TO GO THROUGH ANY OF THAT.
ZU
ZU
ZU (LOOM)
ZU
BIKU (TWITCH)
SFX: ZUDODODODO (CHAAAARGE)
WHY...?
WHY DOES EU ALWAYS HAVE TO BE SO PESSIMISTIC ABOUT EVERY-THING!?
DAMMIT!
DA (DASH)
SERA, HARUNA, AYUMU.
YOU ALL HAD NOTHING BUT KIND WORDS FOR ME THE ENTIRE TIME I KNEW YOU.
IT MADE ME SO HAPPY...
PO
PO (PLIP)
...AND I CAME TO DEPEND UPON YOUR KIND-NESS.

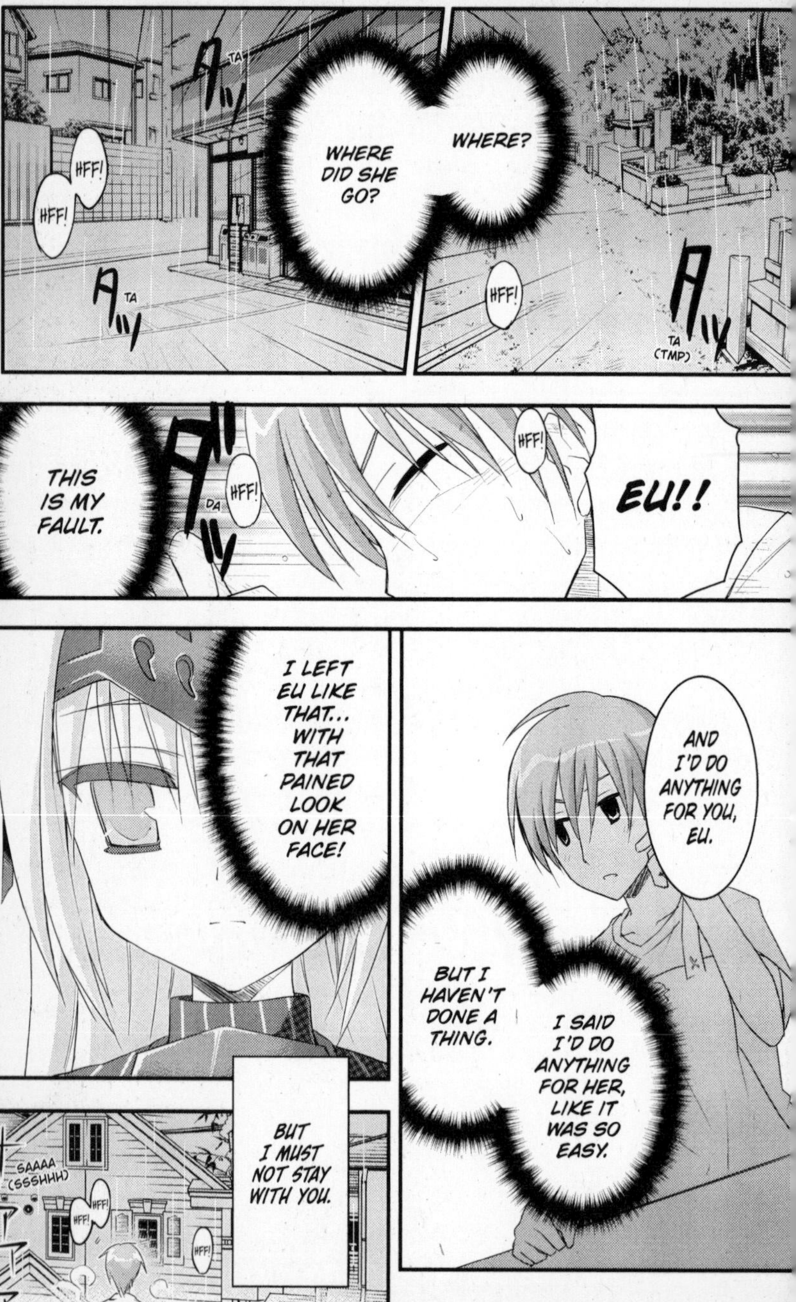
WHERE?
HFF!
TA (TMP)
WHERE DID SHE GO?
TA
HFF!
HFF!
TA
EU!!
HFF!
HFF!
DA
THIS IS MY FAULT.
AND I'D DO ANYTHING FOR YOU, EU.
I SAID I'D DO ANYTHING FOR HER, LIKE IT WAS SO EASY.
BUT I HAVEN'T DONE A THING.
I LEFT EU LIKE THAT... WITH THAT PAINED LOOK ON HER FACE!
BUT I MUST NOT STAY WITH YOU.
HFF!
HFF!
HFF!
SAAAA (SSSHHH)

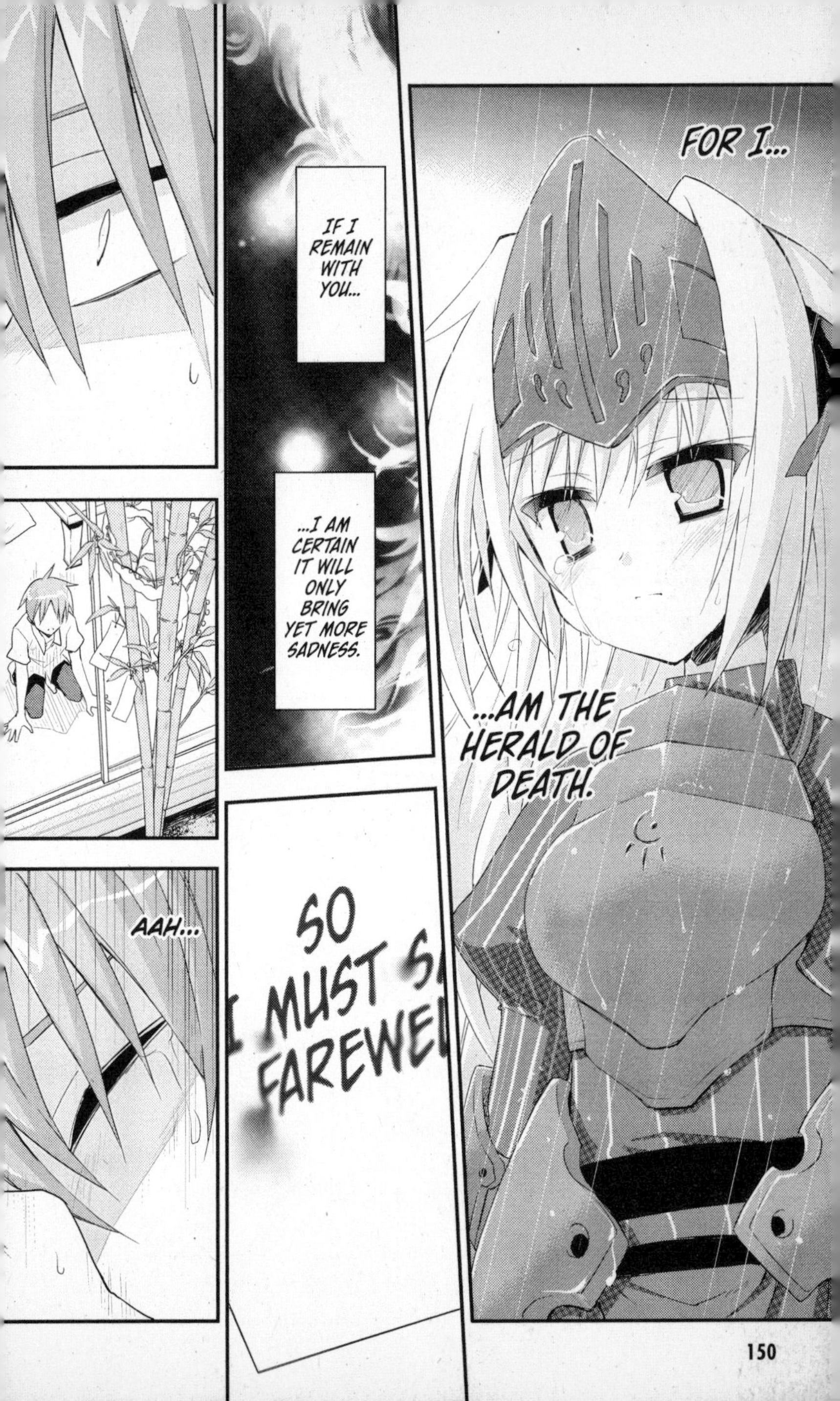
FOR I...
...AM THE HERALD OF DEATH.
IF I REMAIN WITH YOU...
...I AM CERTAIN IT WILL ONLY BRING YET MORE SADNESS.
SO I MUST S
FAREWE
AAH...

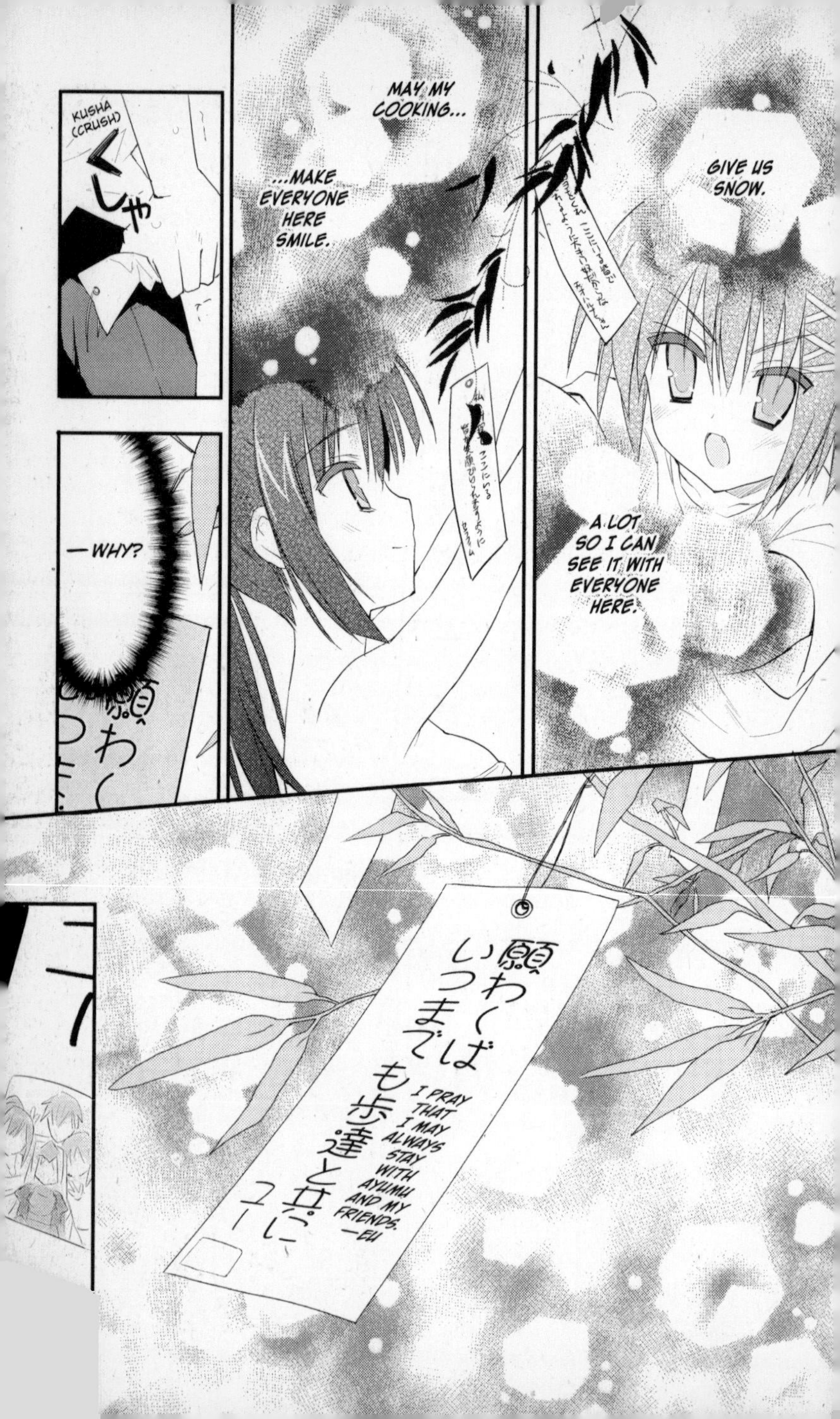
GIVE US SNOW.
A LOT SO I CAN SEE IT WITH EVERYONE HERE.
MAY MY COOKING...
...MAKE EVERYONE HERE SMILE.
KUSHA (CRUSH)
くしゃ
—WHY?
願わくば いつまでも歩達と共に ユー
I PRAY THAT I MAY ALWAYS STAY WITH AYUMU AND MY FRIENDS. —EU

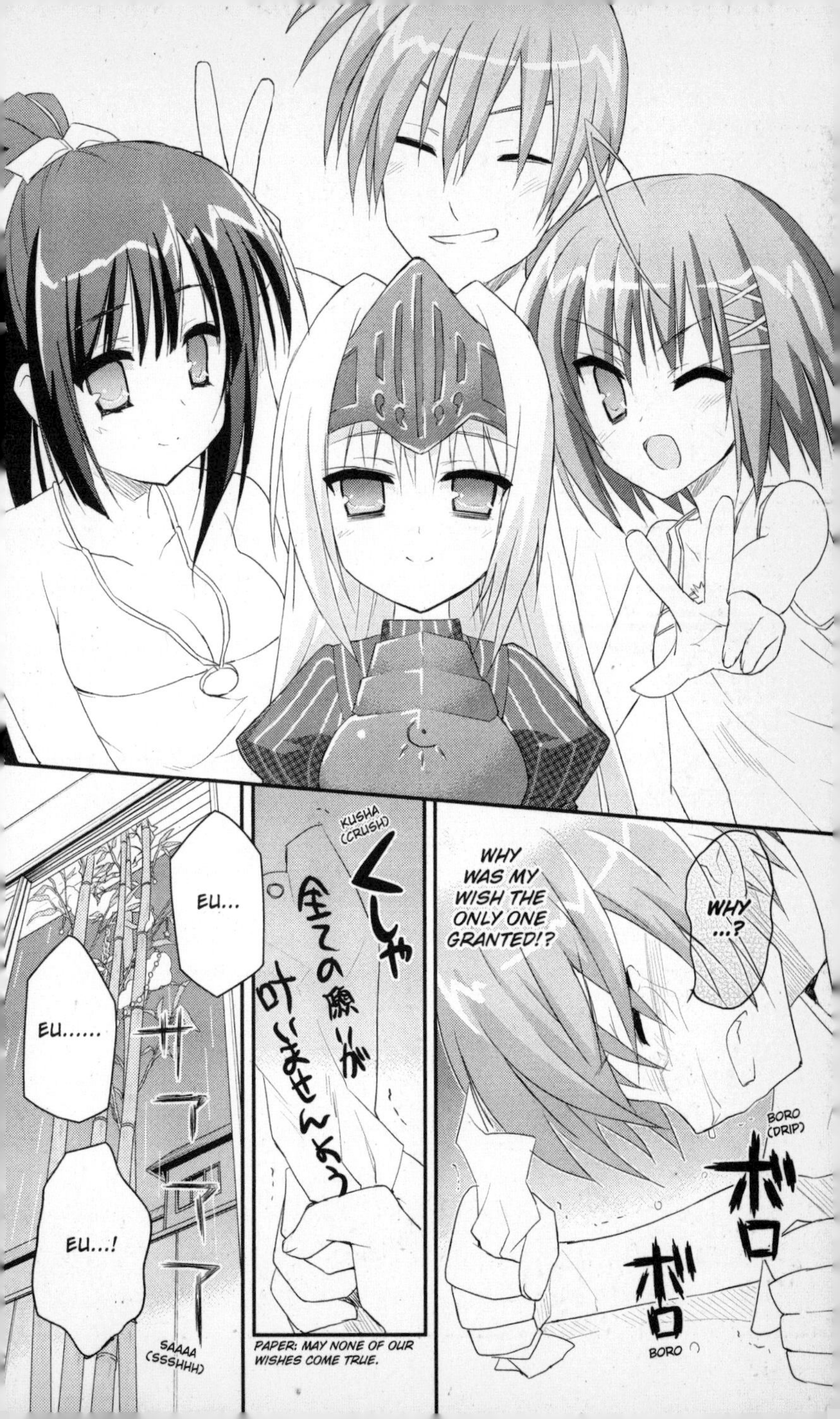
WHY ...?
WHY WAS MY WISH THE ONLY ONE GRANTED!?
BORO (DRIP)
ボロ
ボロ
BORO
KUSHA (CRUSH)
くしゃ
全ての願いが 叶いませんよう
PAPER: MAY NONE OF OUR WISHES COME TRUE.
EU...
EU......
EU...!
サーーー
SAAAA (SSSHHH)

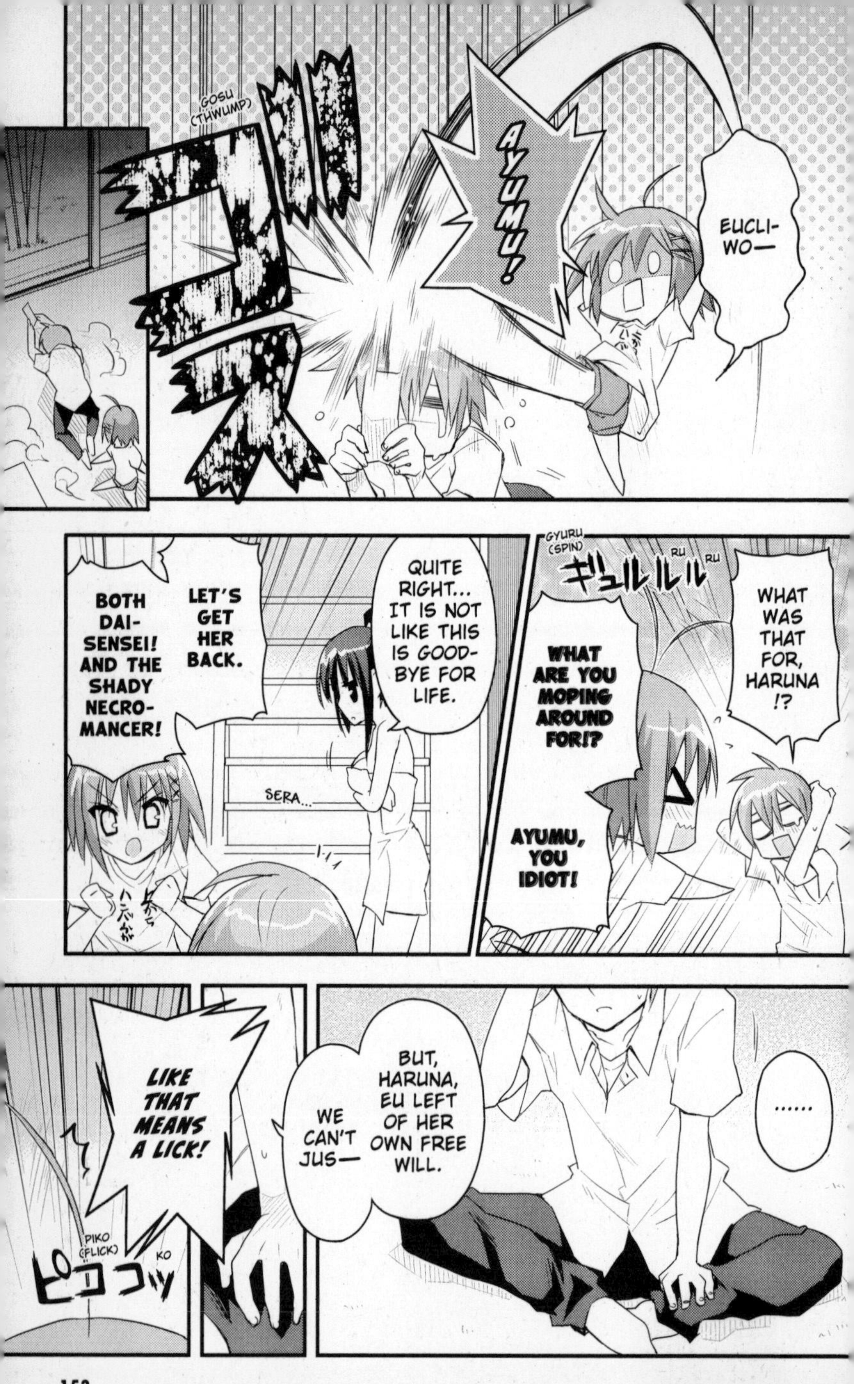
EUCLI-WO—
AYUMU!
GOSU (THWUMP)
GYURU (SPIN)
ギュルルル
RU RU
WHAT WAS THAT FOR, HARUNA!?
WHAT ARE YOU MOPING AROUND FOR!?
AYUMU, YOU IDIOT!
QUITE RIGHT... IT IS NOT LIKE THIS IS GOOD-BYE FOR LIFE.
LET'S GET HER BACK.
BOTH DAI-SENSEI! AND THE SHADY NECRO-MANCER!
SERA...
......
BUT, HARUNA, EU LEFT OF HER OWN FREE WILL.
WE CAN'T JUS—
LIKE THAT MEANS A LICK!
PIKO (FLICK)
KO

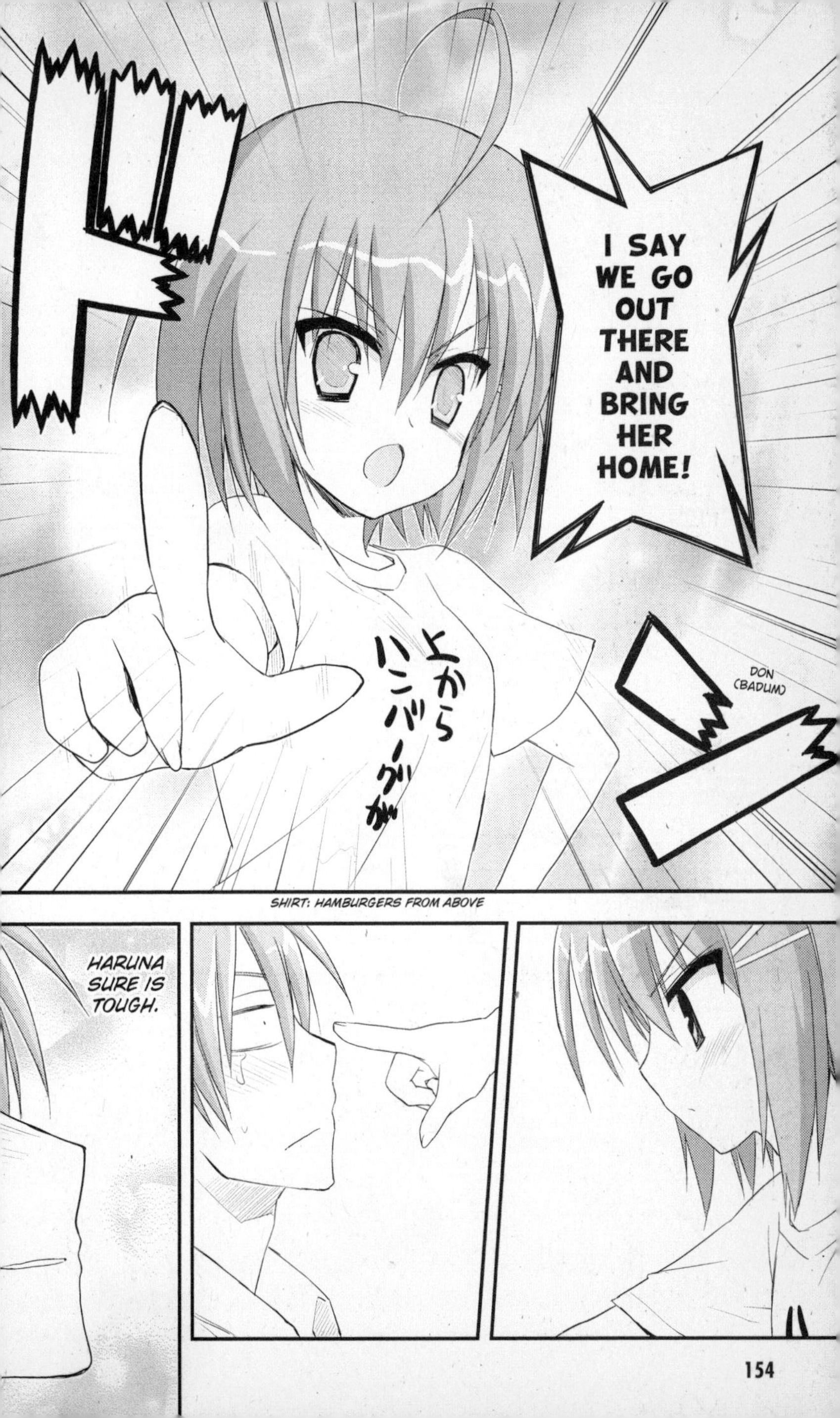
I SAY WE GO OUT THERE AND BRING HER HOME!
DON (BADUM)
上から ハンバーガーが
SHIRT: HAMBURGERS FROM ABOVE
HARUNA SURE IS TOUGH.

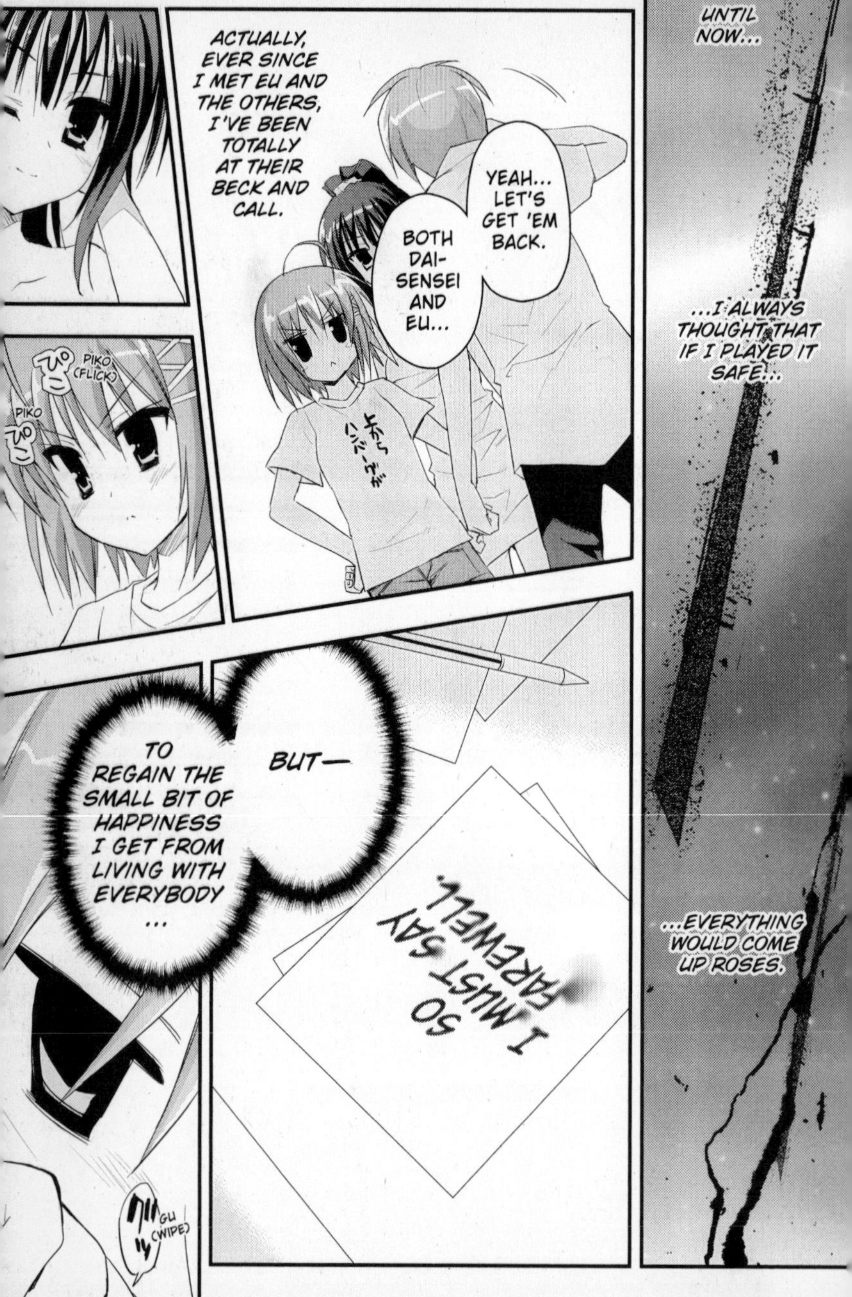
UNTIL NOW...
...I ALWAYS THOUGHT THAT IF I PLAYED IT SAFE...
...EVERYTHING WOULD COME UP ROSES.
YEAH... LET'S GET 'EM BACK.
BOTH DAI-SENSEI AND EU...
ACTUALLY, EVER SINCE I MET EU AND THE OTHERS, I'VE BEEN TOTALLY AT THEIR BECK AND CALL.
上から ハンバーグが
ぴこ PIKO (FLICK)
ぴこ PIKO
BUT—
SO I MUST SAY FAREWELL.
TO REGAIN THE SMALL BIT OF HAPPINESS I GET FROM LIVING WITH EVERYBODY ...
グイ GU (WIPE)

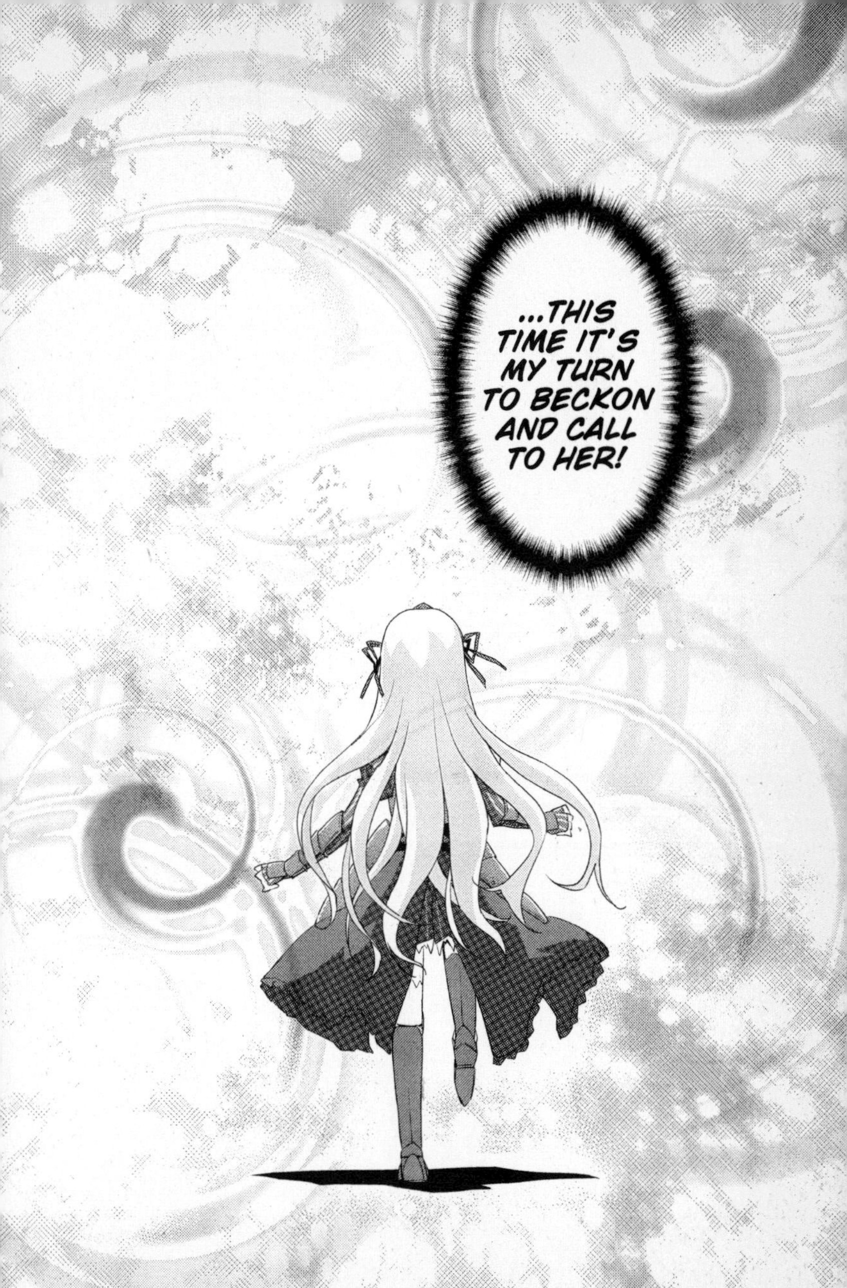
...THIS TIME IT'S MY TURN TO BECKON AND CALL TO HER!

TO BE CONTINUED

IS THIS A ZOMBIE?

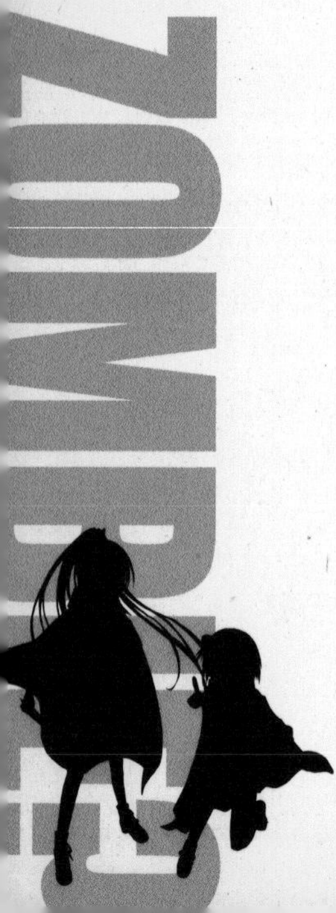

Is this a page of TRANSLATION NOTES?

PAGE 23 - Tanabata: A holiday every July 7th in which two mythological deity lovers (Vega and Altair) are said to cross the Milky Way and spend their one and only night of the year together. People celebrate by writing wishes on small pieces of paper and hanging them on bamboo trees.

PAGE 60 - Golden Eggs: The Japanese on Haruna's apron is a play on words. It reads *kintama*, the common word for "testicles," but the second character in the word has been changed to the *tama* of *tamago*, or "egg."

PAGE 68 - Mandom: A line of men's care products that combine the words "human" and "freedom."

PAGE 71 - Blizzaga: A very strong ice magic spell in the *Final Fantasy* universe.

PAGE 82 - Futae no Kiwami: A fighting technique used by the character Sanosuke Sagara in Nobuhiro Watsuki's manga series *Rurouni Kenshin*.

PAGE 84 - Shuwatch!: The famous character Ultraman's trademark saying.

PAGE 84 - Haruna's popsicle: A parody of the popular Japanese popsicle brand Gari-Gari-kun. Some of their popsicles have what is known as an *atari* (アタリ) stick; they have *atari* ("winner") written on them. If you get one, it means you get a free popsicle. Unfortunately for Haruna, the first two letters in *atari* and *attack* are the same in katakana, and she turns out to be a loser instead!

PAGE 143 - Hamburgers From Above: A reference to a popularly misheard lyric from the song "Passionate Fate" by Ryu☆, which appeared in the arcade game *Beatmania IIDX*. The actual line from the song was "We're gonna have fun tonight!" in English, but was misheard as *ue kara hanbaagu ga*, or "hamburgers from above."

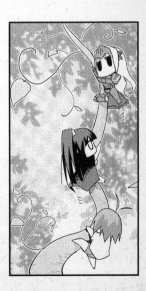

SERA'S FASHIONISTA LEVEL CHECKLIST

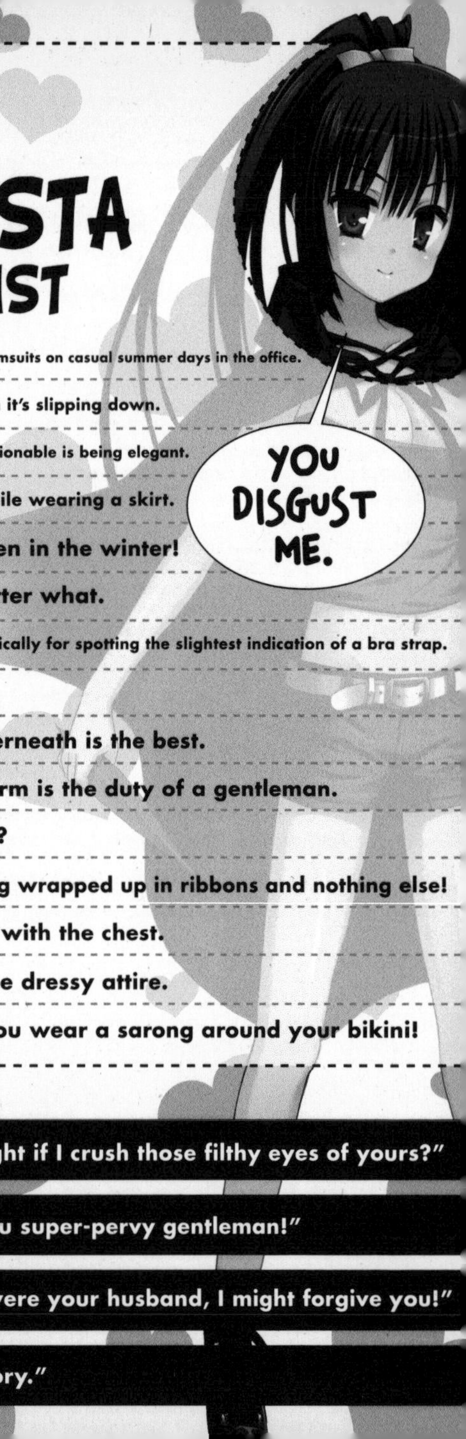
YOU DISGUST ME.

- ☐ You believe girls should be able to wear swimsuits on casual summer days in the office.
- ☐ You love Sera adjusting her top when it's slipping down.
- ☐ You believe the foundation of being fashionable is being elegant.
- ☐ Please crouch down innocently while wearing a skirt.
- ☐ You aim to go sleeveless even in the winter!
- ☐ You wear kneesocks no matter what.
- ☐ You come with a search function specifically for spotting the slightest indication of a bra strap.
- ☐ Cat ears? Yes, please.
- ☐ An apron with nothing underneath is the best.
- ☐ Lending out his school uniform is the duty of a gentleman.
- ☐ Is a cowlick a fashion point?
- ☐ You wouldn't at all mind being wrapped up in ribbons and nothing else!
- ☐ Being fashionable all starts with the chest.
- ☐ You consider full armor to be dressy attire.
- ☐ Your dad would never let you wear a sarong around your bikini!

Score	Results
15	Sera "Is it all right if I crush those filthy eyes of yours?"
8~	Haruna "Y-y-you super-pervy gentleman!"
1~	Tomonori "If I were your husband, I might forgive you!"
0	Eu "Unsatisfactory."

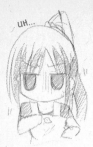

UH...

IS THIS AN AFTERWORD?

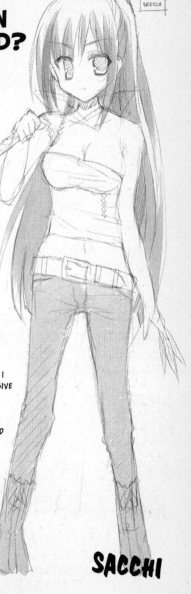

SKETCH

THANK YOU VERY MUCH FOR BUYING VOLUME THREE OF THE MANGA!!

"SERA'S FIGHT SCENES ARE SO IMPRESSIVE!"
I FEEL LIKE I HAD A CONVERSATION LIKE THAT WITH THE EDITOR BEFORE.

"WHAT IF WE TOOK A LITTLE OUT OF THIS AREA?"
"AH, I SEE WHAT YOU MEAN."
"AS FAR AS HER ATTACK NAME, I THINK MAYBE IF WE MAKE IT THIS, IT'LL HAVE MORE OF AN IMPACT."
"ROGER. SO LET'S MIX A LITTLE LOVE COMEDY INTO IT."
"OKAY...WAIT, WHAT?"
"EMPHASIZING HER BOSOM."
"INDEED..."

NOTHING BEATS BOOBIES!!

I CAN'T HELP IT. I'M A MAMMAL...
WHEN ORITO SAYS THAT IN THE STORY, IT REALLY DOES SOUND RATHER PERSUASIVE. THAT PERV.

SEGUEING FROM THAT, I WANT TO LET YOU KNOW THAT I AM GRATEFUL FOR THE UPLIFTING POWER MY READERS GIVE ME WHILE I DRAW THIS STORY.

I SERIOUSLY TRY MY BEST AT THIS COMIC VERSION SO THAT YOU CAN ALL ENJOY IT IN ITS GRAPHIC FORM, AND IT WOULD MAKE ME TERRIBLY HAPPY IF YOU WOULD CHEER ME ON IN THE NEXT VOLUME TOO!

THANK YOU VERY MUCH TO BOTH KIMURA-SENSEI AND THE EDITORS OF THE NOVEL AND MANGA FOR ALWAYS SUPERVISING DOWN TO THE SMALLEST DETAIL.
AND THANK YOU FOR YOUR DRAWINGS AND COMMENTS EVEN WHEN YOU ARE SUPER-BUSY, KOBUICHI-SENSEI AND MURIRIN-SENSEI.
AND THANK YOU FOR ALWAYS COLORING EVERYBODY SO CUTELY, STUDIO HIBARI!

★SPECIAL THANKS TO★
MIMIZU-SAN, TOMITA-SAN, AND EKAKIBITO-SAN

SACCHI

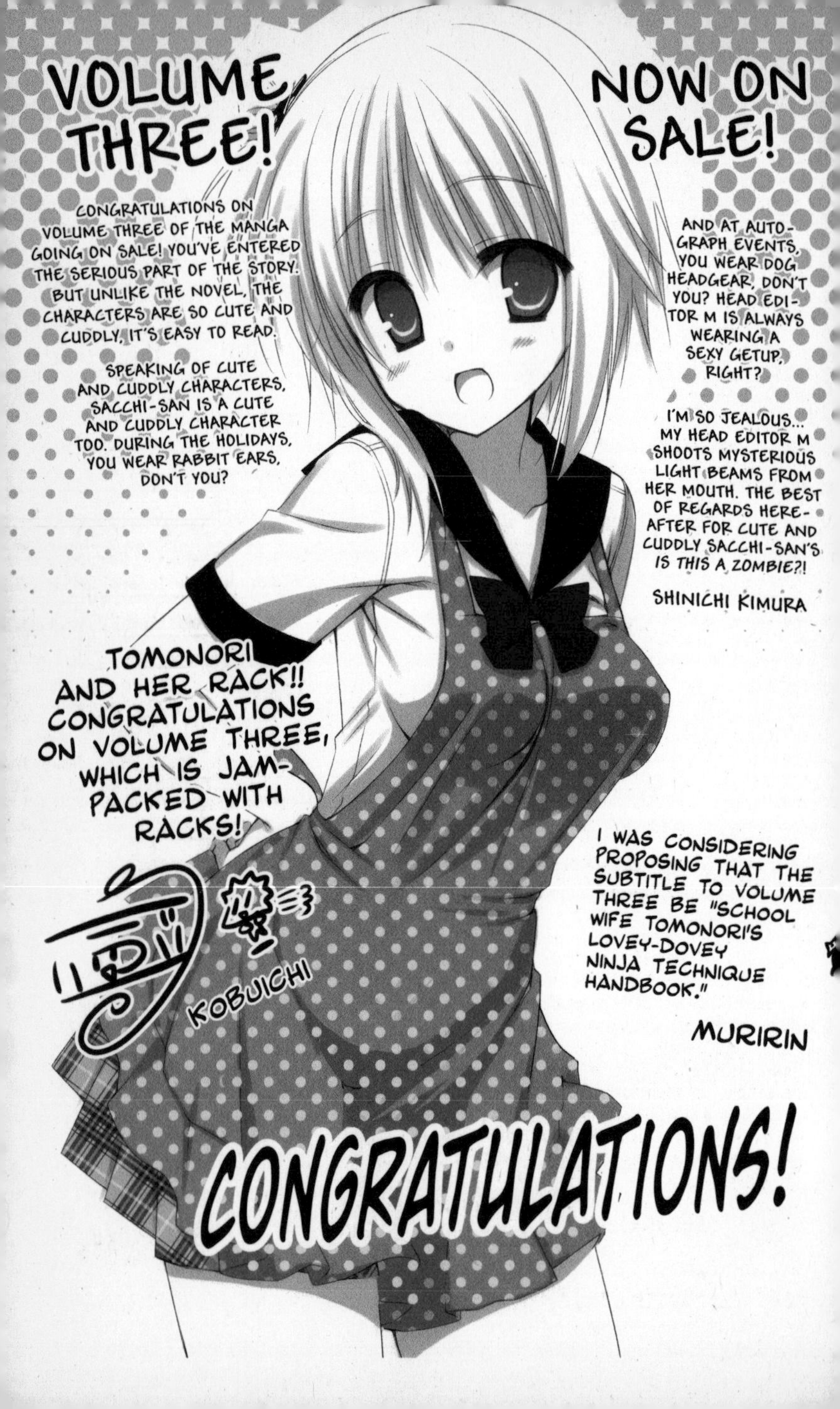

VOLUME THREE!
NOW ON SALE!
CONGRATULATIONS ON VOLUME THREE OF THE MANGA GOING ON SALE! YOU'VE ENTERED THE SERIOUS PART OF THE STORY. BUT UNLIKE THE NOVEL, THE CHARACTERS ARE SO CUTE AND CUDDLY, IT'S EASY TO READ.
SPEAKING OF CUTE AND CUDDLY CHARACTERS, SACCHI-SAN IS A CUTE AND CUDDLY CHARACTER TOO. DURING THE HOLIDAYS, YOU WEAR RABBIT EARS, DON'T YOU?
AND AT AUTO-GRAPH EVENTS, YOU WEAR DOG HEADGEAR, DON'T YOU? HEAD EDI-TOR M IS ALWAYS WEARING A SEXY GETUP, RIGHT?
I'M SO JEALOUS... MY HEAD EDITOR M SHOOTS MYSTERIOUS LIGHT BEAMS FROM HER MOUTH. THE BEST OF REGARDS HERE-AFTER FOR CUTE AND CUDDLY SACCHI-SAN'S IS THIS A ZOMBIE?!
SHINICHI KIMURA
TOMONORI AND HER RACK!! CONGRATULATIONS ON VOLUME THREE, WHICH IS JAM-PACKED WITH RACKS!
KOBUICHI
I WAS CONSIDERING PROPOSING THAT THE SUBTITLE TO VOLUME THREE BE "SCHOOL WIFE TOMONORI'S LOVEY-DOVEY NINJA TECHNIQUE HANDBOOK."
MURIRIN
CONGRATULATIONS!

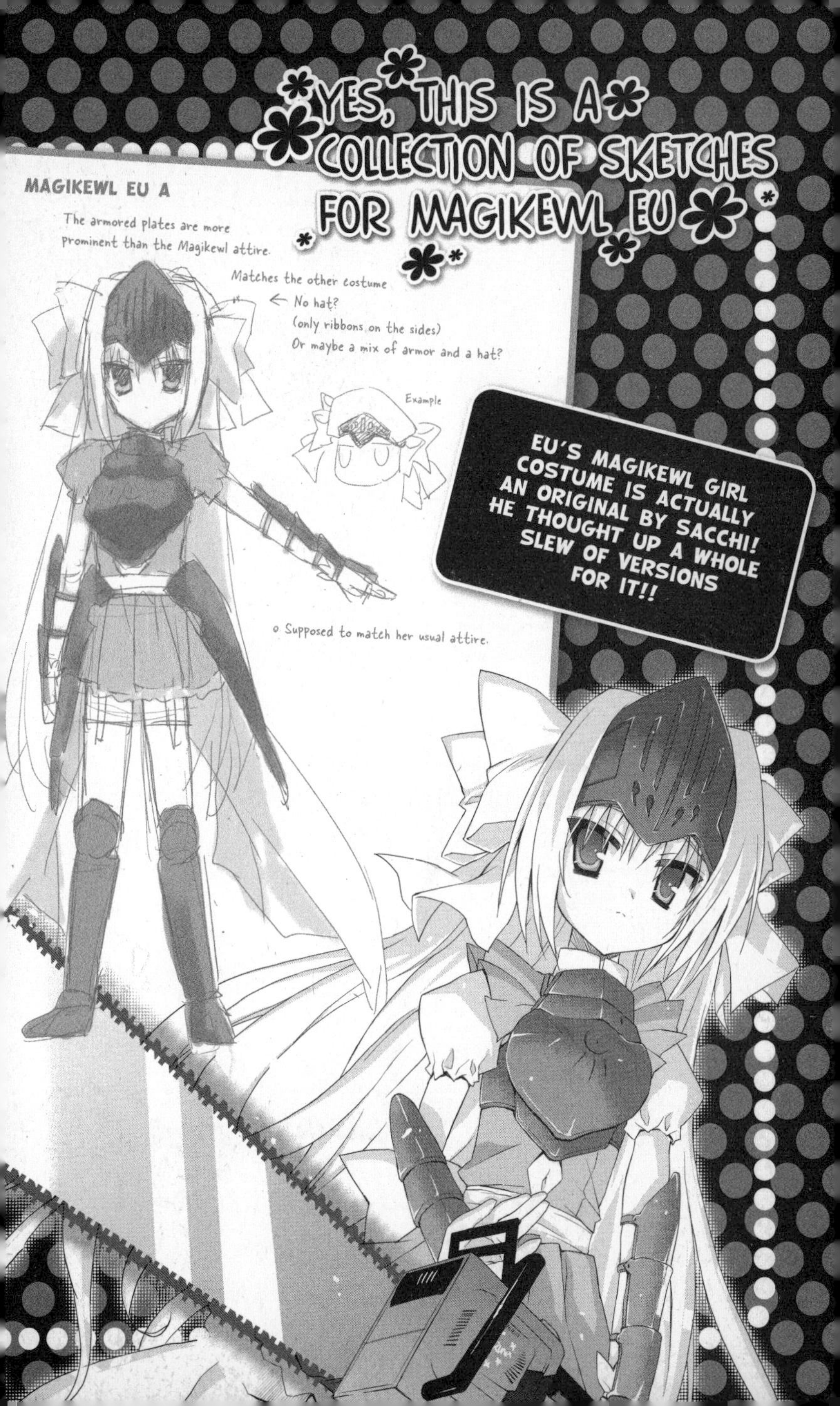

YES, THIS IS A COLLECTION OF SKETCHES FOR MAGIKEWL EU
MAGIKEWL EU A
The armored plates are more prominent than the Magikewl attire.
Matches the other costume
No hat?
(only ribbons on the sides)
Or maybe a mix of armor and a hat?
Example
EU'S MAGIKEWL GIRL COSTUME IS ACTUALLY AN ORIGINAL BY SACCHI! HE THOUGHT UP A WHOLE SLEW OF VERSIONS FOR IT!!
o Supposed to match her usual attire.

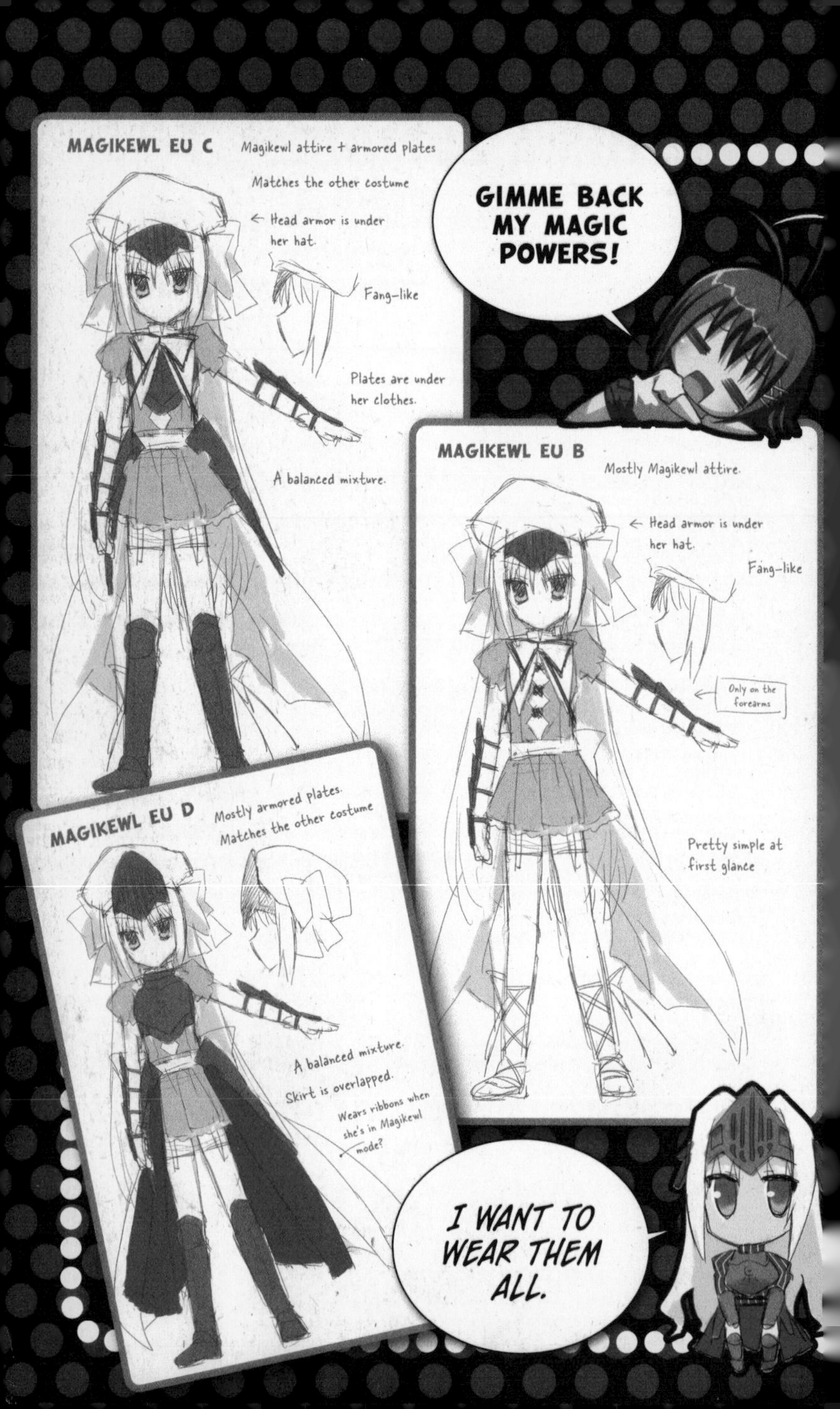
GIMME BACK MY MAGIC POWERS!
MAGIKEWL EU C
Magikewl attire + armored plates
Matches the other costume
← Head armor is under her hat.
Fang-like
Plates are under her clothes.
A balanced mixture.
MAGIKEWL EU B
Mostly Magikewl attire.
← Head armor is under her hat.
Fang-like
Only on the forearms
Pretty simple at first glance
MAGIKEWL EU D
Mostly armored plates.
Matches the other costume
A balanced mixture.
Skirt is overlapped.
Wears ribbons when she's in Magikewl mode?
I WANT TO WEAR THEM ALL.

IS THIS A ZOMBIE?  3 *

SACCHI
SHINICHI KIMURA
KOBUICHI • MURIRIN

Translation: Christine Dashiell

Lettering: AndWorld Design

KOREHA ZOMBIE DESUKA? Volume 3
© 2011 SACCHI © 2011 SHINICHI KIMURA • KOBUICHI • MURIRIN.
First published in Japan in 2011 by FUJIMISHOBO CO., LTD., Tokyo.
English translation rights arranged with KADOKAWA SHOTEN Co., Ltd., Tokyo through TUTTLE-MORI AGENCY, INC., Tokyo.

Translation © 2012 Hachette Book Group, Inc.

Yen Press
Hachette Book Group
237 Park Avenue, New York, NY 10017

www.HachetteBookGroup.com
www.YenPress.com

Yen Press is an imprint of Hachette Book Group, Inc. The Yen Press name and logo are trademarks of Hachette Book Group, Inc.

First Yen Press Edition: November 2012

ISBN: 978-0-316-21038-6

10 9 8 7 6 5 4 3 2 1

BVG

Printed in the United States of America